THE GOLDEN STATE PHANTASTICKS.
The California Romantics and Related Subjects.

D. Sidney-Fryer has produced, or helped to produce, the following books and booklets whether authored by himself or by others:

Poems in Prose, by Clark Ashton Smith (1965)

Etchings in Ivory, poems in prose by Robert E. Howard (1968)

Other Dimensions, short stories by Clark Ashton Smith (1970)

Songs and Sonnets Atlantean, The First Series (1971)

Selected Poems, omnibus by Clark Ashton Smith (1971)

The Last of the Great Romantic Poets, i.e., Clark Ashton Smith (1973)

Emperor of Dreams, A Clark Ashton Smith Bibliography (1978)

The Black Book of Clark Ashton Smith, his commonplace book (1979)

A Vision of Doom, poems by Ambrose Bierce (1980)

The City of the Singing Flame, by Clark Ashton Smith (1981)

The Last Incantation, by Clark Ashton Smith (1982)

The Monster of the Prophecy, by Clark Ashton Smith (1983)

Strange Shadows, The Uncollected Fiction and Essays [i.e., miscellanea] *of Clark Ashton Smith*, edited by Steve Behrends with Donald Sidney-Fryer and Rah Hoffman (1989)

The Hashish-Eater; or, The Apocalypse of Evil, 1922 edition, by Clark Ashton Smith (1990, with CD 2008)

As Green as Emeraude, The Collected Poems of Margo Skinner (1990)

The Devil's Notebook, epigrams, apothegms, etc., by Clark Ashton Smith (1990)

Songs and Sonnets Atlantean, The Second Series (2003)

Gaspard de la Nuit, by Aloysius Bertrand, translation (2004)

Songs and Sonnets Atlantean, The Third Series (2005)

The Atlantis Fragments, The Trilogy of Songs and Sonnets Atlantean, omnibus collection (2008, 2009)

The Outer Gate, The Collected Poems of Nora May French (2009)

The Averoigne Chronicles, by Clark Ashton Smith, edited by Ron Hilger with Donald Sidney-Fryer

The Case of the Light Fantastic Toe, The Romantic Ballet and Signor Maestro Cesare Pugni, A Chronicle and Source Book, edited by Adam Lopez

Donald Sidney-Fryer with his bass lute.
Photo: Robert W. Thompson, 2007

THE GOLDEN STATE PHANTASTICKS.
The California Romantics and Related Subjects.

Collected Essays and Reviews

Donald Sidney-Fryer

Associate Editors
Leo Grin and Alan Gullette

Hippocampus Press

New York

Published by Hippocampus Press
P.O. Box 641, New York, NY 10156
www.hippocampuspress.com

ISBN-13: 978-1-61498-037-7

Cover and book design by Alan Gullette.
Cover production by Barbara Briggs Silbert.
Frontispiece photograph by Robert W. Thompson.
Hippocampus Press logo designed by Anastasia Damianakos.

Originally published by Phosphor Lantern Press,
Westchester, Los Angeles, California.

Dedicated to the Trimurti of special friends whose assistance and encouragement have made this and other books of mine possible, Leo Grin, Don Herron, and Alan Gullette.

Contents

Foreword/Forward in a Phantastick Mode!

The present author began his literary career as a published writer back in the early 1960's with several essays, and he now closes it with his last book by gathering those essays, along with quite a few others, into the present collection, including various reviews, introductions to books by other authors, and sundry pieces.

Otherwise complete, this collection does not include *Arthur Machen and King Arthur: Sovereigns of Dream*, published by Silver Scarab Press as the last half of No. 12 for *Nyctalops*, No. 11–12, the special double issue dated April 1976. At twice the length of *The Last of the Great Romantic Poets*, it ranks as a separate monograph, albeit of short book length. Whether or not it deserves a separate republication as its own book or booklet, need not concern us here.

Apart from the above monograph the only exception to the otherwise complete is the three essays that appear by Donald Sidney-Fryer in *The Freedom of Fantastic Things: Selected Criticism on Clark Ashton Smith*, edited by Scott Connors (Hippocampus Press, New York, 2006). "Klarkash-Ton and Greek" / "James Blish versus Clark Ashton Smith" / "Brave World Old and New"—these essays form an integral part of this first anthology devoted to critical pieces on the Bard of Auburn.

Apart from reading the writings of Edmund Spenser, especially his epic *The Faerie Queene*—which summoned me during the first half of 1961 to my vocation as a poet and poet-performer—it was the poetry and prose of Clark Ashton Smith that changed me into a writer. This happened in a simple, straightforward way, but it required not quite a decade to move me to become one.

I first became acquainted with Ashton Smith's prose fictions, along with those of other Arkham House authors, in the mid-1950's. Thanks to owner-editor August Derleth and his biographical sketches of these authors, I learned that many of them had begun their careers with one or more collections of poetry, not exactly unconventional behavior for beginning writers. As I acquired copies of their Arkham House collections of short stories, I also began reading or collecting sporadically their poetry volumes.

However, I had not gone far in that subsidiary direction when in the spring of 1958 I managed to get hold of Ashton Smith's four early poetry collections, *The Star-Treader* (1912), *Odes and Sonnets* (1918—this I had actually acquired in September of 1957 at San Francisco), *Ebony and Crystal* (1922—the subtitle significantly reads *Poems in Verse and Prose*), and *Sandalwood* (1925), all at incredibly low prices, particularly as compared to those that these volumes command from determined collectors today.

I had already purchased *The Dark Chateau* (1951) directly from Arkham House. It did not take me very long to perceive the four early collections as the epochal achievements that they remain. Unlike most of his fellow Arkham House author-poets, Ashton Smith stood out, stood apart from them in his own poetry. In fact he looms as a major poet, a great poet, one of unique, profound, and wide-raging vision, no less than of impeccable craftsmanship. Inherited and developed from George Sterling, it is Ashton Smith's bleak and uncompromising cosmic-astronomic-mindedness that makes the real difference between him and other poets and scriveners.

By mid-1960, having made what became for me this life-changing realization, I had launched myself on into the enormous but inspiring task of researching and compiling an Ashton Smith bibliography, such as would end up as a compendium of all manner of lore associated with this poet-author, not only what I was to discover myself but what I would manage to invite from a good many of his friends, such persons who had known Ashton Smith very well indeed, and furthermore, over a very long period of time in most cases.

I realized that, if Smith could ever achieve critical acceptance and recognition from the mainstream, a bibliography (but only of an unconventional type) would play perforce an essential role, and would form the foundation for such critical recognizance, not to mention future evaluation and scholarly research. In a critical sense the 1950's represent the absolute nadir of Smith's career; the 1960's improved somewhat. Between 1958 and 1970 Arkham House published five hardcover titles of his thanks to the astute management of August Derleth.

As a poet and fictioneer Smith acknowledged obvious influences from the poetry and prose of Edgar Allan Poe, the poetry of his mentor George Sterling, the *Pastels in Prose* (Harper and Brother, 1893) as translated and presented by Stuart Merrill, *The Arabian Nights*, William Beckford's *Vathek*, as well as the fiction of Ambrose Bierce and Robert W. Chambers. Smith had already read an immense amount of books of all types by the time that *The Star-Treader* appeared, and then between 1912 and 1922, apparently he read an even greater amount of material. This continued from the early 1920's on through the middle to latter part of that decade. More than an omnivorous reader, he remained a highly discriminating one all his life, first in English, then in Latin, next in French, and finally in Spanish.

My earliest essays dealt with what I had identified as a vexing (if not irritating) problem. Several well-intentioned but ill-informed critics had falsely perceived certain influences on Smith's fiction from writers whom he himself had not acknowledged, such as Lord Dunsany and Lovecraft himself. However, in my first major essay, devoted to Smith's life and the entire corpus of his work (poetry and pictorial art, prose and sculpture)—given my own background in French and other European languages and literatures—I was able to do justice for the first time ever to all of Smith's remarkable *oeuvre*.

First published in August 1963 as part of the commemorative booklet *In Memoriam: Clark Ashton Smith*, this major essay *The Sorcerer Departs* has now undergone two separate booklet publications, first by Tsathoggua Press at Los Angeles in 1997, and then (currently) by Silver Key Press (la Clef d'argent) at Dole (France) in 2007. This essay has now become the standard short account of Smith's life and writings. In the first major collection of essays ever assembled about Smith and his *oeuvre*, *The Freedom of Fantastic Things* mentioned above, Scott Connors in his introduction refers to the present author, inter alia, as follows: "After Smith's death in 1961, his study was largely the private preserve of one man, Donald Sidney-Fryer...." That same present author can only comment on this obvious truth, sic: *Faute de mieux*—for lack of anything or anyone better. He had no real critical company until Steve Behrends appeared, above all with the volume that he researched and edited, *Strange Shadows, The Uncollected Fiction and Essays* [i.e., miscellanea] *of Clark Ashton Smith*, published by Greenwood Press, Westport, Connecticut, 1989. To recapitulate, his early poetry had led to an invitation to contribute to *Weird Tales, The Unique Magazine*, in the 1920's and then the 1930's. From there he had moved on to hardcover publication by Arkham House, above all thanks to August Derleth. Founded by Derleth in 1939, Arkham House in Sauk City, Wisconsin (not far from Madison, the state capital), became as it remains to this day the first major specialized and alternative press vis-à-vis the publishers on either the west or the east coast of the U. S. A. It was not until 1970 that the foundational work done by Arkham and by Derleth on behalf of Ashton Smith found an even greater scope and impetus, including both a national and international mass market, no less than mainstream recognition of a kind. Thanks to the extraordinary success worldwide enjoyed by Ballantine Books' paperback edition of J. R. R. Tolkien's trilogy *The Lord of the Rings* both popularly and critically, the same publisher had hired and empowered the very well-read and well-informed Lin Carter to act as the over-all editor for the new Adult Fantasy Library, which would result in the creation of new imaginative fiction as well as in the resurrection of much older and unjustly neglected classics of the literature.

Along with many volumes by other authors as well, Lin Carter compiled and edited with outstanding taste and literary savoir-faire four mass-market paperbacks featuring Smith's idiosyncratic short stories: *Zothique* (1970), *Hyperborea* (1971), *Xiccarph* (1972), and *Poseidonis* (1973). The series editor had planned a fifth paperback, *Averoigne*, but his fatal illness and premature death forestalled what might have emerged as the most popular title of all, not to mention other books by other authors. Carter had also prominently featured Smith's work in several anthologies published in the early 1970's as part of the Adult Fantasy Library. All these volumes appeared planet-wide throughout the English-speaking world.

By the 1980's and 1990's Ashton Smith had become firmly re-established, at least in regard to his prose fictions. This new readership and recognition has by now far surpassed Smith's earlier poetic fame, 1912–1930, whether on the West Coast or the East Coast of the United States or in Great Britain. Thanks to the heroic and sustained efforts of S. T. Joshi, David E. Schultz, and Derrick Hussey, the three monumental hardcover volumes of Smith's complete collected poetry (including all his translations) made their appearance during 2007–2008 from Hippocampus Press. Since 2006 Night Shade Books has been publishing all of Smith's fiction in a series of no less monumental hardcover volumes. Four have appeared and one further volume and one final booklet (this last will contain the very small body of his non-fantastic fiction) are planned. Thus by the current end of the first decade in the twenty-first century Smith's writings and reputation have reached some kind of genuine acceptance and permanence.

Meanwhile all during the same period from the early 1960's on into the last part of this decade, as my circumstances have permitted, I have continued writing essays long and short elucidating not only Smith's poetry and prose—including especially his poems in prose that directly lead to his original short stories of 1928–1938—but also the general Romance Tradition to which he firmly belongs, no less than Ambrose Bierce, George Sterling, and Nora May French. But I have branched out also to other authors and other subjects, whether in articles, reviews, or introductions. We should mention here, excluding Lovecraft, that Ashton Smith and Robert E. Howard share a certain frontiersman frame of mind. Nonetheless, the main goal of this book remains in place, that of defining in critical terms the survival of not just the Late Romanticism from the 1800's but also the Modern Romanticism of the 1900's on into the twenty-first century. Romanticism of whatever type is alive and well in California!

—DONALD SIDNEY-FRYER
Westchester, Los Angeles
23 February 2010.

THE GOLDEN STATE PHANTASTICKS.
The California Romantics and Related Subjects.

The Sorcerer Departs

I pass ... but in this lone and crumbling tower,
Builded against the burrowing seas of chaos,
My volumes and my philtres shall abide:
Poisons more dear than any mithridate,
And spells far sweeter than the speech of love....
Half-shapen dooms shall slumber in my vaults
And in my volume cryptic runes that shall
Outblast the pestilence, outgnaw the worm
When loosed by alien wizards in strange years
Under the blackened moon and paling sun.

The Sorcerer Departs (Fragment of unfinished poem),
by Clark Ashton Smith (from *The Acolyte*, Spring, 1944)

1. A Biography of Clark Ashton Smith

For those of us who recognize in the late Clark Ashton Smith a poet and a poet in prose as remarkable as the French genius Baudelaire, the above "fragment"—actually far more complete than many a longer poem—cannot but possess certain poignant autobiographical associations. The eventuality stated symbolically in the last lines is devoutly to be wished: that connoisseurs of fantasy, whether in the immediate or the far future, shall indeed come to know the canon of Smith's works and appreciate his quite considerable achievement, and that Smith shall thus come to realize the only type of immortality any human being may reasonably expect.

When Clark Ashton Smith died on August 14th, 1961, his death passed almost completely unnoticed, apart from a few local newspapers in his native state of California. No *Saturday Review of Literature*, no *Atlantic Monthly* devoted an entire memorial issue to the man and his writings. To the knowledge of the present writer, not a single science-fiction or fantasy magazine even mentioned the fact of his death. Smith's connections with the main literary river of his own time were at best tenuous, if not just about non-existent; his connections with the tributary or sub-tributary of the science-fiction and fantasy magazines, proved only a little less gossamer. The echoes of his earlier poetic fame in the bohemian cir-

`cles of San Francisco and Monterey had long since died away, and thus he died, little better than unknown to his own time.

The biography of Smith's external life is relatively uneventful, although still significant; but this relative uneventfulness places a greater importance on the life of the inner man, on the inner life of the literary creator, where such is known to us and where it is revealed in his works. However, it will still serve to some purpose to review the more salient facts of biography with particular emphasis on those details which strongly relate to his creative life.

Smith was born of Yankee and English parentage on January 13th, 1893, in Long Valley, California, about six miles south of Auburn, in the house of his maternal grandparents (the Gaylords) located along the old road leading south of Folsom out of Auburn, and about five miles from the northern reaches of Boulder Ridge where Smith was to spend the major portion of his life. In 1902, his parents, Fanny and Timeus Smith, moved to Boulder Ridge, to a spot about a mile south of Auburn and about one-fourth of a mile east of the Folsom Road. Here his father with the help of the then nine-year-old boy, built a cabin and dug a well, and here Smith lived almost continuously until 1954, apart from visits to Sacramento, San Francisco, Monterey, the neighboring state of Nevada, and a few other places. He almost visited New York City sometime in 1942 under the aegis of his friends Benjamin and Bio DeCasseres.

One can easily imagine the effect that the surrounding countryside had on the sensitive and imaginative boy; a countryside that was and still is a veritable garden of fruit trees—pear, plum, peach, cherry, apple— located on the rolling foothills of the Sierras and alternating with copses of evergreen and deciduous trees and with broad park-like areas; the foothills filled with deserted mines, some of them still containing gold; and arching overhead, the diurnal or nocturnal immensitudes of the heavens rendered remarkably clear in the clean smog-free country air.

He attended the equivalent of the first three grades of grammar school (in Smith's own words) "at the little red schoolhouse of the precinct." He completed the five remaining grades of grammar school in Auburn. Smith wrote later that "As a schoolboy, I believe that I was distinguished more for devilment than scholarship. Much of my childhood was spent in the neighborhood of an alleged gold mine; which may be the reason why the romance of California gold mining failed to get under my skin." However this last may have been, this neighboring gold mine—the "Old Gaylord Mine" close to his grandparents' property—evidently had some influence on the young Smith as his mature literary work, both poetry and prose, abounds in mining and geological terms. Without realizing it, he had succumbed to the greater romance of splendor, as numerous references to precious and semi-precious metals and stones attest in his poems and in his tales.

Smith did not go on to either high school or college; he preferred to conduct his own education and later, when he turned down a Guggenheim scholarship, it was for the same reason. Thus early in his life he manifested what was to be his lifelong independence. To judge by his creative work, we may be sure that Smith—always an omnivorous but discerning reader—proved to be his own best teacher.

From the very first Smith seems to have been attracted to the exotic, the far away, and the literally astronomically far away. The gold mine near his grandparents' home, with its hints of precious, untold wealth, may account to some minor degree for Smith's predilection for the exotic. The fact that his father Timeus Smith had travelled extensively as a young man, and that he may possibly have reminisced to his son, may also explain Smith's early attraction to the far away and the fabled, to the Orient and to those mysterious lands of the imagination so beloved by visionary youth.

The last is somewhat borne out when Smith later wrote that his "first literary efforts at the age of eleven, took the form of fairy tales and imitations of *The Arabian Nights*. Later, I wrote long adventure novels dealing with Oriental life, and much mediocre verse." These "long adventure novels dealing with Oriental life" culminated in Smith's first professional short-story appearances in magazines: "The Malay Krise" and "The Ghost of Mohammed Din" in the then well-known west-coast literary magazine *The Overland Monthly*, the issues for October and November 1910, respectively; and "The Mahout" and "The Raja and The Tiger" in *The Black Cat*, in the issues for August 1911 and February 1912, respectively. Significantly enough, all these tales are laid in the Orient, the first-named in the area of Singapore and the last three in India. "The Ghost of Mohammed Din" is important as being Smith's first professional story in which he features the element of the supernatural (handled with considerable skill, it may be added). In "The Raja and The Tiger" the climactic action of the story takes place in the Jain cave temple where "Huge stone pillars, elaborately sculptured, supported the roof, and around the sides great gods and goddesses of the Jain mythology, called Arhats, glared downward. The torch illuminated dimly, leaving much in shadow, *and in the shadow imagination created strange fantasies.*" (The present writer's italics.) Smith later re-used the theme of "The Mahout," of a mahout who trains and uses an elephant to wreak his revenge upon a hated Oriental despot. When Farnsworth Wright, the editor of *Weird Tales*, came to found in 1930 a companion magazine called *Oriental Stories* (later changed to *The Magic Carpet Magazine*, Smith contributed two tales: "The Justice of the Elephant" in the Autumn 1931 issue of *Oriental Stories*, and "The Kiss of Zoraida" in the July 1933 issue of *The Magic Carpet Magazine*. In the former laid in India, Smith used again, in slightly altered form, the theme of "The Mahout." In the latter, laid in Damascus, appears one of Smith's principal inspirations, the manifestation of death. The Oriental background continued in "The Kingdom of the Worm," a tale of the medieval adventurer Sir John Maundeville, published in *The Fantasy Fan* for October 1933; and it continued in "The Ghoul," published in the same amateur magazine for January 1934; this last is a tale laid in Bagdad during the reign of the Caliph Vathek, William Beckford's fictional "grandson" of Haroun al Raschid.

The four earlier tales of 1910–1912 are written with a control, a sense of selection that would have done credit to a mature writer. If it weren't for the evidence to the contrary, a reader might very easily mistake the four later Oriental tales as being of the same period of his four earlier ones; or vice versa. These four early stories serve as testimony as to the care with which Smith has schooled himself for one of his self-appointed spheres of creation.

Besides witnessing the appearance of the very first of Smith's professional short stories, 1910 was also the very first year that saw Smith professionally in print, whether in verse or in prose. Then, for some reason Smith lost interest in professionally writing short stories, and devoted himself almost wholly to poetry from 1911, from the time he was eighteen, until 1925, when he was thirty-two. Smith's parents proved fortunately sympathetic to their son's creativity all during this time, and indeed up until the time of their death in the 1930's.

In 1906, when he was thirteen, Smith had made an important literary discovery for himself, one which profoundly influenced his own writing. Let Smith tell this in his own words: "Unique, and never to be forgotten, was the thrill with which, at the age of thirteen, I discovered for myself the poems of Poe in a grammar-school library; and, despite the objurgations of the librarian, who considered Poe 'unwholesome,' carried the priceless volume home to revel for enchanted days in its undreamt-of melodies. Here, indeed, was 'balm in Gilead,' here was a 'kind nepenthe.'" Later, and equally important, Smith discovered Poe's short stories. Then, when Smith was almost fifteen, he made yet another important discovery: "Likewise memorable, and touched with more than the glamour of childhood dreams, was my first reading, two years later, of "A Wine of Wizardry," [by George Sterling] in the pages of the old *Cosmopolitan*. The poem, with its necromantic music, and splendours as of sunset on jewels and cathedral windows, was veritably all that its title implied...." Meanwhile and after, Smith was writing the "much mediocre poetry" which served as the practice prerequisite to the creation of his mature poetry. Also, it may have been during this period of poetic apprenticeship that Smith worked out of his system any and all desire to create slavish imitations of Poe's "The Raven," "The Bells," and company. The cosmic-astronomic poetry of Sterling may have suggested to Smith to try his hand at the same theme; that, together with the beauty of the Auburn countryside with its immense blue skies at day and its black profundities of heavens ablaze with stars and planets at night.

Through the suggestion of Emily J. Hamilton, a teacher at the Auburn high school, Smith came into personal contact with Sterling, at that time the unofficial poet laureate of the West Coast and very much the social lion. In Smith's own words: "Several years later—when I was eighteen, to be precise—a few of my verses were submitted to Sterling for criticism, through the office of a mutual friend; and his favorable verdict led to a correspondence, and, later, an invitation to visit him in Carmel, where I spent a most idle and most happy month. I like to remember him, pounding abalones on a boulder in the back yard, or mixing pineapple punch (for which I was allowed to purvey the mint from a nearby meadow), or paying a round of matutinal visits among his assorted friends." This personal friendship and correspondence with Sterling lasted for 16 years, until Sterling's death in November 1926.

It was during these years, 1911–1912, when he was eighteen and nineteen, respectively, that Smith wrote his first mature poetry—the bulk of his first volume *The Star-Treader and Other Poems*. Evidently with some taste for art and literature, Boutwell Dunlop, a well-known property-owner in Placer County (in which both Auburn and Long Valley are located) and an acquaintance of Smith's, assisted the young poet in securing publication for his book. The San Francisco publisher A. M. Robertson, owner of a much-frequented bookshop and publisher of much of Sterling's poetry, agreed to bring the volume out. Sterling himself helped Smith with the reading of the proofs, and otherwise advised him; and in November of 1912 *The Star-Treader* appeared. The leading San Francisco newspapers proclaimed Smith "the Keats of the Pacific Coast," and discerning critics hailed him as a prodigy and a genius. Sterling later wrote that "the story of... [Smith's] triumph with his neighbors, when hundreds of copies of his first book of verses were promptly bought up in a small California hill town is a romance in itself."

Thus, Smith made his début into the bohemian literary and artistic life on the West Coast, centered in San Francisco and the surrounding area, a life that included and had included such notables as Bret Harte, Frank Norris, Jack London, George Sterling, Ambrose Bierce, Joaquin Miller, Edwin Markham, Ella Sterling Mighels, Charles Warren Stoddard, Nora May French, Ina Coolbrith, Gertrude Atherton, and many, many others. As the "discovery," protégé, and a friend of Sterling, Smith may have had access into the charmed circle of San Francisco *haut ton*. However, it is important to remember that for all the éclat of his introduction to this San Francisco literary and artistic life, Smith continued to live with his parents at their cabin on Boulder Ridge. It is interesting to speculate, in lieu of any actual evidence, if Smith ever met "Bitter" Bierce, who with Poe and a few others ranks as one of the greatest masters of the macabre. Before he departed in 1912 for Mexico where he later disappeared, Bierce had been living and working in Washington, D.C. Just before his departure for Mexico, he returned to California for a few months to renew old acquaintances. He did see Sterling again (even though Bierce had broken with both Sterling and Jack London when they had taken up Socialism), since Sterling had been one of the chief protégés of the older writer, who had once enthusiastically championed the younger man and his poetry. On one occasion Smith and Bierce almost met in San Francisco by means of Sterling, but the young Auburn poet was unable to go down to the city at that time. One cannot help but wonder what Bierce might have said in person to Sterling of the young Smith's poems.

Between 1912 and 1922, the year Smith's second major poetry collection appeared, we hear relatively little of Smith. Sometime during this decade Smith first came to know both *Les Fleurs du Mal* and the *Petits poèms en prose* of Baudelaire, possibly about 1914, but not however in the original French but in some English translation, possibly that of Arthur Symons. Smith was not to learn French and come to know Baudelaire in his original language until the middle 1920's. Smith later acknowledged that Baudelaire's poems as well as his poems in prose had had a considerable influence on Smith's work, especially on the latter's poems in prose. However, the Baudelaire influence manifests itself perhaps more in the technique of the *poème en prose* rather than in the subject matter. Also during this decade Smith began to contribute to a wide variety of magazines.

Violet Nelson Heyer, a long-time resident of Auburn as well as a long-term friend of the Smiths, recalls Clark's family during this period in the following words: "our family home adjoined Clark's family acres from the years 1908 until 1919, and the three personalities (Clark and his parents) are well-remembered by us—the dark, reticent father and the happy, light-hearted soul who was Clark's mother... a lady of beautiful spirit and intense dedication to her family."

Sometime after the publication of *The Star-Treader*, Smith suffered a nervous breakdown and an attack of tuberculosis; from the former he fortunately recovered but the latter, while arrested, continued to bother him intermittently the rest of his life. Smith had had terrific nightmares from his early boyhood onward—he bases at least one of his later stories on a nightmare experienced in his early youth (see "The Primal City")—and the terrible nightmares he suffered during this difficult period left a profound impression on his memory: he later recalled for friends that many of his horror stories were based on these nightmares. Vivid dreams and nightmares often accompany the occurrence of fever; and the victim of tuberculosis, alternating as he does between bouts of raging fever and periods when the body temperature falls below normal, experiences dreams and nightmares of even greater intensity. The student of Smith's works may well wonder as to the white-hot intensity of the nightmares suffered at this particular time by Smith, always a highly sensitive and imaginative person. All of this—the nervous breakdown, the attack of tuberculosis, the terrible nightmares, and the dreadful uncertainty of whether he would or would not be cured, whether he would live or die— all of this must have had a shattering effect on Smith: he must have lived an eternity of lives during this period. It would serve to explain the rich and varied emotional background which undoubtedly inspired much of the work in Smith's next major poetry collection, *Ebony and Crystal.*

That he had been putting his inner life to excellent poetic advantage, was demonstrated beyond a doubt when in 1918 the Book Club of California issued fifteen of Smith's poems in an *édition de luxe* of 300 copies, under the title of *Odes and Sonnets*, with decorations by Florence Lundberg of New York City and with a preface by George Sterling. The first four poems were reprinted from *The Star-Treader*, the remaining eleven reappeared in *Ebony and Crystal*. The preface contained not only a discerning appreciation of Smith's genius but also an incidental prophecy that, alas, sadly came to eventualize, that Smith was "unlikely to be afflicted with present-day popularity." Distinguished recognition, however, was immediate. Edwin Markham, a poet now most famous for the poem "The Man With The Hoe," wrote: "These poems have lines of unusual beauty, glints and gleams of true genius. There is something terrific in Smith, as there was in John Martin, the illustrator of Milton's *Paradise Lost*. It cheers me to know that you Californians have honoured yourselves in your honouring of this distinguished poet." Grace Atherton Dennon, editor of the west-coast poetry magazine *The Lyric West*, wrote: "Your poems are rich in feeling and expression. I regard you as a genuine poet, one whose name will endure." And from across the Atlantic the distinguished English poet and essayist Alice Meynell Smith wrote: "I think the imagination in your poems very remarkable, and wonderfully original. They are poems of true genius." In recognition of his services to literature the Book Club of California presented Smith with a bronze plaque designed by the noted San Francisco sculptor Edgar Walter, an honor bestowed only on such literary notables as Sterling and Edwin Markham.

About this time Smith began a number of important correspondences, one with the poet Samuel Loveman, a close friend of Ambrose Bierce and the author of *The Hermaphrodite and Other Poems*; and, about 1922–1923, directly through the auspices of Loveman, with H. P. Lovecraft. This last was the beginning of what must have been a wonderfully rewarding friendship through letters for both men, as it is evident that they held many views, opinions, and tastes in common—in archaeology, astronomy, astrology, languages ancient and modern (and a consequent interest in the systematic invention of personal and place names for fictional purposes), demonology, sorcery, mythology, legendry, folklore, and only Cunthamosi, the Cosmic Mother (in Smith's tale "The Monster of the Prophecy"), knows what else!

As an example of how much Smith and Lovecraft had in common, it is of interest to compare their respective lists of "favorite weird stories." In *The Fantasy Fan*, December 1934, appeared (through the "Courtesy of H. Koenig") the following list of Smith's 10 favorite weird stories: "The Yellow Sign," by Robert W. Chambers; "The House of Sounds," by M. P. Shiel; "The Willows," by Algernon Blackwood; "A View from a Hill," by M. R. James; "The Death of Halpin Frayser," by Ambrose Bierce; "The Fall of the House of Usher," by Edgar Allan Poe; "The Masque of the Red Death," by Edgar Allan Poe; "The Novel of the White Powder," by Arthur Machen; "The Call of Cthulhu," by H. P. Lovecraft; and "The Colour Out of Space," by H. P. Lovecraft. In the preceding issue for October of the same amateur magazine, had appeared (also through the "Courtesy of H. Koenig") Lovecraft's list of favorite weird stories. Six of them duplicate Smith's choices, with only four titles different: "The Novel of the Black Seal," by Arthur Machen; "The White People," by Arthur Machen; "Count Magnus," by M. R. James; and "The Moon Pool" (original novelette), by A. Merritt. Yet for all such similarities in taste and opinion, the creative work of each man is strikingly different from that of the other; and each fully appreciated the other's genius.

In 1922, Smith selected and arranged into book form the best from the work of the years following the appearance of his first volume, and in December 1922, he published in Auburn his second major poetry collection *Ebony and Crystal, Poems in Verse and Prose*, with a preface by George Sterling and dedicated to Samuel Loveman. Again distinguished recognition was immediate. Henry Anderson Lafler wrote: "I wonder that you speak so slightingly of these poems. It seems to me that nothing being written today overtops them. You and George Sterling are two eagles in 'strong level flight,' winging sunward above flocks of sparrows."

The novelist and poet Frank L. Pollock wrote: "I must make you all possible compliments on your magnificent piece of blank verse, 'The Hashish-Eater.' The technique is superb, the verse hard-spun and close-woven. It would be difficult to conceive of greater power and variety of imagination, or a greater splendour of vocabulary. Almost every episode has the material for a long poem in itself—in fact you have used up enough poetical material to make half a dozen volumes of modem poets. As a decorative poem, it seems to me that this is one of the finest things I have ever read. I do not think there are six men living who could have done it—certainly no one else in America. Continually one comes cross absolutely right and infallible lines, giving the joy of a thing perfectly said;

or some burst of metaphor that is like a flash of lightning; or some violent and vivid feat of imagination. I could pick examples by scores; there is only an *embarras des richesses.*"

The secretary of the Book Club of California, Alfred M. Bender, wrote: "Thank you for your wonderful poem, 'The Hashish-Eater.' The subject may seem unappealing to many, but it has such richness of imagination, sustained thought, and stately beauty of expression that I am sure it will enhance your reputation and bring you new laurels. It should be an inward satisfaction to add another star to the firmament of California literature. Your place is growing firmer with each new effort." Smith's great friend and mentor George Sterling wrote: "'The Hashish-Eater' is indeed a most amazing production. It contains more imagination than anything else I have ever read." In the poetry journal *L'Alouette* for January 1924, appeared a highly favorable review of *Ebony and Crystal* by Smith's correspondent living across the continent, H. P. Lovecraft, who gave unstinted and eloquent praise to the volume, especially to its crowning achievement "The Hashish-Eater."

Unfortunately, the fact that *Ebony and Crystal* was privately published in a limited edition (as was the following volume *Sandalwood*), prevented it from reaching a nationwide audience, with the consequent larger critical recognition.. To what extent its poetic originality and excellence, its oftentime extraordinary cosmic vision, would have been appreciated is a moot question, since the year 1922 saw the beginning of the apotheosis of that modernist poet par excellence, T. S. Eliot, who had won the $2000 Dial Award for his 434-line poem "The Waste Land" (1922). It would be interesting and amusing (if nothing else) to compare Eliot's extended ode on sterility and desiccation to Smith's longest poem, the 576-line "The Hashish-Eater." One had summed up in a thoroughly modernist manner the disillusionment, the disenchantment of a postwar generation of the first half of the 20th century of the Christian Era. The other, who rarely bothered himself in the least with his own age, without the manifest gesture of even turning his back on his own times, celebrated in a highly original and inventive manner the eternal, ever-renewing, even if perverse, splendors of the cosmos.

Acclaim of his own age or not, Smith continued on his own supremely independent way, letting no external clamors or censures interfere with the voice of his own personal daemon. During the 1920's Smith was contributing to a wide range of magazines, from those of national or international circulation to the "little" magazines. The poetry journal *The Step-Ladder* honored Smith by devoting its entire issue of May 1927 to his poems (principally from *Ebony and Crystal* and *Sandalwood*). Among this wide range of magazines was one whose founding in 1923 and existence up until 1954, was to play a pivotal role when Smith later came to write short stories. This was *Weird Tales* "The Unique Magazine" (as the subtitle ran), in which Smith first appeared in the issue for January 1924 with the poems "The Red Moon" and "The Garden of Evil" (later collected into *Sandalwood* as "Moon-Dawn" and "Duality," respectively).

During the first half of the 1920's, Smith became a "journalist" and contributed to *The Auburn Journal* 101 installments of a column entitled "Clark Ashton Smith's Column": the first column is dated April 5, 1923, the last is dated January 7, 1926. To this column Smith contributed both poetry and epigrams, largely the former: in all, 81 poems (59 original poems and 22 translations from Baudelaire) and 329 original, and 17 selected, epigrams and pensées. (To the *Journal* overall, Smith contributed 84 poems) The majority of the poems in *Sandalwood*—that is, 49 of the total 61 poems in that collection (37 of the 42 original poems and 12 of the 19 translations from Baudelaire)—appeared in this column of Smith's, most of them previously to their publication in *Sandalwood*. While most of the poems first published in the *Journal* have since appeared elsewhere, virtually all of the 329, or 346, epigrams and pensées have not, although publication of a selection of them (made by Smith) was tentatively considered by an eastern publisher in the early 1940's. The epigrams and pensées appeared in the *Journal* under the following titles: *Epigrams* (once), *Cocktails and Crème de Menthe*, *Points for the Pious*, *Unpopular Sayings* (once), *New Teeth For Old Saws* (once), *The Devil's Note-Book* (which title has its obvious analogy with that of *The Devil's Dictionary* by Ambrose Bierce, originally entitled *The Cynic's Word-Book*), and *Paradox and Persiflage*. In 1990, Starmont House brought out a complete edition—or as complete as then possible—of Smith's epigrams and pensées under the title *The Devil's Notebook*, edited by Don Herron.

In October 1925, again in Auburn, Smith published his third major poetry collection *Sandalwood*, dedicated to George Sterling; a volume distinguished not only for its many beautiful love poems but also for the 19 translations from the French of Charles Pierre Baudelaire. The 19 translations are indeed a remarkable accomplishment in view of the fact that Smith knew virtually nothing of the French language a year prior to October 1925, and hence had learned the language in something less than a year, beginning his study of it and subsequently of Baudelaire in November or December 1924, or during the very first part of 1925. This volume, because of its private printing in a limited edition, has shared the fate of *Ebony and Crystal* of being little better than unknown. In addition to the recognition given Smith's poetry of 1911–1925 by divers distinguished literary persons, the newspapers of the San Francisco area accorded long, elaborate, and over-all excellent reviews to at least the first 2 of Smith's 3 major early poetry collections. As the result of *Ebony and Crystal*, one critic wrote apropos of Smith that "Among the living [poets] he stands alone."

The year 1925 also saw a new development in Smith's creative evolution: in this same year he had written 2 short stories, "The Abominations of Yondo" and "Sadastor," stylistically and thematically growing out of his earlier poems in prose as well as out of his poems in verse. He submitted them to Farnsworth Wright, the editor of *Weird Tales*. The latter, always wary as to reader reaction to something overly new, rejected both stories, which he very well may have considered a little bit of too much, since both tales are essentially extended poems in prose. Later Wright did accept "Sadastor," printed in *Weird Tales* for July 1930; and *The Overland Monthly* accepted "The Abominations of Yondo," printed in the issue for April 1926, with the following note on Smith in the section entitled "April Contributors": "Clark Ashton Smith is a California poet and he proves something else in his 'Abominations of Yondo.'" Indeed, he had proven himself an unique poet in prose—that is, a practitioner of the poem in prose—and had proven the possibility of writing an extended poem in prose, in the manner of Poe's "The Masque of the Red Death," that unique creation in the canon of the elder writer's works. In fact, it is not too much to say that technically Smith had almost created— or at least re-created—the genre of the extended poem in prose.

In November 1926, at the Bohemian Club in San Francisco, occurred the death of George Sterling, Smith's great friend and mentor, ostensibly by suicide, a theory with which Smith never agreed: "...As Smith points out in his article [of personal reminiscences of Sterling written in 1941], the evidence indicating suicide was largely circumstantial. At the time of his death, Sterling had in his possession not only the fatal poison (cyanide) but also a morphine derivative that he had sometimes taken against sleeplessness. He was ill and perhaps suffering the profound mental confusion that often accompanies illness. What could have been more probable than a mistake? Sterling's last letter, written to Smith less than a week before his death, gave no evidence of mental depression or a failing of his vital interests." (From *The Auburn Journal*, Dec. 15, 1941: see article "Notes on Clark Ashton Smith.") Moreover, Sterling had been eagerly awaiting a visit from H. L. Mencken.

His death was a source of great bereavement to Smith, who paid a beautiful and moving tribute to his friend in the memorable poem "A Valediction to George Sterling," published in *The Overland Monthly* for November 1927. Earlier in the same year had appeared in the same magazine, in the issue for March, an article of reminiscences by Smith of Sterling entitled "George Sterling—An Appreciation." In it Smith recalled Sterling in the following words: "Always to me, as to others, he was a very gentle and faithful friend, and the kindest of mentors. Perhaps we did not always agree in matters of literary taste; but it is good to remember that our occasional arguments or differences of opinion were never in the least acrimonious. Indeed, how could they have been?—one might quarrel with others, but never with him: which, perhaps, is not the poorest tribute that I can pay to George Sterling.... But words are doubly inadequate, when one tries to speak of such a friend; and the best must abide in silence." Later (in 1941), Smith recalled Sterling in these words: "He was essentially lovable, gave himself without stint and assisted scores of young poets." Smith remained devoted the rest of his life to Sterling's memory and to his poetry.

A few weeks before his death, Sterling had said to David Warren Ryder: "Clark Ashton Smith is undoubtedly our finest living poet. He is in the great tradition of Shakespeare, Keats and Shelley; and yet, to our everlasting shame, he is entirely neglected and almost completely unknown." Also shortly before his death, Sterling had advised Smith, apropos of the latter's poems in prose of death and similar subject-matter, to give up "this macabre prose," a piece of advice Smith fortunately ignored. One of the very last services which Sterling performed for Smith and the cause of his poetry occurred when the elder poet brought an article for publication into the editorial offices of *The Overland Monthly* in San Francisco. This article was a highly enthusiastic, almost ecstatic essay on Smith's poetry entitled "The Emperor of Dreams" and written by the then 18-year-old Donald A. Wandrei. The monthly subsequently published the essay in its issue for December 1926.

Sometime after the publication of *Ebony and Crystal* or *Sandalwood*, Vachel Lindsay had read some of Smith's poetry and had begun a correspondence with him. This correspondence-friendship lasted until Lindsay's death in 1931. But it may have begun somewhat earlier.

After *Sandalwood*, Smith had evidently given up the creation in quantity of poetry. He had now turned his attention once more to the writing of fiction. Earlier, in 1924, in the August issue of *10 Story Book*—a magazine which featured a piquant combination of short stories with what are now known as "girly pictures" had appeared Smith's first professional short story since his contributions to *The Overland Monthly* and *The Black Cat* in 1910–1912: this is an amusing, deft, and very brief short story entitled "Something New," in which Smith incidentally mocks the extraordinarily rich style of imagery characteristic of *Ebony and Crystal*. In 1925 he had written the two extended poems in prose "The Abomination of Yondo" and "Sadastor." As we have seen, Farnsworth Wright rejected them.

However, Smith continued to contribute to *Weird Tales* his own original poems in verse as well as translations from Baudelaire, all of an expectedly high quality. The issue for August 1928 included Smith's first appearance in prose in *Weird Tales*; this was in the form of prose translations of 3 poems originally in verse by Baudelaire—"L'Irréparable," "Les Sept Vieillards," and "Une Charogne"—presented to the readers as *Three Poems in Prose, by Charles Pierre Baudelaire* and *Translated by Clark Ashton Smith from the French*. Smith had translated the verse originals of the poet into a supple and idiomatic English prose. In the succeeding issue for September 1928 appeared Smith's first short story in *Weird Tales*; a strange parable of love and death entitled "The Ninth Skeleton," but giving relatively little indication of the shape of things to come. The tale is significant, however, in that it is one of the very few laid by Smith in his general natal area: the action takes place on Boulder Ridge not far from the narrator's cabin; and the description of the area in the story is a poetic but exact one of the area around Smith's own cabin.

However, Smith did not begin the writing of fiction in any quantity until the beginning of the Depression in 1929. We must postulate the years 1925 to 1929/1930 as the period in which Smith was carefully preparing in his imagination the divers backgrounds for his stories. In the poem in prose entitled "To The Daemon" and dated December 16th, 1929, Smith wrote: "Tell me many tales, O benign maleficent daemon. . . .

Tell me tales of inconceivable fear and unimaginable love…." And tell him many tales the *daemon* veritably did. Between 1929 and August 1936 Smith wrote more than one hundred short stories and novelettes.

His next story to appear in *Weird Tales* was "The End of the Story," laid in Smith's imaginary province of medieval France, Averoigne; this was in the issue for May 1930. The tale proved immediately popular with the readers of "The Unique Magazine," and the distinguished writer and critic Benjamin DeCasseres, in "The Eyrie" for July ("The Eyrie" was the readers' letter department in *Weird Tales*), commended Smith's tale "as a story which is not only a philosophic thriller but possesses real literary quality, which is not lost (quite the contrary) on readers, such as you have, of imaginative tales." The majority of Smith's tales appeared in either *Weird Tales* under Farnsworth Wright or *Wonder Stories* under Hugo Gernsback. To the latter Smith contributed a highly imaginative, not to say unique, type of science-fiction story. To the former he contributed all manner of tales, many of them laid in Smith's carefully constructed backgrounds: the primeval continent Hyperborea; "the last isle of foundering Atlantis," Poseidonis; medieval Averoigne; the last continent Zothique; the planet Xiccarph; and many other worlds. Although these stories may have been known only to a specialized audience, they introduced a new dimension in the art of the short story: many of the more characteristic tales are actually extended poems in prose in which Smith has united the singleness of purpose and mood of the modern short story (as first established by one of Smith's literary idols, Edgar Allan Poe) together with the flexibility of the *conte* or tale; an entire short story being unified and, in part, given its powerful centralization of effect, mood, atmosphere, etc., by a more or less related system or systems of poetic imagery. This ranks as a technical achievement of the first order, although it has received relatively little or no recognition.

It is indeed fortunate that both *Weird Tales* and *Wonder Stories* existed during this period of intense creation in Smith's life: by providing a more or less ready market for Smith's stories, they served as the necessary commercial incentive which Smith, genius or not, financially needed. Smith paid tribute to the existence of such magazines for writer and reader alike in a letter published in "The Eyrie" in the December 1930 issue of *Weird Tales*: "Speaking as a reader, I should like to say that *Weird Tales* is the one magazine that gives its writers ample imaginative leeway. Next to it comes three of four magazines in which fancy can take flight under the aegis of science; and after these, one is lost in a Boeotian desert. All the others, without exception, from the long-established reviews down to the Wild West thrillers, are hide-bound and hog-tied with traditions of unutterable dullness." Hugo Gernsback, the editor of *Wonder Stories*, appears to have welcomed Smith's stories quite enthusiastically. However much Farnsworth Wright may have appreciated their literary excellence (Wright himself was a considerable scholar who professionally edited, among other things, a fine version of Shakespeare's play *A Midsummer Night's Dream*), the editor of *Weird Tales* appears always to have been rather anxious as to how his readers would react to Smith's extended poems in prose. Undoubtedly this is what caused Smith to publish privately six of his finest tales in his first collection of short stories *The Double Shadow and Other Fantasies*, in February 1933, at Auburn.

Outwardly during this period Smith led a quiet, uneventful life. However, in August 1934, Smith successfully fought a severe wood and grass fire on his ranch. All during this time (1929–1937) Smith continued to write verse but necessarily in a much smaller quantity. In 1933, George Work, the author of *White Man's Harvest*, and one of the then best-known writers in the country, declared Smith "the greatest American poet of today" whose "poems do not compare unfavorably with those of Byron, Shelley, Keats or Swinburne." In *Controversy* for November 1934 appeared the article "The Price of Poetry," by David Warren Ryder. In this article Ryder acclaimed Smith as "a great poet" and as being "in our generation... the fittest to wear the mantle of Shakespeare and Keats," thus adding his considered opinion to the similar one of George Sterling, George Work, and the well-known and respected educator and man-of-letters, Dr. David Starr Jordan, one-time president of the University of Indiana and the first president and "the builder" of Stanford University. Ryder's article was reprinted in June 1937 to accompany the slender collection *Nero and Other Poems*, published in the preceding month of May by The Futile Press, Lakeport, California: this volume included 10 reprints (somewhat altered from their original versions) from *The Star-Treader*. The California poetry journal *Westward* in the issue for January 1935 honored Smith by making numerous quotations from poems in *The Star-Treader* and *Ebony and Crystal*. This magazine featured in its early issues, at the bottom of the pages carrying poems, quotations from the works of the established poets of the past, including the great names in the poetry of the English language.

In 1936 the output of Smith's tales started to drop off, and by the latter 30's, during the 40's and the 50's, Smith had virtually stopped writing fiction. However, he continued writing verse until his death in 1961. The reasons for this cessation of Smith's writing fiction are not clear: it could have been that he had exhausted even his seemingly inexhaustible fancy; or perhaps the daemon no longer told him "tales of inconceivable fear and unimaginable love"; or Smith may have found the production of his small sculptures more interesting. This last seems likely as Smith once wrote, in a brief autobiography published in *The Science Fiction Fan* for August 1936, that he found "the making of these [small sculptures] far easier and more pleasurable than writing" He had begun the carving of these small sculptures possibly in the early 1930's, and it may have been that this was now the new step in Smith's further creative evolution; he made besides hundreds of paintings and drawings, starting in the early 1920's or earlier. Also, the death of his parents, as well as that of his correspondent and friend Lovecraft, may have removed some of Smith's incentive for creating fiction. His mother, Fanny Smith, died in 1935; his father, Timeus Smith, died in 1937; and in March of this same year Lovecraft died, and death thus robbed Smith of one of his greatest, most sympathetic and understanding friends. H.P.L. had always proved an enthusiastic and perceptive audience for Smith's short stories: both Smith and Lovecraft had been in the habit of exchanging manuscripts of stories before their publication, and mutually commenting on them.

Smith paid homage to H.P.L. in the lovely and moving memorial poem "To Howard Phillips Lovecraft" and in a letter in "The Eyrie" in *Weird Tales*, both published in the issue for July 1937. Two tributes in prose had also appeared earlier: "In Memoriam—H. P. Lovecraft, in *Tesseract* for April 1937; and in a letter published in *The Science Fiction Critic* for May 1937, in "A Note From The Editor." His last tribute appeared in 1959, the sonnet "H.P.L.," published in *The Shuttered Room and Other Pieces* (Arkham House) and dated July 17th, 1959.

Lovecraft before he died had paid his homage to Smith in the sonnet "To Clark Ashton Smith" (published posthumously in *Weird Tales* for April 1938), which concludes with the lines: "Dark Lord of Averoigne— whose windows stare / On pits of dream no other gaze could bear!" In his essay "Supernatural Horror In Literature," Lovecraft concludes the section "The Weird Tradition In America" with a paragraph of high and perceptive praise of Smith's fictional art.

During the late 1930's Smith began another of his notable correspondences, this one with Lilith Lorraine, the founder and principal poet
of the Avalon Poetry Foundation. In Lilith Lorraine's volume of science-
fiction poetry *Wine Of Wonder*, she pays Smith a lovely and worthy tribute
in the poem "The Cup-Bearer." Also during the late 1930's Universal
Studios considered the possibility of filming two of Smith's most extraordinary tales "The Dark Eidolon" and "The Colossus of Ylourgne."
This project never materialized, and this may have been a blessing rather
than a misfortune, howevermuch Smith could have used the money from
the movie rights. To have adapted either of these tales would have required not the typically conventional treatment of Universal Studios but
such combined talents as those of Vincent, Alexander, and Zoltan Korda
as demonstrated in their classic fantasy film *The Thief of Bagdad* with its
excellent score by Miklos Rozsa. Conrad Veidt, the evil Vizir and archimage in this film, would have been superb as the archimage Namirrha in
"The Dark Eidolon" or as the medieval sorcerer Nathaire in "The Colossus of Ylourgne." Alas, the might-have-been....

Whatever may have been the reasons for the cessation of his writing
fiction—the continued production of his quintessential sculptures or the
loss of his parents and of his literary *frère et semblable* H.P.L.—Smith only
wrote little more than a dozen stories between the late 1930's and his
death in 1961. Also, he had returned to his first love, the creation of poetry in verse: by late 1941 Smith had three collections or cycles of verse
in preparation: *Incantations*, *The Jasmine-Girdle*, and *Wizard's Love and Other
Poems* (later retitled *The Hill of Dionysus*). Thus, it was during the penultimate decade of his life that Smith composed and/or assembled his final
poem-cycles. *Incantations* contains mainly poems composed during the
1920's and 1930's, hitherto largely uncollected, as well as many unpublished poems. *The Hill of Dionysus* and especially *The Jasmine-Girdle* both
contain many poems never-before published; both are cycles of love poems. And if all the preceding mass of poetry, much of it new, were not
already quite enough for a man in his fifties—a man who had moreover
in the early part of his career created three major collections of poetry—
Smith also experimented with such miniature forms as the quintrain and
the haiku, the last surely the quintessence of quintessential forms. All-
told, he now created over one hundred miniature poems, a small sampling of which is presented in *Spells and Philtres* (Arkham House, 1958).
(These divers collections are included in the *Selected Poems* Smith was con-

currently engaged in assembling during the 1940's.) In addition, Smith learned Spanish during this decade, made translations from Spanish poets, and even wrote a small number of poems in Spanish. Such productivity, much of it in new forms and in new directions and some of it even in a new language for Smith, must be considered remarkable indeed for a man in age already past the half-century mark. Phoenix-like, the poet had been reborn out of the ashes of the fiction writer.

The foundation of Arkham House in 1939 by August Derleth assured the publication of the so-far 4 collections of Smith's short stories in book form: *Out of Space and Time* (1942), *Lost Worlds* (1944), *Genius Loci and Other Tales* (1948), and *The Abominations of Yondo* (1960). Upon publication of *Out of Space and Time*, the well-known writer and man-of-letters Benjamin DeCasseres in his syndicated column "The March of Events" dated Sep. 23, 1942 (this column appeared on the editorial page of the Hearst newspapers), commented briefly on Smith's first major prose collection and hailed Smith not only as a great poet and a great story-teller but as "a great prose writer" as well.

Only to the encouragement of his publisher do we owe the existence of the omnibus volume of Smith's first Arkham House poetry, the *Selected Poems*. This volume was originally entitled *The Hashish-Eater and Other Poems* and was intended by Smith's publisher to be a complete collection of all of Smith's poetry. Subsequently Smith decided instead to make it a selective volume. Produced during the period 1944–1949, it contains about 500 poems, virtually 5/6 of the 600 poems or so extant at the time of Smith's death. (The over-all count of his poems just created while he was an adult is probably much higher.) Delivered to his publisher in December 1949, this collection of collections contains the following sections: *The Star-Treader and Other Poems*, *Ebony and Crystal* (minus the 29 poems in prose), *Sandalwood*, *Translations and Paraphrases* (from Baudelaire, Verlaine, Victor Hugo and other poets both French and Spanish), *Incantations*, *Quintrains*, *Sestets*, *Experiments in Haiku* (Strange Miniatures, Distillations, Childhood, Mortal Essences), *Satires and Travesties*, *The Jasmine-Girdle*, *The Hill of Dionysus*. (*Incantations* and *The Jasmine-Girdle* between them contain some 10 examples of the small body of poetry Smith composed in French.)

This omnibus collection had to wait until November 1971 to see publication. During that long wait of 22 years, a large sampling of the *Selected Poems* appeared in Smith's first published Arkham House poetry collection *The Dark Chateau* (1951), which Smith dedicated significantly "To the Memory of Edgar Allan Poe" and which contains many remarkable poems: 18 of its 40 poems are taken from the omnibus volume. A further and still larger sampling of the *Selected Poems* may be had in Smith's second published Arkham House poetry collection *Spells and Philtres* (1958): 51 of the 60 poems in this last collection are taken from the same volume.

About the end of August 1953, Smith received a personal visit from his publisher, correspondent, and friend August Derleth, in company with his then wife, the former Sandra Evelyn Winters. Before his death in June 1971, Derleth managed to bring out under his Arkham House imprint three more volumes by Smith: the two final collections of short stories *Tales of Science And Sorcery* (1964) and *Other Dimensions* (1970), and an almost complete collection of his unique prose-poems under the title *Poems in Prose* (1965).

A near lifetime of celibacy, brightened here and there by the bowers of divers "enchantresses" (as Smith was wont to call them), came to an end in 1954 when Smith married Carol Jones Dorman, the last and "The Best Beloved" of Klarkash-Ton's enchantresses. To his wife he pays a delicate and a gallant tribute in the sonnet which opens "From this my heart, a haunted Elsinore, / I send the phantoms packing for thy sake:" This sonnet, originally entitled "The Best Beloved," was used by Smith under the title "Dedication/to Carol" to preface *Spells and Philtres*, which in its entirety is dedicated to his wife. Between 1954 and his death in 1961 Smith maintained his residence alternately in Pacific Grove and near Auburn. The old cabin of the Smiths, in which Clark had lived for over half a century, from 1902 to 1954, burned down to the ground in August 1957. This was understandably a source of deep distress to Smith, even though he had sold the major portion of the Smith ranch, about 40 acres, in 1937 (to a local contractor for the purposes of a private airport), sometime after the death of Smith's father. This left about two and a half acres, including the land upon which stood the cabin.

Smith still chopped wood and did gardening during the last decade of his life, in addition to working on his quintessential sculptures. However, these last years saw relatively little literary activity on Smith's part, although he did continue to write poetry, even if sparingly. During the 20's, the 30's, and the 40's, in addition to his literary work, Smith had done much hard manual labor. Among other things, he had been a fruit-picker, a fruit-packer, a cement-mixer, and a hard-rock miner, mucker and windlasser, as well as a wood-chopper and a gardener. Smith did this work primarily in order to earn enough money to support himself while writing his poetry and his prose. However, his literary output shows no or very little reflection of this manual labor.

It was toward the latter part of these last years in Smith's life that the present writer—on two different occasions—had the pleasure of meeting Smith and his wife Carol at their home in Pacific Grove: in August of 1958 and in September of 1959. I recall with warmth and gratitude the unstinted way in which the Smiths gave of their hospitality to me, and made me feel perfectly at home. I had become so accustomed to the strong statement characteristic of much of Smith's poetry in verse and prose that, prior to meeting Smith, I am afraid that I somewhat naively anticipated the poet to speak in a voice of brass and in a manner as sententious and orotund as that of a sorcerer in one of Smith's tales. To my considerable surprise Smith spoke in a deep, quiet, pleasant voice that put me instantly at my ease. With his trim mustache and his handsome, distinguished features, he seemed a perfect gentleman, affable but not unctuously so, civilized and tolerant, about whom there hovered a certain aura of individuality that would have set him apart anywhere but not in any blatant, affected manner: that true individuality which comes from within and has nothing of the theatrical in it.

Of that first visit I recall in particular a delightful picnic we held on the beach about a block and a half east of their home. It was literally a "golden afternoon" with but a few fleecy clouds high overhead, with the gulls crying about us and the waves lisping among the rocks. Smith wore his beret and Mrs. Smith an immense straw hat which gave her the piquant appearance of a 20th-century enchantress. With Mrs. Smith generously purveying the food from a straw hamper, we ate a simple but tasty repast of good, crumbly wheaten bread piled with miniature slabs of a sharp cheddar cheese, all washed down with one of the good red wines of California poured into paper cups: a wine of pomegranates from Hyperborea held in goblets of crystal and orichalch could not have tasted any better. Our conversation was informal and covered a wide range of topics, occasionally spiced by some wise, witty, and often ironic comment from Smith on the contemporary political and international scene.

Of my second visit I recall, among other things, a lengthy discussion Smith and I had apropos divers literary figures, especially Poe and Baudelaire. The discussion reached its climax when Smith, with an unforgettable intensity, read aloud in French one of the powerful sonnets of Baudelaire. Smith commented afterwards: "That's terrific stuff!" I nodded my head in agreement and said, "Well, it certainly wasn't written by Alfred Lord Tennyson!" Then we both laughed, breaking the tension. Earlier, upon my noticing and commenting upon a "complete works" of Poe in some 8 or 10 volumes on a bookshelf in the dining room, Smith had confided to me that he had read virtually everything written by Poe that he had been able to obtain.

However, it was during my first visit that Smith showed me his portfolio of drawings and paintings. I must confess myself somewhat taken aback by their deliberately primitive technique, having become somewhat spoiled by the technical excellence of Smith's verse and prose; but there were a number of demonic heads which struck me as powerful and original. Smith's sculptures, on the other hand, as deliberately primitive as the paintings, impressed me far more favorably and suggested something Egyptian or Mayan or Peruvian of the Inca period, without being quite the same as those. These carvings of Smith's possess a quality rare in sculpture, which generally surrenders its essence at once to the beholder, especially sculpture of a conventionally technical perfection. Smith's carvings grow gradually in the onlooker's appreciation: the more one sees them, the more fascinating they become, adumbrating an essence never fully revealed but extending itself infinitely.

Smith was as generous and fine a friend as Sterling must have been. I happened to lack only one of Smith's volumes of poetry, the slender reprint collection *Nero and Other Poems*, published by The Futile Press. Smith took a copy he had given and inscribed to his wife, cut out the inscription page, wrote in a new inscription to me and them gave me the book gratis. I protested—somewhat feebly, I admit—but Clark and Carol insisted I keep it. Thanks to their dual generosity, today I have in my personal library this copy of *Nero and Other Poems* or, in the words of Smith's inscription, "this relic from an ironically named printing press."

Smith died on the 14th of August 1961, and in the latter part of the same year Arkham House published its second anthology of macabre poems, *Fire and Sleet and Candlelight* (the first had been *Dark of The Moon*). This included 6 largely hitherto-unpublished poems by Smith, in many respects the equal of much of his earlier verse, as all or most of them were evidently composed during the years 1911–1925. Smith demonstrates his admiration for Baudelaire and his works to the very last, as witness the title of the last poem in this group of posthumously published verse: "The Horologe," which title is the English equivalent of the French *L'Horloge*, which Baudelaire uses as the title for the last poem in the first section *Spleen et Idéal* of *Les Fleurs du Mal.*

Thus, death finally came to him who had been, in part, one of death's most lyrical celebrators. As stated earlier, no *Saturday Review* or *Atlantic Monthly* devoted an entire memorial issue to him and his works; and while Smith was alive, no New Yorker had ever allowed him into the charmed and perilous circle of its "profiles." Neither the science-fiction nor fantasy magazines even mentioned Smith's death. He died as he had lived for the most part, as an outsider.

As far as the present writer has been able to determine, Smith left comparatively little unpublished material at his death. Apart from his juvenile fiction, only some two dozen stories, including "The Face by the River," "Mohammed's Tomb," "Secondary Cosmos," "Told in the Desert," "The Red World of Polaris," "A Good Embalmer," "Strange Shadows," "Nemesis of the Unfinished," and "The Dart of Rasasfa." An unfinished novel, *The Infernal Star*, begun about 1936 with about 10,000 words written. Some incidental poetry. A play in blank verse (written before 1951), *The Dead Will Cuckold You*, telling in six tableaux a tale of necromancy in Zothique. Most important of all, *The Black Book*, the notebook used by Smith from about 1930 to 1961. Although some of this material appears irretrievably lost, much of it has appeared in published form, whether in collected form or individually between 1961 and the present day.

To judge by *The Hill of Dionysus—A Selection* (published in November 1962), this penultimate poem-cycle of Smith's must be pronounced the equal of the earlier *Sandalwood*, if not perhaps in some respects the superior of the two collections.

Smith was by no means a prolific writer, except in the sense of creating many writings of a high literary merit. Over-all, there are about 140 tales extant, about 40 poems in prose, and probably about 800 poems in verse, with 300 still uncollected (this is only an educated guess: the overall figure probably totals much higher). For a person who dedicated most of his life to poetry, Smith issued comparatively few volumes. He maintained only about ten or fifteen correspondences of any importance or length. Smith, with his relatively small output of art in various form, provides a striking contrast to those authors whose complete collected works fill one, two, or three full library shelves, or sometimes even more. But if the quantity of his over-all output is negligible, the quality is the reverse.

2. Some General Remarks on Smith's Poetry and Prose

When Smith died at the age of sixty-eight, he left behind him an unique body of work; a body of work remarkable for its consistency in theme and quality from the very first to the very last. It serves as a notable example of an artist who, in his mature creative work, has remained faithful to the ideals, the dreams, and even the creations of his childhood. Fortunately, Smith never betrayed his enchantments.

His poems in verse and prose and his tales and/or extended poems in prose form the integral complement of each other. It is impossible fully to understand or appreciate the tales without some knowledge and understanding of the poems. Conversely, a knowledge of the stories aids toward a richer, a fuller understanding of the poems. Stylistically and thematically the tales grow out of the rich and varied emotiono-imaginative life of the poems.

If Smith had written nothing else but his first volume of poems, *The Star-Treader*, he would still take rank as an unique poet. The very title of the title poem forms a quintessential poem all in itself, a poem filled with amazing imaginative overtones. It seems incredible that such a poem as "Medusa" could have been written by a youth of only eighteen, or even more incredible, that such a hymn to death, destruction and night as "Nero," so mature and controlled in concept and composition, could have been written by Smith before his 18th year. In. "Nero," the very first poem of his very first volume, Smith gives expression, for the very first time, to one of the principal concepts uniting his entire output, the concept or theme of the Man-God, first given crystallized expression by Baudelaire in his study *Les Paradis Artificiels*, although it is actually a very ancient concept. In other poems Smith celebrates the astronomic splendors of the cosmos, or hymns the gods of antiquity, or combines the cosmic-astronomic with the mythological in striking and original fashion. The divination or evocation of past epochs, places and peoples appears for the first time, later to reappear in Smith's unforgettable tales of necromancy. The theme of lost continents appears for the first time in the sonnet "Atlantis." The sonnets are all of a uniformly high quality. Some of the sonnets as well as some of the other poems manifest powerfully

Smith's early and continuing preoccupation with death, destiny and doom. In the extraordinary sonnet "Retrospect and Forecast," Smith strikes for the first time the superb baroque antithesis of life feeding on death, and death feeding on life; a concept that, alone with metamorphosis, continues throughout a goodly proportion of Smith's entire output. At the opposite pole there are charming nature vignettes, in addition to poems celebrating ideal beauty. Marked by an astonishing technical command and assurance, and by an immense vocabulary used with unerring and creative precision, *The Star-Treader* is as remarkable an achievement today as it was over fifty years ago when it was published in 1912.

While it may have obvious affinities with *Les Fleurs du Mal* of Baudelaire as well as with the work of the Symbolists on the one hand and on the other with that of the Parnassians; yet *Ebony and Crystal*, published in 1922, remains an unique collection, quite unlike any other body of poetry whether in French or in English or in any other language. All the themes and background in *The Star-Treader*—the cosmic-astronomic, the mythological, the implicitly necromantic, and the themes of splendor, death, beauty, nature, and of lost continents—reappear in the present volume. But, with what a wealth of difference. For not only have the poet's technical and metrical skills attained their perfection, but a new and undeniably universal theme manifests itself—that of love. The poet uses an even larger vocabulary than in *The Star-Treader*, and with the same extraordinary precision. He has mastered the Baudelairean technique of treating a perverse or unpleasant subject (i.e., from a conventional viewpoint) with the utmost lyricism of imagery and language: such sonnets as "Love Malevolent" and "Laus Mortis" form worthy companion-pieces to Baudelaire 's "Une Charogne." Over-all the sonnets reach a high-water mark of classical perfection and romantic fervor and, sometimes, baroque intensity and complexity. Smith's handling of blank verse—especially in "The Hashish-Eater" and in the dramatic dialogue "The Ghoul and The Seraph"—is nothing less than supreme. The final speech of the Ghoul Necromalor in the last-named piece provides a quintessential example of Smith's unique literary baroque both as to subject and as to style, besides brilliantly illuminating his highly baroque philosophies of death and change, of life feeding on death, and death feeding on life; with everything informed by a burning romantic fervor, and controlled by a classic sense of tone and form. Much of the fascination of Smith's poems (as well as of his poems in prose and of his extended poems in prose) stems from their baroque, shifting and kaleidoscopic imagery; such imagery as appears in the sonnets "Eidolon," "Ave Atque Vale," "Mirrors," "The Orchid," and others. An important technical innovation is Smith's revival of that unjustly neglected and deprecated metre in English, the alexandrine. The most outstanding poem employing this metre, appositely entitled "Alexandrines," is perhaps one of the single most perfect poems Smith ever penned; although it is admittedly difficult to point out even a few outstanding poems amid the plethora of excellent ones.

Standing apart from the volume and Smith's over-all output of poetry, the compressed epic "The Hashish-Eater; or, The Apocalypse of Evil" remains an unparalleled masterpiece of cosmic invention and imagination. It stands as the unique example of the seemingly impossible combination of the epical with the lyrical. Its apparently endless pageant of wonders and episodes forms a veritable catalogue of things to come in Smith's tales of 1929/1930 and 1936/1937. Even more than that sovereign poem "Nero," it exemplifies in an unique manner the all-important concept of the Man-God in the person of the hashish-eater, "the emperor of dreams," impanoplied with demiurgic powers. Arranged into 10 clearly-defined sections, the epic, with an apocalyptic splendor of imagery and language, plunges *in medias res* and relates the already-begun "supreme ascendance" of the Man-God (through the supreme drug or liberating agent of imagination) to his archsublime throne of "culminant omniscience manifold" wherefrom in a series of visions or "memories" and "dreams" he surveys the divers pageantries of the cosmos; the epic then relates the muffled threat to the Man-God's omnipotence by some innominate evil; then the brief but evil-omened respite enjoyed or endured by the Man-God; then the first full-scale apocalypse of evil in the form of the monsters of classical mythology cosmically extrapolated; then, ever pursued by "the dragon-rout," the flight of the Man-God to the utmost edge of the cosmos beyond which plunges the arch-abyss of the void or of chaos; then, rising up from the very depths, the ultimate revelation or realization of evil: the "huge white eyeless Face" "With lips of flame that open," which involves into it (but logically without destroying either) both the Man-God and the rout of now rather childish monsters however macrocosmic.

"The Apocalypse of Evil," the subtitle of this epic (for such it is in everything but length—it satisfies all the desiderata of an epic), has a considerable significance since it indicates for the poem a literary tradition stemming in part directly from "The Flowers of Evil" by Baudelaire. Whatever this compressed epic may owe apropos of general structure and style of imagery to its ultimate model, "A Wine of Wizardry" by George Sterling (which is essentially a brief travelogue of imaginary wonders, a literal "flight of fancy," which Smith first read in late 1907 when he was almost fifteen—the poem was first published in *The Cosmopolitan* for September 1907), yet "The Hashish-Eater" has no true parallel in cosmic concept or in sustained power of imagination. It stands alone. Perhaps the closest thing to Smith's compressed epic is that highly poetic prose-piece in semi-dramatic form by Gustave Flaubert, *La Tentation de Saint Antoine,*—with its saintly anchorite-hero Anthony who undergoes a series of fantasmagoric visions instigated by the Devil to tempt him. Ignoring the overall differences in narrative-purpose of the 2 pieces as well as the differences in symbolic intent of the endings of both, yet these endings do outwardly have a considerable resemblance.

The *Poems in Prose* which concludes *Ebony and Crystal* possess a paramount significance in terms of the over-all canon of Smith's work, for these twenty-nine poems in prose—representing a logical continuation of the thematic material in the preceding poems in verse—lead directly to Smith's two extended poems in prose of 1925, "Sadastor" and "The Abominations of Yondo," and on through them to the tales and/or extended poems in prose of 1929–1937. Many of these poems in prose are essentially condensed or implied tales, and two of them, "The Flower Devil" and "From the Crypts of Memory," served as the inspiration or nuclei (in regard to the over-all plot, atmosphere and even as to actual phrases) for the later extended poems in prose, "The Demon of the Flower" and "The Planet of the Dead," respectively. Smith is one of the very, very few poets in English who have fully understood the technique of this difficult and eminently French genre (the *poème en prose*) more or less created by Baudelaire (under the dual influence and/or suggestion of that unique collection of prose ballads *Gaspard De La Nuit* by Aloysius Bertrand, published in 1842, and of such poems in prose by Poe as "Shadow—A Parable," "Silence—A Fable," "Eleanora," and "The Masque of the Red Death"). Indeed, it is not too much to say that as a practitioner of the poem in prose Smith has no peer in English, and that, considering his achievement in this genre from a universal literary viewpoint, he takes equal rank with Baudelaire, the technique of whose *Petits poèms en prose* influenced Smith in the technique of his own. These poems in prose clearly pave the way toward the highly baroque prose of Smith's later tales and/or extended poems in prose, as of where the latter designation applies. The eventual publication of Smith's over-all more than forty poems in prose in one volume should serve to establish his preeminence in the literature of this genre, his output in which is only a little less than the 50 examples extant by Baudelaire.

The remarkable love poems in *Ebony and Crystal* find their complement on an extended scale in the even more remarkable love poems that make up most of *Sandalwood*, published in 1925, and concluding with 19 translations from *Les Fleurs du Mal* of Baudelaire. After the cosmic and exotic splendors of *The Star-Treader* and *Ebony and Crystal*, and the oftentimes monumental tone of those two volumes; the tender, muted, vertumnal or gently autumnal tone of this third major poetry collection by Smith, comes as a surprise, almost—paradoxically—as a quiet shock. Many of the love poems, as well as some of the non-love poems, Smith has cast into many beautiful forms of his own invention that suggest the old French forms of the rondeau, the triolet, the ballade, and the villanelle, without actually being the same. The poems in *Sandalwood* are above all remarkable for haunting song-like effects, with all manner of refrain and echo-like devices. Smith's successful experimentation with lines of differing lengths and metres suggests on the one hand the similar experimentation by the poets of the Pléïade and on the other the same by the most eminent Elizabethan poet influenced by the Pléïade, Edmund Spenser. Perhaps the single most beautiful and artistic poem in the entire volume is the incomparable "We Shall Meet." But the entire collection is rife with excellent poems, haunting, unforgettable, of a rare poignance, charting as many of them do the course of love that runs disastrously and ultimately perishes. Like *Ebony and Crystal, Sandalwood* is a talismanic, touchstone volume. The 19 poems from Baudelaire, as well as Smith's Baudelaire translations elsewhere, establish Smith as a sovereign translator of the French genius, far superior to Edna St. Vincent Millay or even Arthur Symons.

Of Smith's tales and/or extended poems in prose there is little that one can say in this brief space save that they are prodigies of invention whose style is integrally one with their themes. They synthesize and extrapolate the themes, backgrounds, concepts and stylistic elements of Smith's three major early poetry collections. Smith's unique type of science-fiction (contributed mostly in the 1930's to *Wonder Stories*) represents a return to the cosmic-astronomic material of his very first volume of some twenty years earlier. As a perfectly logical consequence Smith's tales employ the same immense vocabulary to be found in his poetry; a vocabulary used with a precision fully as creative and as masterly as that evident in his poems. Not only does the same vocabulary used in his poetry reappear but even the same or similar phrase-patterns and mannerisms. Such tales as "The Dark Eidolon," "The Empire of the Necromancers," "The Last Hieroglyph," "The Isle of the Torturers," "Xeethra," "The White Sybil," "The City of the Singing Flame," and so many, many others, have no parallel in the creations of any other writer. They are unique like the genius that created them. They form in their entirety a worthy congener to "The Hashish-Eater." In them Smith again gives striking embodiment to the concept of the Man-God, whether personified in such archimages as Malygris, Maal Dweb, Avyctes and Namirrha or in such necromancers as Mmatmuor, Sodosma, and Vacharn or in such kings as Adompha, Euvoran and Xeethra. Such protagonists of Smith's, like true heroes Baudelairean, despite their oftentime sovereignty of temporal and/or necromantic power, are yet paradoxically often impotent to escape that ultimate bane of godhood or of the Man-God, to wit, ennui or spleen. (This last is, of course, one of the central Baudelairean themes, both in *Les Fleurs du Mal* and in the *Petits poèmes en prose*, the alternate title of which is *Le Spleen de Paris*.) The poet-author himself may be seen in an ideal sense as a literary Man-God creating and peopling many worlds of his imagination; the tales and/or extended poems in prose may be seen as the complement and fulfillment of the seemingly endless procession of visions or episodes that make up the compressed epic "The Hashish-Eater".

Smith's tales, because of their efflorescent richness and their baroque combination of seemingly contradictory and incongruous elements, become very difficult to characterize. The love poems in *Ebony and Crystal* and *Sandalwood* find their fictional counterparts in the love interest in a great many of Smith's so-called "tales of horror." But the label of "tales of love" is also inadequate. What should one call them? Tales of death? Tales of splendor? Tales of beauty? Tales of deathly beauty? Tales of necromancy? Tales of demonology? Tales of magic? Tales of the supernatural? Tales of sorcery? Tales of metamorphosis? Tales of wonder? Tales of cosmic irony? Tales of deity, destiny and nemesis? Perhaps, after all, the label "weird tales" serves as well as any. Smith's weird tales were certainly among the most ineffably weird ever to appear in the magazine *Weird Tales*.

And then there is the "magic" of Smith's style. One seems to be reading some sort of incantation or litany with measured invocations and responses. Just as Smith's subject-matter, his symbolism and his philosophies, so may his style be defined as baroque—a literary baroque quite unlike any other. By literary baroque we intend a style wherein certain Gothic elements—such as savageness, grotesqueness, antithesis, changefulness or metamorphosis, redundance or, in Smith's case, largely pseudo-redundance—have evolved from an ultimately classic matrix. To these we might also add the preoccupation with illusion, sometimes manifested in the use of the mirror, the mirage, the mask, and the maze; the fascination and obsession with death and gruesome physical detail; the love of paradox; the use of symbolic ambiguity; the emphasis on extravagance of color and an often outrageous efflorescence of vegetation and decor; the preference for objects and words and imageries of splendor; the element of the theatrical, often manifested in a kind of theatrical spotlighting on crucial objects or persons at critical moments; and a delight in what Leon Edel once termed "the familiar symptoms of decadence" but which are equally as well those of literature in its primal stages—a delight in the wonderful, the marvelous, the strange, the exotic, the bizarre, the hypernatural, and we might add, the unknown and the unknowable.

For all the poetic denseness of his prose style—a style which makes heavy and deliberate use of the technique of poetic compression—Smith's syntax remains remarkably clear, and with striking rhythmical effects. In his poems in prose and in his tales and/or extended poems in prose, there are prose rhythms that challenge comparison with those of the finest stylists in the language, including those of Sir Thomas Browne; whom, in sheer sustained stateliness and sombre splendor of style and subject, Smith surpasses in many instances, or at the very least fully equals. Smith's genius for creating and sustaining a powerful mood—partly through a more or less related system of imagery and through a lucid, even if elaborate, syntax—simplifies the baroque antithesis and complications inherent in his tales, and thereby succeeds in giving his tales their characteristic tense unity. The prose of Clark Ashton Smith features, as does the prose of Sir Thomas Browne (and as does, of course, Smith's own poetry), a skillful, often uncanny juxtaposition of Anglo-Saxon words with those of Graeco-Latinate polysyllables—this creates an effect approximating the incantatory effect of poetry. The prose of Smith's tales is as studied and deliberate as the prose of his poems in prose and as the language of verse. It goes without saying that such a prose demands an unusual and a careful quality of reading to be fully grasped and appreciated. While Smith's style is based in part on Poe, and suggestive in certain respects of Sir Thomas Browne, yet the result is wholly original, quite unlike the style of any other writer. And despite its elaboration and seeming excess, it is essentially a highly compressed, compact, and economical prose. Without such a prose style it would have been impossible for Smith to have created the illusion of reality so characteristic of his tales of superficial unreality.

As poetic and mythical considerations of death and mortality, such poems in prose as "The Memnons of the Night," "From the Crypts of Memory," and "The Shadows," together with such extended poems in prose as "The Planet of the Dead," "The Empire of the Necromancers," or "The Death of Malygris," form worthy twentieth century companion-pieces to the last chapter of Sir Thomas Brown's *Urne-Buriall,* i.e., *Hydriotaphia.*

Merely regarded as short stories told in a heavily poetic style, Smith's fictions would appear extraordinary. Regarded more exactly as extended poems in prose, which is what many of them are in all actuality, his tales are nothing less than astonishing. To sustain a poem in prose for one or two pages is not an impossible feat; but to sustain one for ten, fifteen, even twenty pages, as Smith has undeniably done on many occasions, must be accounted a technical achievement of genius.

Smith's finest tales are in the nature of condensations, distillations, quintessences. They have all the richness of element usually associated with the novel; indeed, many of them could well have been told as novels; in fact, at least one of them (to wit, "The Chain of Aforgomon") Smith did first project as a novel; but the poet-author preferred to condense his stories into as small a space as possible. A few of Smith's tales are allegories; but many are parables of emotional truth, although often allegorical in part. Regarded as strange parables of love and death, or as quintessences of beauty, fear, love, wonder, ineffable strangeness, and much, much else; the tales of Clark Ashton Smith must in all truth take rank as something unique in the annals of prose fiction.

3. The Sorcerer Departs

Smith remained the poet to the very end. He composed his last poem, the sonnet "Cycles," (to quote his own words) "in the midst of the Sabbath pandemonium of dogs, brats and autoes" of June 4th, 1961. A little more than two months later, on the 14th of August, Monday night, at the age of sixty-eight, Clark Ashton Smith died quietly in his sleep at his home in Pacific Grove, attended to the last by his devoted wife Carol.

Smith's true literary affinities have been given little serious recognition. The affinity with Poe manifests itself primarily in a certain weirdness, in certain phrase mannerisms, and in the extreme musicality of much of Smith's verse and of his prose. Indeed, for sheer gorgeousness of sound the student of poetry must go back to the lyrical beauty of Edmund Spenser's strikingly baroque epic *The Faerie Queene* for a just comparison. In the cosmic range of their fancy Spenser and Smith have much in common, as well as in an inexhaustible sense of wonder. Smith's tale "The Garden of Adompha," with its infernal and sentient vegetation, seems like a curious amalgam and extrapolation of "The Garden Of Proserpina" (Book II: Canto VII) and of "The Garden of Adonis" (Book III: Canto XII) in *The Faerie Queene*. There is an interesting evolution from the idyllic medieval dream-garden in *Le Roman de la Rose* to such examples of the Spenserian garden as "The Garden of Proserpina," "The Garden of Adonis," and "The Bowre of Blisse" (Book II: Canto XII) and then the garden of venomous flowers in Hawthorne's tale "Rappacini's Daughter" and then to "The Garden of Adompha".

Smith's affinities with Baudelaire are so obvious as to pass almost without mention. However, we must allude to one fundamental affinity between Smith and Baudelaire. The French poet sought to create beauty out of the filth, the squalor, the disease, the evil and the horror of a great metropolis (Paris). Similarly, Smith sought to create beauty not so much out of the filth, the evil, the implicit or actual horror of one great city as he did out of the ugliness of death and decay and destruction, out of the horror of an irrevocable doom, out of the terror of an ultimate nothingness beyond death (what Sir Thomas Browne terms "the uncomfortable night of nothingness"), or paradoxically out of the possibility that there is no death, that all animate things whether in life or in death as well as all things inanimate—in short, absolutely all things—by virtue of their theoretically indestructible atoms are part and parcel of an inconceivably monstrous and perverse arch-life-form without beginning and without end whether in space or in time that involves not only the cosmos but also the void beyond the cosmos. (This last is given its most powerful symbolic embodiment in the "huge eyeless Face, / That fills the void and fills the universe, / And bloats against the limits of the world / With lips of flame that open:" in the tenth and final section of "The Hashish-Eater.") If, as averred by Victor Hugo, Baudelaire did introduce into the literature of poetry "un frisson nouveau," then Smith has in his own turn introduced "le frisson cosmique".

Smith also has a certain similarity with such Jacobean dramatists of death and the perverse as Cyril Tourneur and John Webster and their arch-imitator of the early 19th century, Thomas Lovell Beddoes. However, Smith has far more than the single string of death on his harp; there are also, among others, the strings of love and beauty. His love poems alone would rank Smith as a poet of unique attainments. For form, for originality of imagery, for originality of created poetic forms, for choice of line length, and for depth of emotion, such collections or cycles of love poems as *Sandalwood* and *The Hill of Dionysus* compare favorably with the best of the series of love poems and sonnets by such English poets as Sir Philip Sidney, William Shakespeare, or Ernest Dowson or by such poets of the French Renaissance as Pierre de Ronsard and Louise Labé.

There is besides an unmistakable resemblance between Smith and the French Protestant, eminently baroque poet Agrippa d'Aubigné, in their love of antithesis and their preoccupation with death and destruction. For example, d'Aubigné devotes at least two, "Les Feux" and "Les Fers," of the seven principal divisions of his epic "Les Tragiques," to catalogues of people meeting violent deaths through civil war and the tortures of martyrdom. Such a poem by Smith as "The City of Destruction," published in *The Arkham Sampler*, Winter 1948, seems especially d'Aubignésque: its long lines, strong rhythms, relentless piling-up of images, all suggest the forceful alexandrines of d'Aubigné, with their realization of emotional intensity through the steady accumulation of synonyms and phrases of a similar nature.

The much "quaint and curious…forgotten lore" to be found in the canon of Smith's works, especially of his tales, has extended parallels in the works of Sir Thomas Browne, particularly in the latter's *Pseudodoxia Epidemica* or *Vulgar Errors* (1646)—with its inquiry into and consideration of the basilisk, of griffins, of the phoenix, of the salamander living in fire, of the chameleon living only upon air, of the unicorn's horn, of the ostrich digesting iron, of "the musical note of swans before their death," of "the pictures of mermaids, unicorns, and some others," etc., etc. That which Lytton Strachey once cited as the peculiarities of Browne's style— "the studied pomp of its Latinisms, its wealth of allusion, its tendency toward sonorous antithesis"—could be cited just as well as being the peculiarities of Smith's own style. However, there are far more than stylistic affinities between these two highly baroque literary creators. Browne's works demonstrate a sense of wonder and a taste for wonders real or imaginary equal to the same demonstrated by Spenser or by Smith. Browne was a great student of Dante's theological fantasy in epic verse *La Divinia Commedia*. Just as *Hydriotaphia* (1658) with its theme of death and of implicit hell connotes with Dante's *Inferno*; and just as *The Garden of Cyrus* (1658) with its implicit theme of life eternal and ever-renewing connotes with the Italian poet's *Paradiso*; so does *Hydriotaphia* connote with the emphasis in Smith on death, on funereal monuments and paraphernalia, on deserts, on desolation, on an ultimate nothingness; and so does *The Garden of Cyrus* connote with the emphasis in Smith on verdure, on the vernal, on extravagance of color, on an ultimately outrageous efflorescence, or on the green fire of "the singing flame."

In Smith's compressed epic "The Apocalypse Of Evil" the ultimate conclusion, that immortality is part of an infinite and eternal arch-life-form of the cosmos and of the void, is similar to but yet distinct from— due to Browne's over-all Christian perspective—the sentiments implicit in some of the concluding pensées in *Urne-Buriall*, such as: "Life is a pure flame, and we live by an invisible Sun within us" and "Ready to be anything in the extasie of being ever...." Such a phrase by Browne as "The night of time far surpasseth the day..." could serve as the motto or moral of Smith's poem in prose "The Memnons of the Night." Such a phrase by Browne as "The number of the dead long exceedeth all that shall live," finds an unexpected similarity to the phrase "...the dead had come to outnumber infinitely the living," in Smith's poem in prose "From The Crypts of Memory," and to the phrase "...its immemorial dead, who had come to outnumber infinitely the living," in Smith's extended poem in prose "The Planet of the Dead." And the following selection from Browne's posthumously published *Christian Morals* (1716), Part the Third, Section XIV, is amazingly similar to the spirit animating so much of Smith's verse and prose, and could easily have been written by Smith himself: "Let thy Thoughts be of things which have not entered into the Hearts of Beasts: Think of things long past, and long to come: Acquaint thyself with the choragium of the Stars, and consider the vast expansion beyond them. Let Intellectual Tubes give thee a glance of things, which visive Organs reach not. Have a glimpse of incomprehensibles, and Thoughts of things, which Thoughts but tenderly touch."

The extended short story by William Beckford, *The History of the Caliph Vathek*, and much of Oriental fiction as exemplified in *The Arabian Nights*, connote with the extravagance of color, incident, and décor or background in many of Smith's tales. For sheer color and bizarrerie the extended poem in prose "The Dark Eidolon" out-Vatheks "Vathek." If Poe did create the extended poem in prose in such masterpieces as "The Masque of the Red Death," it remained for Smith to re-create the genre and create extensively within it. Stylistically the tales of Clark Ashton Smith are, in part, a continuation and a fulfillment on the one hand of the work of Edgar Allan Poe (the Poe of "Shadow—A Parable," "Silence—A Fable," and of course "The Masque of the Red Death") and on the other of the *Petits poèmes en prose* of Baudelaire, as well as of Smith's own earlier *Poems in Prose* in *Ebony and Crystal*.

The critical pontiffs of the twentieth century have so far passed over the work of Smith in verse and prose through a peculiar series of circumstances. Smith's poetry, because it was published mainly in private and limited editions, has become the property of only a fortunate few. His prose has been known principally to a specialized audience. The reviews of *Out of Space and Time* and *Lost Worlds* in *The New York Times Book Review* proved almost completely inadequate: one cannot help but wonder as to the reception that would be given to Sir Thomas Browne if he lived today in the twentieth century, with its distaste for an elaborate style and for anything that might seem a little bit of too much. And there is much else in Smith's work to make an adequate larger critical recognition difficult, at least during the present century with its oftentime and tasteless emphasis on creative literature primarily as autobiographical revelation or as a happy hunting ground for "specialists" in critico-psychoanalysis or for "professors with a system" (to quote in part an early epigram of Smith's). It is, alas, the age of "the brave hunters of fly-specks on Art's cathedral windows" (to use George Sterling's phrase). But, like the ones antecedent, this convention as well as its fostering age will in their own turn pass on to the special nirvana reserved for such, leaving the way clear mayhap for better, more generous ones to take their place.

In an admirable and perceptive essay on Baudelaire first published in 1875, the great English critic George Saintsbury once stated: "It is not merely admiration of Baudelaire which is to be persuaded to English readers, but also imitation of him which is with at least equal earnestness to be urged upon English writers." He then states further, rather ruefully, that "we have always lacked more or less the class of *écrivains artistes*— writers who have recognized the fact that writing is an art, and who have applied themselves with the patient energy of sculptors, painters, and musicians to the discovery of its secrets," and that if the sense of a distinguished prose style has been lost in English, nothing could be more effective for its rediscovery than a study of Baudelaire's prose as a model and a stimulant to writers in English. Less than half a century later, in 1922, as if in answer to this earnest exhortation, appeared *Ebony and Crystal* with its 29 *Poems In Prose*. Alas, Saintsbury is dead, and critics of his stature, of his broad culture and perspective, are rare indeed in this present day and age. Perhaps somewhere in the long circle of eternity there will come a people who will take unhesitatingly to their hearts Smith's brilliant creations in verse and in prose. As the barriers of space and time are steadily removed through the white magic of modem science, Smith with his emphasis on the cosmic and the astronomic could easily become "the poet of the space age".

The poetry and the prose of Clark Ashton Smith represent, in part, a continuation of the humanities of the Renaissance and of classical antiquity. But by giving them a cosmic framework, that is, by emphasizing the surrounding cosmos, Smith has indicated a new avenue of approach to those old, old, old human values and relations. And at the same time, for a literature tending toward an over-anthropocentrism, he has indicated an avenue toward the stars, toward the outer cosmos, and toward possible other universes. He thus avoids the greatest pitfall, the greatest handicap of so much of the serious creative literature of the 20th century, as well as of the attendant serious literary criticism, "that introversion and introspection, that morbidly exaggerated prying into one's own vitals—and the vitals of others—which Robinson Jeffers has so aptly symbolized as 'incest.'" (From Smith's letter to the editor, *Wonder Stories*, August 1932.) Curiously, much of Smith's literary work certainly satisfies the thesis put forth by Arthur Machen in his study *Hieroglyphics* (1902) "that great writing is the result of an ecstatic experience akin to divine revelation." Much of Smith's works also satisfies the present writer's contention that great writing should give the reader a sense of cosmic universality and, above all, a sense of unlimitedness.

The first major poet in English to be influenced by Poe and very likely to remain the last as well, Smith certainly does not belong to any *Weird Tales* "school"—nor yet does he belong to any Gothic or neo-Gothic tradition except, in part, that of his own synthesis and creation. He is essentially *sui generis*. In the words of his own epigram: "The true poet is not created by an epoch; he creates his own epoch." Never lived a poet more than Smith of whom this could be said: Smith, the creator par excellence not only of one epoch or of one world but the creator of many epochs, of many worlds. A deliberate independent and outsider, he belongs to no particular time nor literary period or school: only to that mystical mainstream of literature and art which is one with all cultures and all ages. His tales and/or extended poems in prose are far more than mere exotic "divertissements." They represent a return to the fantastic fictions of serious intent of the Renaissance—to the Utopia of Sir Thomas More, to the *Gargantua et Pantagruel* of Rabelais, to *The Faerie Queene* of Spenser. They are informed with the seriousness of theme and concept and with the wealth of artistry, of technique, of invention that distinguish Smith's finest poems or that distinguish any great poetry. His finest poems, poems in prose and extended poems in prose are deliberate gestures toward the infinite and the eternal, toward those legendary eternal verities which ultimately can be neither proven nor disproven, and which in that sense are indeed timeless. He uses fantasy both in his poems and in his tales deliberately and manifestly in order to transcend the prosaic and unstable reality of a mere ephemeral contemporariness, and to attain to a greater and eternal reality beyond. He searches not only the ultimate meaning of man and his principal emotions of love and fear but, far more than those, the very significance of life and of the cosmos itself.

Smith, in translating himself and his readers to the elaborate worlds created of his imagination, seems to be fulfilling the Baudelairean aspiration to be transported "Anywhere! Anywhere! so long as it be out of this world!" In Baudelaire's poem in prose "Anywhere Out of This World," the poet asks his soul where they should go: to an idealized and picturesque Lisbon, Rotterdam, Batavia, Torneo, the Baltic, or the North Pole with its splendors of the aurora borealis. After the poet has finished his inquiry, the soul shouts in answer: "Anywhere! Anywhere! so long as it is out of this world!" This aspiration Smith embodies in one of his own poems, the sonnet "To the Chimera," wherein the poet cries out: "Unknown chimera, take us, for we tire / Amid the known monotony of things!" and then entreats the chimera not to pause "Till on thy horns of planished silver flows / The sanguine light of Edens lost to God." The first complete publication of Baudelaire's *Petits poèmes en prose* (the French poet's last work, one which in many respects he regarded as his most important) took place posthumously, in 1869, two years after his death in 1867. The third poem in prose from the end of the book is the one entitled "Anywhere Out of This World." This fact has considerable significance as three has been, from primal times down to the present, the mystical number of creation, re-creation, and of life eternal. Thus, in one sense, Smith takes up where Baudelaire has left off. Nor can we overemphasize here—in regard to this inspired aspiration toward the unknown and the otherworldly—the essential trinity of souls formed by Poe, Baudelaire and Smith; for the title of this *poème en prose* is a quotation by Baudelaire out of the canon of the works of the elder American poet.

There are certain things in the works of a literary creator of which the industrious and systematic student can cite catalogues of examples, in which he can discern principal themes and concepts, of which he can analyze the style, of which he can trace the evolution, and in which he can trace or discern the influence of other writers. But there is something which cannot be treated or understood in this way; and that something is the genius which in Smith manifests itself as the "sheer daemonic strangeness and fertility of conception" (to use Lovecraft's happy and perceptive phrase). It is almost as if Smith were literally from another sphere than our own, or at least were literally inspired by some cosmic of otherworldly genius or daemon; and ultimately these 2 words have meanings remarkably alike: genius, a tutelary spirit; and daemon, a tutelary spirit or divinity.

In the crystal of his mind's eye Smith beheld strange, ineffable things. His consummate art was the arch-magician's mirror through which he permitted others to view and share his visions: those curious pageantries of doom, of death, of beauty, of love, of wonder, of destiny, of stars and planets, and of the cosmos. Let us therefore be grateful to him for the enchantment and ecstasy and revelation he created for kindred souls. And let us salute the passing of a generous and a noble spirit whose like we shall not see again.

[Quotations from Smith used in this article, unless otherwise noted, are principally from "George Sterling—An Appreciation" in *The Overland Monthly* for March 1927, and from "An Autobiography of Clark Ashton Smith" in *The Science Fiction Fan* for August 1936. Quotations from Sir Thomas Browne, unless otherwise noted, are all from Chapter V of *Urne-Buriall*.]

Cycles

The sorcerer departs ... and his high tower is drowned
Slowly by low flat communal seas that level all...
While crowding centuries retreat, return and fall
Into the cyclic gulf that girds the cosmos round,
Widening, deepening ever outward without bound...
Till the oft-rerisen bells from young Atlantis call;
And again the wizard-mortised tower upbuilds its wall
Above a re-beginning cycle, turret-crowned.

New-born, the mage re-summons stronger spells, and spirits
With dazzling darkness clad about, and fierier flame
Renewed by aeon-curtained slumber. All the powers
Of genii and Solomon the sage inherits;
And there, to blaze with blinding glory the bored hours,
He calls upon Shem-hamphorash, the nameless Name.

June 4th, 1961
Clark Ashton Smith

Afterword

Reading again after many years this biographico-critical essay that I wrote in the early 1960's, I discover that there is very little about it that needs correction or other changes except the purely statistical data (mostly found at the end of the first and longest of the essay's three major sections) and other material of a similar nature. These few corrections and changes (some of them still involving an educated guess) I have accordingly made, but for the most part the essay remains more or less as it was when it made its first appearance in August of 1963. Other tributes and memorial publications in honor of Clark Ashton Smith have since presented themselves to the interested reader. However, the Klarkash-Tonophiles (that solid core of Smith's admirers both inside and outside the U. S. A.) remain indebted to Jack L. Chalker and his associates, then centered at Baltimore, Maryland, for sponsoring and publishing their chapbook *In Memoriam: Clark Ashton Smith*, that initial and large-scale tribute, during that long-ago summer of 1963. Apart from the few corrections and changes deemed fundamentally needed, the opinions and evaluations expressed in this essay by me concerning Smith's output in verse and prose remain the same. I formulated these in my latter twenties, and albeit I am in my early seventies now, I have not changed my mind in regard to the general or specific uniqueness, beauty, and worth of his poetry and fiction. At least on this one subject I still hold the same opinions now that I held back then, and (if such is possible) even more obdurately.

Looking back on the person that I was then—in that era just before the arrival of the Beatles in the U. S. A.—I note how concerned I was, and with very good reason, to give Smith his just critical due. Apart from those articles and reviews (1911–1927) resulting from his early poetic career (beginning in 1910 and ending in the latter 1920's), there existed in the early 1960's very little critical writing on C.A.S., especially material that interrelated the poetry with the later fiction. That Smith like H. P. Lovecraft had become by the time that he died one of the great outsiders of his over-all period, seemed obvious enough, and I made this condition the solid basis for my critical evaluation. If he did, or does, not quite compare with anyone else born in the latter 1800's, and expiring sometime in the 1900's whether early or late—except perhaps his poetic mentor and progenitor George Sterling, as well as his counterpart in fiction, H. P. Lovecraft—then that fundamental condition freed me completely. I could thus roam through the literary history of the Western World—from the Middle Ages and the Renaissance on through the nineteenth and twentieth centuries—to find those writers and poets with whom I sincerely felt that Smith could honestly compare.

As a poet in verse and in prose Klarkash-Ton (as H.P.L. playfully dubbed him) ranks as a great and unique artist, particularly in view of all the profound changes that have happened in the hundred years between 1893 and 1993 just in the art or science of verse technique, that is, of prosody, in the English language. Smith remained true to the poetic tradition to which he was born, and which he learned, painstakingly, with genius and originality, to use from the time of his early adolescence until his death. Such a poet does not change his practice to suit the latest fad or fashion of the passing moment—a poetic tradition, moreover, inherited from hundreds of years of experimentation as well as of genuine achievement. At this late date in time one is constrained to admire such rare integrity, no less than the solid belief that he maintained in the poetic tradition that he received and that he mastered. As he was in life, so is Smith in death: *sui generis*.

Tsathoggua Press rendered a real service by republishing this essay in January 1997 as a separate booklet, thirty-three years after its first appearance, just as Silver Key Press, the English-language imprint of the French nonprofit small press La Clef d'Argent, renders a no less valuable service by republishing it again today. On behalf of Klarkash-Ton I personally give the successive publishers of this essay—Mirage Press, Tsathoggua Press, and Silver Key Press—all possible credit and gratitude.

DONALD SIDNEY-FRYER
Westchester, Los Angeles
February 2007.

Clark Ashton Smith, Poet in Prose (1893–1961)

When Clark Ashton Smith died at the age of 68, on 14 August 1961, at his home in Pacific Grove, California, he left behind him, among other things, some twoscore poems in prose scattered in divers collections and publications. Here for the first time are gathered in one volume not only all the poems in prose by Smith known to exist but probably all that he cared to compose, including one left uncompleted. Five poems have never seen publication before in any form—*The Crystals, The Touchstone,* the fragment *The Image of Bronze and the Image of Iron,* the dialogue *The Corpse and the Skeleton,* and *The Sun and the Sepulchre.*

The integrity of the series of the twenty-nine *Poems in Prose* first published in December 1922 in Smith's third collection of poetry *Ebony and Crystal,* has been respected here; this series begins with *The Traveller* and ends with *The Shadows.* Likewise the integrity of the series of the ten *Prose Pastels* first published in two amateur magazines of the thirties and the forties, *The Fantasy Fan* and *The Acolyte,* has been respected: this series begins with *Chinoiserie* and ends with *The Peril that Lurks among Ruins.* One of Smith's earliest poems in prose, although not necessarily the earliest, *The Crystals,* with its interesting opposition of microcosmic and macrocosmic points of view, has been used to link the two series. *The Abomination of Desolation* and *The Touchstone,* composed at the same time as most of the *Prose Pastels,* have been placed at the end of the second series; and the unfinished poem in prose *The Image of Bronze and the Image of Iron,* as well as the dialogue *The Corpse and the Skeleton* (composed after the preceding fragment), and *The Sun and the Sepulchre* (composed sometime before Jan. 10th, *1926),* have been placed before the final selection, the extended poem in prose *Sadastor.* The fragment is possibly the earliest poem in prose by Smith extant; to judge from the manuscript and from internal evidence, it was composed circa 1914 or possibly earlier. It will be noted that the *Prose Pastels* as a series are for the most part much lighter in tone and in concept than the initial series first published in *Ebony and Crystal,* the few exceptions furnished possibly by *The Passing of Aphrodite* and *The Muse of Hyperborea* do not necessarily disqualify Smith's use of the designation of "prose pastel."

The period of composition of the poems is circa 1912–1929. Those included among the initial twenty-nine were composed circa 1912–1922, and most of the prose pastels were composed in December 1929. In a letter dated Jan. 9th, 1930 and addressed to his friend, confrere, and correspondent H. P. Lovecraft, Smith writes: "I wrote some 8 or 10 prose-poems just before Christmas. . . ." The precise dates of composition so far known are as follows: *The Crystals,* Jul. 27th, 1914; *The Corpse and the Skeleton,* Apr. 5th, 1915; *The Garden and the Tomb,* Jun. 9th, 1915; *The Memnons of the Night,* Dec. 18th, 1915; *Ennui,* Feb. 26th, 1918; *The Passing of Aphrodite,* Feb. 26th, 1925; *To the Daemon,* Dec. 16th, 1929; *The Abomination of Desolation,* Dec. 16th, 1929; *The Mirror in the Hall of Ebony,* Dec. 17th, 1929; *The Lotus and the Moon,* Dec. 18th, 1929; *The Touchstone,* Dec. 18th, 1929; *The Forbidden Forest,* Dec. 20th, 1929; *The Mithridate,* Dec. 21st, 1929; *The Muse of Hyperborea,* Dec. 22nd, 1929. *Chinoiserie,* although the precise date of the day is not known, was also composed in December 1929. The extended poem in prose *Sadastor* was composed in the year 1925 as was also another extended poem in prose *The Abominations of Yondo.*

(For most of these dates and other details, the author of this essay is indebted to Roger E. Stoddard, Curator of the Harris Collection of the American Poetry and Plays, at Brown University, The University Library, Providence, Rhode Island, for his courtesy in allowing him to inspect the manuscripts and typescripts of the poems in prose as well as of other materials by Smith in the same library's [then] Lovecraft Collection.)

The poems in prose in this volume afford a brilliant addition to the literature of a genre that began in the nineteenth century with Aloysius Bertrand, Edgar Allan Poe, and Charles Baudelaire. It is a type of literature generally misunderstood, poorly defined (if defined at all), and largely unchronicled in English. The poem in prose should not be confused with any merely "poetic prose"; the term "prose-poem" is often employed to designate any loosely atmospheric, vaguely rhythmical, usually decorative, often undisciplined, and rather pretty-pretty type of prose. The true nature of the poem in prose is revealed by a brief consideration of its history and of a few selected poems.

It was the poet Aloysius Bertrand (1807–1841) who introduced the genre of the prose-poem into French literature with the collection *Gaspard de la Nuit* posthumously published in 1842, an event that passed almost unnoticed; but by the end of the century, during the Symbolist movement, the *Gaspard* had become recognized as a masterpiece, and included among its admirers such distinguished figures as Stéphane Mallarmé and Maurice Ravel (who composed a suite of piano-pieces bearing the same title). *Gaspard de la Nuit, Fantaisies à la Manière de Rembrandt et de Callot*, is a series of prose ballads in which Bertrand evokes in vivid tableaux the life, the thought, the imagination of the Middle Ages, especially of the medieval city of Dijon. The book has never been widely known outside France, and has never been translated in its entirety into English. It is divided into seven sections or books (the numeral seven is important to the medieval imagination) which are as follows: *Flemish School (École Flamande); Old Paris (Le Vieux Paris); Night and its Marvels (La Nuit et ses Prestiges); Chronicles (Les Chroniques); Spain and Italy (Espagne et Italie); Sylves (Silves);* and *Miscellaneous Pieces (Pièces Detachées). A* typical prose ballad contains four, five, six, sometimes more, short paragraphs or staves of more or less equal length, arranged somewhat in the manner of the King James Bible, although without being numbered. Some of the ballads make skillful use of repetition (essentially a device of lyrical poetry); for instance, the last paragraph or stave will often repeat the first with a few slight but effective changes. From the final section of *Miscellaneous Pieces,* I cite as a typical example the prose ballad *Evening on the Canal (Le Soir sur l'Eau)* which I give in my own translation below:

Shores where Venice is queen of the sea.
ANDRÉ CHÉNIER.

The black gondola went gliding past the marble palaces, like a bravo hurrying forth to some nocturnal adventure, a stiletto and a lantern underneath his cape.

Aboard the gondola, a cavalier and a lady spoke of love:—"The orange-trees so heavenly sweet, and you so indifferent! Ah! signora, you are a statue in a garden!"

"This kiss, is it from a statue, my Georgio! why do you sulk?"—"You love me then?"—"There's not a star in the sky that does not know it and thou knowest it not?"

"What's that noise?"—"Nothing, doubtless the splashing of the waves rising and falling on some steps of the stairways along the Giudecca Canal."

"Help! help!"—"Ah! mother of God, someone's drowning!"—" On your way, he has confessed his sins," spoke a monk who came into view on the terrace.

And the black gondola quickened its oars, gliding past the marble palaces, like a bravo returning from some nocturnal adventure, a stiletto and a lantern underneath his cape.

To Baudelaire, the *Gaspard* seemed to have inaugurated the genre of the *poème en prose,* and in his dedication to his own collection, the *Petits Poèmes en Prose,* he acknowledges his indebtedness to Bertrand; there can be no doubt that the *Gaspard* "suggested to Baudelaire the idea of elaborating short pieces of prose with the unity, precision, and adornment of verse."[2] It also suggested to Baudelaire to attempt for modern Paris what Bertrand had done for medieval Dijon and the Middle Ages in general. The painstaking craftsmanship of Bertrand, similar to that of Baudelaire, inspired the distinguished critic Sainte-Beuve to think of a medieval *orfèvre* or goldsmith. And there is much in Bertrand's *petits poèmes en prose* (most of them are very short), with their vividly delineated, almost chiseled tableaux, that anticipates the laborious striving-after-perfection of Gautier, of Baudelaire, and of the Parnassian and Symbolist poets. One thinks instinctively of a poet like José-Maria de Heredia and his calculatedly perfect sonnets which evoke, in a highly sculpturesque and painterly manner, brilliant historical or mythological settings.

It has been stated, and with considerable justification, that *Les Fleurs du Mal* (first edition published 1857) and the *Petits Poèmes en Prose* of Baudelaire would not be what they are if it were not for the prose and verse of Edgar Allan Poe (1809–1849). This is indisputable but, more than that, we may point to certain specific pieces by Poe that must have had a direct influence on Baudelaire's *poèmes en prose* as regards the actual form. During 1848–1865 Baudelaire was working at what was to become the classic translation of Poe's prose works in French, and circa 1857–1864 he was also working at the composition of his own poems in prose. He could hardly have failed to have noted those two "*petits* poèmes en prose" by Poe, *Shadow—A Parable* and *Silence—A Fable,* as well as those two *extended* poems in prose, *The Masque of the Red Death* and *Eleanora* (in contradistinction to the *little* poems in prose). Thus, in a sense, it was Poe who introduced the prose-poem into English; his innovation, independent of Bertrand's, seemed to have passed unnoticed during the nineteenth century, although it had a direct effect on Clark Ashton Smith.

Baudelaire (1821–1867), who was one of the earliest and most fervent of the admirers of both Bertrand and Poe, was probably the first to use the designation of "poème en prose." In a sense, by terming it thus, he defined and created the genre, even more than did Bertrand. Baudelaire discarded Bertrand's division of the poem in prose into more or less equal staves, employing instead a more fluid and subtle system of paragraphing dictated by the actual needs of the subject-matter. The *Petits Poèmes en Prose* did not see their first complete publication until 1869, two years after Baudelaire's death; in many respects he regarded this collection as his most important work, and in time the *poème en prose* became a standard and favorite form in French literature. Its single most important early convert was the precocious genius Arthur Rimbaud (1854–1891), who employed the form to embody the powerful fantasies included in *Les Illuminations* (written circa 1871, published 1886), and who in sheer force of imagination surpasses both Bertrand and Baudelaire, and anticipates much of Smith, especially the latter's unique cosmic vision; although, like Baudelaire, Rimbaud was more the singer of metropolitan dissonances. Rimbaud's fertility of invention is easily equalled by Smith's own, although Smith's is possibly of a more abstract and even more imaginative nature.

As Baudelaire had acknowledged the influence of Bertrand, so Smith in turn acknowledged the influence and inspiration of Baudelaire on his own work, especially of the *Petits Poèmes en Prose* on his own poems in prose. Sometime during 1912–1922 Smith first came to know and to study Baudelaire, not however in the original French but in some English translation, most likely that of Arthur Symons; Smith did not learn French and come to know Baudelaire in his original language until 1925 when Smith made his first translations from Baudelaire, as painstakingly as the elder French poet had once done for Poe. Smith had first discovered Poe at the age of thirteen, and this early influence is directly traceable in much of Smith's work. Such pieces as *Shadow—A Parable, Silence—A Fable,* and *The Masque of the Red Death,* with their unity, their word-artistry, and their powerful evocation of mood, made a profound impression on the young Smith, But apart from these poems in prose by Poe, and some of the work of William Beckford and Sir Thomas Browne, there was little to guide Smith in his own language.

However, he did have one single small model which he had probably encountered before his discovery of Baudelaire, and which was written by a poet of his own native California. The poet in question was Nora May French (1881–1907), that tragic, Sappho-like figure who died by her own hand in 1907 at the age of twenty-six. Her body was cremated, and the ashes were scattered into the Pacific from Point Lobos. Her posthumously published collection of *Poems* (The Strange Co., San Francisco, 1910), edited by Henry Anderson Lafler, includes the following selection:

THINK NOT, O LILIAS

Think not, O Lilias, that the love of this night will endure in the sun. Hast thou beheld fungi, white, evil, rosy-lined, poisonous, shrivel in the eyes of day?

In this wilderness of strange hearts it is not thine alone that concerns me. Many brave hearts of men are more to me than thine. The hearts of men breathe deeply. As for thy heart, it runs from me, it is quicksilver, it does not concern me greatly.

This *petit poème en prose,* the only one such in the entire collection, and curiously anticipatory of Smith's work in the same genre, was recalled out of a dream and written down verbatim. With good reason both Smith and Sterling, Smith's great friend and mentor, admired Nora May French; they both composed tributes in verse to her memory; and Smith could hardly have failed to have noted the excellent effect achieved by her one and only poem in prose.

Despite the few models already extant in English, Smith most likely did draw his understanding of the systematic application of the theory of the poem in prose from the *Petits Poèmes en Prose.* In his admirable and perceptive essay on Baudelaire first published in 1875, the great English critic George Saintsbury, when discussing the poems in prose, offers us this definition of the genre: ". . . It is prose employed to serve a new purpose, the presentation of a definite and complete image, thought, or story in a definite, complete, and above all, brief form. The precise presentation within contracted limits, and the employment of an extraordinarily refined and polished style, are the sole differentiating factors [between ordinary prose and the poem in prose], but the variety and originality which their introduction produces are unmistakable." (This essay, *Charles Baudelaire,* first appeared in the *Fortnightly Review* for October 1875.) So far as this definition goes, it is a valid one, but there are a number of important points it fails to make or emphasize.

The beauty of the poem in prose lies in its offering the poet the opportunity to present and develop an idea, image, story or emotional experience without having to bother with rime or strict metre or the arbitrary line length of the traditional forms of verse, thus endowing the poet with the consequent flexibility of prose. Thus, the *poème en prose is,* with all proportions guarded, a sort *of poème en vers libre* (to which it is closely related) or *poème en vers* freed from rime, strict metre and line length; but at the same time it is a form which imposes on the poet the necessity, nay,

the obligation to avoid the often inherent laxness, the undisciplined prolixity and formlessness of prose. This Smith understood supremely well;
and this constitutes one of his most important debts to Baudelaire, primarily one of technique. However, if the poet is freed from strict metre,
he must nonetheless pay rigorous attention to the element of rhythm:
here Baudelaire had less to teach Smith save indirectly through translation, and here Smith had to turn to such masters of rhythmical prose in
English as Edgar Allan Poe and Sir Thomas Browne.

The poem in prose at its best is characterized by a tense and artistic
unity in which style, subject-matter and imagery all work toward the central effect, whether subtly or overtly. It is odd that comparatively so few
poets in English, apart from Smith, have availed themselves of the use of
such a magnificent form, offering as it does excellent opportunities for
poetic expression but with complete freedom from the formal strictures
and requirements of traditional verse-forms. But nonetheless, just as
much as any strict verse-form, the *poème en prose* possesses its own inherent discipline, that indispensable discipline which, working together with
the image, idea and/or emotion, creates that tension from which derives
the work of art, literary or otherwise.

Perhaps the best definition of the prose-poem, even if very subjective (and probably the best for that very reason), is to be found in Baudelaire's dedication to the *Petits Poèmes en Prose:* "Who is there of us who has
not, during his hours of ambition, dreamt of the miracle of a poetic
prose, musical without metre and without rime, supple and abrupt
enough to adapt to the lyrical agitations of the soul, to the pulsations of
reverie, to the sudden starts of the conscience?"

If, apropos the poem in prose, Smith's principal debt to Baudelaire
is technical rather than of subject-matter, there still remain at least two
fairly close textual correspondences. The second and less significant of
these is between the *poème en prose L'Invitation au Voyage* and Smith's poem
In Cocaigne: in the first the poet describes to his beloved the fabled and
planturous land of Cocaigne and then finishes by discovering to her that
Cocaigne is really herself; in the second we follow on an April afternoon
the promenade of two lovers seeking the land of Cocaigne which they
find at last in their embrace. The first and far more important of the textual correspondences is between *The Stranger (L'Étranger),* the opening
poem of the *Petits Poèmes en Prose,* and *The Traveller,* the opening poem of
the *Poems in Prose* in *Ebony and Crystal.* Rhetorically similar, both poems

deal powerfully with the theme of alienation and of the outsider, in a series of questions and answers, or invocations and responses. The reader
will find it of interest to compare Smith's *Stranger* (the first word of *The
Traveller)* with Baudelaire's (especially with the lines placed in italics),
which I give in my own translation below:

> "What lovest thou the most, man enigmatical, say? thy father, thy
> mother, thy sister or thy brother?"
>
> "I have neither father, nor mother, nor sister, nor brother."
>
> "Thy friends?"
>
> "There you employ a word whose significance has remained for
> me up to this day unknown."
>
> "Thy native land?"
>
> *"I know not in what latitude it lies."*
>
> "Beauty?"
>
> "I would worship her willingly, goddess and immortal."
>
> "Gold?"
>
> "I loathe it in the same way that you loathe God."
>
> "Then, what dost thou love, stranger extraordinary?"
>
> "I love the clouds...the clouds that pass...down there...down
> there...the marvellous clouds!"

The reader will also note the striking coincidental similarity between
Smith's traveller and the "weary wight forwandring by the way" (actually
Archimago in disguise as a pilgrim) in Canto VI of Book I of Spenser's
epic *The Faerie Queene,* as described in stanza XXXV:

> A silly man, in simple weeds forworne,
> And soild with dust of the long-drièd way;
> His sandales were with toilsome travell torne,
> And face all tand with scorching sunny ray,
> As he had traveild many a sommers day
> Through boyling sands of Arabie and Ynde,
> And in his hand a Jacobs staffe, to stay
> His weary limbs upon; and eke behind
> His scrip did hang, in which his needments he did bind.

Thus, Smith in his own poem has taken one of the stock figures of
the medieval world, with all its traditional elements, and employed it to
express his own alienation, an alienation even more extreme than that of
Baudelaire or than that of Poe. This has proven to be one of the central

themes in the serious literature of the first half of the twentieth century, even more than it was of the nineteenth. The novel *The Stranger* or *The Outsider* (*L'Étranger,* 1942), by Albert Camus, bearing thus the same title as the *poème en prose* by Baudelaire, presents a powerful study of alienation. However, in Smith's poem, it is not so much an individual merely alienated in earthly time or space as it is rather a sentience exiled on the planet Earth from some other and possibly higher sphere.

Apart from the textual correspondences already cited, there remain only one or two other specifically Baudelairean resemblances; these revolve around Smith's use of the Man-God, a concept first crystallized by Baudelaire in his study *Les Paradis Artificiels* (although it is actually a very ancient one). We find its first exemplification in the poet-visionary of *The Crystals,* and its second in the emperor Chan in the prose-poem *Ennui,* a Baudelairean theme par excellence (we need only remember that the alternate title of the *Petits Poèmes en Prose is Le Spleen de Paris,* and that the first section of *Les Fleurs du Mal* bears the title *Spleen et Idéal*). Chan, despite his sovereignty of temporal power and wealth, is yet paradoxically impotent to escape that ultimate bane of godhood or of the Man-God, to wit, ennui or spleen. However, Smith probably gives more forceful embodiment to the concept elsewhere in the canon of his works; in such poems as *Nero* and especially the compressed epic *The Hashish-Eater; or, The Apocalypse of Evil* (the hero of which is "the emperor of dreams," informed with demiurgic powers), and in many of his later tales, the principal actors in which are often archimages and kings, derived ultimately from tribal witch-doctors and chieftains, respectively.

One could make a very interesting and detailed comparison between Spenser, Coleridge, Poe, Baudelaire, Rimbaud, and Smith in their use of the dream-landscape, although Smith is probably closer to Poe and Coleridge than to Baudelaire, especially to Poe. Compare the landscape of the "dreary region in Libya, by the borders of the river Zaire," in *Silence— A Fable,* and the landscape of the Valley of the Many-Colored Grass, in *Eleanora,* among many others created by Poe, to the landscapes in *The Flower-Devil, A Phantasy* or *The Shadows.* One may make other rewarding comparisons between Smith and Poe in the genre of the poem in prose. Structurally the beginning of *Sadastor* and *The Peril that Lurks among Ruins* bears a strong resemblance to that of *Silence—A Fable.* The Demon who narrates this fable of Silence is indubitably some sort of ancestor or possibly cousin to the titular demon of *The Flower-Devil,* to the Demon in *The*

Demon, the Angel, and Beauty, to the demon Charnadis in the extended poem in prose *Sadastor,* to the Daemon in *To the Daemon* and *The Peril that Lurks among Ruins;* and to the manifold demons in Smith's later tales such as the archdemon Thasaidon in *The Dark Eidolon,* and the demoniac entity, "the featureless Shadow," in *The Ice-Demon,* the soul of the great Hyperborean glacier. Indeed, much of Smith's later fiction could be read, at least in part, as a veritable manual of demonology. *Sadastor,* even more than *The Abominations of Yondo,* is a true, even if extended, poem in prose, in the same manner as Poe's *Eleanora* and *The Masque of the Red Death;* and it anticipates many of Smith's later tales (1928–1938), or extended poems in prose, as of where the latter designation applies. Stylistically the early poems in prose in *Ebony and Crystal* clearly pave the way toward the highly baroque prose of the later tales; more than that, two of them served as the inspiration or nuclei, in regard to over-all plot, atmosphere, and even as to actual phrases, for two later extended poems in prose: *The Planet of the Dead* draws largely upon *From the Crypts of Memory* for its nucleus, with the germ of its ending in the close of *The Shadows;* and *The Demon of the Flower* draws largely upon *The Flower-Devil* for its nucleus, with the plot to poison the flower-demon from lines 65–72 of the compressed epic *The Hashish-Eater:*

> And I see,
> In gardens of a crimson-litten world
> The sacred flow'r with lips of purple flesh,
> And silver-lashed, vermillion-lidded eyes
> Of torpid azure; whom his furtive priests
> At moonless eve in terror seek to slay,
> With bubbling grails of sacrificial blood
> That hide a hueless poison.

That Poe and Smith have much in common stylistically, is shown by the following period by Poe from *Eleanora,* which the reader would do well to compare with some of Smith's own periods: "The pomps and pageantries of a stately court, and the mad clangor of arms, and the radiant loveliness of women, bewildered and intoxicated my brain." But while Smith's style is based in part on Poe, yet the result is highly original, not quite like the style of any other writer. However, despite this originality, perhaps the closest correspondence is with the baroque prose of Sir Thomas Browne (1605–1682) wherein certain Gothic elements—such as savageness, grotesqueness, antithesis, changefulness or metamorphosis, redundance or pseudo-redundance,—have evolved from an ultimately classical matrix. That which Lytton Strachey once cited as the peculiarities of Browne's style—"the studied pomp of its Latinisms, its wealth of allusion, its tendency toward sonorous antithesis"—could be cited just as well as being the peculiarities of Smith's own style which, like that of Browne, makes heavy and deliberate use of epithets; this permits both men not only to condense a good deal into a small space but also to achieve certain rhythms, certain emotive and imaginative effects as well as certain effects of bravura, which could not be achieved in any other way. One seems to be reading some sort of incantation or litany with measured invocations and responses.

The prose of Clark Ashton Smith features, as does the prose of Sir Thomas Browne (and as does of course Smith's own poetry in verse), a skillful, often uncanny, juxtaposition of Anglo-Saxon words with those of Graeco-Latinate derivation; especially does it feature a blending and opposition of Anglo-Saxon monosyllables with Graeco-Latinate polysyllables; this creates an effect approximating the incantatory one of poetry in verse. For all the poetic denseness of his prose style, Smith's syntax remains remarkably clear, and with extraordinary rhythmical effects. In his poems in prose, as in his tales and/or extended poems in prose, there are prose rhythms that challenge comparison with those of the finest stylists in the language, including those of Sir Thomas Browne; whom, in sheer sustained stateliness and sombre splendor of style, Smith in many instances fully equals. However, there is more than a stylistic affinity between these two writers. The much "quaint and curious . . . forgotten lore" to be found in the canon of Smith's works, especially of his poems in prose and of his tales, has extended parallels in the works of Sir Thomas Browne, particularly in the latter's *Pseudodoxia Epidemica* or *Vulgar Errors* (1646)—with its inquiry into and consideration of the basilisk, of griffins, of the phoenix, of the salamander living in fire, of the chameleon living only upon air, of the unicorn's horn, of the ostrich digesting iron, of "the musical note of swans before their death," of "the pictures of mermaids, unicorns, and some others."

Such a phrase by Browne as "The night of time far surpasseth the day," could serve as the motto or moral of Smith's poem in prose *The Memnons of the Night*. Such a sentence by Browne as "The number of the dead long exceedeth all that such live," finds an unexpected similarity to the phrase "the dead had come to outnumber infinitely the living," in Smith's poem in prose *From the Crypts of Memory*, and to the phrase "its immemorial dead, who had come to outnumber infinitely the living," in the extended poem in prose *The Planet of the Dead*. As poetic and mystical considerations of death and mortality, such poems in prose as *The Memnons of the Night*, *From the Crypts of Memory*, and *The Shadows*, together with such extended poems in prose as *The Planet of the Dead*, *The Empire of the Necromancers*, *The Death of Malygris*, and others, form worthy twentieth-century companion-pieces to the extended poem in prose formed by the fifth and last chapter of Sir Thomas Browne's *Urne-Buriall* (1658).

The "tendency toward sonorous antithesis" manifests itself not only in the style and imagination of Smith's poems in prose but even in the form of about one fourth of them: two paragraphs, with the first generally longer than the second. Possibly one sixth or one fifth of Smith's total output in verse is in sonnet-form, usually the Italian or Petrarchan sonnet or some variant thereof; and there is a general correspondence between the prose-poems of two paragraphs, with the first usually longer than the second, to the Petrarchan sonnet with its often sharply-defined and opposed octave and sestet. This arrangement permits Smith to contrast one force, person, story, emotion, object, attribute of an object, to another, often with considerable effect.

In explanation of the elaborate style characteristic of most of his poems in prose and of his tales and/or extended poems in prose, Smith once commented as follows, in a letter written in the summer of 1950 to S. J. Sackett:

> ...It is designed to produce effects of language and rhythm which could not possibly be achieved by a vocabulary restricted to what is known as "basic English." As Strachey points out (in his essay on Sir Thomas Browne), a style composed largely of words of Anglo-Saxon origin tends to a spondaic rhythm, "which seems to produce (by some mysterious rhythmic law) an atmosphere of ordinary life." An atmosphere of remoteness, mystery, and exoticism is more naturally evoked by a style with an admixture of Latinity, lending itself to more varied and sonorous rhythms, as well as to subtler shades, tints, and nuances of meaning.... [This comment was first published in the amateur magazine *Fantasy Sampler* for June 1956 in S. J. Sackett's essay on Smith, "The Last Romantic."]

In the essay on Baudelaire mentioned earlier, Saintsbury states: "It is not merely admiration of Baudelaire which is to be persuaded to English readers, but also imitation of him which is with at least equal earnestness to be urged upon English writers." He then states further, rather ruefully, that "we have always lacked more or less the class of *écrivains artistes*— writers who have recognized the fact that writing is an art, and who have applied themselves with the patient energy of sculptors, painters, and musicians to the discovery of its secrets," and that if the sense of a distinguished prose style has been lost in English, nothing could be more effective toward its rediscovery than a study of Baudelaire's prose as exemplified in the *Petits Poèmes en Prose.* In closing he then urges Baudelaire both as a model and as a stimulant to writers in English. Less than half a century later, in 1922, as if in response to this earnest exhortation, appeared *Ebony and Crystal* with its twenty-nine *Poems in Prose,* and now but a little less than a century later, appears the present volume. I think the great English critic would have been among the first to have applauded the distinction of Smith's achievement with these poems for they bear witness to the pen of a remarkable thinker and of a superb and highly-disciplined stylist. Without a high degree of discipline, these poems would have been neither possible nor successful; for insofar as a poem is an incantation or a spell and the poet a verbal sorcerer or necromancer, it is necessary for him to exercise a perfect, almost iron, control if the poem or spell is to succeed, and if the poet is not to invoke the evil and inimical spirits of artistic failure, and hence of the reader's negative criticism.

The reader who makes in this volume his first acquaintance with these poems, will find much to challenge and stimulate him: Smith's unique cosmic perspective, his extraordinary fertility of invention, his equally extraordinary powers of visionary imagination, and equally important—for without such he could not have embodied these poems successfully for others—his artistry, his innate feeling for form and style, his hypersensitivity to tone, and as one of his earliest critics expressed it, his "power over words to make them come winged at his bidding and to make pictures vivid as of an actual impression of objects." Especially for the reader familiar with Smith's classic tales of the weird, and eager to discover and read further tales by him, these poems in prose will prove an interesting and rewarding experience since many of them tell strange stories in an uniquely quintessential manner. Smith is one of the very few poets in English who have fully understood the technique of this difficult and eminently French genre more or less created by Baudelaire, but among those few who have essayed the genre and have done so successfully, he occupies a sovereign position. Indeed, it is not too much to say that as a practitioner of the poem in prose Smith has no peer in English, and that, considering his achievement in the genre from a universal literary viewpoint, he takes equal rank with Baudelaire and with Rimbaud. The publication of Smith's total forty-six poems in prose in one collection will serve to establish his pre-eminence in the literature of this genre, his output in which is only a little less than the fifty examples extant by Baudelaire in the *Petits Poèmes en Prose,* and only a little more than the thirty-eight examples extant by Rimbaud (out of the total forty-two titles) in *Les Illuminations,*

In closing, I wish to invoke the learned doctor Sir Thomas Browne himself, by citing a passage from his posthumously published *Christian Morals* (1716). The passage is taken from Section XIV of Part the Third, and is amazingly similar to the spirit animating so much of Smith's own writings, and could easily have been penned by Smith himself: "Let thy Thoughts be of things which have not entered into the Hearts of Beasts: Think of things long past, and long to come: Acquaint thyself with the *choragium* of the Stars, and consider the vast expansion beyond them. Let Intellectual Tubes give thee a glance of things, which visive Organs reach not. Have a glimpse of incomprehensibles, and Thoughts of things, which Thoughts but tenderly touch."

Pacific Palisades, California
14 August 1964

George Sterling (1869–1926):
Hesperian Laureate

To Whom the unceasing suns belong,
    And cause is one with consequence,—
    To Whose divine inclusive sense
The moan is blended with the song.
    —AMBROSE BIERCE, "Invocation," 4th July 1888.

(This stanza George Sterling quoted to preface his
own and greatest poem *The Testimony of the Suns*.)

1976 was a year of anniversaries in America both big and small. First, the
Bicentennial celebrated the birth of the U. S. A. in 1776. Second, the
Twin Bicentennial in San Francisco celebrated the dual founding in 1776
of the Presidio on the one hand and the Mission Dolores on the other.
1976 also marked the anniversary of at least two outstanding literary figures peculiarly associated with San Francisco as well as with the San
Francisco Bay Area over-all.

One hundred years have now passed since Jack London first appeared on the scene, and within San Francisco, in 1876, and sixty years
since he died of uremic poisoning in 1916 near Glen Ellen. Precisely fifty
years have elapsed since the one-time poet laureate of San Francisco,
George Sterling, died in 1926 by deliberate or accidental suicide while
quartered in the old "Monkey" or Montgomery Block in downtown San
Francisco.

By an odd coincidence, Ambrose Bierce (a most singular fantaisiste)
influenced both these figures to varying degrees, and they each became a
great and good friend to the other. They shared a considerable spectrum
of experience, whether adventuring in San Francisco's pre-Earthquake
night life on the Barbary Coast, or whether hobnobbing on London's estate in the Valley of the Moon, just outside Glen Ellen and now a state
historic park. London influenced Sterling to be a socialist at least for a
while, and introduced him into the City's own Bohemia. They remained
fast friends up to the time of Jack's death.

But, whereas London has become an internationally recognized figure whose writings have appeared in many foreign translations (he has
proven especially popular in the Soviet Union with critic and mass audi-

ence alike), Sterling has primarily remained only a locally known celebrity. His once national reputation has drastically waned since his death, and he owes his continuing regional fame to reasons other than poetical ones. Yet Sterling, like other (Northern) Californian writers and poets, once enjoyed a not inconsiderable reputation among some of England's critics and other men of letters.

Both Ambrose Bierce and (earlier) Joaquin Miller had each helped to establish a Californian literary beach-head (or a Californian "landfall" if you will) in Great Britain in the 1870's, only a hundred years ago. Miller first came to San Francisco in 1870 where he became an intimate friend of Bret Harte, Charles Warren Stoddard, and Ina Coolbrith, as well as others during California's first golden age of literature. In 1871 he sailed for England where as a romantic and "Wild Western" figure (he was a clever and brilliant self-advertiser) he gained the patronage of W. M. Rossetti and others. *Songs of the Sierras*, marked as his first book of poems published in England, won him instant acclaim, an acclaim which has not survived the years. *Songs of the Sierras* has remained his best known book and *Columbus* (which isn't half-bad, really) his best known poem. However less than gloriously sustained (Miller is unusually uneven), the epic-imaginative sense of adventure that he projects at his best has real *élan*. It places him directly in the solid tradition of Californian romanticism.

Bierce had lived and worked in England from 1872 into 1876. He edited for awhile *The Lantern*, a professionally partisan periodical, for the exiled Eugénie, former Empress of the French, and widow of Napoléon III. In his older age Bierce was to have rather agreeable things to say about the English, and he did enjoy his sojourn in Great Britain. Apart from this extended period in England, however, he stayed in San Francisco (more or less) until 1896. He had first come to the City by the Golden Gate after the Civil War, and his first professionally published writings took the shape of a number of rather Poesque poems first published in the newspaper or journal *The Californian* in the latter 1860's. By the 1890's he had become the acknowledged literary arbiter of the West Coast, and at least as able a critic as the now lesser known Porter Garnett (although Garnett would never have owned to this at the time).

Although somewhat underrated at the moment (an eclipse his work will clearly survive), Bierce has had a minor revival in recent years. *The Devil's Dictionary* has appeared in augmented form, and *Write it Right* has been re-issued in a gorgeous format (its first major re-publication) which might even have pleased the Old Master himself. Several paperbacks of his work (and largely of distinguished academic origin) have also appeared.

His vision and his best works are marked by a love of truth and a total hatred of corruption and hypocrisy. Although not often emphasized, Bierce was nothing if not a genuine and rather tortured romantic of a distinctly poetical sensibility. As expressed aptly in the *Saturday Review of Literature* for January 30th, 1937, "His best, lost in a ton of chaff, was good indeed." Further, "It is the tragedy of Bierce that his finest work should be left to oxidize in the 'complete works' cemented together by a local bookseller."

Be that as it may, Bierce has had a continuing influence on other poets and writers through his protégé George Sterling and then through Sterling's own protégé Clark Ashton Smith. Bierce as well as any had everything to do with later Californian men of letters gaining recognition and serious critical attention from England's own tribe of littérateurs from the 1870's on into the latter 1920's. It will be recalled how the middle to latter 1920's witnessed a major shift in taste away form the highly romantic imagination of decidedly fantastic type which had hitherto proven popular with both elitist and popular audiences. The movement of critical interest (at least in the "Northeast" U. S. A.) was very much away from the intensely "bardic" spirit of awe and wonder and nobility, and very much towards the hard-headed, hard-boiled and hard-edged genus of modern writing (the so-called "realism" of the time) with its stripped style of diction and no-nonsense approach.

Although both Bierce and Coolbrith survived the Victorian Age in which they had been born, artists such as George Sterling, Hermann Scheffauer, Nora May French, Jimmy Hopper, and Jack London represent California's second golden age of literature. But between the generation of Bierce, Miller, Harte, Coolbrith, Twain, and others, and then the generation of Sterling, French, London, Scheffauer, and so forth, there existed a palpable and multifaceted connection, giving continuity and some (necessary) sense of tradition. In a literary sense the older generation did give form and shape (more or less) to the younger, and the younger generation clearly continued certain traditions and aesthetics handed over to them (in some cases as teacher to pupil) by the older one.

Until Robinson Jeffers in the middle 1920's, and with the exception of such novelists as Frank Norris and Jack London, the Californian literary and artistic life from 1900 to 1926/1930 seems (at a superficial glance) like a very special hold-over from Victorian times, a Pre-Raphaelite preserve, with distinct Parnassian and/or Arcadian overtones. There was not that sharp immediate break with the Victorian past that happened in England and in the "Northeast" U. S. A. For that reason the writers and artists of California's second golden age of literature maintained certain traditions and attitudes which elsewhere had virtually gone out of critical favor and fashion by the 1920's; and which survived thus longer in California than almost anywhere else.

Sterling had the good fortune to die virtually in the afternoon of his national fame and thus before he was forced to witness its decline and sunset. Something of his genuine "ancient" renown lingered still in obscure nooks and crannies, however. Clearly growing out of Sterling's generation in an artistic sense, but following the demise of Northern California's older Bohemia (symbolized perfectly in Sterling's death), the melancholy and majestic figure of Clark Ashton Smith emerges, and very much like a lone survivor from lost Atlantis. He remained resolutely faithful up until his death to his Sterlingesque tradition, his "elder inheritance" of wonder and marvel, terror and beauty. All the same elements that we find in Sterling we find also but in a particularly acute and intensified form within the highly compact *oeuvre* of Ashton Smith, whether ode, sonnet, soliloquy, prose-poem, weird story, painting, drawing, or sculpted head.

Although his *oeuvre* has at the minimum survived (in a sense that Sterling's has not, at least yet) so that he has definitely outlasted hostile criticism on the one hand, or critical neglect and indifference on the other—it is a perfect compendium of everything that the informed critical temper of the latter 1920's, and then the 1930's, 1940's, 1950's, and the early 1960's, definitely did not find of interest or concern or value. The shift in critical temper that happened in the middle 1960's, and later, has indirectly benefited the cause of Smith's life and art, and has unwittingly rendered unto Caesar something of that which properly belongs to Caesar: a growing recognition, a little honor and respect, and a little round of applause for one of America's foremost creators of pure poetry, pure romance, and pure fantasy. But interest in Smith will help to keep some interest in Sterling alive, and therein lies a choice bit of literally poetic justice.

Just as the elder poet had once done all he could to help his younger protégé, something of what Sterling had once given to Smith—the thoughtful assistance and the prompt consideration—will eventually return to Sterling from Smith, to help save the elder poet's works from total oblivion. In fact, Ashton Smith and the increasing recognition accorded him will probably serve to keep attention focused on the West Coast or California Romantics over-all (Bierce, Sterling, French, et alia).

It is indeed curious that the current "Renaissance" or "Neo-Renaissance" or "Romantic Revival" (the reader may pick his own label) has not yet caught up with George Sterling and brought him back into the general recognizance. And if it is not yet quite the time for a major revival relative to Sterling, it is time for some general re-evaluation of him both as poet and as a public figure. And it is also time to review some of the major facts of his biography, as well as something of the conditions and aesthetics peculiar to his period of mature productivity lasting from about 1900 to 1926. He was a far better poet than what one would gather from reading the rather slighting references to him (as a poet but not as a personality) in the columns of San Francisco's current poet laureate in prose, to wit, Herb Caen.

Born in 1869 in Sag Harbor, Long Island, New York, George Sterling spent his formative years in the northeast USA. Long Island, although politically a part of New York State, is geographically a part of New England, and much of the island (certainly the eastern extremity) underwent an early maritime development akin to that of neighboring Connecticut, Rhode Island, and southeastern Massachusetts, including Nantucket and Martha's Vineyard. Sterling counted sea-faring men (whether aboard the clipper or whaling ships) amongst his immediate New England forebears.

Then as a young man he came west in 1890 and went to work as a clerk in the business of his mother's brother, a wealthy real-estate operator in Oakland, California. This brought him his first contact with the haut ton or "upper crust" of San Francisco Bay Area society. George worked in his uncle's office from 1890 on into 1905—he had begun writing his first mature poetry around the turn of the century—and then his wealthy aunt came to his rescue and gave him his "freedom" money.

With this money he bought land at Carmel-by-the-Sea on the Monterey Peninsula, built a house there, and proceeded to devote his full time to his writing, both prose and poetry, but mostly poetry; that is, when he wasn't socializing, womanizing, or heavily drinking. (Alcoholism was to pose something of a problem for him much of his adult life.) This was in 1905. In 1896 he had married Caroline Rand, but later best known as Carrie Sterling. For many years she proved remarkably tolerant and forgiving both of George's drinking and his erotic philandering.

What with fishing for abalone and hunting small game such as quail and rabbit, the living in Carmel was easy, and at George's urging and under his aegis various artists came down from the City and set up camp on the Monterey Peninsula where many of them later built regular homes. Thus the artists' colony at Carmel came into being, and (although the local cast of characters has changed sundry times since then) thus it remains to this day.

All things considered, the early Bohemian life there now seems in retrospect wonderfully protected and pastoral, if not Arcadian, even if on occasion punctuated by tragedy or comedy, beginning with that high romantic chronicle: the tragic suicide of the uniquely beautiful and highly gifted poet Nora May French in November 1907. (Curiously, both London and Sterling were also to die in the "ninth" month of November, suggesting the possibility of some arcane and mystically fatal numerology mysteriously at work.) Nora May (or "Phyllis" as her intimate friends called her, an appellation which she adopted whilst growing up in the Los Angeles area, and which she preferred to her regular given name) had been staying at Sterling's place. At the time of her final and successful attempt at suicide George was up in the City, but Carrie was home during the night of Nora's death. Her untimely demise created a shock in the City's Bohemia, and the San Francisco dailies treated it in terms of sensational and melodramatic romance. A poetry reading had been arranged to be given by her at the rebuilt Fairmont Hotel on the crest of Nob Hill to which some of the City's "upper crust" were to have come.

Nora May and her sister Helen Augusta had come from Los Angeles up north to San Francisco in the latter part of 1906 and thus after the disastrous Earthquake and Fire of the preceding April which had almost totally destroyed a major fraction of the City (roughly the area bounded by Van Ness Avenue on the west and by Market or Mission Streets on the south), that is, San Francisco's business and financial districts, as well as its finest residential area along California Street and particularly on Nob Hill.

Shortly after Nora's death, poet George (who immediately came down to Carmel from the City upon learning the sad news) and her sister Helen (who had returned to Los Angeles before Nora's death but who came back up especially for her obsequies), together with a group of fellow artists resident in the Carmel area, staged a strange but aesthetically appropriate and surely touching ceremony in Phyllis's honor on one of the headlands at Point Lobos. After her body's cremation, the ashes were scattered into the western sea.

Although regarded in the last 10 years of his life as the City's great poet laureate, the prince of poets on the West Coast—in short, *the* poet of the West (that is, before Robinson Jeffers)—Sterling in fact created his two single greatest poems (e.g., *The Testimony of the Suns* and *A Wine of Wizardry*) early in his (mature) poetic career.

At the very beginning of the 1900's, George had forwarded (through the regular mail service) one of the early drafts of *The Testimony of the Suns* (his single greatest poem) to Ambrose Bierce, the acknowledged literary master of the Bay Area and Northern California. Bierce immediately perceived the poem's grandeur and imaginative genius. He also assumed the responsibility of helping to refine and strengthen Sterling's creative ability, and to give him precise technical advice in poetics. Bierce was a master in a technical sense of the traditional prosody, the art and science of the inherited forms of poetry. In a more important sense, he posed as the guardian and curator of the classicistico-romantic traditions and aesthetics of his time and, more specifically, of the then West Coast.

George showed himself a willing and acquiescent pupil, and there can be no doubt but that Bierce's help (poetic and career-wise) proved of strategic value to Sterling. The Department of Rare Books and Special Collections at the San Francisco Public Library preserves the original Sterling typescript of *The Testimony of the Suns*, together with the manuscript comments, critiques, and creative counsellings of Ambrose Bierce. This typescript of Sterling's with marginal notes in Bierce's own hand (later published by The Book Club of California in 1927 in facsimile in a singularly handsome édition de luxe indeed) bears witness to their close collaboration, as well as to the almost fatherly devotion and care which Bierce lavished on this greatest single poem by Sterling. But it is typical of the precise and highly technical help (often with acute attention focused on the most minute details) that Bierce characteristically gave to Sterling as well as to other poet-pupils.

Bierce enthusiastically acclaimed Sterling as "the poet of the skies." Heralded by Bierce's praises, *The Testimony of the Suns* created something of a stir when first published (in a periodical of the time), and when later gathered as the title-poem in Sterling's first volume (first put out by Wood, San Francisco, 1903, but later taken over by A. M. Robertson, the San Francisco bookseller, who published most of Sterling's volumes of poetry), the critics appeared suitably impressed. A few (those not cowed by Bierce's justifiable trumpetings) seemed even somewhat annoyed at the specific poem and the book over-all. In the same year as Sterling's first collection there appeared *Shapes of Clay*, Bierce's own second compilation of poems.

In the tradition of Edgar Allan Poe, the American and now largely underground school of "pure poetry" had been peculiarly associated with Bierce, directly or indirectly. In form and in language, he was a traditionalist, a purist, and of the most unbending type. Here we may perceive (perhaps) something of an all-embracing life-attitude that he gained from his military experience during the Civil War. In his critical theories he was a proponent of *la poésie pure*. Much of his taste and preference in verse may be gauged from the fact that he considered Coleridge's *Kubla Khan* the most nearly perfect poem, *qua* poem, in the English language.

> In Xanadu did Kubla Khan
> A stately pleasure-dome decree;
> Where Alph the sacred river ran
> Through caverns measureless to man
> Down to a sunless sea.
> So twice five miles of fertile ground
> With walls and towers were girdled round;
> And there were gardens bright with sinuous rills
> Where blossomed many an incense-bearing tree;
> And here were forests ancient as the hills,
> Enfolding sunny spots of greenery.
> * * *
> But O, that deep romantic chasm which slanted
> Down the green hill athwart a cedarn cover!
> A savage place! as holy and enchanted
> As ever beneath a waning moon was haunted
> By woman wailing for her demon-lover!
> [&c.]

As a poet but more as a poetic mentor, Bierce proved a great and beneficial influence on Sterling, who became the unofficial (but universally acknowledged) poet laureate of the West Coast. Actually, Ina Donna Coolbrith (born 1842)—that beloved survivor from the generation of Mark Twain, Bret Harte, and Joaquin Miller—was made the official poet laureate of California by the governor and legislature of the state in 1915 (the year of the Panama-Pacific Exposition in San Francisco), a position she filled with deserved prestige until her death in 1928. First offered the position himself, Sterling instead insisted that the position go to Coolbrith.

Bierce not only influenced and encouraged Sterling; as we have already seen, he commented and criticized extensively Sterling's first mature poetry, e.g., *The Testimony of the Suns*. There does inhere in Bierce's own *Invocation* a cosmic perspective and understanding, even if not overtly articulated throughout.

Apart from the fact that both poems employ the octosyllabic quatrain (riming a / b / b / a) made famous by *In Memoriam* of Tennyson, *Invocation* clearly anticipates the richer harmonies and the greater vision of Sterling's own magnum opus. *The Testimony of the Suns* curiously previsions the current Age of Space with humanity's increasing exploration into the stars. Bierce also encouraged and influenced the German-born Hermann Scheffauer (1876 or 1878–1927). He indicated the high esteem in which he held his two principal pupils by dedicating to them the first edition of *Shapes of Clay*.

Bierce praised the early poetry of Edwin Markham (1852–1940) and encouraged him long before Markham became famous or infamous for *The Man with the Hoe*. He did not influence, although he did encourage, the fine and unjustly neglected lyric poet Samuel Loveman (born 1887 and but recently deceased) The record of his interest in, and his encouragement of, Loveman as a poet may be read in *Twenty-One Letters of Ambrose Bierce*, edited with a note by Loveman and published by (bookseller) George Kirk, Cleveland, 1922. Mr. Loveman's own poetry has been collected into *The Hermaphrodite and Other Poems* (The Caxton Printers, Ltd., Caldwell, Idaho, 1936).

Sometime in the spring or early summer of 1910, Ezra Pound (that later revolutionary modern poet par excellence) sent *The Ballad of the Goodly Fere* in manuscript to Bierce, evidently in the expectation that he would commend it, and might be able to place it for Pound in some periodical, in the same way that Bierce had placed Sterling's poem *A Wine of Wizardry* with *The Cosmopolitan* Magazine. Commend it Bierce did, and highly, but before he could place it anywhere, Pound withdrew the ballad. Some other verses that Pound had earlier submitted in manuscript to Bierce had, to use the elder poet's own pungent phraseology, "escaped my approval by a wide margin."

Through his poems, through his aesthetico-poetic theories (as gathered in, and revealed by, the essays in *The Opinionator*, one of the volumes in Bierce's massive *Collected Works*, published 1909–1912), and above all through his pupil Sterling, Bierce exercised an important influence on Sterling's own pupil or follower, Clark Ashton Smith (1893–1961). Smith was to surpass his immediate master, just as Sterling had surpassed his own master Bierce (in a purely poetic sense). The "Devil's Lexicographer" read and praised some of Smith's first mature poetry, and on one occasion publicly came to Smith's defense. During the summer and autumn of 1912, Bierce's last visit to California (before his bizarre disappearance in Mexico in late 1913 and early 1914), the two almost met.

Sterling in turn praised, encouraged, and influenced not only Ashton Smith but likewise, apropos of cosmic-astronomic vision and consciousness, the great poet Robinson Jeffers (1887–1962); although this last has received little recognition and attention. Significantly it was under Sterling's aegis that Jeffers set up shop as a poet (as it were) in Carmel, building himself his home as well as his tower into the stars, and creating his remarkable modem lyrics and powerful narratives of a doomed and diseased humanity.

The Biercean influence lingered on through both Sterling and Ashton Smith. It must be noted that, sometime before his mysterious disappearance into the "wilderness" (Mexico), as it were, rather in the manner of the Biblical prophets, Bierce had bequeathed his figurative Cloak of Elijah to Sterling; and Sterling in his own turn bequeathed it to Ashton Smith, in the opinion of some, and/or to Robinson Jeffers in the estimate of others.

Sterling's uniquely outstanding protégé (but not pupil) before Ashton Smith was that strangely gifted and tragic girl Nora May French (born 1881), whose only collection appeared after her death simply as *Poems* published by The Strange Company, San Francisco, 1910. Undoubtedly, had she lived longer, this fine and subtly imaginative poetess would rank today with Emily Dickinson and Edna St. Vincent Millay as one of the few major American women poets.

In turn, Ashton Smith in large part encouraged and to some extent appears to have influenced at least one poet of his native Auburn-Long Valley area, Susan Myra Gregory, as evidenced by her collection *Shadows of Wings* as published by The Troubadour Press, San Diego, 1930. Susan Myra Gregory (of both Monterey and Auburn) was the sister of the popular novelist Jackson Gregory (b.1882) who lived for many years in Auburn in his impressive studio-home high above the north fork of the American River, and who personally knew, respected, and admired "the Bard of Auburn" (as one San Francisco critic once dubbed Ashton Smith). Both Nora May French and Susan Myra Gregory belong to that tradition of Californian poetesses begun by the state's first woman poet in English—to wit, Eulalie—and continued by Ina Coolbrith (that doyenne of Hesperian poetesses), a tradition somewhat analogous to that of Dickinson and Millay on the opposite side of the continent.

But before Robinson Jeffers, George Sterling was great in the land, at least the Californian sector, thanks above all to the influence of Ambrose Bierce, and he definitely loomed as one of the more notable literary figures on the West Coast, from at least 1907, until his death in late 1926. We single out 1907 because this was the year in which Bierce's influence bore its greatest harvest on behalf of his most gifted pupil. He had placed Sterling's second greatest poem *A Wine of Wizardry* with *The Cosmopolitan*. In the issue for September 1907, Sterling's glittering and imaginative effusion made its première appearance in print, accompanied with a trenchant essay by Bierce himself. A considerable controversy developed, and this really put Sterling on the poetic map of the U. S. A. It proved instrumental in setting him up in the City's consciousness as the great poet laureate of San Francisco and (by extension) of the entire West Coast: from that time on, people recognized him as the public figure of a "great poet" for the West Coast, but (again) before Robinson Jeffers.

Just as he quotes a stanza from Bierce's *Invocation* at the head of *The Testimony of the Suns*, Sterling similarly quotes the single best passage from his Master's briefer lyric *Geotheos* at the start of *A Wine of Wizardry*:

> When mountains were stained as with wine
> By the dawning of Time, and as wine
> Were the seas.

Having thus established the dominant "color" or "key" for his poem, he then proceeds with the first main section:

> Without, the battlements of sunset shine,
> 'Mid domes the sea-winds rear and overwhelm.
> Into a crystal cup the dusky wine
> I pour, and, musing at so rich a shrine,
> I watch the star that haunts its ruddy gloom.
> Now Fancy, empress of a purpled realm,
> Awakes with brow caressed by poppy-bloom,
> And wings in sudden dalliance her flight
> To strands where opals of the shattered light
> Gleam in the wind-strewn foam, and maidens flee
> A little past the striving billows' reach,
> Or seek the russet mosses of the sea,
> And wrinkled shells that lure along the beach,
> And please the heart of Fancy; yet she turns,
> Tho' trembling, to a grotto rosy-sparred,
> Where wattled monsters redly gape, that guard
> A cowled magician peering on the damned
> Tho' vials wherein a splendid poison burns,
> Sifting Satanic gules athwart his brow.
> So Fancy will not gaze with him, and now
> She wanders to an iceberg oriflammed
> With rayed, auroral guidons of the North—
> Wherein hath winter hidden ardent gems
> And treasuries of frozen anadems,
> Alight with timid sapphires of the snow.
> But she would dream of warmer gems, and so
> Ere long her eyes in fastnesses look forth
> Over blue profounds mysterious whence glow
> The coals of Tartarus on the moonless air,
> As Titans plan to storm Olympus' throne,
> 'Mid pulse of dungeoned forges down the stunned,
> Undominated firmament, and glare
> Of Cyclopean furnaces unsunned.

And thus the poem proceeds through all of its 207 lines, a master-piece of highly colored imagery and exotic music. The poem closes as quietly as it begins:

> But evening now is come, and Fancy folds
> Her splendid plumes, nor any longer holds
> Adventurous quest over stainèd lands and seas—
> Fled to a star above the sunset lees,
> Over onyx waters stilled by gorgeous oils
> That toward the twilight reach emblazoned coils.
> And I, albeit Merlin-sage hath said,
> "A viper lurketh in ye wine-cuppe redde,"
> Gaze pensively upon the way she went,
> Drink at her font, and smile as one content.

This work had a profound effect on the young beginning poet in Auburn, the then almost 15-year-old Clark Ashton Smith. But its complete continuation or sequel did not appear until Smith himself published in December 1922 his third poetry collection *Ebony and Crystal*. He included in this volume a poem similar to *A Wine of Wizardry* in imagery, music, and over-all construction, but more than 300 lines longer than Sterling's opus, and surely a towering masterpiece of cosmic-astronomic-mindedness. This was *The Hashish-Eater*, which surpassed the older poem just as its author Ashton Smith was to surpass his immediate master and mentor. Be that as it may, Sterling's own poem is a considerable achievement, equal in many respects to Coleridge's *Kubla Khan*, that piece of Holy Writ for the Late Romantic poets of the fin-de-siècle. And it really did put Sterling on the poetic map of the U. S. A. He later used it as the title-poem for his second book *A Wine of Wizardry and Other Poems* which appeared in 1909 and to a generally good critical reception. This volume demonstrated anew the poet's mastery of the sonnet-form, especially as exemplified in the excellent *Three Sonnets on Oblivion*, and above all *The Night of Gods*. 1909 also witnessed in England the passing of one of the greatest Victorian lyric poets, to wit, Algernon Charles Swinburne, a particular favorite with both Sterling and Smith but not necessarily with Bierce who, while he certainly did respect Swinburne, complained that the English poet's verse often set his teeth on edge.

In 1911 Sterling's third book *The House of Orchids and Other Poems* appeared. Next to his later volume of *Selected Poems* this must rank as probably Sterling's single finest collection. It proved an enduring success with Ashton Smith who justifiably cited as excellent the title-poem, then the long narrative *Duandon*, the cadenced Biblical prose of *The Forty-Third Chapter of Job*, the various odes, and particularly the divers sequences (*The Night Sky*, *The Sea's Voice*, *The Night Sea*, etc.) of superb sonnets crafted by Sterling's magisterial hand.

In 1918 Carrie Sterling, estranged from husband George, committed suicide. Her passing marks a further stage in the cavalcade of death inaugurated by that of the poet "Phyllis" or Nora May French.

In 1914 one of Jack London's last novels appeared in serialized form, and was then published in book form in 1915. This was *The Star Rover* which features (among its divers episodes) a brief but powerful cosmic-astronomic section. Both the section in question as well as the title itself betray a considerable affinity with *The Star-Treader*, Smith's first published book (1912), as well as with its general cosmic-astronomic type of imagination. London was always on the watch for promising young writers, and he had of course been immediately aware of young Ashton Smith. Through Sterling, from about 1911 virtually up to the time of his death, he invited Smith on quite a few occasions to travel from Auburn over to London's estate in the Valley of the Moon. But the young poet, probably due to diffidence or actual shyness, never made the trip over to Glen Ellen.

The specific influence of the young Clark Ashton Smith and his first volume *The Star-Treader* (if influence is really the operative word here) on the veteran novelist Jack London is readily perceived in the following cosmic-astronomic episode from Chapter Eleven of London's novel *The Star Rover* (serial, 1914; book, 1915). Needless to say, this particular passage gains by being seen as part of the over-all frame provided by the main story. Interestingly enough, it forms in its entirety the perfect paradigm of a drug experience, and with the usual strong symbolic overtones often associated with, or often arriving in the midst of, such an experience. The passage in question is a literally neat little fable of "ineffable pristine joy" and existential angst where "aeons of star-wandering" alternate with "aeons of dread".

> I was only a mind, a soul, a consciousness—call it what you will—incorporate in a nebulous brain that, while it still centered inside my skull, was expanded, and was continuing to expand, beyond my skull.

And then, with flashings of light, I was off and away. At a bound, I had vaulted prison roof and California sky, and was among the stars. I was a child. I was clad in frail, fleece-like, delicate-colored robes that shimmered in the cool starlight. These robes, of course, were based upon my boyhood observance of circus actors and my boyhood conception of the garb of young angels.

Nevertheless, thus clad, I trod interstellar space, exalted by the knowledge that I was bound on vast adventure, where, at the end, I would find all the cosmic formulae and have made clear to me the ultimate secret of the universe. In my hand I carried a long glass wand. It was borne in upon me that with the tip of this wand I must touch each star in passing. And I knew, in all absoluteness, that did I miss but one star I should be precipitated into some unplummeted abysses of unthinkable and eternal punishment and guilt.

Long I pursued my starry quest. When I say "long," you must bear in mind the enormous extension of time that had occurred in my brain. For centuries I trod space, with the tip of my wand and with unerring eye and hand tapping each star I passed. Ever the way grew brighter. Ever the ineffable goal of infinite wisdom grew nearer. And yet I made no mistake. This was no other self of mine. This was no experience that had once been mine. I was aware all the time that it was I, Darrell Standing, who walked among the stars and tapped them with a wand of glass. In short, I knew that here was nothing real, nothing that had ever been or could ever be. I knew that it was nothing else than a ridiculous orgy of the imagination, such as men enjoy in drug dreams, in delirium, or in mere ordinary slumber.

And then, as all went merry and well with me on my celestial quest, the tip of my wand missed a star, and on the instant I knew I had been guilty of a great crime. And on the instant, a knock, vast and compulsive, inexorable and mandatory as the stamp of the iron hoof of doom, smote me and reverberated across the universe. The whole sidereal system coruscated, reeled and fell in flame.

I was torn by an exquisite and disruptive agony. And on the instant, I was Darrell Standing, the life convict, lying in his straight jacket in solitary. And I knew the immediate cause of that summons. It was a rap of the knuckle by Ed Morrell, in Cell Five, beginning the spelling of some message.

And now to give some comprehension of the extension of time and space that I was experiencing. Many days afterward I asked Morrell what he had tried to convey to me. It was a simple message, namely: "Standing, are you there?" He had tapped it rapidly, while the guard was at the far end of the corridor into which the solitary cells opened. As I say, he had tapped the message very rapidly. And now behold! Between the first tap and the second, I was off and away among the stars, clad in fleecy garments, touching each star as I passed in my pursuit of the formulae that would explain the last mystery of life. And as before, I pursued the quest for centuries. Then came the summons, the stamp of the hoof of doom, the exquisite agony, and again I was back in my cell in San Quentin. It was the second tap of Ed Morrell's knuckle. The interval between it and the first tap could have been no more than a fifth of a second. And yet, so unthinkably enormous was the extension of time to me that in the course of that fifth of a second I had been star-roving for long ages.

Now, I know, my reader, that the foregoing seems all a farrago. I agree with you. It is farrago. It was experience, however. It was just as real to me as is the snake beheld by a man in delirium tremens.

Possibly, by the most liberal estimate. it may have taken Ed Morrell two minutes to tap his question. Yet to me aeons elapsed between the first tap of his knuckle and the last. No longer could I tread my starry path with that ineffable pristine joy, for my way was beset with dread of the inevitable summons that would rip and tear me as it jerked me back to my straight jacket hell. Thus my aeons of star-wandering were aeons of dread.

The cosmic-astronomic influence from the young Clark Ashton Smith upon Jack London adumbrated in this episode is, of course, ultimately (at least in part) that of London's long-term, great, and good friend George Sterling. It points up the faintly paradoxical fact that, whereas George with something like *The Testimony of the Suns* never (or at least rarely) directly influenced Jack in Jack's creativity, he should have done so, and so unmistakably, via the first mature work of the young Smith, his own foremost poet-pupil-protégé.

Also in 1914 Ambrose Bierce (who had disappeared mysteriously into Mexico in late 1913) was evidently shot to death by a firing squad, although this has never been verified. His disappearance and presumed death marked the passing of one of California's greatest literary personalities; his final years had not proven especially happy; and his manner of death might possibly be interpreted as his own original kind of suicide.

In 1915 Sterling received the greatest public accolade of his entire career in connection with the spectacular and splendiferous Panama-Pacific International Exposition celebrated in San Francisco during that entire year. The official fair buildings proudly bore engraved quotations not only from Shakespeare, Milton, Dante, Firdausi, etc., but just as much from San Francisco's own great poet laureate. This represented the high watermark of Sterling's career in an external or public sense, although of course neither he nor his many admirers and friends knew this at the time. The classicistic Late Romantic tradition which Sterling's poetry embodies perfectly was to become a fading legend by the late 1920's: those years witnessed a whole new taste, an entirely new fashion, established in the arts and elsewhere.

When the governor and legislature of the state appointed Ina Coolbrith as the official poet laureate of California in 1915, it was largely on the unanimous recommendation of Sterling and other eminent artists that she was chosen for this honor. Sterling himself had been nominated first of all for the official position but with characteristic modesty, self-effacement, and generosity he declined, and warmly and unselfishly recommended Coolbrith instead.

On 22nd November 1916 George's great and good friend Jack London died, and George himself entered the final decade of his life. Books and booklets continued to come from his pen and to be published, again to generally good critical notice. However, some were now beginning to complain of his archaisms, his purple patches, his overblown rhetoric, etc., and that he had lost contact with the larger pulse of the then modern times, even though his taste continued to fit well enough into the Pacific Coast culture.

In 1919 his romantic allegory *Lilith* appeared (an opus he had been working on since at least 1911), the best of his various dramatic poems, and a lasting favorite with his protégé Ashton Smith. Other volumes were also appearing, and Sterling had certainly by this time become one of the cultural institutions of the City.

In 1923 (published by both A. M. Robertson, his usual publisher in San Francisco, and the Macmillan Company in New York City) there appeared the definitive volume of Sterling's *Selected Poems*, containing the best of his previous books. It is a fine personal anthology of his own work, ranking as his best single collection, with *The House of Orchids and Other Poems* running a close second. A decade or so later, Ashton Smith (discussing Sterling's poetry in general with a correspondent, and mentioning this book in particular) summed up his feeling about it simply by calling it "Grand stuff," and justifiably.

However, by this time not only was a new direction becoming apparent in American and English poetry, taking its lead from Ezra Pound and T. S. Eliot, but a new strong impulse was beating in Californian poetics. This impulse derived from Robinson Jeffers who had set up shop (as a poet) in Carmel in 1916, and significantly under Sterling's aegis. It must not be forgotten that George had praised, encouraged, and influenced not only Ashton Smith of Auburn but also, particularly in terms of cosmic-astronomic vision and consciousness, Jeffers himself. Now in the middle 1920's Jeffers began to attract attention increasingly by his remarkable modern lyrics and (above all else) by his powerful narratives of a doomed and diseased humanity. Sterling, it must be said to his credit, had not only recognized Jeffers' earlier ability, but now became the first, or among the first, to hail the vitality and originality of Jeffers' increasingly mature and individual manner.

Also during the middle 1920's George was passing through a personal artistic crisis of his own, and was toying with styles other than his own previous characteristic ones in an attempt to get himself out of his creative impasse. (This is revealed in the correspondence between Sterling and Ashton Smith in the possession of the New York Public Library's Berg Collection since the early 1950's. The correspondence also reveals that both poets were acutely, if not painfully, aware of the major shift in artistico-critical taste and fashion that was happening at this time.) He paid Jeffers the compliment of imitating him by writing *Strange Waters* (published 1926), which one critic termed a stylistic and thematic parody of Jeffers' own proper and personal poetic modus operandi. Sterling also wrote the first (relatively) full-length discussion of California's "new poet" under the title simply of *Robinson Jeffers* (published in the very last part of 1926, but after George's death).

Also during the middle 1920's George had been contributing a regular column or department to *The Overland Monthly*, called *Rimes and Reactions*, which featured both prose and verse. Moreover, he had been responsible for other special articles and features by other writers appearing in the same periodical. In 1925 the *Monthly* accepted, upon Sterling's recommendation, Ashton Smith's extended prose-poem *The Abominations of Yondo*, a highly individual short story, and one of Smith's earliest prose fantasies. In 1926 the *Monthly* accepted, again upon the elder poet's recommendation, the extraordinary and highly encomiastic essay on Ashton Smith's poetry, *The Emperor of Dreams*, by the then 18-year-old Donald A.

Wandrei (who was later to become a well-known and respected writer in the field of fantasy and science-fiction). This essay appeared in the issue for December 1926.

Thus, right up to the time of his death, Sterling unselfishly and characteristically continued to help younger writers. In this case he helped the young Wandrei achieve his first major periodical appearance, and he continued to publicize the poetry and reputation of his friend and former protégé Ashton Smith. Indeed, Sterling's last recorded telephone call on the day of his death was to B. Virginia Lee, the editor of the *Monthly*, and concerned itself not only with the galleys for his own column but primarily with those for Wandrei's essay, which George himself was to proof. He had asked to see the galleys, and arrangements were made for the editor to get them into his hands (by messenger from the *Monthly's* offices to his room in the Montgomery Building). Sterling had made the telephone call on Wednesday morning, 17th November 1926. Sometime that following afternoon or evening he died.

So now have we come at last to the "still-vexed" question of just how Sterling died. Was it then a deliberate or an accidental suicide? The question has never been satisfactorily answered, and probably never will be.

The official verdict was that Sterling had (presumably) died as a deliberate suicide as the result of swallowing the poison cyanide of potassium which he kept in his personal possession. This verdict the coroner based on purely circumstantial evidence. There was no suicide note left behind, but there were some half-destroyed pieces of a small manuscript. An examination of these bits and pieces revealed what might have been Sterling's last piece of verse, an opus which he was working on sometime immediately before his death but which he did not finish. This was appositely enough a rather despairing poem in blank verse on the subject of death and the indifference of the cosmos to the search, struggle, and final extinction of the human individual. This evidence would seem at a superficial notice to be the clincher that would make definite the fact of Sterling's deliberate intention to commit suicide. But poetic statement is indeed notoriously equivocal, and may be interpreted in many different ways. It is a kind of personal statement, admittedly, but not necessarily tantamount to an ordinary personal note.

This poem on death and the futility of the human condition can be more cautiously and (possibly) more correctly accepted simply as evidence to the fact of Sterling's being depressed at the time. It is a fact that he had been sick before he died (with no major malady, however), and it is a fact that sick people are often depressed as a natural concomitant of being sick. But it is a fact that not all sick people who are also depressed commit suicide.

Various motives for Sterling's committing suicide have been adduced and brought forward as correlation of his successful suicide intent. Thus, he owed H. L. Mencken a sum of money that Mencken had given him as a loan, but being unable to pay it back, Sterling took his own life in despair, being too ashamed and embarrassed to face his friend. Mencken really didn't care about the money, and Sterling had borrowed money from him before (as well as other persons) without paying it back and without being overly disturbed at his inability to do so.

Thus, George was getting older, he was losing his looks and health, and alcoholism was now a major problem. Life had ceased for George to be pleasurable or meaningful, and according to his "pagan" credo, when life became too uncomfortable, then one had the right to take oneself off. And thus the poet promptly took himself off at the most opportune moment.

Thus, George had exhausted his muse, he no longer believed in his own kind of poetry, he had no more to say, or no more to sing. Therefore, washed up as an artist, and overwhelmed with insoluble personal problems, he took the suicide's way out.

These were all some of the main lines of argument and reasoning which various writers and other well-meaning commentators brought forward to elucidate the possible causes or reasons for Sterling's death. Subsequently, critics and literary historians, whatever reservations they may have had about his poetry, applauded his apparently deliberate suicide as a fittingly "romantic" way to end his life.

However, there were other individuals who had been very close friends to George and who did not follow these lines of thinking at all. Chief among the doubters of the official verdict, Clark Ashton Smith proposed the following interpretation of Sterling's death, and he remained faithful to it until he died. It forms the principal argument against the idea of deliberate suicide on Sterling's part.

Ashton Smith remarked the lack of any failing in Sterling's vital interests as expressed in his correspondence to his former protégé. He pointed out that George kept the poison cyanide of potassium on his person or among his personal effects in his room, and that in the depression and confusion often attendant upon illness he could easily have mistaken the poison for a medicine and taken that instead. Who really would have known except Sterling? And there's no asking him now!

The two poets had been corresponding since 1911, and while on occasion they may have disagreed, they did so as gentlemen and friends, allowing no disharmony to disturb the over-all even tenor of their epistolary or personal relationship. While Ashton Smith certainly still believed in the primacy of imaginative literature above all (a belief originally demonstrated and exemplified of course by the older poet), Sterling had now come to doubt this as he had come to doubt his own ability and his own characteristic former styles of composition in poetry. This increasing doubtfulness on Sterling's part is clearly reflected in the very last segment of their correspondence, but it may be seen simply as a natural concomitant of the elder poet's own personal ageing process. However, this very last phase of their correspondence up through Sterling's last letter to Ashton Smith also reveals (as pointed out by the younger poet) no failing whatsoever of Sterling's vital interests. Yes, increasing doubtfulness as to the validity of his own former style of poetry but, no, not any failing of his vital interests. Now, that is significant.

Ashton Smith's own theory is bolstered, incidentally, by the personal memoirs and the documentary evidence from other close friends and associates of Sterling. (The Department of Special Collections at UCLA has quite a good compilation of such evidence.) B. Virginia Lee in one memoir took as her point of departure the last recorded telephone call from Sterling to her at the offices of *The Overland Monthly*. This demonstrates even further (and especially cogently) the lack of any failing in his continuing vital interests. Others also busily recorded their doings and dealings with Sterling virtually up to "the last minute" (as it were) apart from the final mysterious afternoon and/or evening.

The possibility of course exists that the suicide (if such it were indeed) was the unpremeditated, spontaneous act of a given moment. Otherwise, Ashton Smith's theory or interpretation has much to recommend it.

Sterling's death (whatever the cause or reason) was widely mourned, but principally in Northern California, where it made (for the most part) the front page of the local newspapers. It provoked considerable comment (most of it admiring and appreciative) on Sterling as a poet and a person, but really with very little on him as a poet per se. Although his death provided a convenient opportunity for a general evaluation or re-evaluation of his poetry, relatively few took advantage of it to do so, and to fix his place in modern poetics.

By the time of his death in 1926, Sterling had had over twenty books published, eleven of them being of poetry. He had made many contributions to periodicals and ephemeral publications, especially in San Francisco and on the West Coast in general. All manner of people had come to him for pieces in verse or prose for special occasions, and George had almost never sent anyone away without something. Relatively little of his ephemeral appearances later received permanent publication or collection, and much of them remains scattered in obscure sources.

Editor B. Virginia Lee devoted *The Overland Monthly* for March 1927 to a collection of articles, memoirs, and memorial poems all honoring the late poet laureate of San Francisco. Chief among these memoirs was a piece by Ashton Smith, *George Sterling—An Appreciation*, in which the younger poet fearlessly and forthrightly defended the over-all style of Sterling's poetry in general, and singled out some of his greatest poems for specific praise.

Robinson Jeffers also contributed a memoir on his friendship with Sterling but he carefully avoided making any real comment on his poetry. However, almost ten years later, Jeffers allowed himself to make some (reasonably favorable) "public" remarks on Sterling's poetry in an otherwise obscurely known source.

In January 1935 the Book Club of California published for its members "Number One" in a series of *The Letters of Western Authors*. This first specimen on display was by "George Sterling / with Comment / by Robinson Jeffers." Addressed to Albert M. Bender (that notable patron of artists and writers), the letter itself—dated "The Lambs / 130 West 44th Street / New York / Nov. 24th, 1914."—embodied Sterling's warm and unselfish recommendation of Ina Donna Coolbrith (rather than himself) as the proper person officially to ask to write an ode for the Panama-Pacific Exposition. After first discussing his generosity and kindness—two principal qualities of his personality—Jeffers concluded with an interesting and quite significant comment on Sterling's poetry. We quote here Jeffers' pertinent remarks in full (there is no copyright visible in the publication):

> Qualities we ask of our poets, at least the lyric poets, that they be persons as well as writers. The novelist may be somebody or anybody and generally it matters little; his persons are in his novels, but a lyric

poet, besides having some talent and some degree of originality, is expected to represent for us specific qualities—and weaknesses also, for humanity's sake—as Burns and Catullus do, or a distinctive way of life and feeling, as Wordsworth does. The person as well as the work ought to have quality, or else we feel cheated, as when one thinks of Coleridge and wonders who wrote *Kubla Khan*—perhaps the laudanum?

George Sterling was my friend, and no one who knew him will forget the special qualities of his nature. Generosity was chief among them; the word means more than loose-handedness, it carries the sense of well-born too, joining nobility with liberality. He was always poor, and never complained, and what he had he gave freely.

His generosity is somewhat instanced in the letter reproduced in this folder. [....] But I think of innumerable other instances of his generosity; of his kindness to unknown authors; of his continual thoughtfulness in friendship; [....]

Looking at the handwriting of this letter, I am reminded of the first that I received from him, some ten years later than the date of this one. When I took it from the box in the dark Carmel post-office of that time, an old friend of Sterling's, standing thirty twilight feet away, instantly recognized the handwriting on the envelope. "Ah: you have a letter from George."

I think it is quite so with Sterling's poetry. Like his penmanship it is too close to copperplate for the fashion of the time (fashion?) and perhaps he used too conscientiously the "seive for noble words" that Dante speaks of, banishing surprise and the vernacular; perhaps his metronomic ear too constantly preferred rhythmical faultlessness to expression: nevertheless his work is individual as well as beautiful, you recognize the best of it instantly, for his own and no other person's, all the way across the dusty post-office of authorship.

Somehow, Sterling's penmanship and poetic style had both become unfashionable. To the innovative taste of the latter 1920's and then of the 1930's, Sterling's poetry seemed no longer up-to-date and relevant; it belonged (presumably) to the outmoded attitudes of the fin-de-siècle; and most critics and commentators rather amazingly overlooked the specifically twentieth-century element, or elements, in his best work. But, as Jeffers charmingly and generously qualifies his considered opinion, "nevertheless his work is individual as well as beautiful, you recognize the best of it instantly, for his own and no other person's, all the way across the dusty post-office of authorship."

Let us regard then at least a few of the main elements in Sterling's poetry, and examine what affinities it may possess with some of the other arts of the same period, roughly 1900–1926/1930 (although the 1900 could be pushed back at least to 1890 as well).

The *Ladies Home Journal* around the turn of the century featured a number of covers painted by that wizardly artist Maxfield Parrish, who was one of the single most popular as well as distinctive commercial artists during the first two decades of the twentieth century in America. One of the magazine's covers for 1904 features *Air Castles* by Parrish, a composition of clouds, cloud-castles, and large soap-pipe-type bubbles with the seated boy in the lower left-hand corner giving (in that classicistic manner of Parrish's) the de rigueur sense of scale. An almost primordial feeling of serenity, wonder, and marvel permeates and informs the entire conception (and this feeling typifies much of Parrish's work from the 1890's up to 1930). Fantasy radiates from this painting in every brush-stroke and in every glaze. The clouds in Parrish's composition evoke an image very similar to those which open *A Wine of Wizardry*:

> Without, the battlements of sunset shine,
> 'Mid domes the sea-winds rear and overwhelm.

First, however, Sterling has established his own dominant theme of Fancy, or Fantasy, by his magisterial quotation from Bierce's lyric *Geotheos*:

> When mountains were stained as with wine
> By the dawning of Time, and as wine
> Were the seas.

Then Sterling continues with his catalogue or narrative of images, fashioning an immediate color-link with the quotation from Bierce:

> Into a crystal cup the dusky wine
> I pour, and, musing at so rich a shrine,
> I watch the star that haunts its ruddy gloom.

Each of these three passages evokes a highly "painterly" composition in which the vocabulary and the rhetoric (the generalized "allegorical" style of posing the objects in a visually opulent presentation) are quite reminiscent of the modern romantic manner of Maxfield Parrish. This seems especially true of the next lines which clearly suggest the "allegorical" style of such works by Parrish as *Enchantment, Ecstasy, Content-ment*, etc. –

> Now Fancy, empress of a purpled realm,
> Awakes with brow caressed by poppy-bloom....

The main difference between Sterling and Parrish as "pictorial" art-ists lies in Parrish's avoiding almost completely the macabre, which is of course such a. dominant theme in Bierce, Sterling, N. M. French, and Ashton Smith. But, apart from that, there is always the same romantic obsession with marvel and wonder, and the skillful suggestion of exalta-tion, ecstasy, and sublimity.

About this same period of time in the lives of the West Coast or California Romantics on the one hand and of Parrish on the other, the symphonist and singularly serious innovative contrapuntist Franz Schmidt (born 1874) had just had his First Symphony (a monumental summing-up of the Romantic Century which had then run its course) performed and acclaimed in Vienna and was presently working on his first opera (a truly super-romantic work) based for its narrative upon Vic-tor Hugo's novel *Notre-Dame de Paris* (as well as drawing its notablest in-spiration from Schmidt's first visit to Paris along with the entire Vienna Philharmonic under the direction of conductor-composer Gustav Mahler). Schmidt, too, posed as one of the guardians of the classicistico-romantic heritage common to all these artists.

But one of the most fruitful areas of comparison and affinity betwixt Sterling and his contemporary world is less betwixt him and other artists than it is betwixt him and his contemporary and specifically West Coast world, and (more particularly) the then world formed by the City of San Francisco. Especially is there a close correlation betwixt Sterling's poetry and the San Francisco existing before the Earthquake and Fire of April 1906.

Pre-Earthquake San Francisco was at its showiest and most impres-sive within the major area bounded by Van Ness Avenue and Mission Street. This is exactly the area that was almost completely devastated by the great Fire following immediately upon the Earthquake. Within this area there lay the City's business and financial districts, as well as its most highfalutin residential district, running alongside California Street and es-pecially atop Nob Hill, and then continuing on into Pacific Heights west of Van Ness. Many of the large commercial buildings downtown were of course reconstructed within whatever outer shells and frameworks out-lasted the destruction. Something of their earlier grandeur survives in such edifices as the Hibernia Bank (not far from 7th and Market), and the then-main U.S. Post Office on 7th (miraculously untouched by the general devastation), the Flood Building (at Powell and Market), the Emporium just across the way, and then the Phelan Building, the Hobart Building, and the Hearst Building, all on "lower" or eastern Market, and then the Ferry Building at the very end of Market, facing directly southwest.

Nob Hill sported some of the most grandiose mansions, or palaces, on the West Coast. The Flood mansion (rebuilt and converted into the Pacific Union Club) and the "Old" Fairmont Hotel almost alone survive from the pre-Earthquake days, to give us an approximate idea of their former and highly substantial splendors. The Mark Hopkins mansion just across from the Fairmont (and looking for all the world like a Victorian Camelot) survived but was later leveled to make space for the present Mark Hopkins Hotel. But all the other bayed, towered, turreted, and gin-ger-breaded palaces that once stood atop Nob Hill (that eminence of "nobs" and "nabobs") are irretrievably gone apart from photographs (and in some instances the architectural plans) remaining to haunt the reveries and fantasies of posterity.

If these mansions' exteriors created an imposing and wonderfully crazy fantasia, then their interiors correspondingly revealed living quarters at once grandiose and plush. The over-all architectural effect then (whether indoors or outdoors) was overwhelmingly ponderous and opulent. The Charles Crocker mansion (whose site is occupied by Grace Cathedral and associated ecclesiastical structures) in particular can typify for us the Hill's Victorian magnificence and elaboration with its main mass, its turrets and towers and finials, its bays and balconies, its colonnades and pediments, its outbuildings and enclosing fence of stone and metal.

Most of these pre-Earthquake buildings, whether situated on Nob Hill, along Market Street, or within the less pretentious neighborhoods (which ironically furnish us today with our stereotypic image of what San Francisco's Victorian houses should look like), were principally designed by architects who had studied at the notably classicistic Académie des Beaux Arts in Paris, or (if they had not) at least reflected the prevailing influence of those who had. The classicism (if it may still so be termed) which thus resulted, owed then almost nothing to the earlier and "purer" Greek Revivalism as it did to the free-wheeling eclecticism characteristic of the latter 1800's. This school of thought, or frame of mind, did not hesitate to mix elements from all the known historical periods (Moorish, Byzantine, Tudor, Gothic, Renaissance, Romanesque, California Mission, and other even more disparate styles of architecture), whilst yet maintaining the over-all classical (and absolutely de rigueur) concern with symmetry, balance, and form. The result was truly a new architecture (and possibly as authentically Californian as the Mission style) of bewildering variety and with an inexhaustible sense of play, or fantasy.

The edifices thus conceived and constructed were often singularly un-classical in their final appearance, and their purely conventional classical ornamentation (where such was still applied) simply stood out as just one more bizarre element of detail in a larger bizarre assemblage. But this bizarreness, or truly liberated fantasticality, may owe its existence to an otherwise ill-defined factor, or series of factors, which have lain largely ignored, unknown, or overlooked. And we refer here to what we can only call (with all due proportions guarded) a considerable Oriental influence. It is of course a cliché that within San Francisco east is east and west is west and ever the twain do meet. Although the City is literally at the western edge of the North American continent, marking the effective (continental) end of the old American frontier, it very definitely draws much of its energy (spiritual and otherwise) from the Pacific Ocean. From this fundamental condition there has come a pronounced Far Eastern and Polynesian influence (but seldom recognized as such), subtle but (once recognized) pervasive. There is a resemblance of sorts between certain Far Eastern and Polynesian forms of wooden architecture, and some of the more fanciful examples of San Francisco Victorian constructed of wood (and most of the houses are made of wood), especially those conceived in the Eastlake, Stick, and Queen Anne sub-styles. Indeed, the over-all feeling and mood of the Victorians made of wood are much "lighter" than those constructed of stone, and without satisfying all the conditions for such a proper definition, the Victorian style in San Francisco qualifies as a kind of "pre-" or "proto-" Art Nouveau.

The more substantial buildings of brick or some other kind of stone were more obviously classical in a Graeco-Roman sense than the wooden edifices, but the richness of detail, and particularly the inventiveness of the over-all synthesis, betray the same exuberant fancy, verging on the exotic. Although the reconstructed parts of the City could no longer be considered Victorian from a strict chronological point of view, yet the new construction fit in beautifully with the old: there was a definite continuity both in general form and in specific detail. This kind of continuity (architectural or otherwise) has proven rare in the USA.

The continuity of classical "rhetoric" in the other arts (painting, sculpture, literature, etc.) on the West Coast proved no less marked. The type of grandiose Western panorama perfected by the painter Albert Bierstadt (with his obvious indebtedness to, and affinities with, the earlier Hudson Valley school of painters) appeared highly exotic at first to many of his contemporaries east of the Mississippi, in the same way as indeed much of the West was then unknown and exotic. Such a painting as *Rainy Season in the Tropics* (1866) by Frederic E. Church (1826–1900) forms an even more exotic example of a large-scale work with a magical or glamorous content. Howevermuch this type of painted grandeur (with its emphasis on wonder and marvel) fell into disfavor with the more straight-laced critics later in the same century, it did continue very much in popular appeal, as witness the more purely imaginative "landscapes of fantasy" painstakingly crafted by Maxfield Parrish, whose vogue virtually dominated the first two decades of the twentieth century in the USA.

Sculpture on the West Coast during this same period may seem perhaps of itself less interesting in a stringently artistic sense but as part of an architectural setting it also contributed its own unmistakable note of idiosyncratic grandeur.

The love of luxuriant living detail and efflorescence is perhaps best exemplified in a literal sense by the enormous preserve of Golden Gate Park, the inspired creation of the Scots landscape-gardener John McLaren. This extensive forested garden with its plantations and conservatories is the perfect corollary of Sterling's "house of orchids" (even though the original for this was located in a private estate called "Lloyden" and situated itself on the Peninsula far south of the City). Whereas the greatest mansions from before the Earthquake and Fire did not survive, the lovely and endlessly variegated gardens and groves of trees which today make up the Park, have endured and waxed even more beautiful.

As much as the general style and tone of Sterling's poetry had befitted the old pre-Earthquake days, they continued to suit the new reconstructed ambiance just as well. The destroyed parts of the City were completely rebuilt by the time of the Panama-Pacific International Exposition in 1915, which celebrated both the opening of the Panama Canal and the successful rebuilding of such of San Francisco as had undergone devastation. This proud moment in the City's career marked a proud moment indeed in the careers of the various artists and public figures associated with the Exposition.

Architects, painters, sculptors, landscape gardeners, and even poets contributed their various arts to the creation and enrichment of the Exposition buildings and grounds. The land itself consisted of tidal flats filled over and then further built up. Located due north of Pacific Heights, west of Fisherman's Wharf and east of the later Golden Gate Bridge, this area (thus reclaimed from San Francisco Bay) made a dramatic setting indeed for the rare architectural fantasmagoria which soon rose up on the site as though by some Ashton Smithian necromancy. As noted earlier, the official fair buildings bravely bore elegantly engraved quotations from Shakespeare, Milton, Dante, Firdausi, etc., no less than from George Sterling, the City's own great poet laureate.

With its grand courtyards, its towers and other spires, its halls and pavilions, its colonnades and sculpture, the Exposition architecture itself (a very gracious and imaginative extrapolation from Graeco-Roman models) seemed a final glorious synthesis and recapitulation of the classico-romantic fantasies peculiar and proper to the self-respecting architects involved in the project. But more than that, the Exposition rang true to the inner vision, the unabashed idealism, of an entire generation. Probably better than anything else, it captured the romantic idealism common to many people of that time in history, and it also caught the almost universal preference for the "grand manner" and the "solemn tone" inherited from the late 1800's.

When the Exposition officially closed at the end of 1916, and even as it yielded to the crews demolishing it, in order to make the area ready for the new residential district that became known as the Marina, the fair nevertheless lived on in a vast photographic iconography and in a broad spectrum of written accounts but (most of all) as a splendorous memory in the hearts and minds of all who had seen it.

One group of buildings and lagoon had been chosen to survive: the unusually handsome Palace of Fine Arts designed by the fashionable Bay Area architect Bernard Maybeck. Later reconstituted in poured concrete (replacing the original wood, wire, and plaster), it has become a permanent attraction to tourist and resident alike. The achievement in "classical" architecture by Bernard Maybeck here (a classicism imaginatively perceived and extrapolated) has a striking similarity to the achievement in "classical" poetry by George Sterling elsewhere (again, a classicism imaginatively conceived and developed).

The Exposition also lived on in a brief series of substantial verses by Sterling done in his best grandiloquent manner, and published as a small book. *The Evanescent City* remains the perfect corollary of the event itself, intimating as it does the building, the life, and then the demolition of the fair grounds.

The vast "barn" of the Civic Auditorium (especially built for the City at the time of the Exposition, and now bordering the southern side of the present Civic Center) also survived. Other buildings constructed at this same general time (or shortly thereafter), which reflect the same frame of mind and which still survive, are the main Public Library downtown (with its grand and opulent inner staircase) and the Palace of the Legion of Honor in Lincoln Park (and near the northwestern extremity of San Francisco which projects into the Pacific Ocean). These are all eminently classicistic or "classical" edifices, even if a long way from both Greece and Rome.

The carefully chosen and regularly marshalled lines of Sterling's poetry, with their luxuriant images and sententious vocabulary, are then the perfect equivalent of the fanciful domes and colonnades, the massive pavilions and high-soaring spires, as well as the elaborate horticulture which surrounded them, of the Panama-Pacific International Exposition and (before that) of the Late Victorian and Late Romantic metropolis destroyed by the 1906 Earthquake and Fire.

Sterling's best work has real substance, outrageous imagination, flamboyant emotionalism, delicate and precise observation, enraptured attitudinizing, as well as a profound and inspired cosmic pessimism, together with the eternal pursuit of Beauty (not beauty, but Beauty) whether on our planet Earth or out into the cosmos at large. Of course, in many salient respects, his poetry belongs to another age, but part of it belongs to ours as well. In a special way (whether overt or subtle) its best attributes live on in the poetry and prose of his follower and protégé Ashton Smith. However, it is safe to say that Sterling's best (at least) will live on in its own right. It remains one of the more potent expressions of the type of imagination characteristic of the fin-de-siècle as well as of the early 1900's. In addition to his considerable "natural" talent or genius for poetry, it must be emphasized that Sterling for all his occasional and often amusing jackanapes was nonetheless a true artist, a highly dedicated and disciplined craftsman. The current "Romantic Revival" may discover and acclaim him yet.

Of course, his poetry is cast (for the most part) in the forms and themes of the traditional prosody which Sterling inherited and accepted, and within which he worked. Nonetheless it does have modem elements, and one can find them if one takes care to search. Indeed, Sterling allows far more immediate topicality into his work than does his brother bard Ashton Smith. The older poet did strive (even if not that successfully) to incorporate some allusions to contemporary events and modes of thinking. Ashton Smith, on the contrary, tended to regard most contemporaneity as anathema, and deliberately refused (with but rare exception) to make such "concessions" in his own work. But it is their cosmic-mindedness, or cosmic-astronomic-mindedness—above all else—which marks both Sterling and Ashton Smith as specifically modem poets. Independent of the trends and currents which later became fashionable in poetry (particularly in the 1920's), the *oeuvre* of George Sterling and then Ashton Smith, taken together, represents the logical final extension and extrapolation of the Late Romanticism cultivated by Tennyson and Swinburne but out into the unending frontier of cosmic space.

The single greatest poem by Sterling, *The Testimony of the Suns*—created in two main parts—grew directly from the turn of the century and from the type of thinking and reflection that such a time engendered. Part I is dated "December, 1901." Part II, following immediately in time of composition, is dated "February, 1902."

> The winter sunset fronts the north....
> The light deserts the quiet sky....
> From their far gates how silently
> The stars of evening tremble forth!

In the tradition of Tennyson's *In Memoriam*, Ambrose Bierce's own *Invocation* clearly anticipates the richer harmonies and the greater vision of Sterling's magnum opus. Indeed, *The Testimony of the Suns* does curiously anticipate the current Age of Space with humanity's increasing exploration into the stars.

Cosmic space with its infinity of suns and planets, if we attain to them, may yet prove to be humanity's salvation. If we do not attain (in a truly large-scale way) beyond our own planet—which even now we continue to develop and destroy in the name of a constantly increasing human population—and if the forces that we ourselves long since have set in motion do annihilate us here, then the final seven stanzas of Sterling's magnum opus can serve as well as any as a just and not inappropriate epitaph.

How vast the gulfs of man's desire!
    Children of Change, we dream to share
    The battle-vigil of Altair,
And watch great Fomalhaut expire;

To live, where darkened suns relume
    Their kingdoms in the abysmal haze—
    Where nearing Night attends the blaze
Of high Antares red with doom;

To hear within the deeps of Law
    The Word that moves her causal tides;
    To know what Permanence abides
Beyond the veil the senses draw.

And such the hope that fills thy heart,
    O Life! on some allegiant world
    Round Procyon's throne of thunder whirled
Or poised in Spica's gulf apart.

So dreamt thy sons on worlds destroyed
    Whose dust allures our careless eyes,
    As, lit at last on alien skies,
The meteor melts athwart the void.

So shall thy seed on worlds to be,
    At altars built to suns afar,
    Crave from the silence of the star
Solution of thy mystery;

And crave unanswered, till, denied
    By cosmic gloom and stellar glare,
    The brains are dust that bore the pray'r,
And dust the yearning lips that cried.

FINIS

A Garland of Poems by George Sterling

Selected, with notes, by Donald Sidney-Fryer

The White Rose
Nora May French
The Siren's Song
The Night of Gods
Sonnets on the Sea's Voice (IV)
The Black Vulture
Memory
The Huntress of Stars
The Ashes in the Sea
The Coming Singer
Ocean Sunsets (I)
To a Girl Dancing
The Forty-Third Chapter of Job

SOURCES

A White Rose is taken from *The Testimony of the Suns* (1903); *Nora May French* and *The Night of Gods* are both taken from *A Wine of Wizardry* (1909); *The Coming Singer* appears from *Beyond the Breakers* (1914); *Ocean Sunsets* (I) and *To A Girl Dancing* both appear from *Sails and Mirage* (1921); and all the other poems are culled from *The House of Orchids* (1911). All the collections cited were published by A. M. Robertson of San Francisco.

NOTES

This gathering from the verses of George Sterling is representative of his better work. His manner like that of Swinburne never basically changed: he just got better, and more supple, at it, accordingly as he developed a better sense of how and where it was best and most appropriate to apply it. However, in his later collections there is far less of such obviously outmoded poetic diction as "o'er" and "e'er" and so forth—and much more of deliberate simplicity and (comparative) modernism, at least for Sterling.

Both of Sterling's deeply touching and very special tributes to Nora May French—the sonnet whose title is formed by her full name, and then the longer series of quatrains, *The Ashes in the Sea* / *N. M. F.*—are

97

included here. Half of the present selection consists of a generous sampling of George's magisterial sonnets with their unique mingling of long-breathed Late Romantic melody, strikingly pictorial imagery, exalted emotionalism, adroitly defined atmosphere, and skillful suggestion of various metaphysical and philosophical issues, but always imaginatively conceived and "classically" modulated.

Just as the body of thought and metaphysical/imaginative speculation of Bierce, as well as of Sterling and Smith in their turn (each building upon, but still individually modifying, the work of his predecessor), is thus "cross-pollinated" from within itself (with many "cross references" and additional, purely accumulative meanings), so are there innumerable linguistic, rhetorical, and metaphysical linkages among the work of the three authors.

"So shall thy seed on worlds to be, / At altars built to suns afar, / Crave from the silence of the star / Solution of thy mystery;" but then "And crave unanswered, till, denied / By cosmic gloom and stellar glare, / The brains are dust that bore the pray'r, / And dust the yearning lips that cried." Both the thought and even the language here of Sterling finds an echo and continuation in (at least) such lines as these from Ashton Smith's *Ode to the Abyss* (a poem which Bierce isolated for especial praise and even for some discussion of individual details): "What spheres that now essay / Time's undimensioned vast, / Shall plunge forgotten to thy gloom at length / With life that cried its query of the Night / To ears with silence filled."

The cosmic-astronomic "catastrophe" adumbrated in these lines by Sterling and Ashton Smith finds a reverse echo in the extended simile which opens Bierce's sonnet *To Maude*, and which comprises exactly and symmetrically the first four lines of the poem's octave (note how nicely classicistic his verse procedure now becomes): "Not as two errant spheres together grind / With monstrous ruin in the vast of space, / Destruction born of that malign embrace, / Their hapless peoples all to death consigned—"

Both Sterling and Smith were acquainted in some considerable depth with the bulk of Bierce's output in verse, and both poets were acquainted with, and admiring of, this particular sonnet.

It is interesting to note how the concept of planets as both spheres and/or (spherical) space-ships is utilized by Bierce in this sonnet as well as in the tercet *Creation*. This finds echoes in Sterling's work in at least *The*

Testimony of the Suns and in some of the work by the Mid-West dramatist and poet William Vaughan Moody, who is the only poet contemporary with Sterling whose work contains close parallels to that of the Californian poet, but which definitely developed independently of the *oeuvre* created by the West Coast Romantics. The three poets (Bierce, Sterling, and Moody) thus anticipate the use of the same concept (in virtually the same terms) in the two pivotal science-fiction (or science-fantasy) "novels" *Last and First Men* and *Star Maker* by Olaf Stapledon.

Equally lovers of the prose and poetry of Edgar Allan Poe, both Sterling and Ashton Smith knew and appreciated Bierce's uneven but still over-all rather potent exercise in the macabre, the long poem in blank verse, *A Vision of Doom*, with its effective opening: "I stood upon a hill. The setting sun / Was crimson with a curse and a portent, / And scarce his angry ray lit up the land / That lay below, whose lurid gloom appeared / Freaked with a moving mist, which, reeking up / From dim tarns hateful with some horrid ban, / Took shapes forbidden and without a name. / Gigantic night-birds, rising from the reeds / With cries discordant, startled all the air, / And bodiless voices babbled in the gloom— / The ghosts of blasphemies long ages stilled, / And shrieks of women, and men's curses."

(Linguistically the use of "freaked" here is quite similar to that by Ashton Smith in the following "episode" or subsection of *The Hashish-Eater*: "I know the blooms / Of bluish fungus, freaked with mercury, / That bloat within the craters of the moon, / And in one still, selenic hour have shrunk / To pools of slime and fetor....")

Bierce intones further in his own poem: "As I stood, a voice, / But whence it came I knew not, cried aloud / Some words to me in a forgotten tongue, / Yet straight I knew me for a ghost forlorn, / Returned from the illimited inane. / Again, but in a language that I knew, / As in reply to something which in me / Had shaped itself a thought, but found no words, / It spake from the dread mystery about."

Ashton Smith then writes many years later in his miscellany *The Black Book* the first draft of the poem *Broceliande* (not otherwise finished), where there are many close similarities (in word, phrase, image, and rhythm) between Smith's vision (or "audiovision") and that of Bierce.

"As a child, I wandered beside a fen / Where the sunset, falling through cloudless air, / Stained with scarlet the still and sedgy pools. / There I entered a silent evening wood / (Knowing not that the wood was

Broceliande.) / Then, in the twilight of / great oaks, a voice that I / heard and yet heard not / seemed to dictate un- / known words, and I, / constrained by some weird / power, repeated them aloud. / .... / In the same sunset (or / was it haply in another?) / I came forth again from / the wood beside the / fenland where the / tarns and ponds were still crimson / with a flaring afterglow. / And peering into a / pool, I saw not the / face of a child neglected, / but the hoar and / many-wrinkled visage of / the ancient warlock Merlin!"

(This poem is quoted in full from *The Black Book of Clark Ashton Smith* where it forms item 186 in the late 1961 transcript-edition made by R. A. Hoffman and Donald Sidney-Fryer.)

After intimating the increasing and general corruption of human-kind, Bierce continues on in his own vision of doom: "Then the great poet, touched upon the lips / With a live coal from Truth's high altar, raised / His arms to heaven and sang a song of doom— / Sang of the time to be, when God should lean / Indignant from his Throne and lift his hand, / And that foul city be no more!—a tale, / A dream, a desolation, and a curse! / No vestige of its glory should survive / In fact or memory: its people dead, / Its site forgotten, and its very name / Disputed." Thus the disembodied voice finishes its tale, and when the poet-narrator asks "Was the prophecy fulfilled?"—his only answer is the initial landscape or tableau which opens the vision, but with this confession: "But not to me came any voice again; / And, covering my face with thin, lean hands, / I wept, and woke, and cried aloud to God!"

Bierce's breathtaking little masterpiece of boldness and compression *Creation* ("God dreamed—the suns sprang flaming into place, / And sailing worlds with many a venturous race! / He woke—His smile alone illumined space.") finds a close affinity with Ashton Smith's opus *The Motes* (only a little less compact):

I saw a universe today:
Through a disclosing bar of light
The motes were whirled in gleaming flight
That briefly dawned and sank away.

Each had its swift and tiny noon;
In orbit-streams I marked them flit,
Successively revealed and lit.
The sunlight paled and sifted soon.

(This poem is quoted in full from its appearance in the Smith volume *Selected Poems*, Arkham House, Sauk City, Wisconsin, 1971.)

Bierce's sonnet *One Morning* could easily pass as part of Ashton Smith's own cycle of poems *The Hill of Dionysus*:

> Because that I am weak, my love, and ill
> 　　I cannot follow the impatient feet
> 　　Of my desire, but sit and watch the beat
> Of the unpitying pendulum fulfill
> 　　The hour appointed for the air to thrill
> 　　And brighten at your coming. O my sweet,
> The tale of moments is at last complete—
> The tryst is broken on the gusty hill!
> O lady faithful-footed, loyal-eyed,
> 　　The long leagues silence me; yet doubt me not:
> Think rather that the clock and sun have lied
> 　　And all too early you have sought the spot.
> For lo! despair has darkened all the light,
> And till I see your face it still is night.

Indeed, this sonnet could easily fit in with Ashton Smith's own *Twilight Song* (again quoted in full from the *Selected Poems* where it forms part of the complete cycle *The Hill of Dionysus*):

> O heart, be sad, be still!
> She that we love is far,
> Veiling her face with folded plain and hill
> Below the vesper star.
>
> Breathe only one wild sigh
> On winds of sunset gone -
> Flown like the exile, brief, October cry
> Of oread and faun.
>
> Mute evening wanes in mist....
> Our feet have lost the way
> Leading to that inviolable tryst
> In dells of yesterday.
>
> O night! upon thy stream
> Obliviously to float

And haply find in westward-flowing dream
Her place and face remote.

Bierce's epitaph in honor of a friend *Light Like the Earth Upon His Dear Dead Heart* (with its concluding line "Forever and forever!") finds an exact echo in Sterling's own work:

Light lie the earth upon his dear dead heart,
And dreams disturb him never!
Be deeper peace than Paradise his part,
Forever and forever!

Sterling was haunted by the music of that "Forever and forever!" to such an extent that he included it in his first sonnet of the series *Ocean Sonnets*: "Along the mighty rondure of the world / Forever and forever sweeps that wave, / From Arctic mountains to the southern floe...."

However, the best affinities between Bierce and Sterling (in terms of cosmic outlook and philosophy) can probably be found in the latter's own cadenced Biblical prose comprising *The Forty-Third Chapter of Job*. This opus, together with *The Testimony of the Suns*, exercised a profound influence on the younger Ashton Smith.

The affinity between Bierce and Smith in the domain of the weird and macabre has been given a token demonstration already through the example of their poems *A Vision of Doom* and *Broceliande*, respectively; and the affinity between Bierce and Sterling in the same area is demonstrated by a general comparison between *A Vision of Doom* and *A Wine of Wizardry*, respectively. Bierce's own obsession with, as well as attitude towards, death and the macabre is neatly capsuled for us in the quatrain *Dead* taken from *The Devil's Dictionary*:

Done with the work of breathing; done
With all the world; the mad race run
Through to the end; the golden goal
Attained and found to be a hole!

Additional artistic expression of the same preoccupation is provided by the sublime quatrain *Man is Long Ages Dead* (this is taken from one of Bierce's essays gathered into his *Collected Works*, published 1909–1912):

Man is long ages dead in every zone,
The angels all are gone to graves unknown;

The devils, too, are cold enough at last,
And God lies dead before the great white throne!

Further correlation between Bierce and Ashton Smith, as well as between Ashton Smith and Sterling, in the domain of both the cosmic and
the macabre, is abundant, howevermuch their individual styles may
sometimes differ from each other and then at other times resemble each
other closely.

There is not only a general resemblance among the love poems of
Bierce, Sterling, and Smith but a particular affinity between Sterling's fine
lyric *To A Girl Dancing* (a poem which Ashton would have known and
loved) and the complete cycle making up *The Hill of Dionysus*, inspired for
the most part by Smith's dancer-friend Madelynne Greene (and wife of
the poet Eric Barker). For just one salient example, the alternation of
long lines with short ones that we find in George's lyric, we also find in
such poems by Ashton as *Dancer*, *Bacchante*, *Wizard's Love*, *Paean*, *Interim*,
Wine of Summer, *Ode*, *For An Antique Lyre*, *Silent Hour*, *Supplication*, *Erato*,
The Hill of Dionysus, *Anodyne of Autumn*, *Nocturne: Grant Avenue*, *Even in
Slumber*, *De Profundis*, *Calenture*, and *Do You Forget, Enchantress?*

However, it may be maintained that in the best of the Sterling poems assembled herein it is either the cosmos at large or the sea (that
lesser cosmos) which serves as the keenest inspiration, and which acts as
the true renewing element, within Sterling's classicistic prosody.

The quotations of Bierce's poetry made in these notes are taken
from *A Vision of Doom*, a selection (by poet-author Donald Sidney-Fryer,
who edits and introduces them) of "fifty best" poems culled from
Bierce's over-all output in verse (which totals over 800 pieces). [*A Vision
of Doom* was published by Donald M. Grant, West Kingston, Rhode Island, 1980.] Sidney-Fryer's introduction *A Poet Called Ambrose Bierce* was
first dated 23 November 1967, which marked the one hundredth anniversary of Bierce's premier professional appearance in print with the two
rather Poesque poems *Basilica* and *A Mystery* in the early San Francisco
weekly newspaper *The Californian*.

The White Rose

How pure the light thy petals hold
  In fragrance on the tideless air!
How gently come the hands that mold
  Nor break the sleep of color there!

How mutely on the richer day
  Thy wafture floats of patient breath!—
We cannot hurry nor delay
  The feet of Time and Love and Death.

Ah, calm thy day, ere evening take
  Her misty throne, upbuilt anew
Of starlit gloom, till dawn awake
  The topaz hidden in the dew.

And sweet thy night, ere, uncontrolled,
  The restless winds of dawn depart;
And, cast from sudden heights of gold,
  The shadows tremble at thy heart.

O brother-life! the silent Pow'r
  Constrains thy wings with other bars;
Remote from human time thine hour,
  Thine evening fair with alien stars.

Our senses light a little arc,
  Beyond whose twilight, vague, untrod,
The reaches of denying Dark
  Withhold the infinity of God,

Whose range of unrecorded night,
  And distance of eternal plan,
Isle in equality of light
  The stars of life in flower and man;

And waken to recurrent morn
  Of bee or blossom, bird or leaf,
The life that in the days unborn
  Shall sorrow in the halls of Grief;

When I, afar from human fears,
    Illusive hope or joy intense,
May yet, beyond estranging years,
    Attain the blossom's innocence.

Nora May French

I saw the shaken stars of midnight stir,
    And winds that sought the morning bore to me
    The thunder where the legions of the sea
Are shattered on her stormy sepulcher,
And pondering on bitter things that were,
    On cruelties the mindless Fates decree,
    I felt some shadow of her mystery—
The loneliness and mystery of her.

The waves that break on undiscovered strands,
    The winds that die on seas that bear no sail,
    Stars that the deaf, eternal skies annul,
Were not so lonely as was she. Our hands
    We reach to thee for Time—without avail,
    O spirit mighty and inscrutable!

The Siren's Song
(From *Duandon*)

Far down, where virgin silence reigns,
    In jasper evenings of the sea,
    I toss my pearls, I wait for thee.
The sea hath lent me all its stains:
    It is but treasure-house for me.

The corals of the deep have caught
    A Titan shell whose fragile dome
    Is crimson o'er mine ocean home
Mine opal chambers subtly wrought
    In semblance of the shaken foam.

Oh come! and thou shalt dream with me
    By violet foam at twilight tost
    On strands of ocean islets lost
To prows that seek them wearily,
    O'er seas by questing sunsets crost.

All dreams that Hope hath promised Love,
    All beauty thou hast sought in vain,
    All joy held once and lost again,
These, and the mystery thereof,
    I guard beneath the sundering main.

The Night Of Gods

(from Three Sonnets on Oblivion)

Their mouths have drunken the eternal wine—
    The draught that Baal in oblivion sips.
    Unseen about their courts the adder slips,
Unheard the sucklings of the leopard whine;
The toad has found a resting-place divine
    And bloats in stupor between Ammon's lips.
    O Carthage and the unreturning ships,
The fallen pinnacle, the shifting Sign!

Lo! when I hear from voiceless court and fane
    Time's adoration of Eternity—
        The cry of kingdoms past and gods undone—
I stand as one whose feet at noontide gain
    A lonely shore; who feels his soul set free,
        And hears the blind sea chanting to the sun.

Sonnets on the Sea's Voice, IV

O thou unalterable sea! how vast
    Thine utterance! What portent in thy tone,
    As here thy giant choirs, august, alone,
Roll forth their diapason to the blast!—
Great waters hurled and broken and upcast
    In timeless splendour and immeasured moan,

As tho' Eternity to years unknown
Bore witness of the sorrows of the Past.

Thou callest to a deep within my soul—
    Untraversed and unsounded; at thy voice
        Abysses move with phantoms unbegot.
What paeans haunt me and what pangs control!—
    Thunders wherewith the seraphim rejoice,
        And mighty hunger for I know not what.

The Black Vulture

Aloof upon the day's immeasured dome,
    He holds unshared the silence of the sky.
    Far down his bleak, relentless eyes descry
The eagle's empire and the falcon's home—
Far down, the galleons of sunset roam;
    His hazards on the sea of morning lie;
    Serene, he hears the broken tempest sigh
Where cold sierras gleam like scattered foam.

And least of all he holds the human swarm—
    Unwitting now that envious men prepare
        To make their dream and its fulfilment one,
When, poised above the caldrons of the storm,
    Their hearts, contemptuous of death, shall dare
        His roads between the thunder and the sun.

Memory

She stands beside the ocean of the Past,
    A diver. Pearls and hydras can she bring,
    Shells for the child and crystals for the king.
Prone on her reefs the sea-essaying mast
And keels that dared the hurricane are cast—
    Trophies of tides invincible that swing
    Around the islands where the Sirens sing,
The magic of whose song is hers at last.

Some shadow of the glory she restores,
    Tho' wave and wind devour the Ships of Dream;
        For many mark her ere the fall of night,
When the surf's sound is mighty on her shores,
    Singing, as wildly on her bosom gleam
        The sea-dews, and the rubies of the light.

Three Sonnets of the Night Skies

III. The Huntress of Stars

Tell me, O Night! what horses hale the moon!
    Those of the sun rear now on Syria's day,
    But here the steeds of Artemis delay
At heavenly rivers hidden from the noon,
Or quench their starry thirst at cisterns hewn
    In midnight's deepest sapphire, ere she slay
    The Bull, and hide the Pleiades' dismay,
Or drown Orion in a silver swoon.

Are those the stars, and not their furious eyes,
    That now before her coming chariot glare?
        Is that their nebulous, phantasmal breath
Trailed like a mist upon the winter skies,
        Or vapors from a Titan's pyre of death
Far-wafted on the orbit of Altair?

The Ashes In The Sea

N. M. F.

Whither, with blue and pleading eyes,—
    Whither, with cheeks that held the light
Of winter's dawn on cloudless skies,
    Evadne, was thy flight?

Such as a sister's was thy brow;
    Thy hair seemed fallen from the moon—
Part of its radiance, as now
    Of shifting tide and dune.

Did Autumn's grieving lure thee hence,
    Or silence ultimate beguile?
Ever our things of consequence
    Awakened but thy smile.

Is it with thee that ocean takes
    A stranger sorrow to its tone?
With thee the star of evening wakes
    More beautiful, more lone?

For wave and hill and sky betray
    A subtle tinge and touch of thee;
Thy shadow lingers in the day,
    Thy voice in winds to be.

Beauty—hast thou discovered her
    By deeper seas no moons control?
What stars have magic now to stir
    Thy swift and wilful soul?

Or may thy heart no more forget
    The grievous world that once was home,
That here, where love awaits thee yet,
    Thou seemest yet to roam?

For most, far-wandering, I guess
    Thy witchery on the haunted mind,
In valleys of thy loneliness,
    Made clean with ocean's wind.

And most thy presence here seems told,
    A waif of elemental deeps,
When, at its vigils unconsoled,
    Some night of winter weeps.

The Coming Singer

The Veil before the mystery of things
    Shall stir for him with iris and with light;
    Chaos shall have no terror in his sight
Nor Earth a bond to chafe his urgent wings;

With sandals beaten from the crowns of kings
    Shall he tread down the altars of their night,
    And stand with Silence on her breathless height,
To hear what song the star of morning sings.

With perished beauty in his hands as clay,
    Shall he restore futurity its dream.
Behold! his feet shall take a heavenly way
    Of choric silver and of chanting fire,
Till in his hands unshapen planets gleam,
    'Mid murmurs from the Lion and the Lyre.

(Dedicated privately by Sterling to Clark Ashton Smith.)

Ocean Sunsets

I.

Men watch the wide magnificence uprolled,
    A deathless surf of glory down the zones—
    Ancient as that with which the sea intones
Its undelivered sorrow. Fold on fold
The foam of splendor deepens, far and cold,
    Below the stars' imaginary thrones,
    Till on the twilight of those sapphire stones
Are ashes of the sun-deserted gold.

Along the mighty rondure of the world
    Forever and forever sweeps that wave,
        From Arctic mountains to the southern floe,
In soundlessness on purple islands hurled,
    With opalescent wash of hues that lave
        Old summits, sacred in that afterglow.

To a Girl Dancing

    Has the wind called you sister?
Sister to Kypris, who, as the far foam kissed her,
    Rose exquisite and white.
For seeing you, we dream of all swift things
    And of the swallow's flight,—

Of sea-birds drifting on untroubled wings,
And incense swaying at the shrine of kings,
In gossamers of violescent light.
In what Sicilian meadows, cool with dew,
 Ran rosier girls than you,
 With tresses dancing free,
To tell how beautiful the world might be?
 In what high days unborn,
Will sheerer loveliness go forth at morn,
To wave a brief farewell to night's last star?
For you, we envy not the lost and far,
 As now you make our day
As happy and imperial as they.

More than the ripple of grass and waters flowing,—
 More than the panther's grace
Or poppy touched by winds from sunset blowing,
 Your limbs in rapture trace
An evanescent pattern on the sight—
Beauty that lives an instant, to become
A sister beauty and a new delight.
So full you feed the heart that hearts are dumb.
Those little hands set back the hands of time,
Till we remember what the world has dreamed,
 In her own clime,
Of Beauty, and her tides that ebb and flow
Around old islands where her face has gleamed,
The marvellous mirage of long ago.

 Ah! more than voice hath said
They speak of revels fled—
 The alabastine and exultant thighs,
The vine-encircled head,
The rose-face lifted, lyric, to the skies,
The loins by leaping roses garlanded.
 The sandaled years return,
 The lamps of Eros burn,
 The flowers of Circe nod,
And one may dream of other days and lands,

Of other girls that touch unresting hands—
    Sad sirens of the god,
    To some forgotten tune
Swaying their silvern hips below the moon.
    Dance on, for dreams they are indeed,
    A vision set afar,
But you with warm, immediate beauty plead,
And fragrant is your footfall on our star.

O flesh made music in its ecstasy,
Sing to us ere an end of song shall be!
    O fair things young and fleet!
    White flower of floating feet!
Be glad! Be glad! for happiness is holy!
Be glad awhile, for on the greensward slowly
    Summer and autumn pass,
    With shadows on the grass,
    Till in the meadow lowly
November's tawny reeds shall sigh "Alas!"

    Dear eyes,
What see you on the azure of the skies?
    Enchanted, eager face,
Seek you young Love in his eternal place?
Round arms upflung, what is it you would clasp—
    What far-off lover?
    Hands that a moment hover,
What hands unseen evade awhile your grasp?
Ah! that is best: to seek but not to find him,
For found and loved the seasons yet will blind him
    To this true heaven you are—
That moth unworthy of your soul's white star.
Dance on, and dream of better things than he!
Dance on, translating us the mortal's guess
At Beauty and her immortality—
Yourself your flesh-clad art and loveliness.

Dance, for the time comes when the dance is done
    And feet no longer run

On paths of rapture leading from the day.
    Release not now
The vine that you have bound about your brow:
Dance, granting us awhile that we forget
    How morrows but delay,
Yet come as surely as their own regret.
    Through you the Past is ours,
    Through you the Future flow'rs
In you their dreams and happiness are met.
    Through you we find again
    That birth of bliss and pain,
That thing of joy and tears and hope and laughter
        That men call youth—
    A greater thing than truth,
    A fairer thing than fame
        In songs hereafter,
A miracle, an unreturning flame,
The season for itself alone worth living,
And needing not our patience nor forgiving.

O heart that knows enough, and yet must learn
    The wisdom that we spurn!
    The years at last will teach you:
    May now no whisper reach you
Of noons when pleading of the flutes shall cease
And not for rapture will you beg, but peace.
To-day it seems too harsh that you should know
    How soon the wreaths must go
    And those flower-mating feet
Be gathered, even as flowers, by cruel Time,
        Their flashing rhyme
No more to mingle with the blood's wild beat.
Dance, with no wind to chill your perfect grace,
    Nor shadow on your face,
Nor voice to call to unenduring rest
The limbs delighting and the naked breast.

THE FORTY-THIRD CHAPTER OF JOB

1. Moreover, the Lord made question of Job, and asked,
2. To what end dost thou search Me, seeing that My wisdom is not as thine?
3. Shalt thou question My ways, or have dreams concerning My justice? Am not I the Lord?
4. Who hath strange laughter, Whose judgments are not as those of the elders;
5. Who leadeth the lamb from the den of the she-wolf, and armies to the quicksand;
6. Who slayeth the prince in his youth, and rulers at their marriage-feast, but maketh the slave to grow old in his bondage;
7. Whose rains go forth on bitter waters, tho the land thirsteth; Who delivereth thee from the javelin thou beholdest not;
8. Who maketh the king in his secret place and him that the vultures did devour to sleep the same sleep;
9. Who confoundeth the sea, but leadeth the ant to her desire.
10. Have not I sharpened the beak of the kite against the day of thy hope; the raven's beak against the eyes of thy young men?
11. I shall bar thee from thy joy with a thread of gossamer; I shall bind thy sin to thy children's children with ropes of adamant.
12. The rock is a bolt for My treasure-house. Thou knockest in vain upon the doors thereof.
13. Who art thou that eternity should hold parley with thee, or the pits of the sky be thy fortress?
14. Thou abidest in My sight as the smoke of a sacrifice, or as the grey moth in the conspection of the stars.
15. What hast thou if thou hast not Me? Thou takest to thee strange wine, and the kiss of the asp that it comfort thee.
16. Awake, let it be always day with thee! Know that I am the Lord,
17. Who ordaineth His truth as the mountains, and the dust as stars that conceive;
18. Who teacheth fear with an arrow, and bitter wisdom to thy young men of war;
19. Who boundeth pain by peace, and setteth a term unto love;
20. Who hath no truce with the day, and slayeth the dark with the sword of mighty mornings;

21. Who buildeth the house of life with colored beams, and the house of death without a door;
22. Who hath set harps in hell, and given pure gold for the winding sheet of kings;
23. By Whose breath are the Signs shaken; as a swarm of gnats are they troubled by the wind of His passing;
24. Who yoketh stars to His harrow, and the whirlwind to drag his plough on great waters.
25. Take counsel of Me; behold what shapes I have set as My servants.
26. The sun is a coal of My hearth, the moon an ember that I have quenched;
27. Shall not I make her a desolation, and a rock where devils worship?
28. Shall not My gulfs conceive, and Mine angels whet their scythes against the day of My reaping?
29. Be thou abased, for they are yet unborn that shall lay thee out; the worm is unhatched that shall consume thee.
30. Wilt thou hold forth to Me thy heart in thy hand; or turn for Me its leaves that thou hast writ?
31. Thy wisdom profiteth thee nothing, neither the guards within thy citadels.
32. Shall I consider for long the mighty, or the habitations of the strong?
33. Behold! blood shall be in their courts for wine, and the moaning of their concubines for the voice of the viol.
34. I shall break their temples as a shard; their high pillars shall be snapt as a bow-string.
35. My tempests shall neigh in the walled cities; My grass shall lift up her sword against them;
36. The toad shall be judge there; the jackal shall collect the tax;
37. The owl shall feed her young on their altars; the dung of lions shall be thereon for a testimony.
38. Wert thou upon the flint when I confirmed it, or upon the granite when I laid its sheets?
39. The thunder, was it thou that didst call? Was the rain the tears of thy bringing-forth?
40. Be thou bowed down, nor question the pains that I have set over thee: for each thing have I ordained its shadow.
41. My thoughts are from eternity; I change not by reason of thy dismay. Thou shalt know Me for the Lord.

42. Who setteth Capella and Achernar to be gods for a term, and a guide upon the deep to strange peoples;

43. Who maketh Altair and Rigel the captains of His host; Who leaneth His spear upon Sirius ere the trumpets call;

44. Who holdeth Vega His armor-bearer, and hangeth his buckler upon Alderbaran;

45. Who hath convoked their chariots against the lamps of Evil, and their swords against the abyss.

46. Who healeth the day with night, and thy heart's wound with the hands of little children;

47. Even they that seek the breast in darkness, hushing the voices that were aforetime.

48. The wind cometh, the dust is troubled for a season, but hath rest when the wind departeth.

A Memoir of Timeus Gaylord:
Reminiscences of Two Visits with
Clark Ashton Smith, &c.

Prefatory Note: I suppose that it should seem incumbent upon me to apologize for the plethora of references to myself and my own activities, presumably quite apart from Smith and his *oeuvre*, within the present memoir; but because the thread or threads of my interest in this poet of unique and major vision have been so closely interwoven with my own life, I do not see how else I could have lucidly presented these memories. Much of this memoir may not be of unusual value to my own contemporaries; but to Smith scholars a hundred years from now, many of the details recorded herein (that might seem at this time too trivial to note) may prove of genuine interest. Needless to add, my interest in Smith and his work has been one of many during the last twenty-four years of my life; however, it certainly has been one of the dominant interests. (Final version, 1978.)

Among the divers pseudonyms used by Smith during his lifetime (1893–1961) or used for him since his death by others, there is none more logical or appropriate than that of "Timeus Gaylord"—constituting as it does a delicate and subtle tribute to both his parents. Just as the poet himself was derived in equal parts from his parents, so does this *nom de plume* derive equally from their names: the "Timeus" was the first name of Smith's father, and the "Gaylord" was the maiden name of his mother before her marriage to Timeus about 1888. Born in Iowa in 1850 as Mary Francis Gaylord, Fanny Smith died on September 9, 1935, at the age of 85. Born in England in 1855, Timeus Smith died on December 26, 1937, at the age of 82. Their son Clark did not use the pseudonym of "Timeus Gaylord" until after their death, and thus it seems he clearly intended it, in some small way, as a memorial gesture.

The death of Smith's parents in 1935 and in 1937, respectively,—as well as the death of his great friend, confrère, and correspondent H. P. Lovecraft (born 1890) on March 15, 1937, at the age of 47,—coincides almost perfectly with the gradual cessation of his fictioneering. Between 1937 and 1961, the year of his death, he evidently wrote less than a dozen stories, or just a little more than a dozen. Why this happened, provides what at first seems one of the major mysteries in Smith's creative life. The answer lies not with any one specific factor as it does with a complex of factors. The chief reason was Smith's growing disgust with pulp-magazine fantasy and with the restrictions imposed upon its writers. The death of his mother in 1935, that of his great friend Lovecraft in 1937, and that of his father later in the same year, had taken from him some of his chief sources of immediate encouragement. Also, Smith found the production of sculptures much easier and more enjoyable than that of fiction; he had begun sculpting circa April of 1935. There was also the desire, nay, the *need*, to get away from Auburn for awhile, and to experience a different pattern of living.

During the years 1929–1937, Smith had been tied to his home just outside Auburn not only by his intensive creation of short stories but possibly just as much by the fact that he had increasingly to provide for, and take care of, his ageing and ailing parents, especially during the years 1934–1937. Although his existence had certainly been brightened by the bowers of divers enchantresses (as he termed them), the son had never married. Accordantly, the Smith family had always been very close, and to this day persons in Auburn who were friends of the Smiths will still bear witness to the extra-ordinary closeness and harmony in which the three lived—the father, the mother, and the son. With the death of his parents and the consequent cessation of this close relationship, the son was free to do and to go as he pleased; and yet their death had left a large empty place in his life on an immediate personal level. Into this emotional vacuum there stepped some new friends who were to become as important to Smith as had been the old ones now departed.

The middle and the late 1930's witnessed a considerable number of pilgrimages by admirers and fellow writers to the old Smith cabin. Early in 1938, the expatriate Englishman and then beginning poet, Eric Barker, and his wife, the dancer Madelynne Greene (at that time both living in San Rafael) came out to visit him just outside Auburn. In time the three became very close friends—the fledgling poet, the dancer, and the veteran poet and fictioneer. They remained thus for quite some time, at least during the decade of the 1940's, and often exchanged visits; with the Barkers making the long drive to Auburn and then back to San Rafael or San Francisco, whither they later moved; or with Clark taking the bus to San Rafael, then later to San Francisco, and for awhile to Little Sur where Eric had a job as the caretaker of an estate. Previous to the visit from the

Barkers, Smith had received Henry Kuttner, and before Kuttner, E. Hoffman Price—both fellow writers of fantasy and science-fiction. During the 1940's, Smith was to receive many admirers and fellow writers— R. A. Hoffman, C. L Moore, and Fritz Leiber, to name only a few.

From 1938 until July of 1941 particularly, Clark was away from Auburn much of the time and during these years he did more living than writing. As he wrote in his letter to August Derleth dated "July 13th, 1941": "[It] Had got to the point where it was absolutely necessary. Now I'm trying to settle down to literary production again." And settle down to literary production he did, but not of short stories. He had returned to his first love, the creation of poetry in verse; indeed, sometime in 1934, he had started to write verse again on a fairly regular basis.

Starting about 1939 and continuing until about 1946, Smith was deep in the creation of the remarkable cycle of love poems *The Hill of Dionysus*, growing out of his close friendship with the Barkers, and especially out of his love for Madelynne. They were all three a source of inspiration to each other. Clark encouraged and praised some of Eric's fledgling poetic efforts, and would often suggest the subjects for Madelynne's interpretative dances. In her turn, Madelynne and her dances directly inspired many of the poems in *The Hill of Dionysus*: "Dancer," "Bacchante," "Witch-Dance," and others.

Meanwhile, August Derleth and Donald Wandrei, two of his friends, correspondents, and fellow writers for *Weird Tales*, had established Arkham House principally to preserve the fiction and other creative work of H. P. Lovecraft. The first book, Lovecraft's *The Outsider and Others*, appeared in 1939. The second book to appear was Derleth's *Someone in the Dark* in 1941. Now Derleth wrote to Smith, suggesting as the third Arkham House book a collection containing at least part of his best short stories. This of course proved to be a great impetus to Smith's creative self. Accordantly Smith selected the stories for the first hardcover collection of his fantasies, *Out of Space and Time*, which appeared in August of 1942 and to largely favorable reviews during 1942–1944.

Two years later, Arkham House brought out Smith's second hardcover collection of fantasies, *Lost Worlds*, which appeared in October of 1944 and again to largely favorable reviews. A little before this, Derleth and Wandrei had suggested to Smith the future publication of a complete or near-complete collection of his published and/or collected poems, whether in verse or in prose. At that time Derleth and Wandrei hoped to bring this collection out in 1945 or 1946 in an edition that was to be uniform in size and format to Smith's prose collections *Out of Space and Time* and *Lost Worlds*. The original title of this collection was *The Hashish-Eater and Other Poems*. Following this there would appear a third volume of Smith's fantasies, to have approximately the same number of pages, etc., as the first two. But the poetry collection proved to take longer for Smith to compile than any of the three had thought, and the contents of what was to have been the third volume of short stories were more or less divided between *Genius Loci and Other Tales* (1948) and *The Abominations of Yondo* (1960).

Early in September of 1944 (according to his letter to R. A. Hoffman dated "Sept. 9th, 1944"), Smith started what was to become the tremendous task of putting together his poetry collection of collections by retouching old manuscripts, typing new copies of old poems, etc. During the 1940's, Clark was plagued off and on with eye trouble, which made it difficult for him to do any typing or much typing at one time. Of course, he could not afford to hire a typist, so that the publisher's manuscript of the *Selected Poems*—Smith's final choice for a title—was achieved as the result of at-times considerable physical discomfort to the veteran poet. In terms of sheer creativity, the poems in his early collections of poetry for the period 1910–1926 had of course cost him much. Now, merely in terms of retouching and/or copying for what was to become virtually a complete collected poems, they were to cost him only a little bit less. [As now known, only half of it.]

Even if Smith might have returned exclusively to fictioneering, after his vacation from writing during 1938–1941, it is doubtful if he could have attained again the productivity of 1929–1937, when he was creating stories at such a comparatively white heat and with comparatively such great speed. Given his characteristic method of writing stories, which was painstaking, and involved three or four re-writings per story, and given the eye-trouble with which he was plagued off and on during the 1940's, Smith's rate of production would have proven much reduced.

Yet in many respects the period of 1939–1951, especially the decade of the 1940's, became as fruitful a period of poetical creativity as the earlier one of 1910–1926, which had more or less come to an end late in 1926 with the death of his great friend and mentor, the poet of the West Coast, George Sterling. In addition to preparing the manuscript of the *Selected Poems*, creating the poems in *The Hill of Dionysus*, touching up old poems, etc.—Smith sometime in the late 1940's helped Kenneth Yasuda with the Englishing of haiku from the Japanese. He became fascinated with the form's possibilities and created well over one hundred haiku, most of which he included in the *Selected Poems*, in the section "Experiments in Haiku." In October of 1948, Arkham House published the third hardcover collection of Smith's fantasies, now only about one-half its original size, under the title *Genius Loci and Other Tales*. Most of the remaining stories, promised but not collected, found their way into the eventual fourth volume of short stories *The Abominations of Yondo* (1960).

In late 1948 or early 1949, Smith learned Spanish, made his first translations of Spanish poetry, and wrote his first poems in Spanish. Thus, from September of 1944, in addition to odd jobs such as fruit-picking and fruit-packing, he stayed hard at work on the manuscript of the *Selected Poems*. Finally early in December of 1949, he finished it, and sent it on its way to August Derleth; the manuscript was delivered to Arkham House later in the same month. Alas! the volume that had been enthusiastically solicited and promised in an expanding market of fantasy and science-fiction during 1944, was now delivered to one that had already started to fall. Also, the expense of publishing such a large volume of verse had become almost prohibitive for such a small house as Arkham because printer's costs had spiraled since the early 1940's. The manuscript had to be shelved for an indefinite period of time. But Smith was patient and could wait. The volume's dedication reads "For Eric and Madelynne"—a token of the great friendship that once existed between Clark and Eric and Madelynne. To the best of my knowledge, this is the only publisher's manuscript that Smith ever prepared in toto for Arkham House. Those of his short stories were all typed either by Derleth's quondam secretary Alice Congdon or some other typist, from magazine tear-sheets or from typescripts assembled and then sent on by Smith to Arkham House. The *Selected Poems* was finally published in 1971.

Thus, the *Selected Poems* is actually Smith's first Arkham House book of poetry, but not his first published one. This distinction lies with *The Dark Chateau*, his second Arkham House book of poetry, but first *published* one. During 1950–1951, Smith continued to create new poems both in English and in Spanish. Many of these new poems he included in *The Dark Chateau* which appeared in December of 1951 as Smith's over-all sixth collection of verse. Eighteen of the forty pieces therein come from the *Selected Poems*. Most of the others, created thus after the omnibus volume, include some outstanding poems.

At the time I first came to know of Arkham House, almost none of the preceding facts were at my disposal. I discovered most of them principally during the years (1960 through 1965) when I was doing the research for the Smith bibliography.

The Arkham House editions, published by August Derleth, had the merit not only of saving many fine stories from the oblivion of pulp magazines but also of bringing such fiction to the attention of many people who had never come into contact with it when originally published in the respective periodicals. Also instrumental in attracting the attention of new readers and critics, the excellent anthologies of fantasy, supernatural horror, or science-fiction that Derleth commenced editing in the mid-1940's, beginning with *Sleep No More* (1944), played a strategic role. Many of these anthologies were bought by public and university libraries and added to their shelves, thus coming to the attention of many people who had never previously heard of Arkham House. Also, strangely enough, many libraries on military bases were sufficiently enlightened to buy not only many of the Derleth anthologies but even books published by Arkham House, to the undoubted delight of many a serviceman. One such serviceman to whose delight I can testify with absolute certainty was none other than myself, to wit, Donald Sidney-Fryer. At the time that I discovered Arkham House, and through its publications both H. P. Lovecraft and Clark Ashton Smith (amongst other authors) I was in the Marine Corps, and stationed at the Marine Corps Air Station, formerly a Naval Air Station, at Opalocka, in northwest Miami.

In late October of 1953, I entered the Marine Corps, and did my basic training at the Marine Corps boot camp on Parris Island—midway between Charleston, South Carolina, and Savannah, Georgia. I finished my "boot" training mid-January of 1954; then I was assigned to the Air Supply Clerk School at the U. S. Naval Air Station, Jacksonville, Florida, which I attended from February through May. After graduation from this school of basic office procedures (typing, filing, bookkeeping, etc.), I was assigned to Opalocka where I arrived early in June. One of the first things I did there during my own time was to check out the resources of the base library. Besides the standard reference works, the library was very well stocked with fiction, and some of it fiction such as I had never encountered before. It soon became a fixed habit of mine to spend as much of my lunch period (an hour and a half), as well as much of my evenings, as I could, reading in the library, filling my head with all manner of fact or fiction.

During the summer of 1954, I took off the shelves, from under the "D's" (the fiction was arranged alphabetically), an anthology edited by August Derleth, *Sleep No More: Twenty Masterpieces of Horror for the Connoisseur*. The anthology intrigued as well as impressed me, particularly three stories which I list in the order of descending impressiveness as they appeared to me at the time. "The Rats in the Walls," by H. P. Lovecraft; "The Black Stone," by Robert E. Howard; and "The Return of the Sorcerer," by Clark Ashton Smith. The Lovecraft and the Howard stories especially gave me an unexpected thrill of horror as well as of delight. These were both vivid, poetic, powerful tales. The fiction by Smith impressed me most for a certain obliquely somber quality and for its deliberately understated manner of telling.

The next Derleth anthology I read was one of science-fiction, *The Other Side of the Moon*. The volume over-all seemed impressive, but unforgettable proved the overwhelming experience of reading the science-fantasy by Smith contained therein under the title "The City of the Singing Flame." I started reading this fantasy of fantasies a little before lunch. and surreptitiously at my desk in the office where I worked; this office was located in a large hangar. I became so enthralled with this tale that instead of putting it down and finishing it after lunch, I read on and on, until I came to the end, thoroughly shaken and exhilarated all at once. Although I did not realize it at the time, I had taken my first "trip" via one of the most powerful drugs known to man: imagination. I was thrilled, and double-thrilled, and triple-thrilled, by one of the greatest stories and one of the greatest flights of the imagination I ever hope to encounter in my life. It seemed to me at the time of that first reading that I had not merely read the story but had somehow lived it. If it be true that one of the results of profoundly experiencing great art is to alter the spectator's way of looking at the world so that it never is quite the same again, then this masterpiece by Smith surely is great art: I never saw the world again as it had been. Everything around me, including the most commonplace objects, took on a freshness, an interest, and an excitement completely unsuspected hitherto.

Later that afternoon or evening I recall returning to the base library and looking up in an atlas the little city of Auburn, California, outside of which the tale's author reputedly lived. On the map of California to which I was referred. I remember tracing my finger from San Francisco northeast to Sacramento and then northeast again to Auburn, the seat of Placer County.

Thereafter I read all the other Derleth anthologies that I could find in the base library, always looking for stories by Smith as well as by Lovecraft. Indeed, Lovecraft over-all excited my greatest interest at the time, then Smith, then Howard, and then Henry S. Whitehead. I recall reading Smith's "Master of the Asteroid" in the science-fiction anthology *Strange Ports of Call*, and then "The Metamorphosis of Earth" in yet another science-fiction anthology, *Beachheads in Space*. Always I was struck not only by Smith's unique imagination but also by his unique, poetic, and powerful style. I had of course read the standard fantasy classics usually given to children (*The Arabian Nights*, the fairy tales of Hans Christian Anderson, the brothers Grimm, and Charles Perrault, etc.) and in high school I had become enamored of the works of Edgar Allan Poe on one hand and of the novels of Edgar Rice Burroughs on the other. In a way Smith reminded me of both these writers, especially of Burroughs, but Smith was infinitely more exotic and masterful, and purely in literary terms he commanded a skill such as Burroughs could never have, no disparagement intended to the latter. Also, again and again, I was instinctively arrested by what I must call for lack of a better term a certain classic quality in Smith, a certain classic excellence that made me think instantly of the same I had encountered in high school when reading and studying (in Latin, of course) the standard Latin authors then usually studied at that scholastic level: Julius Caesar, Cicero, and Virgil. All of these writings, *The Aeniad* above all, gave me an excellent understanding of style and rhetoric.

In the prefatory material appended by Derleth to each story included in his anthologies, I had of course noticed the constant mention of Arkham House. Gradually it dawned on me that Derleth, a regionalist writer in his own right, owned and ran this publishing house. By the end of September I had exhausted the contents of Derleth's anthologies, as well as of the few books published by Arkham House, on the shelves of the base library. Accordingly, I determined to write to Arkham House and find out what materials by Lovecraft and Smith were available in order that I could purchase them and have further "thrilling adventures of imagination".

In October of 1954, 1 wrote my first letter to Arkham House, enthusing over Lovecraft, Smith, and others. About a week or so later, I received my first letter from Derleth who cordially assured me he understood perfectly my delight in such authors of fantasy and the supernatural as Arkham House was publishing and promoting. He thoughtfully enclosed the current stock-list, plus other advertising material, which I promptly studied, receiving anticipatory thrills merely by reading the different titles and the general descriptions of the books in the stock-list. My initial order, which I made a few weeks thereafter, proved quite a large one, and Derleth had to mail it to me in two cardboard boxes.

Thus, my interest in Smith grew tangentially out of my interest in Lovecraft and the general group of authors published by Arkham House. Although it was Lovecraft who at first had excited my greatest admiration, he was gradually superseded by Smith. The first books by Smith that I ordered from Arkham House, *Genius Loci and Other Tales*, and the volume of verse *The Dark Chateau*, I did not read all at once all the way through but (as it evolved) gradually and over a period of years. This first copy of *The Dark Chateau* that I owned, I shortly gave to one of my former English teachers in high school. Later I bought a second copy which I retained. However, once my interest in Smith became established, it remained definitely established as it does to this day. The passing of time has only increased my respect and admiration for Smith as an author.

The outfit, the Third Marine Air Wing, in which I stayed throughout the period of my military duty, moved in September of 1955 from Opa-locka, Florida, to El Toro, California, where I remained stationed until my release from active duty. In the late spring or early summer of 1956, I bought from Acres of Books in Long Beach a very good used copy of Smith's second Arkham House prose collection *Lost Worlds* for $3. I don't think I ever devoured a book with similar eagerness again! I also tried to obtain a copy of Smith's first Arkham House collection *Out of Space and Time* (1942), but with no success at this time. I took a week's furlough in Spring 1956, and driving up with a friend, made my first trip to Northern California, and visited Carmel, Pacific Grove, Monterey, and then San Francisco. I was discharged from the Marine Corps in August of 1956, and attended the University of California at Los Angeles, beginning in September of the same year.

During my first academic year at U. C. L. A., I had theatre arts as my major but somewhat after the beginning of my second year I changed it to French language and literature, which major I retained through my last regular semester there, ending in January of 1961. The French major did not prove overly difficult, as I had studied both French and Latin in high school. But the revelation of literature in another language—especially French literature with its emphasis on form and style (until recently, I might add)—made me at once more critical and, paradoxically, more appreciative of literature in my natal tongue. Predictably and customarily, I came to regard almost all writing in English as the acme of sloppiness. Later of course I came to re-love English and the literature written in it for their own unique qualities, and not necessarily viewed vis-à-vis French literature. This was all par for the course, and all a necessary education. One thing to remember: as a French major I came into contact with primarily the great French writers whether in verse or in prose, and learned the art of commentary on, and analysis of, literary texts from French models, and from my professors of French language and literature. When I seriously commenced my study of Smith, I brought all these tools, all these literary procedures, to bear upon his *oeuvre*. I might anticipate that Smith was to pass all these tests, all these recipes (as it were) for literary greatness, with flying colors.

In late August and early September of 1957, I went with a friend on a trip to San Francisco. While temporarily based in the city of Saint Francis, I discovered in a used-book store on Polk Street two copies of Smith's second collection of poetry, *Odes and Sonnets*, for $3 a piece. One copy I later sold to Acres of Books in Long Beach for the same price I had paid for it. The copy was going to a person who, the bookstore informed me, was a fellow collector of Smith's books. I felt even then that it was incumbent on follow Smithophiles to aid and abet each other by supplying copies of his books at only a minimal cost. The other copy I retained (this was No. 298 out of an edition of 300). These early poems proved a revelation to me. The technical competence, the vision, the imagination, and especially the imagery, astonished me. I had known Smith chiefly as a writer of short stories; now as a poet he seemed to me, merely from a casual perusal, on an equal with the English Romantics, to say the least. I determined (as time and funds permitted) to search out and obtain copies of Smith's other early books of poetry.

Just before I left to return to Los Angeles, I made a brief trip by bus to Auburn, some 115 miles northeast of San Francisco, intending to visit Smith who reputedly still resided there. Derleth had told me in a letter that Smith still was very much alive, and had recently married. But I did not question Derleth as to whether or not Smith still was living in Auburn. I assumed it for a fact that he was. The bus seemed to take the eternity of all afternoon to travel to my destination but we finally arrived in the former mining town, and the seat of Placer County. Auburn lies amid the rolling foothills of the Sierras, and the countryside is strikingly beautiful, with large park-like expanses alternating with fruit orchards and with stands of pine and oak trees. [The area has changed much since then.]

I went at once to the Auburn City Public Library as the most likely source of information as to where I could locate the general vicinage of the Smith cabin just outside the old part of town. Although the librarian and the girls at the counter (where they checked books in and out) knew of Smith, they did not know where exactly it was that he lived. But they advised me to ask a lady who lived in a little white house just across from the library. This I did, and the lady in question, although she did not know herself, put me in touch with yet another lady, Luzetta Swett, who should know, she assured me. This next call placed me a few blocks north of the library. Mrs. Swett, who was friendliness and courtesy personified and a very fund of information, both knew, as well as knew of, Smith but not as well as yet another lady, whom she promptly contacted over the phone. Mrs. Swett did all the talking, relaying the information on to me. The lady to whom Mrs. Swett was talking was Ethel Heiple, who had known both Clark and his parents for quite some time. From her we learned that only a few days before I had come up from San Francisco, the old Smith cabin on Boulder Ridge (just southeast of the old section of town), in which Clark had lived for over half a century, had burned to the ground—this was in the very last part of August. Also, Clark had moved his regular residence to Pacific Grove near Monterey after his marriage to Carol Jones Dorman in 1954, and fortunately was not living in the cabin at the time of the disaster. Presently Mrs. Swett said good-bye. I thanked her warmly for her assistance, and excused myself as I needed to eat somewhere before returning to San Francisco that night.

I ate dinner at a little restaurant on High Street, one of the main thoroughfares in the town. Afterwards, having a little time to kill before my bus would leave, I decided to phone Ethel Heiple myself. Although I had been unable to see Smith on this attempted visit, it would afford me some consolation at least to talk with a long-term friend of his, someone who had evidently been very close to him. Ethel answered the call immediately, and proved to be a wonderfully warm and friendly person. She invited me to come and see her for a visit that evening, and deciding on the instant to go back to San Francisco the next day, I accepted. I walked south along High Street (her directions were explicit) and came to where Sacramento Street (ascending from Old Auburn that lay just to the west) crossed High.

Here on the northeast corner stood a small attractive frame house embowered in trees and shrubbery. This was Ethel's home, and a warm little light glowed on the porch in anticipation of my arrival. I mounted the porch stairs and rang the doorbell. Ethel came to the door and let me in. We introduced ourselves again, and got along famously: it would have been very difficult to have done otherwise as Ethel was a marvelously encouraging and cheerful person. We spent a most enjoyable evening together (as well as early morning!), and Ethel (who was to become a fine friend and correspondent to me) told me many pertinent and interesting things about Clark as a person. She gave me his then present address at 117 Ninth Street in Pacific Grove, and assured me she would write him on my behalf so that the next time I came up north from Los Angeles, I could visit him in the Monterey area.

Finally, when it was about three o'clock in the morning, we said farewell. I had to get some sleep before going back to the City, and Ethel (who was used to staying up all night) would have invited me to catch a few hours of slumber on the living-room sofa but she already had one guest and there simply was not enough room in her little house for anyone else. We promised to write, and I departed for the Auburn Hotel, located in the modern downtown area. I had no trouble acquiring a room, and soon fell asleep. I arose around nine, ate breakfast, and took the Greyhound bus back to San Francisco, my head buzzing with Smithian anecdotes and with vivid impressions of the Mother Lode country.

During the spring semester of 1958, I did not attend school but worked instead at the office of the Southern Counties Gas Company in Venice (sometimes called Venice West) from March through June. Besides taking a much-needed rest from the monotony of the academic grind, I put this working semester to use in another way. Now I had the time and the funds to prosecute a search, via the U.S. mail, for Smith's other published volumes. I had one copy apiece of *Odes and Sonnets* (1918), *Lost Worlds* (1944), *Genius Loci and Other Tales* (1948), and *The Dark Chateau* (1951). 1 sent a form letter with my Smith wants to antiquarian book-dealers in San Francisco, Berkeley, and Oakland.

The Imperatrix Mundi, to wit, Dame Fortune, certainly favored my search. As the result of my initial inquiry and my subsequent ordering, I obtained a treasure-trove at comparatively little expenditure. A copy of *The Star-Treader and Other Poems* (1912) for $2.25, if my records are correct. A copy of *Ebony and Crystal: Poems in Verse and Prose* (1922) for only $1.25. (This last was No. 23 out of an edition of 500, and Smith had signed and numbered this himself at the end of the volume. But an added bonus was the fact that it had been the presentation copy that the author had given to former Senator James D. Phelan, the benefactor of the San Francisco Public Library, and patron to many artists pictorial or literary. On the right of the inside front cover appeared an inscription by Smith to Phelan.) A copy of *Sandalwood* (1925) for $5. (The copy in question was No. 63 out of an edition of 250, and Smith had autographed and numbered this at the end of the volume.) This was an even rarer item than *Ebony and Crystal*. But still eluding my search and possession were *The Double Shadow and Other Fantasies* (1933), *Nero and Other Poems* (1938) and *Out of Space and Time* (1942).

Far greater than the comparative cheapness at which I had obtained these volumes, proved the impact of their unique and original contents. But of these last one could write simply books and books, and this is presumably a memoir of Smith and of matters relating to him, not an exposition and explication of his *oeuvre*.

In May of that same spring, I acquired a copy of *Spells and Philtres* which Arkham House had just published in March of 1958. This was Smith's third Arkham House book of poetry, but the second *published* one. Later (after Smith's death), I was to discover that fifty-two of the sixty selections were taken from the *Selected Poems*. Apparently only seven of the other eight pieces turned out to be new.

Meanwhile Ethel Heiple had written the author of these books, mentioning that I would like to visit him next time I came up north. I attended summer school at U.C.L.A. that year to compensate for what I then considered a loss of academic time. At the end of summer school I again went north with a friend, bringing with me my almost complete set of Smith books. We drove along the route between the Coast Highway and the principal route in the San Joaquin Valley. This was on the 26th of August, 1958. We turned west to Monterey, and upon our arrival in Pacific Grove, we obtained a room in a motel not too far from the Smith residence. After getting settled and showered and changed, and before going to dinner, I decided to brave the literary lion in his lair at 117 Ninth Street.

This was my second visit to the Monterey area. It impressed me as much as the Auburn-Long Valley area where Smith was born and had lived so much of his life. But in a way I felt more strongly drawn to this particular bit of Californian coast. With its shoreline of rocky promontories alternating with wide sandy beaches, and with its quaint old-fashioned seaport atmosphere, it reminded me of my natal New England, especially of Maine.

In the very early evening I set off, armed with my set of eight Smith books which I was carrying in a large doubled paper bag. I located the house with no trouble. Despite the sign telling me that strangers were not welcome, I bravely knocked on the door. A portentous pause ensued and in the near-silence I heard someone coming to the door. It opened. A gentleman with handsome, distinguished features, with a trim moustache, and with a high, broad, and "noble" forehead, stood there, saying "Yes?" I asked him if Clark Ashton Smith did indeed live at this address. He said that he did, and that he was the Smith that I sought. I told him my name, and suggested that he might know me as an admirer of his from Ethel Heiple's letters. He said, "Oh, yes," and we shook hands. He then invited me into the cozy, comfortable house he shared with his wife. He had been eating his supper and excused himself while he finished, asking me to sit at the dining room table. A heavy but not unappetizing odor of fried fish hung in the air. I excused myself for interrupting his supper. He said it was perfectly all right, and asked if I wanted anything to eat. I shook my head no, explaining that I was going out to eat shortly at Lovers Point Restaurant with the friend who had come up north with me from Los Angeles.

I'm afraid I was a trifle incoherent, so overwhelmed was I by the experiences of meeting a living author, especially one whom I was gradually coming to recognize as a great thinker and a great poet. My great admiration for his writings made me try to pay him some verbal tribute, but my comparative incoherence made it difficult for him to understand me at first. I vaguely desired some great impact, and when this did not occur, I certainly felt ineffectual. Also, as I have written elsewhere, I had become so accustomed to the powerful mode of utterance characteristic of Smith's best poetry in verse or in prose that, I'm afraid, I naively anticipated the poet to speak in a voice of brass, like one of the djinns in *The*

Arabian Nights, and in a manner as orotund and sententious as that of some sorcerer incanting a rune in one of Smith's tales. To my considerable surprise, almost to my disappointment, Smith spoke in a deep and gentle voice that put me at as much of mine ease as I could muster at what I felt was a deathly historical occasion as a young adult. I had typically expected much too much of this very first meeting.

Clark had cast an inquiring look at the paper bag which I had been carrying and which I had put down on a chair. I explained that I had an almost complete set of his books in the bag, and asked if he would autograph them. He nodded, and asked me to leave them with him, and said he would sign them later that night. As I was taking the books out of the bag to show Clark exactly the titles by him that I did own, his wife Carol came down from their upstairs bedroom, and Clark introduced us. They both seemed impressed by the earnestness of my admiration as well as by the rare Smith titles I had managed to collect. I detailed how and when I had acquired them.

I told them I had gone up to Auburn almost exactly a year before, expecting to find them in the old Smith cabin. Clark had been and was evidently still very much shaken over the cabin's destruction which had climaxed a whole series of vandalistic acts done to the cabin and the property. He told me he had sold most of the Smith ranch (about forty acres) on Boulder Ridge ("Indian Ridge" in legal documents) sometime after the death of his father Timeus in late 1937, in order to pay for the funeral expenses. He had made the sale to a local contractor who desired the property as ground for a private airport and later for a subdivision. This left about two and a half acres including the land on which stood the old cabin.

Both Clark and Carol told me that they had just recently sold the George Sterling and Clark Ashton Smith correspondence, plus related papers, to the Berg Collection of the New York Public Library for a sum in excess of $2000. They had married in November of 1954. Between 1954 and 1961 they maintained their residence alternately in Pacific Grove and Auburn. After the old cabin had burned down, a friend of Clark's, Marion Schenck, gave them during the summers the use of a cabin on the fruit ranch owned by Marion and her husband.

Carol presently went into the kitchen, leaving me free to talk to her husband. She was always very considerate this way. As Clark and I were going over his different titles, I confided to him that it would be very difficult for me to pick out a few outstanding favorite pieces of verse or prose by him, but if I had to choose one supreme favorite, it would probably be what I considered his greatest poem *The Hashish Eater; or, The Apocalypse of Evil.* This appeared to please him. That sublime piece of blank verse, *Nero*, also ranked high in my admiration. I had memorized the first stanza of this last poem, and proceeded to declaim. When I came to the end of what I had memorized, Smith continued into the next stanza, and when he paused, we began to discuss the deeper thought and meaning behind the lines declaimed.

Clark then told me he had written the first draft of *The Hashish-Eater* in ten days, averaging around fifty lines a day. A staggering accomplishment, surely. When I remarked on the tremendous vocabulary employed, and so unerringly, in *The Hashish-Eater*, as well as on his vocabulary in general, he informed me that he had once gone through *Webster's Unabridged Dictionary* in its entirety, studying every single word and its origin. A study that served him more than well, since Smith uses words almost invariably in their root-pure sense.

I asked Clark what poet in English, that is, in his own native tongue, did something of the same things for him that he did for me. He answered by turning a little in his chair to some books on the shelves behind him. I saw the name Sterling on most of this particular group of books. He took one entitled *The House of Orchids and Other Poems* from the shelf, and proceeded to read portions of a poem cast in couplets of a Swinburnian flexibility (as in Swinburne's romaunt of *Tristram of Lyonesse*). This was "Duandon," actually a singularly magical short-story told in the form of a poem in verse. Years later, when exploring the *oeuvre* of George Sterling, I was to discover the volume and the poem for myself. (*The House of Orchids*, published in 1911, ranks as the elder poet's most outstanding collection, apart from the *Selected Poems* that Sterling assembled for publication in 1923.) Now I well understand why Smith thought so highly of "Duandon"; it is an achievement only a little below Sterling's two greatest poems, "The Testimony of the Suns" and "A Wine of Wizardry." Upon my further inquiry, Smith mentioned something about Poe, Baudelaire, Swinburne, and Rimbaud as being among his favorite poets.

We discussed these last-named figures briefly. Carol came back out of the kitchen, and said she hoped that we had had a good talk. I excused myself and said I had to go to dinner but I obtained their permission to return afterwards. As I left, I felt myself greatly reassured, if not heartened, by the warmth and friendliness that both Clark and Carol had shown me.

Dinner went its due course, and I returned to the Smith dwelling. A fire was going in the living-room fireplace, and now the lamps and the overhead lights had been switched on. The greater illumination permitted me to note the interior of the house in more detail than what had proven possible during my first visit earlier that same evening. Then the house had been dark with the half-light that follows the setting of a summer sun.

The Smith house faced east, on to Ninth Street which ran north and south. It had two stories, the ground floor and a floor under the peaked roof whose peak ran also north and south, and thus parallel with the street. One entered the house through an enclosed porch (which had a couch-bed in a small bedroom located in its southern half), and then one entered the living room. To the right in the living room stood a fireplace made out of flagstones, a handsome piece of masonry. Through a wide door going directly back from the living room, there lay the dining room. Around the walls of both dining and living rooms there stood low book-cases laden with all manner of books, including (I noticed from the characteristic binding and/or dust jackets) many Arkham House titles. To the left of the living and dining rooms, there lay several rooms. First, a combination bedroom and den; then a bathroom; then the big roomy kitchen. Just a superficial glance at the bookcases and their contents assured me of the breadth and depth of Smith's reading.

Upon the mantelpiece of the living-room fireplace there stood quite a few of what I instantly recognized as some of Clark's carvings; of these I had read much. They were fascinating. Conceived in a bold "primitive" way, they suggested something Egyptian or Mayan or Peruvian of the Inca period. These carvings, as well as all others I have seen in divers collections, possess a quality rare in sculpture, which generally surrenders its essence at once to the beholder, especially sculpture of a conventionally technical perfection. Smith's carvings grow gradually in the onlooker's appreciation, in an almost hypnotic way, as though they were incantations in stone: the more one sees them, the more fascinating they become, adumbrating an essence never fully revealed but extending itself infinitely.

Clark and Carol made me instantly at home, as they had earlier. I noticed that Clark had been reading a book called *Pastels in Prose*, that rare collection of prose-poems translated by Stuart Merrill from the French of

3-and-20 authors and published by Harper and Brother in 1890. (Although born in the United States, this was the only book in English that Stuart Merrill published; all his other work, including his poetry distinguished by a high level of technical accomplishment, is in French.) I could see that Clark and Carol were evidently very much in love, and yet there seemed to be a great ease between them. I understood that there had been three teenagers living in the house, but in deference to the parents' desire for quiet and solitude, they had all decamped and were living elsewhere. They were all Carol's children by a previous marriage. I thought at the time how very obliging of them to leave the house to their mother and their step-father!

The domestic data proceeded from Carol, with an occasional obbligato from Clark, while he and I maintained an over-all literary conversation. I early learned verbatim from Clark what I had suspected from his writings: that he had read virtually everything: literature, mythology, philosophy, etc. He knew Latin and French and Spanish authors and poets in their original languages, having taught himself in these three languages at least. And he knew these writers in foreign languages as well as he did writers in English. No mean feat, that.

We talked a little longer, but I was beginning to feel the strain of a long and overly abundant day, and so I bid them goodnight. Clark assured me again that he would autograph the copies of the eight books I was leaving with him, and Carol invited me to a lunch they were going to have around noon of the next day. Again, as I left, I felt more than reassured and impressed not only by the warmth and hospitality radiating from them both but also, and above all, by Clark's innate kindness and graciousness.

The next morning I woke and arose much later than my wont—I had been much more tired than I had realized the night before—and after a modest late breakfast I returned to 117 Ninth Street. Both Clark and Carol had gotten up long since, and Carol had gone out to do some shopping. It was a glorious day. Light radiated everywhere. There was little wind but the air was fresh and buoyant, charged with a delightful salt-sea tang. The eight books that I had left yesterday, Clark had all autographed, and I think he received as much pleasure as I did as I eagerly perused each book: *The Star-Treader, Odes and Sonnets, Ebony and Crystal, Sandalwood, Lost Worlds, Genius Loci, The Dark Chateau,* and *Spells and Philtres.* Clark has autographed each book to me on the right-hand page of the inner front cover. Beneath the inscription to Senator Phelan, in the copy of *Ebony and Crystal*, there spread out the new inscription to me, written in the author's fine scrawl. I declared firmly that this particular copy at least would never again be found on the shelf of a used book store, that at my death it would go to the Department of Special Collections at U. C. L. A. Clark seemed vaguely amused at the vehemence of my declaration, but I meant it. The autographs in all eight books were dated "August 26th, 1958."

Presently Carol returned from her shopping, and greeted me in a warm and cordial way. Soon everything, and everyone, was ready for lunch, which we had all unanimously decided to have as a picnic on the beach about half a block or so north of the Smith cottage.

A little after high noon, we set out on the short distance to the beach, each of us carrying something for the picnic. We had to cross a street, and then Stevenson's Walk, and then we had to climb down a slight embankment to reach the strand which was liberally strewn with rocks and boulders. We found a little level stretch of sand, spread our blanket, and put the provisions down. Clark had thoughtfully brought a bottle of red burgundy which he soon broached and poured into paper cups, which he handed around. Mr. Smith was wearing his béret (to hold down his fine hair which was easily mussed) and Mrs. Smith wore an immense straw hat which, together with her large one-piece bathing-suit, gave her the piquant appearance of a twentieth-century enchantress.

Carol opened the straw hamper holding the food, and made us all sandwiches with miniature slabs of a sharp cheddar cheese piled on slices of a very tasty, grain-filled wheaten bread. We proposed a toast—to the beautiful day, to friendship, to the wine itself—and after a few swallows of the wine, we voraciously attacked the sandwiches. The tangy salt air had given a zest to our appetites. It was literally a golden early afternoon. A few fleecy clouds rode far overhead. The seagulls were screaming all around us and out over Monterey Bay to the north where the waters were very calm. Accordingly the waves did not thunder on the beach but merely lisped among the rocks.

Our conversation was informal and covered a wide range of topics, occasionally spiced by Smith with some wise, witty, and often ironical comment on the contemporary national and international scene. Clark rarely spoke with any rancor, and repeatedly I was impressed by the fact of his being a perfect gentleman, affable but not unctuously so, civilized and tolerant. There radiated from him an aura of individuality that would have set him apart anywhere but not in any blatant, affected manner; that true individuality which comes from within and has nothing of the theatrical or of the calculated effect about it. His kindness and simplicity registered most strongly in retrospect, since at the time I was so caught up with the charm and mood of the moment that I did not consciously reflect on these qualities of his: everything seemed so natural. And this is not the least of the tributes I could pay Smith today on a personal level: he was a perfectly *natural* man.

The picnic on the beach proved an enchanting interlude. After we had poured and drunk the last of the wine, we picked everything up and returned to the Smith cottage. It was still early afternoon.

We climbed upstairs by means of a ship's ladder, and emerged into Clark and Carol's bedroom, which occupied the southern half of the tallest area provided by the peaked roof which ran north and south parallel with Ninth Street just outside to the east. The northern half was occupied by Clark's upstairs study. The rest of this second floor was attic space, and behind the house (to the west), as I had discovered that morning, there lay a patio embowered with ferns and other plants.

Carol was going to read in bed and maybe take a nap, while Clark was going to entertain me in his study. Before we settled ourselves, he pointed out to me in the attic space, west of the study and the bedroom, some boxes and chests replete with strange treasure: many early issues of *Weird Tales*, as well as of other fantasy and science-fiction magazines. Carol came into the study briefly. She felt badly that Clark, despite paper and writing tools, was doing so little writing, and she somehow felt she was responsible. But, as I was to discover later, a series of strokes, initiated sometime after 1951, had evidently impaired some of Clark's creative powers. During the years 1952–1961 he did only a little literary work, a few short stories and some poetry; he continued to do his sculptures, and on occasion he hired out as a gardener; but that seemed to be the sum of his activities. Certainly Carol was not responsible for his doing so little writing. She had done everything that lay in her power to give him a warm and comfortable home, and to set up a suitable studio for him. As ever, evidently up until the very end, Clark continued to take long walks, and he remained an omnivorous reader, especially of contemporary science-fiction, of which he was rather critical.

We sat ourselves at his work-table, and Clark brought out a weighty portfolio of drawings and paintings. Of his artwork I had read much, but this was the first time I was to see any of it. We went through the entire pile, some of it dating back to the 1920's and before. I must confess myself taken somewhat aback by what I considered at a first viewing as their deliberately "primitive" technique. A number of daemonic heads, archetypically Smithian, struck me as powerful and original. I thought the pile would never come to an end: it was simply too much to absorb in one sitting. And since I did not have the time to become accustomed to their style, I'm afraid that Smith was very much casting pearls before swine, the swine being none other than myself! Since 1958, I have seen some other Smith drawings and paintings many times, and have come to appreciate their excellence and their unique value. Today I can only wish I could go back in time and see the entire portfolio for at least a second viewing. Education is a slow process, alas!

It was now a little after mid-afternoon. We went downstairs. Carol followed us shortly. I explained to them both that I had planned to go out to Point Lobos that afternoon with the friend with whom I had come up north from Los Angeles, and that I would have to be leaving. Clark nodded his understanding. On the morrow early in the morning, my friend and I would he departing for San Francisco before going hack south to Los Angeles, and so this was farewell to Clark and Carol, at least for while. I asked if I might visit them again, and they said that would he fine, but for me to write in advance in order to make sure that they would be at home. I told Clark that I hoped by the time of my next visit to have copies of the titles I so far lacked, especially *Out of Space and Time* and *Nero and Other Poems*. Clark wished me luck in my further search, Carol gave me her best, and we said goodbye.

Oddly enough, I did not think to ask him at the time but I subsequently discovered that Clark had still quite a few copies left of *The Double Shadow and Other Fantasies*. A close friend of Clark's for many years, Genevieve K. Sully (to whom he had dedicated *Out of Space and Time*, and for whom he had done gardening on occasion) had discovered a large cache of copies somewhere on her property in Auburn. This cache she subsequently gave to the author as the rightful owner, and in order that he might derive some profit from them.

Every spring my alma mater, U. C. L. A., together with a leading bookstore in Westwood, sponsored a book-collecting contest, and I decided to enter my collection of fantasy and supernatural horror in the contest of Spring 1959. The first prize was either $50 or $100, I forget which. I didn't win that but I did win the second prize of $25, which could be taken either in cash or in books from the co-sponsoring bookstore in Westwood Village. I decided to take the cash. I had just received from a book-finding agency in Beverly Hills a price quotation on a rare mint copy of *Out of Space and Time* with the original dust-jacket. $35 was the asking price. So, by adding $10 from my meagre funds to the $25 I had won in the book-collecting contest, I could buy this rare book. I was soon its delighted owner. However, *Nero and Other Poems* and *The Double Shadow and Other Fantasies* continued to elude my search. By now, I had learned of the recently discovered copies of the last-named pamphlet in the possession of the author. I determined on my next visit with the Smiths to buy one or more copies.

That summer I worked as a spot-welder in an aircraft and automotive small-parts manufacturing firm in West Los Angeles, and I was planning to take two weeks off before going back to U. C. L. A. in the fall. Ethel Heiple had contracted for the temporary use of an empty residence in the Pacific Gas and Electric power camp at Lake Spaulding in the Sierras, some fifty miles or so northeast of Auburn. I was to meet her there around the 8th of September.

After eight weeks of working in a factory, the distant evergreen-filled Sierras appeared a veritable paradise to me in Los Angeles. I wrote Clark and Carol asking if I could visit them en route to the mountains. They wrote back yes. A friend of mine was driving north, and I was to ride with him to Pacific Grove. There we were to separate, he to drive on to San Francisco, I to visit briefly with them and then to continue on through the Bay Area up to the Sierras via Greyhound bus.

We arrived in Pacific Grove on the 5th of September, Friday afternoon, and had much difficulty and bother in finding a motel room. It was the Labor Day weekend, and virtually every place was filled up. Finally we discovered a vacancy and, once we became settled, I called on the Smiths in the early evening. It was chilly outside, and Clark and Carol were entertaining a small group of friends, with everyone seated around a crackling fire in the living room fireplace. They made me at home at once. I related my success in locating at last a copy of *Out of Space and Time*, and my failure in finding one of *Nero and Other Poems*. I told Clark I wanted to buy some of his copies of *The Double Shadow*. I couldn't stay long as I was on my way to dinner with my traveling companion, and said I'd be back in the morning. The Smiths were as cordial and agreeable as ever, and I bid them an au'voir until tomorrow.

Late Saturday morning, the 6th, I returned to the Smith cottage. My friend was waiting in the car with my bags. Due to the trouble and expense of staying overnight, I was having to shorten my visit in Pacific Grove to an hour or more, and then to go on with my friend to San Francisco, unless the Smiths could put me up for the weekend. Since it was apparent to Clark that I would be terribly disappointed if our visit could not last longer than an hour or so; since he well understood the impecunious condition of a student; and since he was kindness itself; both Clark and Carol with no hesitation agreed to let me stay at least until Monday morning when I could leave for the Sierras via the Greyhound.

Clark helped me bring my few bags into the house after I had said goodbye to my travelling companion. I was assigned the couch-bed in the southern half of the enclosed porch, and my hosts made sure I had plenty of blankets. After I had settled myself and my bags, I brought out my copy of *Out of Space and Time* which Clark obligingly proceeded to autograph to me, including after the inscription the lines from Poe's poem "Dream-Land." "From a wild weird clime that lieth, sublime, / Out of SPACE—out of TIME." The aptness of the quotation charmed me greatly, since this poem by Poe has always been one of my favorites. I thanked Clark profusely, and we briefly discussed the lines in question, and their "wild weird" quality while he was looking the book over, and marveling at its mint condition. The date in his inscription to me reads "Sept. 6th, 1959."

I then bought five of Clark's copies of *The Double Shadow* for a total of $10. It was a definite pleasure to buy them from the author during a time when dealers in rare books were making princely profits from the out-of-print Smith titles while Clark himself had almost at times to go begging for money. He autographed all five copies, and one specifically to me. The extra four copies I was to give away as gifts over a period of years. I still had not succeeded in obtaining a copy of *Nero and Other Poems*, I reported once rather sadly. Clark said he would look to see if he could locate an extra copy for me from among his own titles. I noticed the book he had been reading when I had entered the house, *Five Plays* by Lord Dunsany. Clark had the hook opened to *King Argimenes and the Unknown Warrior*.

That afternoon, whilst seated at the dining room table, Clark and I had a lengthy discussion apropos of divers literary figures, especially Poe and Baudelaire. I had noticed, more vividly than during my visit in August of 1958, and had commented upon, a "complete works" of Poe in some eight or ten volumes on a bookshelf in the dining room. Clark had then confided to me that he had read virtually everything by Poe that he had been able to obtain. The discussion reached its climax when Clark, with an unforgettable intensity, read aloud in French one of the powerful sonnets in *Les Fleurs du Mal.* He commented afterward: "That's terrific stuff!" I nodded my head in agreement and said, "Well, it certainly wasn't written by Alfred, Lord Tennyson!" Then we both laughed, breaking the tension. Clark made the supper that evening. It was a simple meal but very tasty: ground beef fried in a big cast-iron frying pan with onions and green peppers. Plus a huge salad, the lettuce for which I had been enlisted by Carol to wash and shred. I was glad to help.

On my first visit to the Smiths in August of 1958, Clark had shown me some copies of a bibliography of his tales compiled by a New Zealand admirer, Thomas G. L. Cockcroft. I asked if I could use the typewriter in the den-bedroom downstairs to make a copy for myself. He gave his permission, and I proceeded to make a copy. I was still at it when Clark and Carol went to bed. Finally, around midnight, I knocked off and went to bed myself, feeling very warm and comfortable under the woolen blankets, and very eager for the restful oblivion of sleep. I fell asleep within minutes of getting myself tucked-in.

Sunday morning, feeling more than grateful to the Smiths for letting me stay on with them, I asked if I could help them with the cleaning. When Carol made us a breakfast of scrambled eggs, toast, and coffee, I had noticed the coat of grime and soot on the kitchen ceiling, and Carol had said it needed cleaning, but that it was beyond her energy at the time to do it. I volunteered my services, and she promptly accepted. Armed with a bucket of ammonia diluted with hot water, and with some old rags, and mounted on a high stepladder, I proceeded to battle heroically with the dirt. I think my perseverance rather surprised my hosts as they virtually had to force me to take an occasional break. I had about half the ceiling done when Carol suggested round about mid-afternoon that Clark and I go for a walk and buy some wine and ice cream.

We walked along one of the main streets in Pacific Grove but, as I recall, away from the main shopping area. We went by a store specializing in used books and magazines, a store where the people working there seemed to know Clark rather well. We browsed around a bit, and then went on our way to a local ice-cream parlor. We bought ourselves one cone apiece, beside a quart of ice cream for dessert with that evening's supper. The ice cream was delicious, and on the way back home we stopped in at a liquor store, and I insisted on buying the bottle of wine, some inexpensive but good Californian claret or chablis, if memory serves. During our absence Carol had been doing some cleaning, and the house looked spick and span by the time we returned.

We ate an early supper, and after washing the dishes and cleaning up, Clark and I settled down to another discussion. Carol retired upstairs to read and take a nap. She was always insistent—and very thoughtfully so—that I have enough time for serious literary discussion with her husband in private. I started going through his own books, pointing out and reading aloud favorite poems as well as favorite passages in stories. There was more to this than meets the eye, as virtually everything written by Smith was a favorite with me for one reason or another. We both made comments as my choosing and reading of material proceeded apace. Then I came to one of my supreme favorites—and this is one of Smith's greatest stories—the extended poem in prose "The Planet of the Dead."

At first I read only here and there but soon I was reading everything, and gradually that unforgettable pageant of love and death enacted on the planet Phandiom under a dying sun unrolled before our mind's-eye. When I came to the death of the sun, and then to that of the lovers Antarion and Thameera, my voice had sunk almost to a whisper. Tears were welling unashamedly from my eyes. I looked up at Clark, and a thin line of tears had run down his cheeks from both of his eyes. For a moment I was too overwhelmed by the story, and by his reaction to my simple, unaffected reading of his own tale, to continue. I wiped my eyes and blew my nose, and then read the very last part of the tale. It was now late twilight, and quite dark in the house, and I think we both felt like Francis Melchior, the antique dealer and amateur astronomer in the story, as he awoke from his dream of life as the poet Antarion on the dying world of Phandiom.

There was the sound of someone stirring in the bedroom above, and Carol came down. She scolded us for sitting in the cold and the dark— the house had grown chilly—and proceeded to switch on some electric lights, and to start up some heat. I excused myself and said I wanted to continue my copying of Cockcroft's bibliography in the downstairs study. I worked for awhile, but I was beginning to feel very tired. The cleaning of the kitchen ceiling had taken more out of me than what I had thought it would. I said goodnight to Clark and Carol, and then went gratefully to bed.

Monday morning I more or less finished cleaning the ceiling. Smith was as generous and fine a friend as Sterling must have been. He hadn't been able to locate any extra copies of the slender reprint collection *Nero and Other Poems*; so he took a copy he had given and inscribed to his wife, cut out the inscription page, wrote in a new inscription to me, and then gave me the book gratis. I protested—somewhat feebly, I admit,—but both Clark and Carol insisted I keep it. They did have some other copies of the book, so I wasn't leaving them destitute of this particular title, I was quick to console myself. Thanks to their dual generosity, today I have in my personal library this copy of *Nero and Other Poems* or, in the words of Smith's inscription, "this relic from an ironically named printing press." The gift was all the more apt from Clark's giving it to me on the 8th of September, which happened to be my birthday.

In the afternoon I finished copying Cockcroft's bibliography, and then I went for a stroll by myself. When I returned to the cottage, I took a much-needed bath and I shampooed my hair. In the evening after supper, l continued to discuss Clark's writings with him. In particular I went through all of his then three Arkham House collections of short stories, asking his advice as to how to pronounce the names he had invented for persons and places. I was so caught up with his poetry by the time of this second visit that I tended over-all to slight his tales. However, Clark firmly and emphatically declared that his poetry and his fiction were equally valid. And he was absolutely right.

By now I felt that my stay had lasted as long as was tolerable and so I determined to leave on Tuesday for San Francisco and then the Sierras.

Tuesday morning Carol made us breakfast, and then I packed up my few belongings in my bags and got ready to go. I thanked both Clark and Carol for their hospitality, and then I said goodbye to Carol. Clark was accompanying me to the Greyhound bus station in the downtown area of Pacific Grove. He carried one of my bags and I carried the other. It was a beautiful, somewhat chilly day, and excellent for walking. Eventually we arrived at the bus station; I bought my ticket, and Clark waited with me for the bus leaving Pacific Grove for San Francisco about the middle of the morning. I thanked Clark again and again for his kindness and hospitality, and I repeated once more my firm conviction that he was a great poet. I promised I would try to visit him again, possibly next summer. He nodded his head and said that would be fine, but to make sure to write first; I promised. Although I did not know it at the time, the third visit was never to materialize.

The bus came. We said goodbye, and I boarded the bus which was comparatively empty. I walked toward the back, put my bags in the racks above the seat I had chosen, put my jacket down, and then went to the very back seat which spanned the bus's entire width. I looked out and saw Clark still standing there. We smiled at each other, the bus started, I waved to him, and he waved back. He was dressed in a pair of woolen trousers, a woolen sport coat, and some colorful sport shirt, as was his wont. On his head he wore his béret. He turned and slowly walked in the direction of his home. As the bus continued to pull away, his figure became smaller and merged into the motley areas of dark and light which the morning sunlight made as it fell through the shade tress planted along the street; and that was the last I ever saw of Clark Ashton Smith.

As I made my way back to my seat, only the thought that the bright and cheerful presence of my dear friend Ethel Heiple was awaiting me at the end of what was going to be a long, long bus ride, buoyed my spirits up. Otherwise, despite some fascinating books I had with me to read, I felt curiously sad. The mood had of course passed by the time the bus reached San Francisco, but to this day I can recall the inexplicable and shattering sense of desolation that overwhelmed me when I had to say goodbye to Smith on that now far-away Tuesday morning. He was a truly kind and compassionate man.

Shortly after my return from my vacation up north in September of 1959, I began a correspondence with Thomas G. L. Cockcroft, the New Zealand admirer who had compiled a bibliography of Smith's tales. Slowly we evolved the idea of compiling a bibliography of Smith's poems. Cockcroft would publish it; but I would do most of the research, being geographically more conveniently located than Tom, as most of the research materials reposed in the United States, particularly in California. During the spring of 1960, I did some preliminary research but much remained to he done. I had only begun. In February of 1960, Arkham House had finally published the long-promised fourth book of Smith's short stories. I had had my order in with the publishers for some time, and in due course I received my copy with an inscription to me from Clark dated "Mar. 14, 1960." This was the last of his titles that he lived to see published.

After the spring semester of 1960, I went up to live in Auburn for the summer. During July and August, and during the first week in September, I worked as a night-watchman at the Mendelson-Zeller Fruit Company fruit-packing shed on Nevada Street, to the west of the Old Auburn downtown area and just south of the lovely old Auburn District Cemetery, with its picturesque old gravestones and with its abundant shrubbery and trees and thick, springy grass. Somewhere in the cemetery stands a tombstone to Clark's mother, Fanny Gaylord Smith, although neither her ashes nor those of her husband are buried there. In the northeast corner of the cemetery stands a tombstone to the memory of one of Clark's local poetic progenitors, to wit, Eulalie (pronounced YOU-luh-LEE), the Auburn Poetess (as she was called). This was Mary Eulalie Fee, Mrs. John Shannon (1824–1854), California's first woman poet in English whose only collection *Buds, Blossoms and Leaves* appeared just a month before her death in late December of 1854 while in the throes of giving birth to a child.

Ethel Heiple had obtained my summer job for me through the manager of the fruit-packing shed, Angelo Lemos, a long-time acquaintance of hers. Ethel also permitted me the use of the house she and her sister Pearl had inherited from their Grandmother Atkins. Ethel lived on the northeast corner of High and Sacramento Streets; her sister Pearl had her home further up High on the same side of the street; and in between their houses and placed back from the road stands Grandma Atkins' house. This is a delightful, old-fashioned residence furnished at that time with much of the original furniture, including four large reproductions of Maxfield Parrish paintings, the "teacher" of the late great fantasy and science-fiction artist Hannes Bok, who did the dust jacket for Smith's first Arkham House collection.

Although I had an excellent opportunity that summer to do some considerable Smith research in the old bound files of *The Auburn Journal* owned by the Auburn City Public Library, I did not at the time know that Smith had made any sizable contribution to it. I came to do the over-all *Journal* research some little time later.

At the end of the summer and before returning to Los Angeles I did some research at the California State Library in Sacramento. This was but the first of innumerable occasions when I was to use the facilities of the California Section. As always, the staff there proved a joy to work with, whether in person or (later) through correspondence. I had also tried to arrange a third visit with the Smiths on my way south but this did not work out.

The autumn semester of 1960 was my last regular semester at U. C. L. A., and at the end of the semester in January of 1961, I did not receive my baccalaureate in French language and literature. I had received inadequate counseling and had failed to complete some necessary lower-division courses outside my major. Eventually I would have to go back to school if I wanted a degree, but for the nonce I was content to work for awhile at routine jobs while I devoted my real energies to prosecuting the Smith research in full.

During my last semester at U. C. L. A., I had made the acquaintance of that doyen of fantasy and science-fiction fans, Forrest J. Ackerman, at his then home-cum-library in Beverly Hills. Using his extensive collection of professional and amateur publications, I had managed to do considerable research. During January and February, I did the most arduous of this work, going through (virtually page by page) what must have amounted, if piled all on top of each other, to a twenty-five-foot stack of fanzines, i.e., fan magazines. So much new material (much of it of a miscellaneous nature) had come to light that I was by now no longer content with the idea of just a bibliography of Smith's poems: it had to he a bibliography of all Smith's writings, or nothing else. This developed into a compulsion of the first class, a compulsion that would drive me until most of the research had been done, up through Spring 1965.

Spring 1961 marked the début of the really intensive research for the over-all Smith bibliography. To facilitate my search, I was now using the arch-helpful *Union List of Serials*, which gives the data as to which libraries in the United States and Canada have what magazines and which issues—an invaluable aid to a researcher seeking appearances by any particular author in periodicals. I must have easily written over one hundred letters that spring. There were not only the initial inquiries to write and mail, but also the follow-up letters and then, of course, letters of acknowledgement and gratitude. One exciting and unexpected development of both the initial and the later research was the revelation of Smith's early poetic reputation as indicated by the wealth of articles and reviews about him and his early books of poetry.

In February of 1961, I had made the acquaintance of Fritz and Jonquil Leiber, then living in Santa Monica. We rapidly became close friends. They both encouraged me not only in my Smith research; but just as important they provided me with my first (easily and regularly accessible) intelligent, in-depth conversation apropos of fantasy and science-fiction specifically and apropos of literature in general. I had long been an admirer of such of Fritz's writings as appeared in his first collection *Night's Black Agents* (Arkham House, 1947), especially of the adventures of his two heroes or anti-heroes, Fafhrd and the Gray Mouser, some of whose further adventures had also been collected in *Two Sought Adventure* (just recently published by Gnome Press at that time).

Knowing my predilection for great fantasy and great poetry, Fritz urged me to read that unique epic masterpiece, *The Faerie Queene* by the great Elizabethan poet *par excellence*, Edmund Spenser. I started reading it is early March and finished it in late August. Since that first over-all reading, I have subjected the poem's individual parts to intensive study. *The Faerie Queene* proved a great shock and a great revelation, as great as had the writings of Clark Ashton Smith, but it was the poetry of Spenser that gave me the impetus to write my first poetry since the juvenilia I had composed in late grammar school and early high school. The Leibers encouraged me just as much in my own writing as in my Smith research.

During my last visit to Smith, he had shown me the notebook he had used since about 1929, *The Black Book*, and hence during the years of his intensive fictioneering, 1929–1937. He had read to me a number of plot-sketches, including "The Doom of Azédarac" and "The Oracle of Sadoqua." These were tales of Averoigne, his mythical province of medieval France. I instantly realized the great value of this notebook to dedicated students of Smith's writings, and in March or April of 1961 I sent a money-order of $25 to the author, asking him to have a microfilm made of *The Black Book* in order to insure the preservation of this valuable literary material. For some reason he could not agree to this. I changed my commission, and asked him to write for the bibliography a sonnet in alexandrines which would symbolically comment on the canon of his writings. He said he would try.

In May, Clark and Carol went up from Pacific Grove to Auburn to supervise the filling-in by a bulldozer of the old well on the Smith property. Presumably this uncovered well was a menace to any children who might wander through Clark's two-and-a-half acres, and the then District

Attorney of Placer County had ordered Clark to have it filled-in. A mutual friend of Ethel Heiple's and of mine, Helen Farmer, gave them a place to stay while they were in Auburn.

In the late spring of 1961 I had made, via the auspices of Forrest J. Ackerman, the acquaintance of another long-term admirer and friend of Smith's, R. A. (or "Rah") Hoffman who was living at that time in West Los Angeles, and who also was to become one of my best friends.

Finally, in June, when I had really given up hope for a poem, I received a letter from Clark, together with a sonnet in alexandrines called "Cycles," which I found perfect for the bibliography. This was to be his last poem. Again, that spring and summer I had tried to arrange a third visit with the Smiths but again it did not work out. In August Clark suffered a series of strokes, went into a coma, and then died on Monday, August 14, 1961. Three friends each phoned me with the information: Fritz Leiber, Forrest Ackerman, and Rah Hoffman.

Smith's death only strengthened my compulsion that I should carry through the compilation of the over-all bibliography, despite whatever obstacles might arise. It had originally been intended to be a tribute to Smith as a living author; it was now being compiled as a memorial gesture. I also determined to do anything else that lay in my power to further the cause of Smith's life and letters, no matter how difficult or how seemingly trivial.

Following the obsequies, Carol went from Pacific Grove to Auburn to see to the interment of Clark's ashes there. Later, traveling to recover from the loss of her husband, she went to the east coast to visit her daughter. She then returned to California, passing through Los Angeles where she spent several weeks in early October, visiting old friends of hers as well as of Clark including both Forrest Ackerman and Rah Hoffman. She was carrying with her Smith's notebook *The Black Book*. Upon her departure she entrusted the notebook to the temporary possession and care of Rah Hoffman. Rah then contacted me, and together we decided that *The Black Book* should be transcribed and preserved for the benefit of Smith scholars.

Rah and I commenced the decipherment and transcription on the 14th of October—two months after Smith's death—and by the following 14th of November, one month later, we had succeeded in deciphering, transcribing, and editing all the literary materials in the notebook. In the next few weeks subsequent to the last date, together we proof-read with great care our transcription, checking it at all times against the original. Then, during the month of December, we individually proof-read the transcription, checking it against the original whenever any doubt or question would arise as to the accuracy of a given passage or word. Finally, during the last week or January of 1962, during the entire month of February, and during the first week in March, we undertook our ultimate proof-reading of the transcription, again checking it always against the original notebook. Altogether then, we proof-read the text of our transcription a total of *four* times; and we checked it against the original notebook over-all a total of *three* times: the first time during the original decipherment and transcription, the second time during the original dual proof-reading, and the third time during the fourth and ultimate proof reading, not to mention the added checking needed for especially difficult and questionable passages and words. Most of the difficulties we solved eventually with the aid of a magnifying glass. However a few ultimately questionable words remained. Rah and I attempted, in our transcription and editing, to be as faithful as possible to the original notebook, even retaining words crossed out or otherwise obliterated, as well as reproducing all inconsistencies and incorrectnesses made in the original text by the author himself. However, we did permit ourselves the liberty of some very few, very minor editings. During the rest of the spring, I prepared for my own use my own edition of *The Black Book*, with an introduction, an index, various and sundry notes, divers appendices, and with the 248 items (of literary interest) enumerated. I also continued my research for the Smith bibliography. Preparing my own edition of *The Black Book* proved more difficult than I had thought possible: I became so conscious of trying not to make errors that I almost drove myself, unwittingly, to a nervous breakdown. Fortunately, I somehow passed through this difficult period, and came out of it a better as well as a better educated person.

In May of 1962, I went north to visit Auburn, and to do some research in the California Section of the California State Library. I stayed at the house of Helen Farmer where Clark and Carol had also stayed a year earlier when they had come up from Pacific Grove to supervise the filling-in of the old Smith well. Oddly enough, on my previous visits to Auburn, including the summer of 1960 when I had lived there, I had never taken the opportunity to visit either the Smith property or the site of the old Smith cabin.

Helen drove us the short distance south down the old road leading to Folsom, but we did not go into the property by the usual way (east along Carolyn Street after turning off the old Auburn-Folsom road, and then south along Katherine Way through the gate, and then southeast along the old trail that leads up to Boulder Ridge and the site of the old cabin). Instead we went along a series of roads going around the north and then by the east of the main portion of the former Smith property that had been sold to the local contractor. We parked east of the small airstrip, then used for dumping construction debris, and got out of the car. We then walked west along the southern edge of the airstrip and into Smith's two and a half acres.

The wild grass which yellows during the long dry summer had almost completely covered the site of the cabin, now marked largely by some foundation stones and by the stone wall which Clark built to the west and north of the cabin during 1938 after the death of his father in late 1937. It is a beautiful and peaceful spot. To the west, at some little distance, lies the Catholic Novitiate (erected 1940) with its extensive walled gardens—the Nunnery of Averoigne as Clark delighted in calling it. A little northwest of the stone wall is the area where Clark did most of his writing outdoors; the site was marked by parts of an old metal cot, an old table, and an old stove. The blue oaks are everywhere in little copses, and it is at the top of the gentle rise of Boulder Ridge that the cabin once stood. The over-all panorama surrounding the cabin site is truly lovely whether by day or by night. And a great peace inhered over the entire property and its environs. Usually, whenever I go to Auburn, I make the short pilgrimage out to the property on foot. It makes a singularly pleasant walk.

In November of 1962, Roy A. Squires published *The Hill of Dionysus—A Selection*. Smith had made the selection himself before his death from the overall cycle as it appears in the *Selected Poems*. This publication marked in effect the first memorial gesture on behalf of the late poet.

Meanwhile I continued my intensive research for the Smith bibliography. In January of 1963, 1 did the specific research for materials by and about Smith in the bound copies of *The Auburn Journal* at the Auburn City Public Library and at the California State Library. A good month's work, I somehow managed to do it in less than two weeks. I checked *The Auburn Journal* (a weekly) exhaustively for the years 1914–1942, turning over every page and scrutinizing it for Smithian materials. It was a miracle my eyes did not give out on me! My hard work was amply repaid by the wealth of appearances, etc., uncovered. By this time, I was making two trips a year to Northern California, doing research principally in Auburn and in Sacramento, about thirty miles southwest of the seat of Placer County.

In August of 1963, Jack L. Chalker published the large mimeographed booklet *In Memoriam: Clark Ashton Smith*. After its publication I received, anent my biographical-critical essay included in the chapbook, my first fan letter. This was from George F. Haas, who had been Clark's closest living friend in the last eight years or so prior to the poet's death. Subsequently I was to have the honor as well as the delight of meeting both George and his mother, Bertha Maud Boyd, in person, when I was on one of my periodic research trips up north. From that first letter of George's developed a memorable correspondence and a great friendship.

Also about the same general time, my acquaintance and correspondence with Tom Cockcroft came to an end. I was determined as a compiler to do an over-all bibliography. Cockcroft wanted to publish a bibliography of only Smith's poems. Therefore I took the responsibility for publishing the over-all bibliography into my own hands. I was and am grateful to Cockcroft for much of the original bibliographical impetus, and for the loan or gift of many books and periodicals.

On the 27th of February, 1964, there occurred a general panel discussion on Smith at one of the meetings of the Los Angeles Science Fantasy Society. Unfortunately, what might have proven an excellent opportunity to introduce some new scholars to Smith's work, degenerated into an harangue by Leland Sapiro over the relative merits or demerits of specifically Smithian poetry versus other modern poetry in general.

In July of 1964 Roy A. Squires published eight of Smith's original poems in Spanish, in the form of a small chapbook *¿Dónde Duermes, Eldorado? Y Otros Poemas*, as by "Clérigo Herrero" that is, "Clark Smith". In July and August, I worked only part-time, and returned to U.C.L.A. where I attended both sessions of summer school, at the end of which I finally received my baccalaureate in French (dated September, 1964). In November of 1964 Arkham House published its fifth Smith short-story collection *Tales of Science and Sorcery* with a memoir of Smith by E. Hoffman Price used as an introduction.

In January of 1965 died Bertha Maud Boyd, George F. Haas' mother, a gracious and lovely lady who had served for me as one more link in the cycle of Smith lore and friendship. Although I had known her only from two extended visits at the home that she and George shared together, I had come to feel very close to her, so that her death was a source of considerable grief to me. I shall never forget her kindness and hospitality.

In June of 1965 I completed the last of the intensive research for the Smith bibliography. In all, I had visited and used a great many both major and minor research libraries in Northern California: principally the Auburn City and County Public Libraries, the California State Library in Sacramento, both the General Library and the Bancroft Library in the University of California at Berkeley, Mills College Library in Oakland, the San Francisco Public Library, and the Library at Stanford University just outside Palo Alto, to say nothing of the many private collections of books and papers I had utilized courtesy of their kind and gracious owners, especially Forrest Ackerman.

In July of 1965 Arkham House published a complete collection of all Smith's prose-poems known to exist at that time, under the title *Poems in Prose* and with the distinction of twelve illustrations by the Wisconsin artist Frank Utpatel (the first "t" is silent and the accent is on the first syllable). Finally, in September of 1965 I moved myself and my possessions to Auburn, where I lived through most of January of 1966 until I moved once again and this time to San Francisco. Both Northern California and San Francisco have always proven far more to my taste than Southern California and Los Angeles. The move up north was of course inevitable, and I have never regretted it. I only regret I didn't move sooner!

In late 1966 I made the acquaintance of the dancer Madelynne Greene, now a recognized authority on ethnic dance. Madelynne lived, and had her studio, in San Francisco; but her husband, the poet Eric Barker, lived in the general Big Sur area where he had become a well-known literary figure. Madelynne arranged that I should meet Eric on the day following Christmas when we would all share a holiday dinner together. This turned out to be a singularly memorable occasion, and the beginning of a fine friendship. All that afternoon and evening we had quite a discussion: about Clark Ashton and his *oeuvre*, and the many good times that he and the Barkers shared; about Dylan Thomas' last visit to San Francisco when Eric met him and went with him around the city on a splendid carouse; and about many other things poetical and otherwise. A few days after this, and at my request, Eric wrote for reproduction in the Smith bibliography a lovely piece of prose entitled "Clark Ashton Smith—In Memory of a Great Friendship." Both Eric and Madelynne were wonderfully warm and vibrant persons, and through them I have somehow come to know Clark even better than I might have in person had he lived longer. I regret to recall that Madelynne Greene passed away in February of 1970, and Eric some years after that.

The following years continued to see many good things happen for the cause of Smith's life and letters, nothing spectacular but all of them solid achievements. Roy A. Squires put the extensive Smith papers, or archives, into order—a considerable accomplishment; Squires had the papers in his care from about 1964 through the first half of 1968. He subsequently returned them to Mrs. Smith (who had remarried, becoming Mrs. Frank Wakefield). Brown University in Providence, Rhode Island, now maintains the Smith papers in a special collection. Arkham House published its sixth collection of Smith's short stories and novelettes, *Other Dimensions*, in 1970 as well as the long-awaited omnibus collection *Selected Poems* in 1971, the latter dedicated by Smith to Eric Barker and Madelynne Greene. Of equal importance must rank the first book publication (at long last) of Smith's fantasies abroad and in translation and in paperback editions. Neville Spearman in England have republished in hardcover facsimile Smith's first four Arkham House short-story collections: *Out of Space and Time*, *Lost Worlds*, *Genius Loci*, and *The Abominations of Yondo* (1971–1972); they completed their program by republishing the fifth collection, *Tales of Science and Sorcery*, and the last one, *Other Dimensions*; all of these titles had gone out of print and became very expensive and difficult to obtain on the used-book market. Smith has now been translated into French, German, Italian, and Spanish at least. The full impact of these recent translations cannot he gauged at the present time; it will benefit Smith's *oeuvre* in ways undoubtedly unique. Finally, the paperback editions of Smith's stories published in the United States by Ballantine Books in the Adult Fantasy Series under the titles *Zothique*, *Hyperborea*, *Xiccarph*, and *Poseidonis* (1970–1973), along with the British editions bearing the six original Arkham House titles published by Panther Books (1974–1976), represent the greatest publishing event in the history of Smith's writings. Because of their numerically large printings, and because of their widespread distribution, the impact of these paper-covered editions in making Smith's name and reputation better known has proven enormous, far exceeding the éclat of *Weird Tales* and Arkham House combined (no disparagement, of course, to these last).

Even in his native Auburn-Long Valley area Smith is receiving some belated recognition. The housing development that came into place next to the former Smith acres outside of Auburn now features a "Smith Court" on one hand and on the other a "Poet Smith Drive."

The following years, I regret to say, witnessed the deaths of a number of persons intimately associated with Smith or Lovecraft. First, as mentioned above, Madelynne Greene—the inspiratrix of Smith's cycle of love poems *The Hill of Dionysus*—died in February of 1970. Second, Genevieve K. Sully—the inspiratrix of another cycle of love poems, *The Jasmine Girdle*—passed away in March of that same year. Third, August Derleth—Smith's publisher since the early 1940's—died in July of 1971. Fourth, Mrs. Sonia Greene Lovecraft Davis, the quondam wife of Smith's great friend, died in December of 1972. Fifth, Mrs. Clark Ashton Smith passed away in the following January. Sixth, Mrs. Helen French Hunt—the sister of Nora May French, a poetess whom both Sterling and Smith greatly admired—died in April of 1973. Last, Smith's devoted friend George Haas passed away in February of 1978.

My own first book, *Songs and Sonnets Atlantean*—a volume of poetry which continues in part the tradition of three of California's greatest lyric poets, George Sterling (1869–1926), Nora May French (1881–1907), and Clark Ashton Smith (Robinson Jeffers with his long narrative poems is regarded in this context as largely a dramatic and epic poet somewhat like the Greek poets of classical antiquity)—was published in June of 1971 by Arkham House, just before the death of August Derleth. In a sense, it was the last book published (i.e., made public) by Arkham House under his personal aegis; although a number of other titles were in production or had actually been finished at the time of his death, these were not actually published until more than a month after his death and after Arkham House had been reorganized. I owe much to the generous encouragement and assistance given to me by August Derleth.

At long last my bibliography of Clark Ashton Smith made its appearance. Donald M. Grant (the West Kingston, Rhode Island, publisher of deluxe editions of fantastic literature) then issued it under the title *Emperor of Dreams*—over a decade of research having gone into its compilation. Included in this bibliography is a biographical account of Smith. During the interval that elapsed between the publication of *Songs and Sonnets Atlantean* and *Emperor of Dreams* appeared my booklet on Smith (and in particular the *Selected Poems*) entitled *The Last of the Great Romantic Poets,* published by Harry Morris II (Albuquerque: The Silver Scarab Press, 1973).

Now that my Smithian labors have at last borne tangible fruit, and now that I finish this memoir of "Timeus Gaylord" as well as related matters, it is possible that the compulsion, or *geas*—laid upon me by a late and notable enchanter—will at long last be lifted. As I look back over my two visits with Smith, so much of what he said keeps returning to me. One *pensée* in particular: Clark, Carol and I had been discussing divers faiths and philosophies. Both Carol and I were trying to establish a priority for one credo or one body of creeds, but Clark refused to be restricted to one belief or speculation. He summed up his own feelings by saying, "Why couldn't they all be possible?" Then I could not accept this *pensée*; since that time, however, my own experience of life and literature has but convinced me of the incredible wisdom of this… as well as of other *pensées* that he uttered.

I remember then principally his wisdom on one hand and then his kindness, graciousness, and compassion on the other. I felt at the time I visited him, as well as afterwards (for quite some time, I might add), that I was not really communicating with him. I know now that I was mistaken. Smith was fantastically aware. Nonetheless, I am sure that I may have missed much when I met him in person, despite my best intentions and efforts to miss nothing, to be as sensitive as possible to the vibrations of the moment. Still, I shall always treasure these memories of an unique human being as well as an unique artist. And I shall always be grateful to him for the education that his writings—and the compilation of his bibliography—have given me, an education such as I could never have gotten from any college or university.

Whenever I have made the trek up to Auburn from San Francisco or Los Angeles in order to pay my respects to Smith's departed spirit at some appropriate site, I am always reminded of one of Smith's favorite poems by one of his favorite poets in English, to wit, the "Ave Atque Vale" by Swinburne, the memorial verses to Baudelaire, and one of the greatest elegies ever created in any language. It is appropriate therefore—in lieu of any funereal tribute I might make myself—that I quote here at the end of this long memoir the final stanza of this poem…and this stanza is truly just as applicable to Smith as to Baudelaire:

XVIII

For thee, O now a silent soul, my brother,
    Take at my hands this garland, and farewell.
    Thin is the leaf, and chill the wintry smell,
And chill the solemn earth, a fatal mother,
    With sadder than the Niobean womb,
    And in the hollow of her breasts a tomb.
Content thee, howsoe'er, whose days are done;
    There lies not any troublous thing before,
    Nor sight nor sound to war against thee more,
For whom all winds are quiet as the sun,
    All waters as the shore.

Concluding Note: The present author prepared the final version of this memoir-essay sometime during 1978 before its appearance in *The Romantist*, No. 2, dated 1978 but published in 1979. He has revised it again, but slightly, in August of 2010. He wishes to thank his great and good friend George F. Haas, posthumously, for examining (sometime before his death in February 1978) the memoir for any errors in the description of Smith's Pacific Grove home and its enrivons.

A Visionary of Doom:
Ambrose Bierce, Poet (1842–1914)

More than half a century has now elapsed since the death, presumably in 1914, of Ambrose Bierce (born 1842), one of California's authentic literary Titans. Only a short time before his disappearance into northern Mexico in late 1913, the Neale Publishing Company of New York City had finished bringing out Bierce's twelve overly bulky and seemingly unselective *Collected Works* in a sumptuous edition (1909–1912). Today this edition rather resembles a vast Victorian attic stored with apparently endless piles of quaint and curious rubbish, and with the real *trouvailles* lying carelessly scattered about, virtually unheralded, and usually requiring the interested reader to discover and explore them very much on his own. This is certainly true of the two volumes of verse, numbers IV and V, which bear the titles, respectively, *Shapes of Clay* (1910) and *Black Beetles in Amber* (1911).

However, the appearance of these two volumes in the *Collected Works* represents their second, and definitive, editions. *Black Beetles in Amber* first appeared in 1892, published by the Western Authors Publishing Company of San Francisco; *Shapes of Clay* first appeared in 1903, put out by W. E. Wood, Publisher, also of San Francisco. The contents and number of poems in both of these early editions differ somewhat from those in the later ones. Into these two volumes Bierce had gathered evidently most of his not inconsiderable output in verse (exclusive of the more than two hundred original poems and bits of verse included in *The Devil's Dictionary*).

When we consider that his published verse must total somewhere around eight hundred pieces in all, and that this total represents around one fifth or one sixth of his over-all literary output (as assembled in his *Collected Works*), we have ample assurance that Bierce must have placed some value on his verse, whatever he may have said or written to the contrary. Today much of it seems little more than competent versifying, generally light in character and (more often than not) of a satirical nature, attacking the fads, foibles, and personalities of Bierce's day. His best poems lie embedded in a mass of typically Biercean satire in verse mainly apropos of persons who were once celebrities of the West Coast but who are now nonentities except to the specialist in Californian history and literature. Read infrequently and at the rate of a few pieces at a time, this satirical verse is apt and amusing; but read in a large quantity, it rapidly becomes tiresome, if not downright unbearable.

But a modicum remains of real poetry, compact, imaginative, and powerful; or—quite unexpectedly—tender with a tenderness not usually associated with one who has on occasion been called "The Devil's Lexicographer." The present gathering retains this hard core of real poetry, together with a small sampling from the better pieces of satirical verse; in all, half a hundred poems, virtually all taken from *Shapes of Clay* and *Black Beetles in Amber* (their second and final editions, respectively). Since *The Devil's Dictionary* continues to be published, we have included nothing from that lexicon except the quatrain "Dead," which figures here as the penultimate selection. The final sublime quatrain "Man Is Long Ages Dead" appears in Bierce's essay on some of his own dreams "Visions of the Night" (included in volume X, *The Opinionator*). The pieces included in the section "Early Poems" first appeared in the San Francisco weekly newspaper *The Californian* (published in the 1860's): "Basilica" appeared in the issue for September 21, 1867; and "A Mystery" appeared in the issue for November 23, 1867. This represents their first collected appearance.

Thus it has happened that, whereas he has become comparatively well-known as an aphorist, a short-story writer, and an epistolarian, Bierce has remained almost unknown as a poet, *qua* poet. In his own day he was of course best known as a satirist and a critic whom quite a few people had cause to hate and fear and respect. Yet on the basis of his best poems Bierce clearly merits the attention of the discriminating lover and student of poetry.

In the tradition of Edgar Allan Poe, the American and now largely underground school of "pure poetry" has been peculiarly associated with Bierce, directly or indirectly. In form and in language he was a traditionalist, a purist of the most rigid kind; in this we may perhaps see something of an all-pervading life-attitude that he gained from his military experience during the Civil War. In his critical theories he was above all else a proponent of *la poésie pure*. And much of his taste and preference in verse may be gauged from the fact that he considered Coleridge's "Kubla Khan" the most nearly perfect poem in the English language.

As a poet but more as a poetic mentor, Bierce proved to be a great and beneficial influence on George Sterling (1869–1926), who became the unofficial poet laureate of the West Coast. (Ina Donna Coolbrith, by the express act of the California Legislature, was chosen as the official poet laureate of the state in 1915, a position she held with undeniable prestige until her death in 1928.) He not only influenced and encouraged Sterling; he gave him much valuable technical training, and he commented and criticized extensively Sterling's first mature poetry, e.g., "The Testimony of the Suns." There does indeed inhere in Bierce's own "Invocation" a cosmic understanding even if not overtly articulated throughout. Apart from the fact that both poems employ the octosyllabic quatrain (riming a/b/b/a) made famous by the "In Memoriam" of Tennyson, "Invocation" clearly anticipates the richer harmonies and the greater vision of Sterling's truly remarkable poem "The Testimony of the Suns"; which, although created in 1901 and first published in book form in 1903 (as the title-poem in Sterling's first collection), strangely previsions the current Age of Space with humanity's increasing exploration into the stars. Bierce also encouraged and influenced the German-born Hermann Scheffauer (1876 or 1878–1927). He indicated the high esteem in which he held his two principal poet-pupils by dedicating to them the first edition of *Shapes of Clay*.

Bierce praised the early poetry of Edwin Markham (1852–1940) and encouraged him long before Markham became famous or infamous for "The Man With the Hoe." He did not influence, although he did encourage, the fine and unjustly neglected lyric poet Samuel Loveman (born 1887). The record of his interest in, and his encouragement of, Loveman as a poet may be read in *Twenty-One Letters of Ambrose Bierce*, edited with a note by Loveman and published by George Kirk, Cleveland, 1922. Most of Mr. Loveman's own poetry has been collected into *The Hermaphrodite and Other Poems* and published by The Caxton Printers, Ltd., Caldwell, Idaho, 1936.

Sometime in the spring or early summer of 1910, Ezra Pound sent "The Ballad of the Goodly Fere" in manuscript to Bierce, evidently in the expectation that he would commend it, and might be able to place it for Pound with some periodical, in the same way that Bierce had placed Sterling's poem "A Wine of Wizardry" with *The Cosmopolitan*. Commend it Bierce did, and highly, but before he could place it anywhere, Pound withdrew the ballad. Some other verses that Pound had earlier submitted in manuscript to Bierce had, to borrow Bierce's own pungent phraseology, escaped his approval by a wide margin.

Through his poems, through his poetic theories (as expressed in the essays contained in *The Opinionator*), and above all through his pupil Sterling, Bierce exercised an important influence on Sterling's own pupil and follower, Clark Ashton Smith (1893–1961), who as a remarkable lyric poet was to surpass his immediate master, just as Sterling had surpassed his own master Bierce. Although the two never met, Bierce read and praised some of Smith's first mature poetry, and on one occasion publicly came to the younger poet's defense.

Sterling in turn praised, encouraged, and influenced not only Ashton Smith but likewise, apropos of cosmic vision and consciousness, the great poet Robinson Jeffers (1887–1962); although this fact has received little attention and recognition. The Biercean influence lingered on through both Sterling and Smith. It must be noted that the figurative Cloak of Elijah that Bierce bequeathed to Sterling, Sterling in his turn handed on to Ashton Smith.

Sterling's single outstanding protégée before Smith was the strangely gifted and tragic girl Nora May French (1881–1907), whose only collection appeared after her death as *Poems*, published by The Strange Company, San Francisco, 1910. Undoubtedly, had she lived longer, this fine poet would rank today with Emily Dickinson and Edna St. Vincent Millay as one of America's major women poets.

In his own turn Ashton Smith in large part encouraged and to some extent influenced Susan Myra Gregory, a poet who lived in both Auburn and Monterey; she was closely related to the popular novelist Jackson Gregory, who also made his home in the Auburn area. Her one collection, *Shadows of Wings* (with a rare introduction by Ashton Smith), was published by The Troubadour Press, San Diego, 1930. Both Nora May French and Susan Myra Gregory belong to that tradition of West Coast poets begun by Eulalie, California's first woman poet in English.

Most of the persons whom Bierce mentions or attacks in his overtly topical poems are now known largely to the specialist in the history of Californian politics, finance, and literature. But this is not the case with the places he mentions or attacks. Both San Francisco (which figures in the dream-allegories "The Passing Show" and "A Vision of Doom") and Auburn, California (which figures in "The Foot-Hill Resort" and "The Perverted Village") have not only so far escaped the doom or decline Bierce wishfully envisioned for them but have prospered and grown far more than anyone in Bierce's day could have anticipated. The Mission

San Francisco de Asís, founded October 9, 1776, and better known as the Mission Dolores (which figures in the wryly reflective love poem "Again"), was part of the original nucleus around which the later city of San Francisco grew, and was evidently a trysting-place for lovers around the fin-de-siècle.

In the 1880's Bierce lived intermittently in Auburn, the seat of Placer County, and once one of the great Gold Rush towns of California. The fogs and general damp of the San Francisco Bay Area had become too much for Bierce and his asthma. Beginning about 1884, he resided (part of the time at least) in Auburn situated among the foothills of the Sierras, and advertised as "the healthiest town in California" (the town had won the second prize in a national contest for the healthiest town in America). Here in what is now modern downtown Auburn, but then East Auburn Bierce lived a hermitlike existence at the Putnam House, later the site of the Conroy Hotel, and presently that of the Auburn Hotel. He satirized his fellow lodgers in "The Foot-Hill Resort" and Auburn's gossipmongers in "The Perverted Village." In this latter poem Bierce was able to utilize his model, "The Deserted Village" by Oliver Goldsmith, to particular advantage since both villages, the one in California and Goldsmith's "mythical" one in England, bear the same name.

Bierce's favorite place for a promenade in Auburn was the local graveyard, called the Old Cemetery, located not far from the town's hanging tree. This was all quite in character for "The Devil's Lexicographer"—according to the testimony of H. L. Mencken, Bierce was a connoisseur of executions, graveyards, and morgues. He must have enjoyed his stroll in the Old Cemetery as it was an evidently peaceful spot, lovely with overgrown verdure, and much neglected at the time. That the graveyard did have a peculiar fascination and charm for Bierce, is attested by the fact that he later used the place as one of the locations in his short story "The Realm of the Unreal." He devotes an entire paragraph to its description:

> There was at Auburn an old, abandoned cemetery. It was nearly in the heart of the town, yet by night it was as gruesome a place as the most dismal of human moods could crave. The railings about the plats were prostrate, decayed, or altogether gone. Many of the graves were sunken, from others grew sturdy pines, whose roots had committed unspeakable sin. The headstones were fallen and broken across; brambles overran the ground; the fence was mostly gone, and cows and pigs

wandered there at will; the place was a dishonor to the living, a calumny on the dead, a blasphemy against God.

Further on in the same story Bierce refers to the cemetery as "that congenial spot." He then describes the place on a moonlit night:

> The light of the half moon fell ghostly through the foliage of trees in spots and patches, revealing much that was unsightly, and the black shadows seemed conspiracies withholding to the proper time revelations of darker import.

Only a few years after Bierce's intermittent residence in Auburn, and only a few miles south of town, Clark Ashton Smith was born in Long Valley on January 13th, 1893, and later developed into one of California's greatest lyric poets.

It was during one of his later periods of residence in the town, during the late spring or early summer of 1888, that an official committee came from San Francisco to request from Bierce a poem for the City's celebration of the Fourth of July. Evidently flattered, he consented, and "Invocation" was the result. While the traditional parade highlighted the day of the Fourth, the traditional exhibition of fireworks highlighted the evening, together with some official exercises at the then Grand Opera House in San Francisco, the principal features of the program being an oration by the then well-known orator Samuel M. Shortridge, and the "Invocation" by Bierce. The poet himself did not read his own poem; the actor George Osbourne did. The audience received it with applause. Only a few hours later, *The Daily Examiner* (as it then styled itself) printed the poem in its issue for Thursday morning, July 5, 1888. This constituted the poem's first printed appearance. In the same issue appeared the editorial "A Great Poem," an over-all sound appraisal and appreciation. Bierce included the poem in both the 1903 and 1910 editions of *Shapes of Clay*. Later, in 1928, John Henry Nash of San Francisco printed the poem in gorgeous form for separate publication by The Book Club of California, preceded with an explanation by Oscar Lewis and a critical introduction by George Sterling, and followed with a reprinting of the editorial that had first appeared in the *Examiner*. Sterling's "Introduction" (written shortly before his death in mid-November 1926, and therefore one of the very last things he ever wrote), although brief, ranks as one of the best summaries extant of Bierce as a poet: it contains a thoughtful and well-written appreciation of Bierce's poetry in general and of "Invocation" in particular.

Oddly enough, during this same general period that he was in the employ of William Randolph Hearst, Bierce made him the subject of the satirical poem "A Voluptuary," although taking care not to mention him by name. While the "Pleasure-dome down by the sea" would probably rightly cause the reader to think of Hearst and the Hearst Castle at San Simeon, the locale itself could only refer to the large Piedra Blanca ranch purchased in 1865 by his father George and to the spacious Victorian ranch house erected by him upon the property, since the actual construction of the Castle did not begin until about 1924. This poem incidentally permits Bierce to quote from Coleridge's "Kubla Khan," which (as mentioned previously) he considered to be the most nearly perfect poem in the English language.

Other figures of Bierce's day—some internationally known but others only locally—appear in his poems, whether satirical or tenderly personal. "Montefiore" refers of course to Sir Moses Haim Montefiore (1784–1885), the Anglo-Italian philanthropist; "T. A. H." refers to T. Arundel Harcourt; "J. F. B." to James F. Bowman; the "W. F. S." of *Light lie the earth upon his dear dead heart* to William F. Smith; all three were figures of the San Francisco area, and all had been close friends to Bierce.

It would be pleasant but scarcely accurate to claim for his best poetry a spectacular originality. While a good portion of his output in verse—considered as poetry—may seem "negligible" and even "trivial" as some critics have maintained, yet his best is neither, and well rewards sympathetic attention. At his best Bierce as a poet is, beneath a seemingly conventional exterior, very much his own man. In his "Introduction" to the 1928 publication of "Invocation," George Sterling considered the following ten poems by Bierce to be among his poetic master's best: "The Passing Show," "Geotheos," "Invocation," "T. A. H.," " J. F. B.," "The Death of Grant," "Reminded," "Another Way," "Presentiment," and "Light lie the earth upon his dear dead heart," with pride of place being reserved for "Invocation"; although Sterling thought there was "the flash of genius in the great poem, 'The Passing Show.'" The present editor confirms this judgment, and the reader will find all ten poems included in this volume. However, the final quatrain of "The Death of Grant" may strike more than a few contemporary sensibilities as either bathos or falsehood.

Usually personal, Bierce's "sentimental" poems, evidently written during the apogée of late Victorian times, are singularly unsentimental, and refreshingly simple and direct statements of emotion. His love sonnets in particular may come as a surprise to the reader acquainted primarily with Bierce's pungent satire or with his unforgettable supernatural stories. His best serious poetry is largely to be found in *Shapes of Clay*. Apart from a handful of pieces, *Black Beetles in Amber* contains only satirical or humorous verse. The weary reader discovers the few serious poems in the latter collection almost with a sense of relief. However, even his satirical pieces considered collectively, too often like so many peas in a pod both in language and in substance, do not appear unfavorably against the background of late Victorian and of Edwardian poetry, but rather as agreeably nasty cast-iron thorns in the Victorian rose-garden. Thus the poems in the present volume fall principally into three major categories: the macabre, the satiric, and the personal. But even those poems not intentionally macabre are usually shaded by Bierce's characteristic obsession with death.

"Invocation" remains one of the best things of its kind, and far more than a mere *pièce d'occasion*, a mere piece of facile chauvinism made to order. Although not quite a hundred years have now passed since "Invocation" was first proclaimed, most of Bierce's thoughts on the good and evil possibilities inherent in liberty still hold true. The reader will note that the God that Bierce posits in his apostrophe (see particularly quatrains 10 through 25) is not the compassionate deity presented in the New Testament.

Moreover, the reader should not construe from these references to a conventional divinity (as well as from those in other poems) that Bierce was in any sense a strict religionist. Although highly moral—even puritanical—in his own lifestyle, he was of course very much of a freethinker. As he once wittily remarked in a letter to poet pupil George Sterling, God ranked in the sphere of poetic reference as one of the most useful items (or "properties") from the poet's given repertoire of tropes. If God had not already existed as a reality, or merely as a figure of speech, then the poets would have been obliged to have invented Him out of sheer necessity.

Many critics have considered "Invocation" to be Bierce's greatest poem; actually it is not; such an honor should probably go to the tercet "Creation," that little masterpiece of boldness and compression. Nonetheless, "Invocation" does contain a number of magnificent and nominally great passages. With good reason Sterling quoted lines 45–48 (the twelfth quatrain) to preface his first greatest poem "The Testimony of the Suns":

> To Whom the unceasing suns belong,
> And cause is one with consequence,—
> To Whose divine inclusive sense
> The moan is blended with the song,—

Indeed, placed somewhere within the context of the latter poem, this quatrain could easily pass as one of Sterling's own more inspired and artistically modulated stanzas. With equally good reason Sterling quoted lines 26–28 of Bierce's lovely lyric "Geotheos" to preface his second greatest poem "A Wine of Wizardry":

> When mountains were stained as with wine
> By the dawning of Time, and as wine
> Were the seas...

Sterling rightly considered this to be "indelible purple" and it seems quite possible that in this passage from his "Magister's" own work he discovered the germ-nucleus for the glittering, and often breathtaking, imagery of "A Wine of Wizardry," which he sent in manuscript to Bierce early in 1904. (It was first published, under Bierce's aegis, in *The Cosmopolitan* for September 1907, and it reappeared in 1909 as the title-poem in Sterling's second collection.) Although Bierce did not mention it at the time, Sterling's own poetic master had begun not only his career as a poet, but simply his career as a writer, in 1867 with a fantastic and macabre poem which, while not the masterpiece that is Sterling's effort, must rank nevertheless, in terms of structure and imagery, as a remarkable anticipation of "A Wine of Wizardry." This poem was "Basilica" (the name itself is evidently the feminine form of *basilicus*, designating not the ecclesiastical basilica but a basilisk or cockatrice), which Bierce wrote shortly after his arrival in California in 1866. It was published for the first time in the early San Francisco weekly newspaper *The Californian* for September 21, 1867. About two months later, it was followed by a second poem, "A Mystery," which appeared in the issue for November 23, 1867. In style these two pieces are at least equal, if not superior, to the poems usually published in this periodical, whether original or reprinted. In substance they are sombre and surely not at all typical of the verse appearing in periodicals of the time. Both are signed by "A. G. Bierce." Both are especially written "[For the Californian.]" - which device appears at the top of each poem. Both are dated at the bottom with the date of composition, or of completion of composition (a procedure distinctly unusual for verse published in periodicals then or now). Both these poems, Bierce's only such contributions to *The Californian* (even though the newspaper continued to appear through November 1868), have reminded some commentators of Edgar Allan Poe, or of Keats and Coleridge.

In the twenty-two tercets of "Basilica," Bierce relates and develops a comparatively simple story in terms of highly colored and often macabre imagery in the manner of Keats, Coleridge, or Poe. The poet or narrator is walking along the seashore and sees in the midst of some rocks what appears to be a radiant gem but which resolves itself into a weirdly shining cockatrice when the poet essays to grasp it

Thus, Nature or Life leads us ever onward with her external shows of beauty but when we try to plumb the mystery of loveliness we find only evil and corruption. The imagery is notable for its lurid imaginativeness: "The groaning sea, wind-smitten white" / "ocean's leprous agony" / "A glinting gem with lustrous sheen" / "An opal chalice brimming gold" / "dim with amber-tinted air" / "Gem-tinct with gleams of prismic ice." The fulsome description of the basilisk is not without a certain effectiveness:

> O, with Heart of Stone, with eyes of light,
> And ivory throat of pallid white,
> And snaky folds concealed from sight;
>
> With jeweled teeth, alas! and breath
> Whose touch to passion ministreth—
> Sweet-spiced with aromatic death!

This type of vividly colored imagery descends in part from Poe and in part from the English Romantics and, before them and singularly influencing them, from Edmund Spenser and the concentrated, brilliantly hued, and highly symbolic imagery of *The Faerie Queene*; and it anticipates the characteristic, Late Romantic imagery of both Sterling and Ashton Smith. Not only is Bierce's imagery in "Basilica" concentrated but the poem itself is a concentration of such imagery developed on the foundation of a simple narrative. Since he considered imagery to be the heart, the soul, the essence of poetry—to him the imagery *was* the poetry—then in theory a poem successfully constructed along these lines would be the most poetic possible, that is, the most imaginative. Although it remained first for Sterling to create such a poem, Bierce theoretically formulated it in his two essays "A Wine of Wizardry" (originally "A Poet and his Poem") and "An Insurrection of the Peasantry" (he included both of these in *The Opinionator*).

There is one short poem by Keats which, in however modest the way, anticipates the Biercean poem-formula of simple narrative or theme elaborated in vivid and concentrated imagery, and which probably acted as an influence, together with the passage from "Geotheos," on Sterling in the creation of "A Wine of Wizardry." This poem by Keats "Fancy" whose opening line "Ever let the Fancy roam" (later repeated as the penultimate line "Let the wingèd Fancy roam") seems to have given Sterling an immediate (technical) inspiration for his own poem, the narrative of which is literally a flight of Fancy personified as a goddess or a fay. However, where Keats evokes for us an attractive but un-ambitious imagery of his native English seasons and months, Sterling presents an often overwhelming pageant of extraordinarily imaginative and exotic tableaux or episodes. Just as the "Fancy" of Keats apparently prepared the *modus operandi* for Sterling in "A Wine of Wizardry," so in its turn did "A Wine of Wizardry" serve as the model for Ashton Smith in his infinitely greater poem, the compressed epic "The Hashish-Eater; or, The Apocalypse of Evil." Evidently unknown to both Sterling and Smith, Bierce's own poem "Basilica" had anticipated, even if imperfectly, their own later achievement.

Nor should the achievement of Sterling and Smith in these particular poems of theirs be underestimated or overlooked. Both "A Wine of Wizardry" and "The Hashish-Eater" have a grandeur and a real greatness which are unique. Just as "The Testimony of the Suns" is in its own way the equal of Tennyson's "In Memoriam," so is "A Wine of Wizardry" in its own way the equal of Coleridge's "Kubla Khan" in English, or of Arthur Rimbaud's "Le Bateau ivre" in French. "The Hashish-Eater," as an epic narrative and as a study in cosmic-astronomic-mindedness, stands incomparably alone, a towering masterpiece of cosmic invention and imagination. In vision, in theory, and nominally in accomplishment, Bierce had prepared the way for both later poets through his essays and through his best poems.

As among his best and briefest poems we should consider the excellent and highly imaginative titles Bierce chose for his two volumes: *Shapes of Clay* and *Black Beetles in Amber*. Indeed, much of the best of his invention and mordant wit is to be found in his titles. For example, an early prose collection has the vivid and poetic title *Cobwebs from an Empty Skull*. For another example, "To Dog," constructed on the analogy of "To Man" (Bierce apparently detested dogkind as much as he did mankind). For yet a further example, "Oneiromancy" which, in terms of the love poem it entitles, signifies not only divination through dreams but also "O Near Romance, See."

Exclusive perhaps of the two early pieces, which are nonetheless effective, the poems in this selection reveal Bierce as an adroit and facile versifier. He is a master of the run-over line. His handling of rime, metre, consonance, assonance, etc., is assured and often ingenious. He is able to make his poetic statement move through difficult and demanding traditional forms with singular ease. He sometimes achieves some of his best effects—effects of power or of grim humor—simply through his punctuation: "Creation" especially furnishes a good example of this. Although his diction may seem somewhat old-fashioned today, and perhaps overall somewhat conventional, it also possesses here and there subtle little touches of originality. He has a good ear for colloquial speech, and he has a good eye for unexpected and homely detail, as well as a good instinct for the unexpected and homely resolution, usually presented at the end of a given poem in sharp contrast to what has preceded it. In many of his pieces both satirical and personal, he has anticipated the modern poetic temper at once ironical and colloquial. Although "Invocation" shows him as master of the grand manner and the solemn "tense" or tone (a manner and a tone with which much of present-day taste appears to have little sympathy), in most of his poems he simply uses his own conversational style, anticipating the same in contemporary modes of poetic expression. Perhaps not in terms of versification, but at least in terms of "a vision of doom," Bierce is quite a modern poet.

Compared to his better-known poet-contemporaries, and according to their test of sublimity or that of the purple patch, Bierce would hardly qualify as a poet at all, except perhaps on the basis of "Geotheos," "Invocation," and a few other pieces. Bierce often wrote and said that he was not a poet. Too many critics have taken him at his own word, and have examined his two volumes of verse with little diligence, perception, or appreciation. At least one commentator has found him to be a failure as a poet, basing that judgment (it must be admitted) on a very superficial consideration of Bierce's output in verse. Virtually none of his poems continue to appear in anthologies of American poetry, and he is rarely mentioned in American poetic surveys. Surprisingly enough, in *Our Singing Strength* (an outline of American poetry covering the period 1620—1930, and published by Coward-McCann, Inc., 1929), Alfred Kreymborg displays a true comprehension of Bierce's originality as a poet. According to Kreymborg, his poetry "deserves more notice than what it has received of posterity."

Apart from Kreymborg, however, most of Bierce's recognition as a poet has come largely from his fellow Californians, and most extensively from his own pupil George Sterling who himself reigned as a prince of poets on the West Coast for some twenty years before his death in 1926. Sterling paid homage to his master not only in a number of poetic tributes but also in his "Introduction" to the 1928 edition of "Invocation," and in his summary of Californian poetics, "The Poetry of the West Coast—California," published in Braithwaite's *Anthology of Magazine Verse for 1926*. In this latter volume Sterling has written of his master as follows: "Eminent as he was as a critic, narrator and satirist, Ambrose Bierce was equally distinguished in the writing of poetry. ... His 'Invocation to Liberty' is one of the noblest and most thoughtful poems in English literature, even as 'Another Way' is one of the tenderest."

"I'm no great bard," sings Bierce in the last line of "A Voluptuary." But, despite whatever he wrote or said to the contrary, he was a poet, possibly not a great one but surely a good one, and in some respects definitely superior to many of his contemporaries. In his best serious poems Bierce clearly anticipated and influenced two of California's greatest lyric poets, George Sterling and Clark Ashton Smith. Through Sterling he paved the way for Robinson Jeffers with *his* unique cosmic vision and his deliberate disregard of humanity. Thus, the line of general poetic descent runs from Edmund Spenser and the Elizabethans to William Blake and the English Romantics, and then to Tennyson, Poe, Swinburne, and Bierce, and at last to Sterling and Smith and Jeffers. The line of immediate poetic descent runs directly from Poe and Bierce to Sterling and Smith and Jeffers.

While there is less of the sardonic and often grimly playful sense of imagination in his verse over-all than what we find in his best and most characteristic prose fictions; yet many, if not most, of Bierce's best poems are unusually fantastic and macabre. Even those poems not overtly macabre Bierce seems to have written in the Valley of the Shadow of Death. The grim presence of Death stalks through most of his personal poems, even his love sonnets and other pieces. Bierce's verse at its best is austere, even angular, with an most provincial sparseness; rather like a corpse whose bones have been clean-picked by some thoughtful scavenger. As always, there is something harsh and unyielding, and even cold, about Bierce and his best work; a quality well-summarized by the contemporary science-fiction author Fritz Leiber in his phrase "Bierce, the Man with the Phallus of Ice."

For all of Bierce's own personal preference for a rich Spenserian or Shakespearian imagery in the poems of other poets—for the overflowing purple and gold of *The Arabian Nights*—the reader will find little such in Bierce's own poetic works. Instead, he will discover something different, an unique savor not found quite anywhere else. While we must agree with H. P. Lovecraft, speaking of Bierce in the monumental essay *Supernatural Horror in Literature*, that "the bulk of his artistic reputation must rest upon his grim and savage short stories," his best verse clearly deserves more attention and appreciation than what it has received to date. When *Black Beetles in Amber* and *Shapes of Clay* first appeared in 1892 and 1903, respectively, they were virtually ignored. When they reappeared in the *Collected Works*, they were virtually lost in the sheer bulk of that edition. Bierce would have done posterity a great service if he had gone through his output in verse and selected a hundred—or half a hundred—of his best poems for preservation, and simply allowed the remainder to rest uncollected. Since he did not do so, the present editor has attempted the task.

It is therefore all the more fitting that we make this appraisal or reappraisal of Bierce as a poet now on the one hundred and twelfth anniversary not merely of his first published work but, more specifically, of his first published poems. In the memoir "George Sterling—An Appreciation," first printed in *The Overland Monthly* for March 1927, Clark Ashton Smith has remarked that "Bierce, whose own fine qualities as a poet are mentioned with singular infrequency, was an almost infallible critic." It is hoped that the present selection from his best poems will help to call some notice to Bierce's "own fine qualities as a poet."

Sacramento, California
23 March 1979.

Clark Ashton Smith:
The Last of the Great Romantic Poets

The Coming Singer

The Veil before the mystery of things
    Shall stir for him with iris and with light.
    Chaos shall have no terror in his sight
Nor Earth a bond to chafe his urgent wings;
With sandals beaten from the crowns of kings
    Shall he tread down the altars of their night,
    And stand with Silence on her breathless height,
To hear what song the star of morning sings.

With perished beauty in his hands as clay,
    Shall he restore futurity its dream.
Behold! his feet shall take a heavenly way
    Of choric silver and of chanting fire,
Till in his hands unshapen planets gleam,
    'Mid murmurs from the Lion and the Lyre.

From *Beyond the Breakers and Other Poems*, by George Sterling. S. M. Robertson, San Francisco, 1914 (p. 24). This sonnet Sterling dedicated to Clark Ashton Smith but not officially in print, for obvious reasons.

CAVEAT LECTOR

The following review-essay is in large part an attempt to define the overall romance tradition from its beginnings in the Middle Ages on into our own time, and to demonstrate how Smith's own *oeuvre* occupies the principal place in that same tradition for the twentieth century. The essay assumes on the part of the reader some sophisticated knowledge of his prose fictions, most of these being (stylistically) extended poems in prose. These fantasies—somewhat in the nature of allegories, parables, or fables of emotional and psychological truth—represent an unique twentieth-century contribution to the romantic tradition that goes back at least all the way to the metrical romances of the twelfth and thirteenth centuries. Similar to the cycles of tales and legends revolving around King Arthur and Charlemagne, about half of Smith's prose fictions are cycles of tales laid in such imaginary worlds as Hyperborea, Atlantis, Averoigne, Zothique, Xiccarph, and other places. Not only these, but most of his short stories have the same general tone, character, and fictional ambiance of the original metrical romances. These short fictions represent the most serious and successful attempt to adjust the great tradition of romantic story-telling to the twentieth-century sensibility. In the following review-essay's final summary of Smith's unique poetic achievement, the statements are based upon an underlying corpus of meaning woven equally from Smith's poetry as well as from his prose. There is no conventional exposition of this in the text of the review-essay itself, and it is mentioned here only to explain what might otherwise appear as a curious and mysterious deficiency.

Clark Ashton Smith. *Selected Poems*. Pp., xx, 403. Arkham House, Sauk City, Wisconsin, November 1971. $10.00.

El Desdichado
The Disinherited

I am that dark, that disinherited,
That all dishonored prince of Aquitaine.
The star upon my scutcheon long hath fled,
A black sun on my lute doth yet remain.
—Gérard de Nerval.

(This quotation from Andrew Lang's translation, but not the title, appears on the dedication page of Ashton Smith's volume.)

The Last Romantic? The Last of the Great Romantic Poets? How can romanticism die? Is there not a new romanticism alive and well in the world of the 1960's as well as of the present early 1970's? Although we shall define romanticism in general and in specific later on in this essay-review, we must state here that the late Clark Ashton Smith *is* the Last of the Great Romantic Poets, and we mean this in terms of both the *older* romanticism and the *older* prosody. There will never again be any other poet quite like Smith. His own romanticism and his own prosody (which he received by due right of literary and cultural inheritance and in due chronological order), taken together, are the ultimate flowering (in both direct and indirect line of descent) of the great romantic-psychological-ethical-mythological-aesthetic synthesis effected by Edmund Spenser, the first great poet of the First Elizabethan Age. And this ultimate flowering, formed thus by the *oeuvre* of Clark Ashton Smith, derives especially from the American Romantic poet Edgar Allan Poe (and his French admirer and proselytizer Charles Pierre Baudelaire) on the one hand and on the other such English Romantic and Victorian poets as Keats, Coleridge, Shelley, Tennyson, and Swinburne. However, Smith's line of immediate poetic descent is from Ambrose Bierce, George Sterling, Nora May French, etc., that small company of Californians who preceded Smith's own entry into the literary sphere. But now let us return to the beginning of romanticism in (early) modern English, that is, to the encyclopaedic Master Spenser.

In the Poet's Corner of Westminster Abbey, rather centrally located in terms of that portion of the cathedral wall against which it adheres, there uprises the monument erected at the behest and expense of Anne, Countess of Dorset, in 1620, to mark the burial place of Edmund Spenser (1552?-1599). Although too often obscured, the fact remains that to the Elizabethans themselves Master Spenser was the supreme poet, — the supreme literary figure of the age, —the successor to the allegorical splendors of Geoffrey Chaucer, and for us the great Renaissance intermediary who stands betwixt Chaucer and Shakespeare, and betwixt the Middle Ages and (what we like to call) our modern times, and who saved us from too thorough a renascence, a fact most perceptively pointed out by C. S. Lewis.

In the last dozen years or so there have appeared at least two dozen book-length monographs on Spenser, besides a host of papers published in various and sundry scholarly journals, all of which have succeeded in rehabilitating the *critical* reputation of Spenser, who has accordingly once more been recognized as "the Prince of Poets in his tyme" (to quote from the inscription on Spenser's monument in Westminster Abbey mentioned just above). But this has not restored Spenser to the people— which could probably be done best now through a series of dramatic pageants—so that in a very curious and special sense the *oeuvre* of Edmund Spenser, especially in his greatest work, to wit, his idiosyncratic epic *The Faerie Queene*, has become for the average English-speaking reader the lost Atlantis of our older literature, the great "lost" classic of early modern English, the great "unknown quantity" of our early modern culture. It is nonetheless highly significant, symbolically speaking, that the

critical rehabilitation on behalf of the supreme poet of the Age of Elizabeth *the First*, has been effected in this the Age of Elizabeth *the Second*.

With what acclaim, with what éclat, with what universal excitement!—was the "New Poete" received (as he was then known)—when
he came in late 1589, in the company, and under the aegis, of Sir Walter
Raleigh, to the court of Queen Elizabeth to present her with the first
three books of *The Faerie Queene* (dedicated to that "most high, mighty,
and magnificent empresse"). Portions of the poem had circulated in MS.
in England at least during the late 1580's. Marlowe's early dramas, created
about the same time, contain some very significant "plagiarisms" from
Spenser's epic which Marlowe could only have made from the circulated
MS. or from holograph copies of the same but made by some other hand
than Spenser's. In January 1590 the first three of the projected twelve
books of *The Faerie Queene* were published.

Once the news had gone the rounds that the great English epic everyone had been expecting was now at hand, the general interest and enthusiasm in England (Spenser ordinarily lived in Ireland at this time)
could not have been greater than those caused by the news that a great
new continent, a completely hitherto-unknown world, a whole new cosmos of beauty and wonder, had just been discovered. *The Faerie Queene*
was thus instantly recognized as the prime cultural metaphor which
would explain to the Elizabethans themselves the meaning of their own
brave new world. As Tucker Brooke has well summed it up, writing on
the English Renaissance, "Nothing in Elizabethan literature, perhaps
nothing until Byron's time, equaled the over-night fame of the *Faerie
Queene*. Spenser became at once "the only living Homer" and the supreme literary celebrity of the age." But with the passage of time, this tremendous achievement, after being thoroughly subsumed into the oeuvre
of Spenser's literary posterity, became obscured, and fell into that curious
and reverent semi-oblivion reserved for certain great masterpieces, to be
honored but not to be understood especially well.

Then, closer to our own immediate time, since around 1900, more
or less coinciding with the death of Queen Victoria and with the inevitable decline of the British Empire, *The Faerie Queene* has fallen from the
common currency that it once enjoyed in the homes of English-speaking
families all over the world. (This statement, however extreme it might
appear at first, is perfectly true in regard to the homes of the more self-
consciously *cultured* English-speaking families, whether they formed part

of the British Empire or of the United States of America.) How rapidly have we forgotten that at one time Spenser's great myth—uniquely fusing as it does classical epic, medieval epic, medieval romance, and medieval allegory from the firm foundations of English and Continental Renaissance pastoralism—was one of the great family classics, together with the King James Bible and the complete works of Shakespeare, both of which it thus antedates. How rapidly have we forgotten that Spenser's great fairy tale—once universally accepted as the great *English* epic—was the great contemporary classic to Shakespeare and his fellow Elizabethans,—and for them their central cultural metaphor. Just as the King James Bible is the King's English, *The Faerie Queene* is the Queen's English, from which the former derives in direct historical and cultural flux (*culturally* the reign of Elizabeth I continued on into that of James I).

In the medieval sense of "scientia"—that is, "having knowledge"—*The Faerie Queene* is a huge science fantasy, supremely a work of the surrealistic imagination, supremely a work of speculative fiction. In the modern sense of "science" and "science-fiction"—especially as it applies to the modern science of psychology, the study of both *mind* and *behavior*—the metaphysical and psychological depths of Spenser and his "Elvish Queen" (as fellow scholar Gabriel Harvey once called it in a letter to the "New Poete") have been too little explored and charted. *Webster's Seventh New Collegiate Dictionary* (1963) gives as one definition of "science-fiction" the following: "literary fantasy including a scientific factor *as an essential orienting component*" (the reviewer's italics). Since *The Faerie Queene* is flatly intended on one level as an ethical primer—"The general end therefore of all the books is to fashion a gentleman or noble person in vertuous and gentle discipline"—this great epic poem has every cogent reason to be considered under the aegis of science-fiction. And this perspective throws a new and acutely relevant spotlight on Spenser's great poem.

Indeed, although the fact is often overlooked, *The Faerie Queene* is not only the first great fantasy in modern English, having crystallized many of what are now familiar conceptions of faërie and of the light fantastic but it includes moreover—amidst its vast spectrum of tone (word, vibration, energy) and subject—the first delineation of the weird and the darkly fantastic (that is, as we understand such today) in terms of our early modern English. Indeed, properly defined (in terms of a conscious work of fiction, qua fiction), *The Faerie Queene* not only represents the first conscious "olden" style in modern English—or for that matter the first conscious style, or rather spectrum of styles, as we comprehend such today, and as Master Spenser utilizes such in a completely artistically finished manner—but this epic poem also represents the first "Romanticism" (as understood in the original sense of the Arthurian and Carolingian romances) as well as the first great "Gothic" fiction in modern English, in the most inclusive definition of those expressions. *In modern English*, let us emphasize yet again, even if in early modern English.

Indeed, despite all the continuing and widely-publicized protestations of Messieurs Lin Carter and Lyon Sprague de Camp (particularly uttered time and time again by Lin Carter in his present pivotal role of chief editorial consultant for the paperback Ballantine Adult Fantasy Library, in introduction after introduction of volume after volume), it was *not* William Morris and his prose-poetic romances created in the late 1800's that inaugurated the genre of "heroic fantasy" or "weird heroic fantasy" *in modern English*. Shakespeare's own master and the supreme literary celebrity of his time, to wit, Edmund Spenser, had already done this in his greatest work *The Faerie Queene*—amongst many another accomplishment.

Indeed, as a matter of sober historiographical record as well as by virtue of both *The Shepheardes Calender* (1579) and *The Faerie Queene* (1590, 1596, 1609)—at least—the following statements of fact may be recapitulated here. Spenser was the supreme literary celebrity of his own time. *The Faerie Queene* was to the Elizabethans themselves their supreme work of art. Spenser's poetry proved a great and beneficent influence—a source of delight, vision, wisdom, and technical instruction—to virtually all the other great English poets coming after him (starting with Christopher Marlowe and William Shakespeare and continuing on through the English Romantic and Victorian poets). This same poetry, whether directly or indirectly, has continued to be a great and beneficent influence on virtually all of literature in modern English even into our own century. Spenser is in essence the very father—the very fountainhead—of literature, poetry, and fantasy in modern English.

And it is nicely symptomatic of the general cultural decline of our times (in the classical sense of culture), as well as of the lack of precise historical discrimination,—quite independent of their liking or disliking *The Faerie Queene*,—that Messieurs Lyon Sprague de Camp and Lin Carter, being in the forefront of the contemporary movement in fantasy and science-fiction, can thus consistently ignore or depreciate the presence and precise achievement of Edmund Spenser. It certainly does not say much for *their* general perspicacity and intelligence and aesthetic awareness when Spenser's known admirers have included such a diverse lot as Sir Philip Sidney, Sir Walter Raleigh, Kit Marlowe, Will Shakespeare, Sir Kenelm Digby, John Milton, John Dryden, Alexander Pope, Sir Walter Scott, John Keats, Samuel Taylor Coleridge, Percy Bysshe Shelley, Alfred Lord Tennyson, Virginia Wolfe, T. S. Eliot, F. Scott Fitzgerald, Louis MacNeice, and C. S. Lewis, amongst many other persons whether American or English or European.

Now that we have sufficiently established the *fact* of Spenser's great *seminal* influence and his great *cultural* significance, we shall proceed to the principal matter at hand, a discussion of the poetic achievement of the late Californian poet and fantaisiste Clark Ashton Smith, especially as revealed in his recently and posthumously published volume of *Selected Poems*. Before we present some of the salient features of his life, and before we discuss his unique poetic achievement, we must state here the one basic similarity betwixt Spenser and Smith: as poets they are both mythopoeic or mythopoetic, that is, myth-creating; and they are supremely such in a way that no other single poet is; and they both create their own world or worlds as well as their own myths or mythologies. And, supremely, both poets are moralists: both are deeply concerned with the ethical consequences of any particular entity's decision as to where it wants to go. In Spenser's case the majority of his protagonists choose to go down the road marked "Dexter" and in Smith's case most of his protagonists decide to enter the highway marked "Sinister"—and thus the dual vision of both men mutually complements that of the other. There are many other similarities as well as dissimilarities betwixt Spenser and Smith, but these would require a special study of book length, and will not be particularized here.

Also, before we can proceed any further, we must state here another important correlative: what Spenser was to romanticism and pure poetry in early modern English (until the advent of Smith, Spenser was the unique begetter of pure poetry and pure fantasy in English), Smith is the same to romanticism and pure poetry and fantasy in the English of the twentieth century. Smith is in a certain unique and special sense the dead-end of certain characteristics and tendencies and directions first put into motion in modern English by Edmund Spenser. Smith's over-all *oeuvre* (both his poems and his tales) is a great and monumental summing-up of a super-special kind. And some understanding of this achievement is pivotal to us and our spiritually disoriented age. But now, the basic facts of Smith's life and career, and we quote verbatim from the back inner flap of the dust-jacket that wraps around the present volume of *Selected Poems*.

Almost sixty years have now passed since August 1912 when the San Francisco daily newspapers then extant—the *Call*, the *Chronicle*, the *Examiner*, and the *Bulletin*—officially discovered and acclaimed the poetic genius of Clark Ashton Smith. In the uproar that followed, none other than Ambrose Bierce and George Sterling defended the then 19-year-old poet from 'the lions of reaction" (to use Bierce's own phrase).

Born on January 13, 1893, in Long Valley, just outside Auburn, the seat of Placer County,—in the heart of an old gold-mining and fruit-growing area,—Clark Ashton Smith lived all his life in his native California apart from a few visits to the neighboring state of Nevada. In 1954 he married Carol Jones Dorman, and moved to Pacific Grove on the Monterey Peninsula, where he died on August 14, 1961.

After attending the local grammar school, Smith educated himself, and was widely published both here and abroad during his lifetime. He started writing fiction at the age of eleven and poetry at the age of thirteen. From 1911 to 1928 he devoted himself almost completely to poetry, but from 1929 to 1937 he became one of the principal contributors to *Weird Tales*. However, from 1938 until his death Smith was once again primarily the poet. During this last period of time he wrote little more than a dozen short stories. In addition to his distinguished verse and prose he created fantastic paintings, drawings, and sculptures, which he exhibited in Auburn, Sacramento, San Francisco, the Monterey area, and other places.

Called variously *The Bard of Auburn*, *The Poet of Science Fiction*, *The Last Romantic*, *The Last Great Romantic Poet*, etc., Smith was (and is) the leading representative of the West Coast or California Romantics, that small company of romanticists which included Ambrose Bierce, George Sterling, and Nora May French, among others. Although he has never lacked for distinguished recognition, it is only today that Smith, thanks to paperback and foreign publication, is beginning to know that wider public which his earliest admirers first predicted for him more than half a century ago.

Let us now consider the volume at hand—but first in terms of its physical makeup and of its over-all contents. First of all, the book is the same omnibus size as the omnibus editions that reprint the Lovecraft fiction or the omnibus volumes that contain the Lovecraft *Selected Letters*.

The jacket design by Gary Gore is handsome, with a certain austere sumptuousness about it, and admirably restrained. On the back of the dust-jacket is a portrait of Smith by one "Natalae Bixby Carter" and dated "1946." Ten dollars may seem like a lot of money for a book even in this day and age of inflated prices, but the buyer is receiving more than ten dollars' worth of poetry and imagination for his money; the book contains just over 400 pages. The text was edited, and the dust-jacket blurbs were prepared, by Donald Sidney-Fryer, the author of the present review-essay. Over-all, just what does the book contain? Again, we quote verbatim, this time from the front flap of the dust-jacket.

> This first omnibus collection of the poems of Clark Ashton Smith contains over five hundred selections and reproduces entire volumes of verse long out of print as well as complete cycles of poems never before published in their entirety. From September 1944 to December 1949, in one way or another, Smith was involved in the production of this book, revising old poems, creating new ones, and painstakingly preparing the manuscript himself during a time when he was having serious eye trouble.

> Preceded by a notable appreciation of Smith's unique imaginative genius by Benjamin DeCasseres, this book contains the following sections: *The Star-Treader and Other Poems, Additional Early Poems, Ebony and Crystal* (including the final version of *The Hashish-Eater*), *Sandalwood, Translations and Paraphrases, Incantations, Experiments in Haiku, Satires and Travesties, The Jasmine Girdle,* and *The Hill of Dionysus.*

> The distinguished admirers of Smith's Muse have been legion, and have included George Sterling, Ambrose Bierce, Samuel Loveman, David Warren Ryder, Edwin Markham, David Starr Jordan, Senator James Duval Phelan, Vachel Lindsay, Ina Donna Coolbrith, and Albert M. Bender, among others. One of the most verbal and enthusiastic of Smith's early fans was H. P. Lovecraft who wrote to Smith (on a card postmarked February 9, 1923, Salem, Massachusetts): "*Ebony and Crystal* is titanic, cyclopean, marvelous!" He then went on to state: "*The Hashish-Eater* is the greatest imaginative poem in English literature."

> Inspired by the example of his poetic mentor George Sterling and his two greatest poems *The Testimony of the Suns* (1903) and *A Wine of Wizardry* (1907),—long before the early science-fiction and fantasy magazines,—Clark Ashton Smith was creating an unique type of fantasy and science-fiction in verse whose metaphysical and psychological depths have yet to be discovered, charted, and explored.

Here, within the pages of this long-deferred publication, is not only the bulk of Clark Ashton Smith's output in verse, here is testimony indeed to an imagination that has no peer in our time.

At the request of Smith's then publishers August Derleth and Donald Wandrei, the volume now called the *Selected Poems* was originally projected as *The Hashish-Eater and Other Poems*, and as a collection of all Smith's poems whether in verse or in prose, and to be published in the latter 1940's. Subsequently the idea of also including his poems in prose was abandoned. (All of these were compiled, edited, and introduced in 1964 by Donald Sidney-Fryer—that is, all but one, *The Mortuary*, not yet discovered by Roy Squires at that time amongst the Smith Papers—and were published under the title *Poems in Prose* by Arkham House in 1965.) Smith changed the title *The Hashish-Eater and Other Poems* to *Collected Poems*, and then finally to the present *Selected Poems*. Arkham House received the MS. in December 1949, when the postwar market for fantasy and science-fiction books had already started to fall; and because of the expense involved in producing such a large volume, the owner-editor of Arkham House, to wit, August Derleth, shelved the MS. indefinitely. However, 1951 and 1958 saw Arkham House publish (rather as a stopgap for the indefinitely shelved *Selected Poems*) the two slender collections *The Dark Chateau* and *Spells and Philtres*, respectively; the which, while they rank as the poet's first and second Arkham House *published* books of poetry, are technically his second and third books of poetry prepared for Arkham House. About half of *The Dark Chateau* is taken from the *Selected Poems*, and most of *Spells and Philtres* is also taken from the same omnibus collection.

Thus, what was technically Smith's first Arkham House book of poetry had to wait virtually twenty-one years for publication (November 1971). Meanwhile both the poet and his publisher had passed away, Smith on 14 August 1961, and Derleth on 4 July 1971, the latter while the *Selected Poems* had already been set up in type. [Please see note at end in regard to *Songs and Sonnets Atlantean* by Donald Sidney-Fryer.] The page-proofs had been entrusted by August Derleth for editing to Donald Sidney-Fryer during early June and thus before the owner-editor of Arkham House died. Smith in preparing the typescript of the *Selected Poems* had used a very poor quality of paper (most likely for economic reasons— Smith's funds during the 1940's were so meagre that he had to go back to fruit-picking and fruit-packing to supplement his income—hot, miserable, underpaid labor), and the typewriter ribbons he used became very worn, with the end result that both words and marks of punctuation were not always perfectly legible for the typesetter. Added to these factors was the *age* of the MS. The printer's MS. was thus in such a state of disrepair that the text could not be checked and corrected until the book was finally set up in type. The editing, constantly checked against Mr. Sidney-Fryer's own microfilm of the original MS. (technically typescript), was done directly on the page proofs, during the months of June and July 1971. The editor of the text prepared the dust-jacket material during August 1971. Thus, the published text of the *Selected Poems* is not perfect, but the number of gross errors, editorial and otherwise, is minimal. Actually both Arkham House and the Collegiate Press (The George Banta Publishing Company, Menasha, Wisconsin) are to be congratulated on achieving as good a production as they have. The typesetter or typesetters working for The Collegiate Press did not have an easy job getting this book into shape. The editing both by the press and by the present textual editor appears to be careful, even if not perfect. It would be churlish to complain that the typesetter or typesetters did not use all the corrections made by the present textual editor; suffice it to say that they seem to have caught the few inadvertent errors perpetrated by the editor himself! After all, one must give future scholars something to complain about and correct!

Those Smithophiles who know the first editions of his early collections will note that some of the early poems have been altered, a few have been dropped, and quite a bit of new material has been added from the poetic productivity of the same period. To cite some random examples from *Ebony and Crystal*: *The Mirrors of Beauty* has a new octave, *The Mummy* has been dropped, and *Sea-Memory* (although of the same general time) has never seen publication before. *The Hashish-Eater; or, The Apocalypse of Evil*, originally in ten sections, or verse paragraphs, Smith has recast into twelve. Apart from some minor changes in wording here and there, this telescoped and highly compressed epic remains the same; however, the few real changes, whether in word or format, are important to the serious student of Smith's poetry and should not be glossed over. Smith may have recast this his greatest single poem into *twelve* sections for the excellent reason of correlating them to the traditionally desired and demanded *twelve* "books" of the classic epic, as well as for reasons of arcane numerology. There are many other such minor changes but they alter Smith's earliest major period of poetical creativity (1911–1928) relatively little.

The changes are neither for the better nor the worse: they are merely different and equally valid as the original readings. However, they serve as evidence that Smith did not merely *copy* most of his older, that is, *earlier*, poems into the MS.; he quite actively had to re-live the full intellectual, emotional, imaginative, and aesthetic life of the poems in passing them before his careful scrutiny. That is, he had to *re-test* all his older spells; this, coupled with the serious and annoying eye trouble he was experiencing during the latter 1940's, added up to a great deal of work and strain and sustained aspiration. Since he also had to return to mundane work during the hot Californian summers, is it any wonder that Smith created relatively few stories during this particular period of time? Well should Smith have felt that a mountain was lifted from his shoulders when he finally sent the completed MS. off to Derleth in December 1949—a consummation indeed! The *Selected Poems* in its production *both* as a MS. *and* as a published book has passed then through some extraordinary "ordeals" as it were. But, the book is here at last, a cause for celebration.

Thus a majority of the over 700 poems in verse by Smith known to have been extant at the time of his death [the figure is now known to be about or over one thousand], the over 500 selections in this magnificent collection of collections add up surely to an extraordinary amount of living and poeticizing. But more than that, what can one say in general about these poems, *qua* poems? For the problem here is that there is too much to say, too much to notice, too much to mention. Where does one begin in the face of such encyclopaedic abundance?! For our first clue we must turn to the dedication-page, where we learn that the *Selected Poems* is dedicated "To Eric and Madelynne"—that is, Eric Barker and Madelynne Greene, Mrs. Eric Barker (deceased February 1970).

Underneath this dedication Smith quotes the first four lines of the sonnet *El Desdichado* (*The Disinherited*) by the great French Romantic poet Gérard de Nerval (and the author of the classic translation of Goethe's *Faust* in French), given here in the older translation by the scholar Andrew Lang. These lines are very important to a full understanding of just what Smith self-consciously has defined as his own unique poetic and historical role. And so let us quote his partial quotation in full; and then let us correlate this poetry with his life and career.

I am that dark, that disinherited,
That all dishonored prince of Aquitaine.
The star upon my scutcheon long hath fled,
A black sun on my lute doth yet remain.
—Gérard de Nerval.

Apart from the favorable reception afforded him as a poet of the general San Francisco literary scene, and apart from the specialized reputation he gained as one of the leading contributors to *Weird Tales* (and as one of the first and best authors to be preserved in hardcovers by Arkham House), Smith clearly felt that he had not received the larger recognition that was his rightful due, at least during his lifetime., as the chief representative of romance for the twentieth century; as truly "the emperor of dreams" for his own time. Especially during the last decade of his life he felt himself to be a "prophet without honor" in his own America. Of course, however much he may have hoped and even suspected his time might eventually come, he had no sure way of *knowing* that he would start to come into his own during the early 1970's. Because of both foreign and paperback publication, it is only today that his work is acquiring that larger circulation and readership which alone can lead to that larger recognition proper to an artist of Smith's calibre. He *knew* that he had rendered an unique and all-important service as a creative artist to the high cause and calling of romance, particularly during a time when the whole concept of romance and romanticism had fallen into contempt, neglect, and near-oblivion. The large-scale discrediting of romance, imagination, and (above all) wonder during (at least) the 1940's, the 1950's, and the 1960's has almost no precedent or previous parallel in the history of intellectualism.

Smith had not only remained faithful to the older verities during a time of great psychic danger and disintegration (when there were relatively few worshippers at the olden shrine) but more than that he had actually expanded the basis for their appreciation and understanding by extrapolating the same verities into the cosmic immensitudes. And in this aspect of his over-all artistic achievement (in spite of the apparent but attractive "old-fashioned" quality of much of his output) his work is more modern and futuristic than many of the most highly acclaimed but narrowly existential "modern" writers. In his particular province Smith's mind and mentality were of Einsteinian dimensions. Building firmly upon his Late Victorian heritage (synonymous here with Late Romantic)—

which, unlike so many moderns, he did not find necessary to deny in order to be himself—he created a physically small but highly concentrated *oeuvre* that has, ultimately, its principle roots in medieval romance and the lyricism of the troubadour-poets (who *sang* their poems whilst accompanying themselves on any of a variety of instruments, especially the medieval lute, plucking the strings with a metal plectrum or a large goose quill). So, there is an undeniable poignance to Smith's own self-conscious recognition that he was "dark" (id est, "unknown") and "disinherited" and "all dishonored"—and that the star upon his "scutcheon" or shield had long agone disappeared, leaving only "a black sun" upon his "lute," that is, his métier as poet. It must be emphasized here that Smith keenly felt the full weight of the Late Romantic inheritance and responsibility, an inheritance that goes at least all the way back to the twelfth century, to the beginnings of romance and modern poetry.

We must now define romance and romanticism both in general and in specific terms. We shall do this primarily through a brief discussion of romance's historical origins and development. However, we must first define the sense of wonder, since this so-called sixth sense is basic to romance and romanticism. "To wonder is to perceive with reverence and love," Sam Keen cogently observes in his brilliant monograph *Apology for Wonder* (page 5, Harper & Row, New York, etc., 1969), which the present reviewer heartily recommends to *everyone* but especially to the lover and student of both imaginative art and literature.

In this monograph (see particularly pages 30 and 31) Mr. Keen makes some important statements about wonder and the wonder-experience which are pertinent not only to romance and romanticism in general but, especially and specifically, to Smith's own genus of romanticism. We quote these relevant statements in full.

> It is important to insist upon the priority of wonder, because otherwise we lose the basis of ethics. If there is nothing wonderful, nothing that is inviolable and sacred (in principle), then ethics can be based only upon a balance of terror.
>
> Wonder is the foundation of values because a wondering encounter is the basis of a nonutilitarian approach to things and persons. In wonder we perceive the other as inexhaustible, as the locus of meanings which are only revealed as we cease to be dominated by the impulse to utilize and possess the other and learn to rejoice in its presence. It is when we cease making imperialistic claims over objects and persons

(structurally similar to neurotic claims) and allow them to be what they are in their own right, that we touch the inviolable strangeness—which is their sacredness. The intuition of the inviolability or sacredness of objects and persons invests them with the character of mystery—which means merely that they stand out in stark outline as themselves and cannot be reshaped to fit our desires and needs.

Language comes near failing when we try to describe the new density and significance that objects and persons take on when encountered in wonder. This is because, in one sense, wonder adds nothing to our knowledge *about* an object. It is rather that the object comes into focus and is respected and relished in its otherness.

The imagery of apocalypse and resurrection is integral to the experience of wonder. Every wonder-event involves a cognitive crucifixion; it disrupts the system of meanings that secures the identity of the ego. To wonder is to die to the self, to cease imposing categories, and to surrender the self to the object. Such a risk is taken only because there is the promise of a resurrection of meaning. To accept the meaning which is given by the object is to find the world redeemed from drabness or staleness. Refreshment or resurrection leaves us reborn but unable to articulate an adequate testimony. There is nothing new to say about the world ("a rose is a rose is a rose")—only a new ability to celebrate its density and meaning.

Keeping the essence of the above quotations in mind, let us continue into our definition or discussion of romance and romanticism. And this brings us to the romance culture of the twelfth century and onward, *the* beginning of romance in our modern sense.

The triumph of grace and beauty in twelfth-century France and elsewhere indicates a period of true renaissance. Speaking on the rise of romance in his monograph *Epic and Romance* (first published by MacMillan, London, 1896, etc.), W. P. Ker states authoritatively that "The change of fashion in the twelfth century is as momentous and far-reaching as that to which the name "Renaissance" is generally applied." The code and Age of Chivalry grew with the songs of the minstrels in the 1000's and 1100's (a development somewhat corresponding to the beginning of the Crusades, which the Christians undertook from the end of the eleventh century to the end of the thirteenth). Troubadours and trouvéres, the cult of the lady fair and of the Virgin Mary, the corresponding cult of the ideal and of the beautiful; music, poetry, and song; had everything to do with the creation of a new attitude, a new way of life, and the form of literature called *romance*, from *romanz*, the language of the common people. It was then that romance gave the first shape to what we have termed earlier as the "older romanticism" and the "older prosody": the upper classes (with a great deal of help from the lower ones) extrapolated an ideal world of romance from their actual world of romance, their courts and courtly life and courtly love. Although the genre of the *roman* grew out of medieval epics and the so-called romanticized epics, and although always narrated at this time in verse, it proved nonetheless (to paraphrase W. P. Ker) a true revolution from which all later narrative and fiction derive in some degree, that is, in the Western World.

The very form of both medieval epic and romance had immediate origins in medieval song and lyric poetry. The creation and use of a prosody different in kind and in degree from that of the ancient Greeks and Romans, plus the invention of rime, guaranteed not only a highly musical poetry but a poetic music such as had never existed before. The English word *rime* itself is Middle English taken from Old French, and is used here to include terminal rime, internal rime, alliteration, consonance, assonance, etc. They fitted the lines of poetry directly to the musical cadences. Minstrels or *jongleurs* accompanied their singing of the verses by playing on a variety of instruments: for example, the little medieval fiddle, the *vielle*; the little medieval harp with metal strings; the lute with four strings or four pairs of strings. The *vielle* was played with its peculiar arched bow which would drone out those long bass notes during which the lines of poetry would be sung or recited (a technique at once monotonous and hypnotic). The lute (derived from the classical Arabian string instrument, the oud) at this time was plucked not with the fingertips but with a metal plectrum or a large goose quill, thus giving the tone of the lute a stronger and sharper resonance. The *jongleurs* and the minstrels would beat the rhythm out with their foot. Since the lute was to become singularly important to song and poetry during the Renaissance, it may be mentioned here that the instrument had come into Europe probably sometime in the twelfth century, but this was only one part of the over-all Oriental influence that happened as a result of the First Crusade.

The wandering minstrels went everywhere and, singing their songs of love and adventure, had access to all spheres of society. In the north of France, the land of the *langue d'oïl*, the trouvères were creating their medieval epics, their *chansons de geste* and *chansons d'histoire*. This school of poet-musicians was to flourish from the eleventh to the fourteenth century. In the south of France, the land of the *langue d'oc*, as well as in the north of Italy, and the northeast of Spain; the troubadours, often of knightly class, were creating that lyric poetry which in terms of form and musicality paved the way for some of the greatest lyricism of the Renaissance and of the nineteenth century. This class of lyric poets and poet-musicians was to flourish from the eleventh through the thirteenth century.

As just one example of how much the form of considerably later poems and songs was influenced by the prosody of this time, we need only to consider the ballad and the ballade: one, a fixed form of folk song; the other, a fixed form of this "older prosody." The ballade (used extensively later on by the French Renaissance poets and then even later by some of the British poets of the late nineteenth century before being largely abandoned by our modern age) was originally a sung and danced narrative poem, usually concerned with heroic deeds or legends. The ballad (similar to the ballade in some respects but distinct from it in others) meant originally a dance danced while singing or a song sung while dancing, and evolved into the narrative in verse with strongly marked rhythm, still to this day often sung. Many, but not all ballads, use the old ballad stanza. The ballad stanza's alternating lines of eight and six syllables found their origin in a dance at harvest or sowing time: a line of males singing the eight-syllable line and dancing to its rhythm, and a line of females opposite them singing the six-syllable line and likewise dancing to its rhythm. From the original ballads there evolved the epic ballad of later times, a sung and often danced narrative of love and adventure.

The musical style and background of this medieval lyric poetry was the vigorous tradition of the Gregorian chant. For further details of this lyric-poetry-with-music of the romance culture, the interested reader should consult pages 96 through 121 of *Music in Western Civilization* by the musicologist Paul-Henry Lang, first published by W. W. Norton, Inc., New York, 1941.

Needless to say, both the knightly class and the class of troubadour-poets reappear in the metrical romances themselves in idealized form. More than that, the medieval epic and the medieval romance had their metrical origin in the forms of medieval lyric poetry; and thus romance began in song and in the glorification both *from* and *of* song. The poet evolved from the musician, and most of the poets were musicians. Is it surprising then that later romantic poetry (i.e., the poetry of the Renaissance and of the nineteenth century) embodies a highly *musical* style?

Evolving thus from both song and the medieval epic, the medieval romance eventually replaced the older narrative form. At this time, epic concerned itself with statement, not with motivation or explanation. But in romance the story required comment, the actions required explanation. As W. P. Ker defines the difference between the two genres; "Whatever Epic may mean, it implies some weight and solidity; Romance means nothing, if it does not contain some notion of mystery and fantasy." Romance is thus distinguished from epic and religious narrative (both of which preceded romance) by its taste for the fantastic, the marvellous, the improbable, the wholly ideal; by its virtual exemption from any didacticism; and by the fact that it recounts fictions for their own sake. Romance is virtually synonymous with adventure; romantic love, the exploits of chivalry, a quest or a voyage to far places, etc., are all staples of romance.

The earliest romances were in verse, the later ones in prose. Typically written in ten-syllable lines, the medieval epic was made up of assonanced stanzas, or *laisses*, with an irregular ballad-like structure. From these ten-syllable lines with assonance rimes of the *chansons de geste* and *chansons d'histoire* it was an easy step to the riming octosyllabic couplets of the medieval romances of which there were several principal types: *romans d'antiquité*, *romans d'aventure*, *romans courtois*, etc.

Everything of the original romance culture found reflection in the romances, usually in transmuted form, often greatly exaggerated: courtly life, courtly love, troubadour lyricism, battles, tournaments, etc., reappeared in the medieval romances in the same way as they had appeared in the medieval epics as well as in the romanticized epics. But what sharply distinguished romance from epic and the other forms was the "matter"—and King Arthur had everything to do with this. In 1155 *Li Romanz de Brut*—Wace's translation into French of the *Historia Regum Britanniae* by Geoffrey of Monmouth (1137)—opened up to the writers of romance a whole new world for their imaginative development: to wit, that of Britain, of King Arthur's court, and of the Celtic *féerie*. Almost all of the romances by Chrestien de Troyes are set in Arthur's fabulous realm, but the behavior of his characters moves in accordance with the code of courtly life and love, rather than what we might suppose to be the ethics of fairyland. The historical Arthur became thus transformed into another Charlemagne with an imperial court and a vast realm.

However, the distinction for having first introduced Arthur into any romance whatsoever, lies with Marie de France in whose Breton *lais* we have for the first time a love element that can be termed "romantic" and understood in our own modern sense of the romantic, a love element that Marie elaborates in a lavishly sentimental and idealistic way. The human male who loves an immortal, usually having to renounce the ideal or to perish thereby unless he does,—this theme was to re-emerge in poignant form with the Romantic Ballet of the early nineteenth century. An archetypal story of this type may be found in Smith's own extended prose-poem *The White Sybil*. And from the purely sentimental interest developed by these early romances there descends such a (degenerate) twentieth-century form as *True Romance* Magazine.

In the early romances (such as the *romans d'antiquité*) we find many of the standard features of later romance writing whether in verse or in prose: for example, the elaborate set pieces describing in great detail the characters, buildings, clothing, tents, gardens, etc., with whom or wherein the action takes place. Some of these romances must perforce be singled out by name.

The celebrated *Roman d'Alexandre* began as a *roman d'antiquité* but evolved into a most fantastic *roman d'aventure*. It was begun by Albéric de Briançon, then supplemented by diverse other author-poets, and then put into final shape by Alexandre de Bernai. This romance became especially popular for the exotic and marvellous elements in the third *branche* (laid in India) composed by Lambert le Tort: for example, the *cynocephali*, the springs of rejuvenation, Alexander's magic ship drawn through the air by griffins, the flower-maidens growing in a forest (as extra-ordinary as *The Flower-Women* by Clark Ashton Smith), etc. Another important feature: instead of being cast in riming octosyllabic couplets, the *Roman d'Alexandre* moves in riming twelve-syllable couplets, and these *alexandrins* (or alexandrines, in English, named thus after Alexandre le Grand), became the classic line for French prosody during the Renaissance and after, on into the early twentieth century.

Then during the 1200's the first great dream-allegory appeared, *Le roman de la rose* by Guillaume de Lorris (but finished considerably later by Jean de Meung). The influence this opus had on later romance writing but especially on allegorized romances (yet another class of the over-all genre) proved enormous, and the final classic form this influence assumed was Spenser's own epic-romance-allegory *The Faerie Queene*.

The metrical romance held sway all over Europe from the twelfth through the fourteenth century, and the purely prose romance then had its own vogue from the fourteenth century onward. In the fifteenth century the *Orlando Innamorato* by Matteo Boiardo and the *Orlando Furioso* by Ludovico Ariosto were based on the later fusion of the Charlemagne legends with the spirit and apparatus of the Arthurian prose romances; on the face of it these poems are obviously metrical romances, but in place of the simpler riming couplets we now have the ottava rima (eight lines of iambic pentameter, riming abababcc). All of this poetic fusion, plus any and all allegorical exegetical tradition, would soon flow into the Spenserian matrix of *The Faerie Queene*.

Meanwhile in England Arthurian romance attained definitive form in English prose for the English themselves with Sir Thomas Malory's prose romaunt *Le Morte d'Arthur*, published by William Caxton in 1485. By Spenser's time Arthur, in addition to being a magisterial figure of romance, had become a patriotic institution for the English themselves, and the English rulers claimed monarchical descent from him. Although Arthur is only one of many strands woven into and throughout the complicated tissue or tapestry of *The Faerie Queen*, it was inevitable that Spenser would have used him in some central mythopoeic capacity in his great epic-romance-allegory. However, Spenser wittily chooses to depict Arthur's exploits in "Faeryland" (a realm even more ambiguous and arbitrary than the fairyland depicted in the first romances)—that is, when Arthur was Prince and before he became the quasi-historical King.

The unique fusion of *The Faerie Queene* sums up the whole history and development of romance before and into the First Elizabethan Age but returns it to romance's authentic provenience by setting this polyphony of tales in the first complete dream-world. Whatever Spenser may have borrowed from other poems and poets, his "Faerie lond" in its final synthesis owes everything to his own syncretistic genius. *The Faerie Queene* is a dream-poem in the manner of the French medieval allegory *The Romaunt of the Rose* by Messieurs Guillaume de Lorris and Jean de Meung; this last poem (as noted above) inspired many similar allegorical romances, and was one of the first major works in literature deliberately to create an imaginary place as a background for a narrative (in the manner of Plato's Atlantis). But whereas the *Romaunt* merely creates an imaginary garden,

The Faerie Queene creates an entire land, an entire world, an entire cosmos of the imagination, and one which somehow reflects the world we know. Indeed, *The Faerie Queene* is a symbolic model of the cosmos constructed in "narrow verse." All of this is in itself a great feat of creative originality with Spenser. Also, whereas the *Romaunt* primarily concerns itself with love courtly and otherwise, the scope of Spenser's epic-poem is enormous: it attempts to reflect all of life, and not just human life.

From the Arthurian and Carolingian mythopoetic cycles of tales and legends, Spenser undoubtedly derived the idea of the cyclic structure and cyclic movement of *The Faerie Queene*. Not only does Spenser's use of the Arthur Mythos return romance to its authentic provenience but the Spenserian stanza likewise does the same and, in addition, sums up the whole complex fusion of music and poetry first crystallized by the troubadour-poets of the twelfth century. The Spenserian stanza is the most involved stanza that romance has ever evolved. Its complicated system of interweaving rimes (eight lines of iambic pentameter with the ninth line as an alexandrine) makes it more difficult than the ottava rima in Italian. (The Spenserian stanza rimes ababbcbcc.) This is all the more remarkable when one considers that the comparative paucity of rime words in English makes it a most difficult language to rime, and Italian—like the romance languages in general—abounds in easy rime words. The whole elaborate medieval tradition of poetry with music finds a perfect expression in the Spenserian stanza: for just as medieval epic and medieval romance had a lyric foundation, each Spenserian stanza is a lyric in itself.

Further, the effect obtained by the typical Spenserian stanza is all part of the cyclic/circular ambiance created by Spenser for *The Faerie Queene*: a deliberate, usually slow-paced music as of a planet moving in its processional-like orbit around the sun; a music that purposes to reflect the order and the harmony of the cosmos, or (more aptly) the music of the spheres; in the same way that the great circular maze which is the over-all structure of *The Faerie Queene*, purposes to reflect the great circular maze of the macrocosmos, of the stars and planets moving in their predestined orbits through the heavens.

Within the proportions established by Spenser's own selective symbology (which is nonetheless encyclopaedic), *The Faerie Queene* sums up, in its all-inclusive metaphor, the entire medieval intellectual and aesthetic tradition, and it looks both backward and forward in the manner of the Roman god Janus. It is the final epic-romance-allegory, the final great medieval poem but created during the Renaissance. It passed on both the spirit and the letter of romance, and it has never been reduced to just one interpretation or one level of interpretation, a most signal feat for a work of the imagination almost four hundred years old, considering the extraordinary changes in taste and fashion since the First Elizabethan Age. *The Faerie Queene* bequeathed incalculable riches and lore to all the poets and writers who came after, beginning with Marlowe and Shakespeare.

Something of the olden trouvères and troubadour-poets lingered on in the great lutenist composers of the Renaissance. Many of them, especially in England, created lute songs (both words and music) and would sing them themselves whilst plucking the lute. They also set to music (both for singing and playing) many lyrics written by Ben Jonson, Shakespeare, and other contemporary poets. John Dowland, Thomas Pilkington, Thomas Campion, etc., must be numbered amongst the distinctive "troubadour-poets" of their day, that "Golden Age of the English lute." At the court of France, subsequent to the death of Spenser, during the reign of Louis XIII (especially during the regency of his mother Marie de Médicis, 1610–1617), the Renaissance lute culminated in the remarkable virtuosity of "Monsieur" Ballard, pupil of Adrien Le Roy. The "Spenser of the Lute," Robert Ballard (1575?-1650?) is to the lute music of the late Renaissance what Spenser is to the metaphysics and poetry of the same time. He taught the young Louis XIII how to play the lute, not an easy instrument to learn (amongst other lutenist monarchs may be mentioned the "Faerie Queene" herself, Elizabeth I of England), and he created some of the earliest French ballet music extant. Monsieur Ballard accompanied virtually all the great court ceremonies and celebrations for the period 1610–1617, and had two books of lute tablature published in 1611 and 1614, respectively. His brilliant improvisations paved the way for the later early-baroque lute, and then fell into almost complete oblivion until rediscovered in the twentieth century.

While Renaissance Italy and Spain had been creating new pastoral never-never lands, the later native Spanish prose romances of approximately the same time—the first and most famous, the *Amadis de Gaula*, was later parodied by Cervantes in his own great romance *Don Quixote*—influenced (from the late fifteenth century on into the sixteenth) the early modern French "novels" of the sixteenth and the early seventeenth century, especially such an extremely long pastoral romance as *L'Astrée* by Honoré d'Urfé. However, with the rise of the neo-classical doctrines promulgated during the reign of Louis XIV, romance disappeared and modern analytical (or "realistic") fiction began. In seventeenth-century France, romance (the product of the courtly life of the twelfth century) paradoxically was no longer considered a "noble" genre.

However, in England, to John Milton (the most important literary figure after Spenser and Shakespeare, and far more influenced by Spenser than Shakespeare), romance remained an honored concept, with Edmund Spenser as the high priest. Later, inaugurated by Horace Walpole's prose fiction *The Castle of Otranto*, the early Gothic romances paved the way for the great romances of Sir Walter Scott, whose influence on Alexandre Dumas *père* and on other writers must not be underestimated. Among important later romance writers may be mentioned A. Conan Doyle, Jules Verne, H. G. Wells, Sir H. Rider Haggard, F. Marion Crawford, Joseph Conrad, Arthur Machen, Edgar Rice Burroughs, Talbot Mundy, Robert Ervin Howard, etc. (this list of names does not pretend to any kind of completeness). Arthur Machen—the high priest of Late Romantic prose fiction, in some respects even more so than Conrad—stands virtually by himself in his profound symbolic and psychological understanding of the moral and ethical responsibilities that had become inherent in modern romance; and this is actually very much in the tradition of Spenser and *The Faerie Queene*. Considerably before Hermann Hesse, Machen pioneered in the romance of alienation, especially as crystallized by his magisterial novel *The Hill of Dreams*.

The indebtedness to the Spenserian music and magic on the part of the English Romantic and Victorian poets cannot be emphasized enough. The Spenserian poets of the eighteenth century, the English Romantic and Victorian poets, and their counterparts in America, all introduced something new into the romance of poetry. The contributions of the American Romantic poet Edgar Allan Poe (1809–1849) and the English Late Romantic poet Algernon Charles Swinburne (1837–1909) proved especially potent; significantly both were outstanding critics and theoreticians. However, it remained for Clark Ashton Smith to innovate a new romantic fusion in his *oeuvre* as cogent and complete as that forming *The Faerie Queene*. In its own turn, Smith's poetry in verse and in prose (and this includes most of his prose-poetic fictions) represents an over-all romantic fusion for the twentieth century as total and unique as that of *The Faerie Queene* for the First Elizabethan Age. Significantly, Smith extrapolates romance into the realms of cosmic-astronomic space: those "other worlds" of fantasy and science-fiction are now to be found on the further shores of time and space.

Thus, romance has now traveled from the Age of Chivalry to the Age of Space. The romance culture of the twelfth century indicates a period of true renaissance and gave birth to its most characteristic art form in the creation of romance as a genre of literature, as a philosophy, and as a way of life. Beginning with the Breton *lais* of Marie de France and the more ambitious romances of Chrestien de Troyes, and with the introduction of King Arthur into the world of romance, the first great romance synthesis came into being. Then in turn the later fusion of the Charlemagne legends with the spirit and apparatus of the Arthurian prose romances, especially as embodied in the Italian epic-romance poems (with their use of the ottava rima), culminated (together with much else, as we have seen) in the ultimate medieval epic-romance-allegory *The Faerie Queene* with its distinctive Spenserian stanza. Thus after that of the Continental Renaissance, the English Renaissance—that is, the First Elizabethan Age—represents the final flowering of the over-all Renaissance. With the Arthur Mythos thus fructifying still the romantic matrix, *The Faerie Queene* symbolizes the second great romance synthesis. The influence this great poem has had on later poets and writers has proven enormous, but the specific romance influence that it has had, after becoming diffused, resurfaced again in the eighteenth-century school of Spenserian poets and then in the English Romantic and Victorian poets. In the tradition of Edgar Allan Poe on the one hand and then in that of Algernon Charles Swinburne on the other (Swinburne must be at the least the Last of the Great British Romantic Poets); but based immediately on the cosmic-astronomic and romantic-imaginative foundation provided by the poetry of George Sterling; the over-all *oeuvre* of Clark Ashton Smith represents the third great romance synthesis. The place occupied by his poetry in this *oeuvre* is ultimately more important (in certain respects) than that occupied by his prose fictions. Out of a total of five decades given to his mature creativity, Smith devoted some four decades to the creation of his poetry, with only one decade given to fiction-writing; accordingly the main regard of critical evaluation must focus on his poetry. Thus, the place occupied in this third great romance synthesis by Smith's monumental volume of *Selected Poems* is nothing less than paramount. It is portentous that this volume should have appeared in this the Second Elizabethan Age—at a time to which some brave and adventurous people have applied, tentatively and hopefully, the name of Neo-Renaissance.

However, in this last new romance synthesis there is one new major ingredient, or body of ingredients, that did not exist in any of the previous romance syntheses, to wit, the Oriental influence added by the translations of *The Arabian Nights* and their numerous imitations. *The Thousand and One Nights* reached Europe in the early 1700's, translated into French by Antoine Galland. William Beckford's remarkable prose romance *The History of the Caliph Vathek* (which represents the subsequent distillation of this new spirit in French and English letters), in addition to the later Sir Richard Francis Burton translation of *The Arabian Nights*, profoundly influenced the young Smith, especially as revealed in his poetry for the period 1911–1928.

The title page of *The Star-Treader and Other Poems*, the first section of the *Selected Poems*, quotes two stanzas from that poet who, more than any other (apart from Edgar Allan Poe), had the greatest immediate influence on the young Smith. From 1903 until his death late in 1926, George Sterling (born 1869) reigned as a prince of poets on the West Coast. One of California's greatest lyric poets, he is second only to his own protégé Clark Ashton Smith. His line of general poetic descent is from the English Romantic and Victorian poets, especially Keats, Tennyson, and Swinburne; his line of immediate poetic descent is from Ambrose Bierce, who performed the role of mentor and theoretician to the over-all group of the West Coast or California Romantics. It may be mentioned here that, in the tradition of Edgar Allan Poe, the American and now largely underground school of "pure poetry" has been peculiarly associated with Bierce, directly or indirectly.

It was largely because of Bierce's influence that Sterling received the recognition in San Francisco that his remarkable talents deserved. Recognition in San Francisco was recognition in the entire west of the United States: from Bering Strait (the northwestern-most projection of North America) down to Tierra del Fuego (the southernmost projection of South America), San Francisco was universally recognized as *the* City. Sterling became the leading figure of the second Golden Age of literary and artistic California (the first Golden Age consisted of writers like Mark Twain, Bret Harte, Joaquin Miller, etc.)—but more than that he was the very embodiment of San Francisco's older Bohemia that more or less ended with his death in late 1926. Because of Sterling, Carmel-by-the-Sea on the Monterey

Peninsula became the artists' colony that it is to this day. Well known and loved and respected, he was a marvelously generous friend who encouraged many writers and poets. Like the present-day San Francisco columnist Herb Caen (who has taken over Sterling's own unofficial poet-laureateship as it were), he knew both great and small, and like Herb Caen served as a vital link between the rich and the poor, between the official San Francisco and its unofficial Bohemia, that is, between the Establishment and the Counterculture of that earlier period.

During the resplendent Panama-Pacific International Exposition of 1915, the official fair buildings proudly bore engraved quotations not only from Shakespeare, Milton, Dante, Firdausi, etc., but especially from San Francisco's own dearly beloved poet laureate George Sterling. And it was largely because of Sterling's influence that the young Smith received the recognition in San Francisco and elsewhere that his genius clearly deserved. The elder poet performed untiringly the role of poetic salesman for his young poetic brother whether with editors or whether with other but better known poets or whether with U.S. Senators! On at least one occasion, when he was due to read from his own works to a distinguished group of poets and celebrities in New York City, Sterling read instead from the poetry of the young Smith. The figurative Cloak of Elijah that Bierce consciously passed on to his protégé, Sterling in his turn passed on to his own protégé. His unceasing activity on the young Smith's behalf shall always reflect with great honor upon the elder poet.

These are the two stanzas that appear on the title page of *The Star-Treader and Other Poems*:

> Eternity! thine awful hands
> Shall blot the Lion from our skies,
> And build thy dark for future eyes
> Where now illumed Orion stands....
>
> A fleeting moment, to thy sight,
> Lamp of thine altar Alphard burns;
> Aldebaran to dusk returns,
> And Betelgeuse is stone and night.
>   George Sterling.

These are from *The Testimony of the Suns* (first published in book form in 1903), which Sterling created just after the turn of the century. It is his single greatest poem. Its new and powerful cosmic-astronomic perspective fascinated and inspired the young Smith, who virtually memorized the entire poem (no mean feat as it is a long one) by dint of endless rereading and study. However, Smith had first discovered Sterling at the age of fourteen through *The Cosmopolitan* for September 1907 when it published (for the first time anywhere) *A Wine of Wizardry* (but first published in book form in 1909). Earlier in 1906 Smith had just discovered the poems and poetic theories of Edgar Allan Poe. Now he discovered Sterling's second single greatest poem together with the strong and trenchant poetic theories of Ambrose Bierce as embodied in the essay *A Poet and His Poem* published along with the Sterling opus. Further poetic theorizing appeared in the essay *An Insurrection of the Peasantry* published in *The Cosmopolitan* for December 1907, wherein Bierce adroitly defended Sterling from adverse criticism. The poem itself Bierce ranked with Coleridge's fragment *Kubla Khan* (which he considered the single most perfect poem in the English language), a judgment more than shared by Smith. Indeed, echoes from *A Wine of Wizardry* and from Sterling's poetry in general resound throughout Smith's *oeuvre*. One quotation from this magisterial and imaginative poem will begin to show the similarity betwixt Sterling and Smith.

> Anear on orange sands,
> With prows of bronze the sea-stained galleys rest,
> And swarthy mariners from alien strands
> Stare at the red horizon, for their eyes
> Behold a beacon burn on evening skies,
> As fed with sanguine oils at touch of night.
> Forth from that pharos-flame a radiance flies,
> To spill in vinous gleams on ruddy decks;
> And overside, when leap the startled waves
> And crimson bubbles rise from battle-wrecks,
> Unresting hydras wrought of bloody light
> Dip to the ocean's phosphorescent caves.

This colorful tableau of the evening beach with the ships and sailors is very much like a scene from one of Smith's own tales of Zothique. But more than that, note Sterling's technique in the rest of the passage where, after having established a concrete scene as his firm point of reference, he only half-reveals his further marvels and wonders. Why "the startled waves" and "the crimson bubbles" arising "from the battle-wrecks," And what of the "unresting hydras" that "dip to the ocean's phosphorescent caves"? What then is the connection between the sailors and the beacon? And what is that which the "radiance" from the beacon awakens, or stirs to movement, in the ocean's depths? This kind of imaginative "teaser" is not only a trademark of this particular poem or of Sterling's poetry in general (although to a lesser extent) but we find it again and again in Smith's own work whether in verse or in prose.

Both poets appear to be saying through this type of device, "Look! Look around you! For everything that you know or that you think you know, there is always something that you don't know, can't know, shall never know. In the end all that you can know is mystery. You are a mystery, made for mysteries, and surrounded by mysteries."

However, Sterling is probably at his best in his sententious and orotund sonnets wherein his genius finds a rare formal and imaginative perfection. The following selection *The Night of Gods* is from *Three Sonnets on Oblivion* included by Sterling in his second collection *A Wine of Wizardry*, etc.— and can serve as an excellent example of how Sterling's own music and magic influenced, and continued on into, the young poet's own work.

> Their mouths have drunken the eternal wine—
>   The draught that Baal in oblivion sips.
>   Unseen about their courts the adder slips,
> Unheard the sucklings of the leopard whine;
>
> The toad has found a resting place divine
>   And bloats in stupor between Ammon's lips.
>   O Carthage and the unreturning ships,
> The fallen Pinnacle, the shifting Sign!
>
> Lo! when I hear from voiceless court and fane
>   Time's adoration of Eternity—
>   The cry of kingdoms past and gods undone—
> I stand as one whose feet at noontide gain
>   A lonely shore; who feels his soul set free,
>   And hears the blind sea chanting to the sun.

The young Smith became especially well acquainted with Sterling's first three collections, all published by the San Francisco bookseller and publisher A. M. Robertson: *The Testimony of the Suns and Other Poems*

(1903), *A Wine of Wizardry and Other Poems* (1909), and *The House of Orchids and Other Poems* (1911). There are not only many echoes of Sterling's poetry resonating throughout Smith's own work, but much of Smith's early mature poetry is an active extrapolation and development of imaginative concepts first found in Sterling—some of these hardly more than suggestions on the part of the elder poet—as the following passage from the narrative poem in heroic couplets *Duandon* (included in *The House of Orchids* etc.) will show:

> Then, wave to wave in deeper anthems roared,
> And realm by realm, the belted sunset soared,
> As tho' a city of the Titans burned
> In lands below the sea-line, undiscerned,
> Till desolation touched it, zone by zone,
> Its splendors gone, like jewels turned to stone,
> And sad with evening sang the ocean-choirs,
> Domed by the stars' imperishable fires.

From "a city of the Titans" in Sterling's line above, we pass to the sonnet *The City of the Titans* from the section *Additional Early Poems* (some of these were created about the same time as *The Star-Treader and Other Poems,* 1911–1912). Note how Smith develops and deepens the elder poet's concept so that it becomes even more imaginative and metaphysical.

> I saw a city in a lonely land:
> Foursquare, it fronted upon gulfs of fire;
> Behind, the night of Erebus hung entire;
> And deserts bloomed or glimmered on each hand.
>
> Sunken it seemed, past any star or sun,
> Yet strong with bastion, proud with tower and dome;
> An archetypal, Titan-builded Rome,
> Dread, thunder-named, the seat of gods foredone.
>
> Outreaching time, beyond destruction based,
> Immensely piled upon the prostrate waste
> And cinctured with insuperable deeps,
>
> The city dreamed in darkness evermore,
> Pregnant with crypts of terrible strange lore
> And doom-fraught arsenals in lampless keeps.

The few quotations from Sterling's poetry that we have cited here in reference to Smith's own verse, will serve to demonstrate not only the similarity of their poetic *music* (much heavier and more deliberate than Swinburne's) but specifically the similarity of their *melody*, a very Late Romantic, post-Swinburnian *melos*, as remarkable and variegated as Spenser's own melody in *The Shepheardes Calender* or *The Faerie Queene*. Indeed, Spenser's melody is the closest to their own that can be found,— yet another indication that what Spenser was to the romantic tradition in early modern English, Sterling and Smith are the same to the same tradition in terms of more recent developments in modern English.

In the next major phase of Smith's poetic evolution, to wit, *Ebony and Crystal* (whose composition covers the years 1912–1922), we see Smith extrapolating his basic premises and concepts even further, to the point of quite self-conscious definition. The science-fiction writer Fritz Leiber in his pivotal essay on H. P. Lovecraft *A Literary Copernicus* (included in the second volume of Lovecraft miscellanea, to wit, *Something About Cats*, Arkham House, 1949) particularized (insightfully and succinctly) Lovecraft's own pioneering achievement in fiction as extending the focus and the background of the supernatural story into the cosmic-astronomic immensitudes. Bierce once prophesied to Sterling that he would be "the poet of the skies"—but Smith, even more than Sterling, has extended both the focus and the background of poetry into the same areas.

As noted earlier, Smith specifically extrapolates romance into the realms of cosmic-astronomic space: those "other worlds" of fantasy and science-fiction are now to be found either deep in the sea of stars or on the further shores of time and space. A perfect example of this (as well as a supernal lyric in its own right) is *Beyond the Great Wall* whereby we may observe Smith as the cosmic troubadour into which he has indubitably matured.

> Beyond the far Cathayan wall,
> A thousand leagues athwart the sky,
> The scarlet stars and mornings die,
> The gilded moons and sunsets fall.
>
> Across the sulphur-colored sands
> With bales of silk the camels fare,
> Harnessed with vermeil and with vair,
> Into the blue and burning lands.

And ah, the song the drivers sing
To while the desert leagues away—
A song they sang in old Cathay
Ere youth had left the eldest king,

Ere love and beauty both grew old
And wonder and romance were flown
On irised wings to worlds unknown,
To stars of undiscovered gold.

And I their alien words would know,
And follow past the lonely wall
Where gilded moons and sunsets fall,
As in a song of long ago.

What a sense of continuity, and yet at the same time what a feeling of almost unbearable nostalgia and poignance, in such lines as "A song they sang in old Cathay / Ere youth had left the eldest king, / Ere love and beauty both grew old / And wonder and romance were flown / On irised wings to worlds unknown, / To stars of undiscovered gold." Note, also, how in this especial poem Smith (and this is very characteristic of his emotional ambiance) seesaws betwixt the past and the future on the fulcrum of a dissatisfying and frustrating present.

But the height of Smith's rhapsodically impassioned emotion is more often attained when he sings of death, especially the death of beauty, one of his primary themes (as it was one of Poe's). Through such a lyric confrontation he makes us realize the beauty of death, and its especial wonder and marvel. A perfect example of this rhapsodically impassioned feeling appears in *Chant of Autumn*, an extraordinary lyric in its own right.

Like the voice of a golden star,
Heard from afar,
Perishing beauty calls
Out of the mist and rain;
Like the song of a silver wind
When the night is blind,
Murmuring music falls
Never to rise again.

Voice of the leaves that die,
Whisper and sigh
Of ruinous gardens waning,
Rose by ungathered rose!
Dolor of pines immortal
That guard the portal
Of a lonely mead retaining
Blossoms that no man knows!

Voices of love and the autumn sun,
In my heart ye are one!
Fairer the petals that fall,
Dearer the beauty that dies,
And the pyres of autumn burning,
Than a thousand springs returning....
O, perishing loves that call
In my heart and the hollow skies!

In the notable appreciation of Smith's unique imaginative genius by Benjamin DeCasseres, to wit, *Clark Ashton Smith: Emperor of Shadows*, which precedes the "selected poems" (what irony in that "selected"!) DeCasseres notes the difficulty in quoting from Smith; for the full impact of Smith's genius is not to be found in ten or twelve or fifty "perfect poems" nor in one hundred or two hundred or five hundred "great lines" but in the totality of his vision. So that the best introduction to that vision can only be found in the totality of the present volume. There is much that could be said about Smith's next major phase of development after *Ebony and Crystal*, that is, *Sandalwood* (whose composition covers the years 1923–1925); and then about the subsequent masterful *Translations and Paraphrases*; and then *Incantations*; and then Smith's unique *Experiments in Haiku*; and then the often uproarious and outrageous *Satires and Travesties*. There is simply too much to quote, and too much to say; as Smith himself once noted, Art is long but criticism is longer-winded. Indeed! But of one thing we can assure the prospective buyer: there are gorgeous adventures everywhere in these *Selected Poems*. Smith, it must be noted here emphatically, is the last major poet in whose lyric effusions the sense of adventure strikes the dominant note, and this almost unceasingly.

After adventuring far and wide, through kalpas of time and infinities of space, Smith comes home to the supreme adventure, the supreme enchantment, love. And so the *Selected Poems* closes with two cycles of love poems: *The Jasmine Girdle* (created circa 1927–1929), inspired by Smith's great friendship with Genevieve K. Sully (deceased March 1970), and *The Hill of Dionysus* (created circa 1938–1946), inspired by his great friendship with the poet Eric Barker and the dancer Madelynne Greene, that is, Mrs. Eric Barker (deceased February 1970). The final poem in the final section, that is, the final poem in the entire book, is the sonnet *Avowal*, at once classic, romantic, futuristic, and modern. In this "little song" or *sonetto*—whilst invoking infinity and eternity in his characteristic manner— Smith bids farewell to us with such a cunningly creative stricture: whatever the future may hold for us, it will all prove in vain if the ancient sense of wonder and romance is not restored.

> Whatever alien fruits and changeling faces
> And pleasances of mutable perfume
> The flambeaux of the senses shall illume
> Amid the night-furled labyrinthine spaces,
> In lives to be, in unestablished places,
> All, all were vain as the rock-raveled spume
> If no strange close restore the Paphian bloom,
> No path return the moon-shod maenad's paces.
>
> Yea, for the lover of lost pagan things,
> No vintage grown in islands unascended
> Shall quite supplant the old Bacchantic urn,
> No mouth that new, Canopic suns make splendid
> Content the mouth of sealed rememberings
> Where still the nymph's uncleaving kisses burn.

After Smith had posted the printer's MS. of the *Selected Poems* off to Arkham House in December 1949, the poetic creativity begun circa 1938 and sustained throughout the decade of the 1940's continued on into the early 1950's. We have already noted that about half of *The Dark Chateau* (published December 1951) is taken from the *Selected Poems*; but the other half of the book (which has not yet seen republication) contains quite a number of outstanding lyrics, especially the opening selection *Amithaine*. Herein beauty and romance and wonder have built them an impregnable fortress on the further shores of the cosmos, and the poem itself becomes an ultimate statement of romance for romance. The poet and the reader become one with those "dream-established sovereignties / Whose princes wage immortal wars / For beauty with the bale-red stars." If ever lyric were a talismanic touchstone, it is *Amithaine*.

Who hath seen the towers of Amithaine
Swan-throated rising from the main
Whose tides to some remoter moon
Flow in a fadeless afternoon?....
Who bath seen the towers of Amithaine
Shall sleep, and dream of them again.

On falcon banners never furled,
Beyond the marches of the world,
They blazon forth the heraldries
Of dream-established sovereignties
Whose princes wage immortal wars
For beauty with the bale-red stars.
Amid the courts of Amithaine
The broken iris rears again
Restored from gardens youth hath known;
With strains from ruinous viols flown,
The legends tell in Amithaine
Of her that is its chatelaine.

Dreamer, beware! in her wild eyes
Full many a sunken sunset lies,
And gazing, you shall find perchance
The fallen kingdoms of romance,
And past the bourns of north and south
Follow the roses of her mouth.

The trumpets blare in Amithaine
For paladins that once again
Ride forth to ghostly, glamorous wars
Against the doom-preparing stars.
Dreamer, awake!... but I remain
To ride with them in Amithaine.

Who hath seen the towers of Amithaine
Swan-throated rising from the main

Whose tides to some remorter moon
Flow in a fadeless afternoon?...
Who hath seen the towers of Amithaine
Shall sleep, and dream of them again.

What then is the unique poetic achievement of Clark Ashton Smith? Let us try to define and summarize it here before we close. Whereas most modern poetry under the guidance of poets like Ezra Pound and T. S. Eliot has followed a course in reaction *against* the old-fashioned and aesthetic romantic tradition, Smith's own tradition of poetry has been a logical *continuation* of that same tradition. There may be other poets of the twentieth century who use the older forms but they are not romantics in the full-blown sense that Smith is. In Smith's *oeuvre* the substance and the form go tightly together. In sheer sensuous musicality alone, his poetry stands virtually by itself in our century, and is fully equal to Spenser's in super-melodiousness. By virtue of his new substance and perspective, and by virtue of his *melodic* renovation, it may be said of Smith that he has renewed the older prosody, that prosody descended—through all its historical evolutions—from the troubadours and trouvères. Smith is the nyctaloptic trouvère whose lute can sing "We have seen the black suns / Pouring forth the night." He is the cosmic troubadour who can claim with perfect justification that "The star upon my scutcheon long hath fled, / A black sun on my lute doth yet remain." Smith's poetry is valuable not only for itself, *qua* poetry, but—infinitely more than that—as the record of a great mind. Smith is thus the chief representative of romance for the twentieth century, truly "the emperor of dreams" for his own time.

Smith's occupation as mythopoeic poet gave him many advantages, merely in regard to style; many of the older poetic usages that he continues (the true second person singular, the older accretions of poetic diction, the melodiousness of tone, etc.) may be seen as the natural stylistic correlative of a sensitive myth-making statement; and he uses them in both his poetry and his prose. His unique cosmic-mindedness (or, more properly, cosmic-astronomic-mindedness, to distinguish it from other types of cosmic-mindedness in these days of "cosmic consciousness") resulted in an encyclopaedic abundance and fertility—how different from the tedious, barren, and unimaginative quality of most modern poetry! His keen sense of artistic discipline and propriety helped him to create an unique polyphony or symphonism of imagery, and to supplement the large poetic vocabulary he had inherited with further old, unusual, and supremely beautiful words, resulting in an almost unsurpassed purity of language. Smith never betrayed the elder worship of beauty passed down to him; and he maintained his sense of wonder and mystery throughout his *oeuvre*, from first to last. His analogies, metaphors, and similes are among the most brilliant to be found in poetic literature: he made use—in both poetry and prose—of some of the most liberated association to be encountered anywhere, and yet this free association is always amazingly precise. For the most part, the metaphysical and psychological depths of his own poetry and prose have really still to be discovered, charted, and explored. His own expansive and humane existentialism makes one realize just how narrow most other types of existentialism really are (a notable exception to this statement being the inspired existentialism of Victor Frankel, the author of "logotherapy"). An Einstein of fantasy and science-fiction in verse, Smith ranks as *the* poet laureate of the imagination.

Smith's poetry in verse and in prose, including his extended prose-poems, represents an over-all romantic fusion for the twentieth century—that is, for the beginning of the Age of Space—as total and unique as that of *The Faerie Queene* for the First Elizabethan Age. Whereas the work of the romancers of the twelfth and thirteenth centuries represents the first great romance synthesis; and whereas *The Faerie Queene* of Edmund Spenser symbolizes the second great romance synthesis; the over-all *oeuvre* of Clark Ashton Smith similarly represents the third great romance synthesis. He has added his own most potent contribution—to wit, the romance of death—to this third great romance synthesis, a synthesis which will play, we feel, a singularly effective role in restoring to "futurity its dream" (to quote from Sterling's own tribute to the young Smith). As a poet and prophet of doom, death, and destruction, Smith has made his most generous gift to the romance tradition by formalizing the romance of alienation, of death, of disintegration. Thus with new fusions and transfusions, he has renewed the archetypal themes and patterns of both poetry and romance. In the manner of Spenser's own great epic-romance-allegory, Smith's entire literary *oeuvre* is a great and monumental summing-up of romance, an encyclopaedical concentrate that, Janus-like, looks both backward to antiquity and forward to futurity.

If Smith is in a certain unique and special sense the dead-end of certain characteristics and tendencies and directions first put into motion in modern English by Edmund Spenser, then he is only thus so that, phoenix-like, his own inheritance of beauty and romance and wonder can be reborn in a renewed and quintessential form, and can thus be handed over to posterity, that is, futurity. In the tradition of such masters of pure poetry as Edgar Allan Poe and Algernon Charles Swinburne—and under the theoretical aegis of Ambrose Bierce—such Late Romantic poets as George Sterling and Clark Ashton Smith have signally helped to safeguard the *flamme sacrée* of romanticism and idealism into an age which, until recently, has proven markedly hostile to such aesthetic manifestations. As an unique creative personality bridging two centuries, Smith (1893–1961) is one with such other last great romantics as the Anglo-Welsh mystic Arthur Machen (1863–1947), the American painter Maxfield Parrish (1870–1966), and the Austrian (post-Mahlerian) symphonist Franz Schmidt (1874–1939). Because of the official hostility of the current intellectual and critical establishment to full-blown romanticism, romance has gone underground in a very special way, like the paganism forced to go underground by the growth and intolerance of Christianity. As the final period of the satyr's farewell speech to Gérard de Venteillon (in Smith's own tale *The End of the Story*) expresses it, "But still, in the cryptic caverns of earth, in places far underground, like the hell your priests have fabled, there dwells the pagan loveliness, there cry the pagan ecstasies." However, this submergence of romance and romanticism underground has only rendered their over-all essence more potent than ever. Smith's legacy is in part, like that of Maxfield Parrish or that of Franz Schmidt, a farewell to the older romanticism and a transition to a modern as well as a future romanticism.

As such phenomena as the Renaissance Pleasure Faire, the Society for Creative Anachronism, the San Francisco popular-music scene indicate; we live at a time of Renaissance or Neo-Renaissance. We are witnessing the birth of a new romantic age. Poetry in our own time has returned to the popular singers and music groups. The olden troubadours and trouvères have re-emerged in the new poets: the folk musicians, the rock musicians, the folk-rock musicians, etc., of the new-style popular music.

Such singers and rock groups as Bob Dylan, Donovan, Judy Collins, Joni Mitchell, Cathy Marion, the Beatles, Pink Floyd, Neil Young, Tim Buckley, Tom Pacheco, etc., fulfill the same function in our "global village" as the troubadour-poets did in the Western European world of the twelfth and thirteenth centuries; indeed, they *are* the new troubadour-poets. In his fourth collection, *Beyond the Breakers and Other Poems* (A. M. Robertson, San Francisco, 1914), Sterling included an inspiring tribute to the young Smith as a cosmic troubadour—this is the sonnet *The Coming Singer*—but as the title itself indicates, it is also an oblique prophecy of the recent developments in popular music. As the new romanticism in popular song and in the other arts grows and develops and deepens, Smith's poetry with its planturous lyricism, its extravagant musicality (harking back as it does to the beginnings of romance in the twelfth century), could form a far more logical link between the old and the new than anything written by Ezra Pound, T. S. Eliot, etc.

Whilst he has had some undoubted influence on fantasy and science-fiction writers (e.g., Ray Bradbury, Harlan Ellison, Donald Wandrei, etc.), Smith will exercise an increasing influence as his reading public expands. This influence (which will follow) will take place principally among the alert and imaginative young people who read fantasy and science-fiction, and who listen *intelligently* to the new troubadour-poets. Romanticism and modernism are not by necessity or by definition incompatible! A sense of wonder and marvel and mystery still endures. As the refrain in one of Tom Pacheco's remarkable science-fiction folk-ballads puts it,

> "Come on through,
> Come on through,
> The stars are waiting there for you."

Smith in a larger sense has been almost as completely ignored so far in his own twentieth century as William Blake (1757–1827) was in his own eighteenth century. And yet it is only in the second half of the twentieth century that Blake himself is really *beginning* to meet with some sort of adequate understanding, over one hundred and fifty years after his death! One of the most potent factors in Smith's being largely unknown (apart from a strong cult of readers and admirers who serve to keep an interest in him very much alive) is the tyranny of the East Coast literary and intellectual establishment over whom or what in literature becomes known: most of the communication-media, the mass-market popular magazines, and the major publishing houses are situated in New York City or the same general area. If the East Coast intellectual establishment wish to ignore someone or something, they can do so very easily. This establishment will tolerate and acclaim only those artists and writers and poets who pander to their own knowledge and perspective and general frame of reference. Like Poe and Lovecraft, Smith will probably have to go abroad to garner some larger, and less provincial, critical recognition; and this foreign recognition will eventually echo back to Smith's own native land. Yes, quite possibly someday the world will catch up with Clark Ashton Smith—even the mainstream literary critics!

Thus it is both appropriate and ironic that at last we should have the music of the *Selected Poems* by Clark Ashton Smith finally resounding in these the early 1970's with all their burden of ecological disaster and catastrophe—with all their prognostications of doom—as though it were the sunset of time for twentieth-century man. This Smithian music is a music of extra-ordinary force and power like the music that "rings to the bronze horizon" in the final period of the poet's early prose-poem *The Memnons of the Night* (created December 18th, 1915, and first collected in *Ebony and Crystal*). And so with this final quotation let us bid a fare-thee-well to the Last of the Great Romantic Poets.

> Only at eve,
> when the west is like a brazen furnace,
> and the far-off mountains smoulder like ruddy gold
> in the depth of the heated heavens—
> only at eve,
> when the east grows infinite and vague,
> and the shadows of the waste are one
> with the increasing shadow of night—
> then, and then only, from the sullen throats of stone,
> a music rings to the bronze horizon—
> a strong, a sombre music, strange and sonorous,
> like the singing of black stars,
> or a litany of gods that invoke oblivion;
> a music that thrills the desert to its heart of adamant,
> and trembles in the granite of forgotten tombs,
> till the last echoes of its jubilation,
> terrible as the trumpets of doom,
> are one with the black silence of infinity.

NOTES

Apropos of the preceding review-essay, the author is indebted to Dr. Ibid Massachusetts Andor, the premier Atlantologist in the world of today, for permission to use as the author's own, verbatim, many statements and phrases from the *Introduction* and *Notes* provided by Dr. Andor for the author's own first book *Songs and Sonnets Atlantean.*

* * *

EL DESDICHADO
THE DISINHERITED

I am that dark, that disinherited,
That all dishonored prince of Aquitaine.
The star upon my scutcheon long hash fled,
A black sun on my lute doth yet remain.
         – Gérard de Nerval.

The "bardic lute" or the "Orphic lute" or any other such phrase has become such a poetic cliché that it is pertinent here to present briefly the historical reality behind such a figure of speech, and just how the lute has actually been used by poet-musicians. The historical evolution of the lute in Western Europe (to say nothing of its evolution in Africa, the Middle East, and the Far East) is a long and fascinating one: this is a brief summary.

The so-called classical lute—which is derived from the oud, the Arabian lute—has a wooden belly, and was introduced into Europe probably sometime during the twelfth century, and was definitely established on the musical scene by the thirteenth. This was only one part of the over-all Oriental influence that came about as a result of the First Crusade and then the later Crusades. However, there already existed as early as the 900's and 1000's, and possibly even earlier, some kind of lute in Europe, including the early membrane or parchment bellied lute (of which we have records from the tenth century onward). There was especially the mandola, or mandora, a smaller and simpler wooden-bellied lute, whose development more or less parallels that of the classical lute. This mandora was particularly popular during the 1100's and the 1200's with the *jongleurs* who used it to accompany their singing, or their reciting of verses, in the manner of the troubadours. However, the oud-originated classical lute became popular with the troubadours during the 1200's. Like the oud, the medieval lute was rounder and smaller than the pair-shaped instrument of the Renaissance. The earliest lutes of all kinds appear to have had four single strings.

Like the guitar, the popular lute—that is, the mandola—usually has the tuning-head as a vertical continuation of the neck. The classical lute usually has the tuning-head bent more or less at a right angle to the neck. The mandolin, mandoline, or mandolino, is descended from the medieval mandola, and like the medieval lute is played with a plectrum and has four pairs of strings. We are discussing in this brief summary the short-necked lute, and can only mention the continuing existence of the long-necked lute from antiquity: the modern banjo with its long neck and four or five strings—whose parchment belly makes it similar to the early European membrane-bellied but short-necked lute—is descended from the ancient Egyptian lute with two or three strings.

At least as popular as the mandora with the *jongleurs* was the little medieval fiddle, the *vielle*, with its three strings. Whereas the *vielle* was hollow, and possessed a pleasing tone; its plebian counterpart, the rebec—also with three strings—was made from a solid piece of wood, and produced a loud, rather grating sound, which nonetheless made them excellent in dance-music ensembles. Rebecs became the instrument of street fiddlers, and have survived into our own century. The three strings of both rebec and vielle appear to have been tuned like the three lower strings of the modern violin, although there were other tunings.

The reader will often encounter in modern romantic usage the expression "wandering minstrel"—which is actually a misnomer. What is meant by this term is the class of *jongleurs*, who were itinerant and were all-around entertainers of the Middle Ages from at least the tenth century into the fourteenth. Minstrels did not wander but were static, and attached to the household of some eminent person such as a nobleman, a high-ranking ecclesiastic, a wealthy merchant, etc. Jongleurs traveled from household to household, from town to town, from kingdom to kingdom. Whilst some *jongleurs* were trouble-makers, and were lazy, shiftless, unprincipled, etc., the majority were highly skilled performers, and many were esteemed and patronized by both nobility and royalty, including the troubadour-poets who were often of knightly and sometimes of royal class themselves.

An accomplished *jongleur* (actually *jongleur*, Provençal *joglar*, Latin *joculator*) could amuse an audience by telling stories or reporting the latest news or reciting narratives in verse or playing on a variety of instruments or singing whilst accompanying himself on mandora or *vielle*. The more athletic *jongleur* could also be a tumbler, sword-swallower, juggler, dagger-thrower, fire-swallower, etc. However, due to changes in social conditions in the 1300's, most *jongleurs* became attached to households and became static like the minstrels; a few continued on in their wonted wandering pattern but in time their status became changed to that of mere "jugglers." From the minstrel of the late Middle Ages there is descended the modern musician, classical or popular.

The troubadours had their equivalents—called by various other names—in all European states during the 1100's and the 1200's. The accomplished troubadour usually sang his own poems or songs, and accompanied himself on the lute. However, for that troubadour who was better at creating songs than in performing them, there were professional singer-instrumentalists for hire to perform them. Some troubadours only sang, and minstrels—usually in attendance upon them—accompanied them on some instrument. However, the ideal of the troubadour, like that of the *jongleur*, was both to sing and play at the same time. We in the twentieth century have become so accustomed to the combination of singer and instrumentalist all in one person, that we often fail to realize what an unusual and often difficult feat it is.

By the middle 1300's, the original four single strings of the lute had evolved into four pairs, or courses. About 1400, a fifth string was added, equivalent to the later top "g" of the Renaissance lute. Writing toward the end of the 1400's, Johannes de Tinctoris (circa 1436–1511) gives the tuning of the five-course lute as (from bottom to top) c f a d g. Whilst some lutenists were still picking the strings with a plectrum or quill, an increasing number had begun using their fingertips, essentially a harpist's technique; this factor is responsible in a large measure for the delicate and arpeggiated quality of much Renaissance and Baroque lute music. The late 1400's saw three important innovations. First, a sixth course, or pair—tuned two octaves below the top "g"—was added in the bass. Second, lutenist composers began to use written tablature to record their improvisations; and the first printed tablatures appeared early during the first decade of the 1500's. Third, the plectrum or quill was definitely discarded. However, players of the mandola continued to use a plectrum or quill until the late 1600's.

Thus, the tuning for the sixteenth-century lute became (from bottom to top) g c f a d g. This tuning was also employed for the Spanish equivalent of the lute, the *vihuela de mano* (to wit, *viola* played *of* or *by* the hand, that is, by plucking), which was shaped like a guitar or cello but strung like a lute. From the late 1400's into the first half or so of the 1600's, the lute was the "regina omnium instrumentorum"—"the queen of all instruments"—the chief solo instrument like the piano or guitar in the twentieth century. Such phrases as "Phoebus's lute, the queen of music" (from Richard Barnfield's famous sonnet, still often attributed to Shakespeare), that often appear in Renaissance poetry of all European countries, are not mere decoration but reflect the considerable esteem in which this beautiful instrument was held. Apart from the great composers of the polyphonic vocal music of the 1500's and 1600's, it was mostly the Renaissance and early-baroque lutenists who developed the art of counterpoint before Bach. The great names of this "Golden Age" are too numerous to mention here, and this period over-all is now particularly well documented. The great lutenist composers were as much lionized and sought-after as any rock-music guitarist of our own twentieth century, all proportions guarded. Whereas formerly *jongleurs* had used both mandola and *vielle* whilst singing or reciting, there arose—in the latter 1500's on into the early 1600's—a considerable number of lutenist composers who sang their own airs (often with their own verses) whilst accompanying themselves on the lute in the manner of the olden troubadours. Especially noteworthy were the early *airs de cour* (as they were called) of Adrien Le Roy, and the lutenist "ayres" of John Dowland, who possessed an excellent singing voice; these last-cited songs, or sung poems, are artistically as fine as the art songs of Franz Schubert.

Although this "Golden Age" lasted only until about 1630, the so-called "Paris School" of (early-baroque) lutenists—evolving from the late Renaissance style of Robert Ballard and Ennemond Gaulthier, and dominated by Denys Gaulthier—enchanted their contemporaries with the new "style brisé" and its abundant ornamentation, and strongly influenced the harpsichordists of the time who sought purposefully to imitate many features of lute-music style.

The first two or three decades of the 1600's had seen the culmination of the late Renaissance lute and, around 1630, its evolution into the early-baroque lute. Since 1590, additional bass courses had been added, at least as many as four, and around 1650 Denys Gaulthier introduced a *nouvel accord* whereby the top six courses were tuned (from top to bottom) a d f a d f, but this was only the first of many new tunings. The late-baroque lute characteristically had thirteen courses, that is, a total of twenty-five or twenty-six strings. Since these lutes had wooden pegs to tune them rather than the gears on modern guitars, putting them and keeping them in tune was no mean feat, indeed, many princes and prelates kept a special lute tuner in their employ who did nothing but keep the lutes in tune.

The late 1500's and early 1600's witnessed the appearance and development of the new theorbo lutes and the archlutes (the largest of these being the chitarrone), principally employed as *continuo* instruments within the purely orchestral consorts or within the early Italian opera orchestras. Both the theorbo lutes and the archlutes survived into the 1700's.

With the death of the last great lutenist composer Sylvius Leopold Weiss, the palmy days of the lute came to a close. Weiss—a super-virtuoso whose style is amazingly like that of Bach—was the single highest-paid instrumentalist of his time, and on at least one occasion competed with his close friend Bach in a contrapuntal improvisatory contest. The early 1790's witnessed some of the very last original compositions for lute, with the sonatas of Johann Friedrich Rust and the solos of Christian Gottlieb Scheidler, both a lutenist and guitarist. By 1800 the lute was virtually extinct, and much of its late-baroque technique had become absorbed into the classical guitar of the 1700's.

No more graphic demonstration of this last phenomenon could possibly be found than the last years of Herr Scheidler, called the Last of the German Lutenists, who died in 1815. He spent the last twenty years or so of his life playing the guitar, teaching the guitar, and composing much guitar music. His set of twelve simple but attractive variations on the melody of the "Champagnerlieder" from Mozart's opera *Don Giovanni*, form part of the lute swansong of the 1790's.

In England, around the middle of the nineteenth century, the old position of court lutenist was finally abolished, but in Germany the lute never completely died out. Also around 1850, as part of the Continental Romantic or Gothic Revival, the *tone* of the lute was restored in an unusual way. In Italy some of the old lutes had their complicated and peculiar stringing removed and then replaced with the six single strings of the classical guitar. Subsequently new lutes were made (usually by German instrument makers) which were strung and tuned like a guitar (or with the bottom e string tuned down to d so as to permit the playing of many old lute chords to which the bottom d, fretted or unfretted, is essential) but with a tuning-head like that of a mandola. These so-called lute-guitars in both appearance and body size actually qualify as mandolas. The six single strings return this medium-sized lute to the original simpler tradition of the early medieval lute with its four single strings.

From the Spanish *guitarra* of the Renaissance—shaped like the *vihuela de mano* but with four pairs of strings tuned to permit the strumming of easily fretted chords whilst the player sings the melody of any given song—there has evolved the modern guitar: flamenco, classical, folk, rock, country western, jazz, etc. The early classical guitar—as developed by French and Italian *maestri* (many of the earliest were virtuoso lutenists as well) such as De Visée, Carcassi, Carulli, Giuliani, Sor, etc.—deliberately imitated the technique of the baroque lute (both early-baroque and late-baroque).

The four courses of the *guitarra* were tuned the same as the four inner courses of the Renaissance lute and the *vihuela de mano*: from bottom to top, c f a d. Later a fifth course was added, and still later a sixth, both of these in the bass, and eventually the six pairs became simplified to the standard six single strings of the classical guitar tuned (from bottom to top) e a d g b e. Thus the four top strings are equivalent to the original four courses of the Renaissance *guitarra*, and to the original four strings (and then pairs of strings) of the medieval lute. During the twentieth century the once-lowly guitar has become the king of the fretted instruments. Derived ultimately from the *kithara* of ancient Greece (the lyre used by professional singers), the guitar has thus fallen heir to all the lore and literature of the lute.

The early 1900's witnessed the beginning of the lute's modern revival. The musicologist and lute enthusiast Oscar Chilesotti did much pioneer research amongst the old lute tablatures, particularly of his native Italy. The fine classical guitarist Emilio Pujol also did much pioneer research amongst the old tablatures for *vihuela de mano* of his native Spain. Both men made effective musical transcriptions for the modern classical guitar from the old tablatures.

Today, thanks to such excellent performers as Walter Gerwig, Julian Bream, and Eugen Dombois, the true classical lute has been thoroughly re-established with authoritative authenticity. The lute today has thus returned both to life and to favor. In Europe, England, and America there is an increasing number of lutenists and lute-makers. For an accomplished guitarist, the lute has much to recommend it as a worthwhile second (fretted) instrument.

For a good general introduction to the lute and its vast literature of music (both in tablature and in modern musical transcription, a total of over three centuries), the reader is referred to the articles *Lute* and *Lute Music* in *Grove's Dictionary of Music and Musicians*, Fifth Edition, 1955: Volume V (L-M), pp. 433–439, and pp. 439–445.

* * *

Donald Sidney-Fryer's own first book, *Songs and Sonnets Atlantean* (June 1971), ranks as the last book published (that is, "made public"— with autographed copies being posted and delivered to customers who had ordered in advance) by Arkham House under the aegis of the original owner-editor August Derleth. The volume is "a deliberate postscript to that specific tradition of 'pure poetry' begun in modern English by Edmund Spenser and more or less ended by such Californian lyric poets as George Sterling (1869–1926), Nora May French (1881–1907), and Clark Ashton Smith (1893–1961)." The book also emphasizes the *continuity* of the over-all romance tradition from Spenser as well as from the Middle Ages up to and *through* the late Clark Ashton Smith.

(The preceding review-essay first appeared as a separate booklet published by Harry Morris II, the Silver Scarab Press, Albuquerque, New Mexico, 1973.)

A Statement for Imagination:
George Sterling and Clark Ashton Smith

On Wednesday, 17th November 1926, the poet and well-known personality George Sterling, by that time one of the acknowledged cultural institutions of "the City," died by deliberate or accidental suicide while residing in the Bohemian Club in downtown San Francisco.

When he died, it would have seemed to those of his contemporaries who interested themselves in such matters that this represented *The Last of Sunset* for his type of fin-de-siècle, classico-romantic art (to quote the title of one of the sonnets that Sterling contributed to *The Smart Set* during 1923)—that with him, its most popular promulgator at that time, the Biercean ethic/aesthetic had also come to an end.

By the time of his death Sterling had reigned as a prince of poets on the West Coast since at least 1915, if not earlier. 1903, the year in which his first collection *The Testimony of the Suns and Other Poems* appeared, or 1907, the year in which his single most famous poem "A Wine of Wizardry" was first published in *The Cosmopolitan*, are other years that might suggest themselves. But he had also been recognized, following Bierce's disappearance and/or death in 1914 somewhere in Northern Mexico, as the principal torch-bearer and promulgator of what we have termed (for convenience) the Biercean ethic/aesthetic.

Although not often defined as such, Ambrose Bierce was nothing if not a genuine and rather tortured romanticist, or "romantist" (to use the term preferred by that magisterial romancer F. Marion Crawford), and of a distinctly poetic sensibility (with an emphasis on the "Poe"). His vision and his best works, especially his highly original short stories, are distinguished above all by a love of truth and a total hatred of corruption and hypocrisy. His genius as a satirist was his principal stock-in-trade as a journalist, but he was also a skilled versifier and, on occasion, a fine poet, although little recognized as such in his own time or since, except by a small company of discerning connoisseurs, including both George Sterling and Clark Ashton Smith.

Despite a growing fame throughout the nation towards the end of his career, despite the solid recognition accorded him on the West Coast (of the United States) as its most influential and incisive arbiter of literary elegance, Bierce's final years did not prove particularly happy. His manner of death in Mexico—which he seems deliberately to have courted, if not engineered—might possibly be interpreted as his own original form of suicide.

For those who value the romantic-imaginative tradition in Anglo-American letters, Bierce's accomplishment as creator, theorist, and critic—to say nothing of his little-recognized but paramount importance as a *continuing influence*—has yet to be assessed at its full value. Bierce as well as anyone else had everything to do with later Californian men of letters gaining serious recognition and critical attention from England's own tribe of littérateurs for the period from the 1870's on into the latter 1920's. This was primarily due to the Californian literary beach-head or landfall, if you will, that Bierce and, a little earlier, Joaquin Miller had each helped to establish in Great Britain in the 1870's.

In the tradition of Edgar Allan Poe, the American (and now largely underground) school of (what is usually called) pure poetry has been peculiarly associated with Bierce, whether directly or indirectly, and chiefly through his two major followers, George Sterling and Clark Ashton Smith (1893–1961). Bierce has had a continuing influence on other poets and writers not only through his own work but just as much through his protégé Sterling and then through Sterling's own protégé Ashton Smith.

When Bierce died in 1914 somewhere in northern Mexico, his figurative Cloak of Elijah (possibly symbolic of his own aesthetic principles, but certainly of his own ethical ones, among divers others) would have passed from him to Sterling, his single best poet-pupil. Before we define something of what this phrase may have suggested to Bierce, Sterling, and Smith, we should ponder the phrase itself. Although *Mantle of Elijah* might possibly better convey the dignity and solemnity that such an imaginative symbol would have possessed for these intrepid artists, *Cloak of Elijah*—while not necessarily surrendering any of this rich association of solemn dignity and ethical imperative—might also imply, as in *Cloak and Dagger*, something furtive, clandestine, or even sinister. At first consideration such an association might seem necessarily lacking in the dignity and grandeur that would gather to *Mantle of Elijah*. But in the concept of *Cloak* in and of itself there exists the suggestion of something *unknown* or *underground*. In view of the fact that, in the tradition of Edgar Allan Poe, the American and now largely underground school of pure poetry has been peculiarly associated with Bierce, this further suggestion is both figuratively and factually appropriate.

Let us now consider something of what *Cloak* of *Elijah* may have meant or suggested to our Californian Romantics. First, it would have meant that love of truth and that total hatred of corruption and hypocrisy which distinguish Bierce's vision and over-all *oeuvre* at their best and most characteristic. Second, and as a natural corollary to this—and very much a part of the Californian Romantics' own initiative in the world of publishing—a total hatred of that type of corruption and hypocrisy sometimes apparent in the world of literary and general artistic endeavor above all, that is, writing in accordance with the formulas or dictates of critic, publisher, or editor, and/or in accordance with the latest interests or preferences of "genteel" or "fashionable" society, rather than in accordance with the artist's own creative conscience and his own self-chosen metaphor or symbol. Third, a love of and unswerving loyalty to the individual artist's own perception of truth: above all, following one's own initiative/intuition or "fantasy" (in the sense of fancy or natural inclination) or imaginative imperative. Fourth—in terms of the particular creative thrust or direction of the leading Californian Romantics—a development of, and an emphasis on, the cosmic/astronomic element such as is found in the collective *oeuvre* of Bierce, Sterling, Nora May French, Ashton Smith, and (not at all incidentally) Robinson Jeffers. This unique (and Californian) cosmic-mindedness or (more exactly) cosmic-astronomic-mindedness, they largely develop in their poetry but Ashton Smith later—and just as potently—developed in his prose. Fifth—and their cosmic-astronomic-mindedness is an excellent example of this—the characteristic and pervasive concern with what we can justifiably term the large (or major) issue or perspective, wherein ordinary humanism is logically relegated to a less than central position.

When Sterling died, Bierce's figurative Cloak of Elijah would have passed to one of two poets at least, or (more likely) to both. One of these was the highly individual and modern romantic poet, Robinson Jeffers, who was already creating quite a stir with his singular lyrics and his powerful narratives of a doomed and diseased humanity. One of the last books that Sterling finished before his death, and that Boni and Liveright of New York City brought out late in 1926 just after the elder poet's demise, was *Robinson Jeffers: The Man and the Artist.* In this publication Sterling (as certainly the first in book form) defined and acclaimed Jeffers' increasingly original manner. On the basis of this, one could make some kind of claim that the elder poet had indeed bequeathed Bierce's Cloak of

Elijah to Jeffers. But the other poet was Ashton Smith, Sterling's own protégé. For those who knew this other poet and what his work represented (as up to that time), it would have appeared that the Cloak had passed rather to him.

Rather than dying out, the Biercean ethic/aesthetic submerged into the mind and literal corpus of Ashton Smith and his *oeuvre*. He was to continue it brilliantly in his unique weird stories of the 1930's and then in his poetic activity of the 1940's, embodied chiefly in his volume of *Selected Poems*, which Smith produced in the middle to latter part of that decade.

The concluding years of Sterling's life paralleled in part a phenomenon that caused him—but not his protégé—to think that he had simply wasted a considerable amount of his earlier and more imaginative creativity. The middle to later 1920's witnessed a major shift in taste away from the highly romantic and often markedly fantastic type of imagination which had hitherto proven attractive to both elitist and popular audiences.

The movement of critical interest in literature was very much away from the intensely bardic spirit of awe and wonder and nobility, and very much toward the hard-edged, hard-boiled, and hard-headed genus/type of modern writing (the so-called realism of the time) with it stripped style of diction and no-nonsense approach.

Sterling directly witnessed the beginning of this shift in taste, with all that it implied for his own best work, but he had the good fortune to die virtually in the afternoon of his national fame and thus before he was forced to witness its decline and sunset. However, something of his genuine ancient renown lingered still in obscure nooks and crannies.

Clearly growing out of Sterling's generation in an artistic sense, but following the demise of northern California's older Bohemia (symbolized perfectly in Sterling's death), the melancholy and majestic figure of Clark Ashton Smith emerges, and very much like a lone survivor from lost Atlantis.

Smith remained resolutely faithful up until his death to his Sterlingesque tradition, his elder inheritance of wonder and beauty and fear. All the same elements that we find in Sterling, we find also, but in a particularly acute and intensified form, within the highly compact *oeuvre* of Ashton Smith, whether ode, sonnet, soliloquy, prose-poem, weird story, painting, drawing, or sculptured grotesque. Of course, by maintaining his loyalty throughout his lifetime to the Sterlingesque tradition, Ashton

Smith was also continuing his own unique exemplification of the Biercean ethic/aesthetic: the imaginative imperative common to Bierce, Sterling, and Smith, among others.

Bierce had most cogently and incisively defined this imaginative imperative for himself and his followers in his essays relative to the publication of, and the ensuing controversy surrounding, one of his protégé Sterling's greatest poems, to wit, "A Wine of Wizardry." By using his influence as an important contributor to the magazine in question, Bierce had been directly responsible for this poem's first published appearance in *The Cosmopolitan* for September 1907. Accompanying this poem was a trenchant essay by Sterling's mentor which he had entitled *A Poet and His Poem* and in which he praised Sterling in the most generous and (withal) discriminating terms, comparing "A Wine of Wizardry" quite favorably to Coleridge's "Kubla Khan," among other universally recognized masterpieces. Both the poem and the essay exercised a profound impact on then almost-fifteen-year-old Ashton Smith living with his parents in their cabin in Boulder or Indian Ridge just outside Auburn on the way to Folsom, and northeast of Sacramento, the state capital. Bierce later included his essay in collected form under the title *A Wine of Wizardry*.

Needless to say, not all the response elicited by Sterling's poem and Bierce's essay proved favorable; indeed, a considerable portion of it took a hostile and controversial form. However, Bierce, that old Civil War veteran, proved more than equal to meeting any and all of this negative reaction squarely on its own terms. In the issue of *The Cosmopolitan* for December 1907 he published his second essay dealing with "A Wine of Wizardry" under the witty title "An Insurrection of the Peasantry." In this he brilliantly dissects and attacks the adverse criticism leveled at Sterling's poem.

These two essays by Bierce add up to a most fascinating and convenient formulation of just what poetry and imagination meant to our Californian Romantics, and that primarily through the medium of that quintessential poetic element, *imagery*. Certainly, in order to exemplify Bierce's definitions and preferences, no poem could have been made more to order than Sterling's opus whether in regard to highly colored imagery or singularly fantastical imagination, and all under the aegis of the cosmic-astronomic.

Not only is Sterling's imagery in "A Wine of Wizardry" admirably concentrated but the poem itself, in structural terms, is an uncompromising concentration of such imagery developed on the foundation of a simple narrative: this is a direct application of Bierce's principal theory in the realm of poetics. Since Bierce considered imagery (and/or imagination) to be the heart, the soul, the essence of poetry—for him the imagery *was* the poetry—then in theory a poem successfully constructed on this model would be the most poetic possible, that is, the most imaginative. Although it remained first for Sterling successfully to create such a poem, Bierce gave it the definitive theoretical formulation in his two essays. While it is true that Sterling's poem provided the immediate reason for Bierce's essays to come into existence, they evidently sum up and formulate something that had been simmering in Bierce's very being for some forty years, that is, since at least the start of his literary career, signalized by the publication of his two earliest extant poems (typically rich in imagery) in the early San Francisco weekly newspaper *The Californian* during the latter half of 1867. It is of definite significance that he later included both essays in a prominent position in Volume X, *The Opinionator*, of his *Collected Works* published 1909–1912.

But far more than the technique of compressing imagery upon the foundation of a simple narrative is the Sterlingesque technique *par excellence* (developed concomitantly along with the previous one) of suggesting or intimating eerie and/or exotic adventures through the series of episodes projected through the imagery. This is a technique that Sterling's protégé Ashton Smith was to imitate, master, and apply over and over again in virtually every collection of his poetry from *The Star-Treader and Other Poems* (1912) through *Spells and Philtres* (1958). It formed the single most important piece of technique that Sterling bequeathed to any pupil, protégé, or follower, and he did so primarily through the medium of "A Wine of Wizardry" (and secondarily through that of his single greatest poem "The Testimony of the Suns") . But Sterling's chief protégé was also to make much use of the technique in his brilliant prose fantasies of the 1930's.

Ashton Smith's own longer and greater poem "The Hashish-Eater; or, The Apocalypse of Evil" (published fifteen years later in his third poetry collection *Ebony and Crystal* in December 1922) continued at once the immediate tradition of Sterling's earlier opus as well as of Bierce's ethic/aesthetic, or (to put it in other terms) of their common imperative. The major shift in critical taste and preference that occurred in the middle to latter 1920's was to consign the work of the Californian Romantics to an unfortunate condition of neglect and near-oblivion until the latter 1960's and afterwards.

Then once again the literary mainstream reopened its collective mind to writers working in modes and metaphors other than of the realism which has flourished in the 1930's, 1940's, 1950's, and early 1960's. Thus, while the Biercean ethic/aesthetic was undeniably passing into a state of decline during the middle 1920's—signalized precisely by the death of George Sterling, Bierce's principal poet-pupil, and the most popular promulgator of Bierce's imaginative imperative at that time—yet this decline was not followed by its demise but, rather, by its submergence into the mind and literal corpus of Ashton Smith and his artistic output. By the latter 1960's the work of Smith, embodying thus the creative/imaginative imperative of the Californian Romantics, had very definitely survived.

This fact of survival, with all its various implications, has been well summarized by Charles K. Wolfe writing in his article "C.A.S: A Note on the Aesthetics of Fantasy" published in *C.A.S—Nyctalops* for August 1972. Although Professor Wolfe is writing primarily about Smith's tales, his remarks (and those of Smith) can apply equally well to Smith's poetry of the 1920's, that is, before Sterling's death:

> Smith perceived that realism was only one tradition, and that romanticism was an equally valid tradition. He rejected the definition that literature was [only or primarily] a study of human reactions and character development; he [quite properly] called such a definition "narrow and limited."

Further on in the same article Professor Wolfe makes the following observation:

> Smith saw the folly of people who equated "realism" with quality in literature; only in the last decade has literature begun to recover from the tyranny of the realism criterion, the assumption that the only function of literature is to tell it "how it is." Smith fought his lonely battle during the height of the realistic movement in the 1930's; only today is the literary mainstream beginning to appreciate the fact that some writers are *not* trying to be "realistic," and that reading them requires a different set of standards. Oddly enough, Smith today is quite at home in contemporary literature in which the most respected writers are neo-romantics like Barth, Borges, Vonnegut, and Hawkes.

In the final stages of the long correspondence (1911–1926) that passed between Sterling and Ashton Smith, the Biercean ethic/aesthetic is redefined at a critical moment in literary and artistic history. Both authors confront the fact of the major shift in critical and (to a lesser extent) in popular taste and preference that more or less began in the early to middle 1920's. This final discussion occurs in their letters for July through November 1926, and was incited through the encomiastic essay on Smith's poetry "The Emperor of Dreams" written by the young writer and poet Donald A. Wandrei (then in his latter teens) and eventually published in the *Overland Monthly* for December 1926. (This latter periodical was the West Coast or Californian equivalent of the *Atlantic Monthly*.) Wandrei was later to become quite well-known for his powerful fantasy and science-fiction tales written during the 1930's and 1940's, many of which are marked with as strong a sense of the cosmic-astronomic as are the writings of Sterling, Ashton Smith, H. P. Lovecraft, etc.

Of course, recognition has always loomed as an important matter for many, or most, struggling, and committed artists, and possibly it proved even more so for the Californian Romantics, located as they were out on the furthest edge of the main part of the North American continent, and often pursuing literary means and ends sometimes acutely different from those in vogue in the Northeastern United States where most of the leading and surely more influential critics lived and worked. Therefore, any intelligent and eloquent appreciation of their work loomed large on the horizon. This is demonstrated not only by the discussion of Wandrei's monograph in the Sterling-Smith correspondence for July through November, but just as well by Ashton Smith's letter of May 9, 1926, wherein he writes in part:

> Ben De C. [Casseres] has sent me his new book, *Forty Immortals*. It is great stuff, like everything else of his that I have read. I understand that he intends to do one some day on you, Jeffers, and myself, under, the title of *Three Californian Poets*. I appreciate the prospective honour, though, in my present mood, I feel inclined to deny that I am a Californian... But I suppose one might as: well be that as anything, since one can't emigrate to Saturn.... Moronism, unhappily, is not confined to California. [Smith's own ellipses.]

Then, in his letter of July 10, Smith first mentions the young Wandrei's essay:

A correspondent of mine in St. Paul, one D. A. Wandrei, has written an article on my work. I appreciate the article, but fear he'll have a hard time getting it published, except at his own expense.

In his letter of August 8, Sterling acknowledges Smith's mention of Wandrei's article via the elder poet's favorable mention of Smith in Braithwaite's poetry anthology for 1926.

I'd have written ere now, but the Jinks [the annual midsummer High Jinks celebrated by the Bohemian Club of San Francisco in the Bohemian Grove on the Russian River north of the City], followed by much work, has tripped me as a correspondent. I've had to write an article for W. S. Braithwaite's 1926 anthology, covering the western section of poetry. Am giving you as good a "send-off" as I've space for. If your St. Paul friend can't get *his* appreciation printed, have him send it to me, and I'll get it in the *Overland*, if it's not very long.

In his letter of September 4, Smith adds a few more details in description of Wandrei's article, and incidentally voices his dissatisfaction with twentieth-century America, expressing his desire to live elsewhere.

Thanks for the mention in Braithwaite's anthology. Wandrei, my St. Paul admirer, may send you his essay before long. He wanted to try *The Bookman* and *The Nation* first!! The essay runs to about 2500 words, including quotations.

[....]

I wish I were in Abyssinia, or Sumatra, or [the] Celebes—anywhere but twentieth century America. I am bored, exasperated and afflicted by everything and everybody—no one was ever so alien and recalcitrant to the "time-spirit."

In this letter of September 12, Sterling responds sympathetically to Smith's complaint about their contemporary U. S. A., and suggests that he might come to San Francisco for technical instruction in painting from Sterling's friend, the portrait-painter Herkomer:

As regards your painting, I think you have immense imagination, as in poetry, but lack technical training. It's a pity you can't come to S.F. for that. Maybe Herkomer could help you . . .

[....]

The Bookman might take Wandrei's essay. *The Nation* would be as likely to run the "Items!...

[....]

> I understand your reaction to this awful country, which will become yearly more detestable. I fancy that all one can do, if too poor to emigrate, is to toughen one's hide. Of course, it's sensitivity that counts, not environment.

In his letter of September 28, Smith states point-blank his prime intent in his artwork. As in his literary creation, it is the play and expression of the liberated and free-wheeling imagination.

> Of course, I lack technical training in the academic sense. But I don't care much more for the literalness of academic painting than I do for the geometrical abstractions of some of the modernists. What I am after is imaginative (some would say emotional) expression through organized design and colour with novel decorative values. [....] Certainly Herkomer, who is, or was, a portrait-painter, would be of little help in teaching me how to paint landscapes in Cocaigne, or Saturn, or Antillia. Like most people, he wouldn't get the idea at all.

In his letter of October 8, Sterling acknowledges the receipt (from Wandrei himself) of Wandrei's essay on Smith's poetry, and makes some cogent objections to it, citing his own experience with "A Wine of Wizardry":

> A matter has come up to that worries me. Your friend Wandrei has sent me an essay on your poetry, perhaps with the intention of having it published in some magazine. That would be impossible in any eastern one, for he is evidently a pretty young man, with a young man's unbridled enthusiasms, and has heaped such extravagant praise on you as not a combination of Shakespeare, Coleridge and Keats could merit. So his adulation could awaken only derision in editorial bosoms, and laughter in readers', if published. I remember what I got in the case of "A Wine of Wizardry"!
>
> However, if you don't mind the incredulity of lesser poets, I can have the essay run in the "Overland," very probably. It would at least attract much attention to your work, and in itself is well-written, however open to argument some of its eulogies may be. Let me know your wishes, and they shall be complied with. Heaven knows you get little enough credit for your exquisite work, and if this will wake folks up, all the better.

The preceding represents the start of the practical redefinition that Sterling and Smith make of the Biercean ethic/aesthetic. In his letter of October 11, Smith does not object to Sterling's objections in regard to

Wandrei's essay but he does invoke the principle of a fair hearing for it. And he does defend Bierce's original opinion of Sterling's best-known poem:

> I agree with all that you say about Wandrei's essay; but after all, his "reaction" is obviously sincere, and it seems to me that he is entitled to a hearing. You might run the essay, if the *Overland* will stand for it. I won't mind the heehaws of the local Fame asses. Anyway, W. means to print and circulate it at his own expense, if he can't get it into any magazine.
>
> I always thought, and still think, that Bierce merely gave "A Wine of Wizardry" it's just due. But good judges of poetry are almost rarer than poets, it would seem.

In his letter of October 24, Sterling informs Smith that the *Overland Monthly* has agreed to run Wandrei's essay and that he is writing to Wandrei for his permission to use it:

> Miss Lee [B. Virginia Lee] is "agreeable" toward using Wandrei's article, knowing that it will attract attention, from the very scope of its claims, not only to you but to her magazine. So I am writing to Wandrei [sending the letter via Ashton Smith] for formal permission to use it. Since he really believes what he has written, he ought to stand by his words, even though they will be received with polite (and impolite) incredulity.
>
> [....]
>
> God guard you, Satan guide you!

In his letter of October 27, Smith makes a very important statement on behalf of imaginative poetry and, by extension, imaginative literature and art in general. Of particular relevance is his point that imaginative art (exemplified in this context by his own poetry), correctly regarded, does not constitute an *escape* from life but an *extension* of it. "Anything that the human imagination can conceive of becomes thereby a part of life," embodies a profound observation indeed.

> I forwarded your letter to Wandrei. He's a strange fellow, but is much more critical than you imagine. I don't know just how young he is; but it's only fair to say that there are men of middle-age (enough of them for a jury, almost!) who would back him up in his contention that my eventual place will be a very high one. He doesn't really contend that I am greater than certain other poets, and the excess of his essay is more in the manner than in the substance. Doubtful though I am my-

self, I think that the people who will laugh at him are fools, and are deaf and blind to all the lessons of literary history. Literary tastes and standards are in a state of perpetual flux, and the narrow, hide-bound "humanism" of the present may seem absurd in some future age. It is absurd to me, and to a few other free spirits. I've no quarrel with the slogan of "art for life's sake," but I think the current definition or delimitation of what constitutes life is worse than ridiculous. Anything that the human imagination can conceive of becomes thereby a part of life, and poetry such as mine, properly considered, is not an "escape," but an extension. I have the courage to think that I am rendering as much "service" by it (damn the pisspot word!) as I would by psychoanalyzing the male and female adolescents or senescents of a city slum in the kind of verse that slops all over the page and makes you feel as if somebody had puked on you.

I don't blame you for writing prose, if you can make money by it. But it's a hateful task, for a poet, and wouldn't be necessary, in any true civilization. Hell speed the ascendancy of the Japs and Hottentotts!

[....]

I'll "start" something somewhere, sometime, somehow in connection with the pictures [Smith's pictorial art]. They provoke the same extremes of dislike and admiration as my poetry, though not always in the same people.

In his letter of October 31, Sterling alludes directly for the first time to the major shift in critical and popular preferences that was happening at that time: "… [It] is disquieting to observe that the whole intellectual (including of course the esthetic) trend is increasingly against admiration of the daemonic, the supernatural." Sterling is quite aware of what this implies for his own creativity:

I wasn't trying to contend that you don't, according to my personal tastes in poetry, deserve a high place in it. I merely thought it uncritical of Wandrei to have you topping the heap, as his essay will lead every reader of it to infer that he believes. No one more than I would like to be able to entertain such hopes, since they involve to a large extent some of my own work, notably "A Wine of Wizardry." But [it] is disquieting to observe that the whole intellectual (including of course the esthetic) trend is increasingly against admiration of the daemonic, the supernatural. Such elements now seem only to awaken smiles, as being childish in their nature and no part of the future vision of the race. I regret that this should be so, for it implies that I've wasted a good deal of creative energy; but only cranks and mental hermits now take my "Wine" seriously, and I feel futile when I use my imagination on "impossible" stuff, the element where it is best fitted to function. Maybe we'll have anarchy in America, some day, with the accompanying reversion to racial childhood. That will come too late for me, but perhaps not for you. For the present, my "blue-eyed vampire" is only an intellectual joke, and to call anyone a fool who smiles back at her is not to win the argument.

Ashton Smith had signed his letter of October 27 as follows: "Yours, in the quest / of the Holey Grail [sic], / Clark." To this bit of whimsy, Sterling—in his letter of October 31—made the following rejoinder in his charming way: "When we find the Grail, it has [sic] in it 'the cool black wine,' Clark!" Smith's letter of November 4 contains his strongest and most extensive statements about the then current literary (and general artistic) humanism in America. One can only regret that neither Sterling nor Smith ever wrote such an eminently Biercean essay as "The Americanization of Intellect":

> Why don't you write an essay on the prevailing trend in thought and aesthetics? You might call it "The Americanization of Intellect." I'd do the article myself, if I knew where Bierce had left his cat-o'-nine tails.
>
> I suppose I'm hopelessly "inadaptable," but I can't attain to that faith in the material values professed by the humanists and other Babbitts. Many attempts have been made to convert me; but I still fail to see that the "impossible"—or problematical—is any more futile than anything else as a poetical topic. Indeed, my fondest dream is to find a Hyperborea beyond Hyperborea, in the realm of imaginative poetry. I have the feeling that my best and most original work is still to be done.
>
> However, I didn't mean to start an argument by what I wrote. We both know the futility of argument. But—whenever you begin to feel that you have wasted your time in writing imaginative verse, remember that poetry such as yours and mine would have found as little favour in the 18th century as it does today. Dr. Johnson and the other Henry Seidel Canbys of his time would scarcely have understood "A Wine of Wizardry." And I'll be dammed if I can see that the present age, for all its scientific discoveries, psychoanalysis, etc., is any smarter or more sophisticated than the 18th. It is, however, equally cock-sure and materialistic,—or more so. But the present orgy of materialism will exhaust itself sooner or later, and perhaps end in some great social *débâcle* after that—since history never does anything but plagiarize itself—there may

be a revival of interest in imaginative literature, and a new Romantic epoch, like that following the French Revolution.

Yes, I get the *Overland*, and always look for your page in it [this was entitled "Rimes and Reactions"]. I'd appreciate an extra copy or two of the issue in which W.'s article comes out. Wandrei has a theory that the literature of the future, since human topics are pretty well worked out, will concern itself more and more with the fantastic and the cosmic. Hence, in part, his enthusiasm for my stuff. Of course, neither he nor I, nor anybody else, can prove anything about the literary tastes and trends of posterity.

Dam' me, I believe I'll do an article myself, in defense of imaginative poetry. One could attack the current literary humanism, with its scorn of all that has no direct anthropological bearing, as a phase of the general gross materialism of the times. If imaginative poetry is childish and puerile, then Shakespeare was a babbling babe in his last days, when he wrote that delightful fantasy, "The Tempest." And all the other great Romantic masters, Keats, Poe, Baudelaire, Shelley, Coleridge, etc., are mentally inferior to every young squirt, or old one, who has read Whitman and Freud, and renounced the poetic chimeras in favour of that supreme superstition, Reality.

Benjamin De Casseres says somewhere that poets pay their debts in stars and are paid in wormwood. But I'll pay some of mine in nitric acid.

Affectionately, Clark.

In his letter of Nov. 9th, George repeats the Biercean aesthetic that "imagination is poetry, or poetry imagination." He rates his own "Wine of Wizardry" rather modestly; Bierce had placed it in the same rank as Coleridge's "Kubla Khan." For all its obvious indebtedness to Sterling's own poem, "The Hashish-Eater" with its unique blend of outrageous fantasy and cosmic-astronomic-mindedness has no true parallel or precedent, and remains a towering pioneer achievement to the everlasting credit of Ashton Smith. But George in his letter reassures Ashton that he has no quarrel with imaginative poetry:

I have utterly no quarrel with imaginative poetry, for as Bierce said, imagination *is* poetry, or poetry imagination. I'd merely want that imagination turned on such themes as have some relation to life, some vital significance, as in Adonais, the Eve of St. Agnes, Ulysses, Dolores, and many other poems I would specify. I've no quarrel with such poems as my "Wine" and your "Hashish Eater," but cannot rank them as high as those I've mentioned. But, as you wisely say, argument is useless in matters of taste. And one's tastes change with advancing years. I only hope I won't find myself calling Whitman a Titan, as Ben De C. does!

George wrote this last letter of his to Ashton on Nov. 9th. Eight days later, on Wednesday, November 17, sometime in the afternoon or evening, he died by deliberate or accidental suicide. With Sterling at last gone, Ashton Smith was left to fight, virtually all by himself, the lonely and often desperate battle for the romantic-imaginative tradition in Anglo-American letters and other art forms against the forces of the new—and almost completely dominant—realistic humanism of the 1920's, 1930's, etc., a realism remarkable for its narrowly anthropocentric perspective.

Sterling's death proved a major loss to Ashton Smith, of course; the two poets had been correspondents and friends since 1911, and the elder bard had indeed performed invaluable services for his young and less worldly colleague. George's death had such an impact on Smith that he wrote little poetry for about a year, apart from the outstanding and profoundly moving elegy "A Valediction to George Sterling" (later published in the *Overland Monthly*). However, he did translate a considerable amount of French verse by Baudelaire into a rich and idiomatic prose (virtually none of these exercises have seen publication), which undoubtedly had some delayed reaction or influence on Smith's prose tales of the 1930's. Now in the latter 1920's the special affection and companionship of the remarkable woman Genevieve K. Sully, the *doyenne* of Auburn's cultural milieu at that time, inspired him to create his single lightest and most song-like cycle of love poems, *The Jasmine Girdle*. She strongly encouraged him to write his prose fantasies, and opened a major source of inspiration by introducing him to the strange, otherworldly ambiance of Crater Ridge in the Sierras. This experience led not only to the specific tales "The City of the Singing Flame" and "Beyond the Singing Flame" but to the strikingly Biercean character of much of Smith's Romantic/macabre fiction written during late 1929 through at least 1934.

Whatever the reigning fashions or cultural preferences, Ashton Smith always believed profoundly in whatever it was his creativity embodied, metaphysically and psychologically. This power of belief was to sustain him during his work of the 1930's and 1940's, outwardly an especially un-opulent period, apart (of course) from the epic-romantic films

mostly made in Hollywood, and remarkable for their luxuriant production values and their often poetic editing. Ironically enough, there is a
definite affinity—above all in the area of "glamourous" presentation—
between such films and Smith's own highly idiosyncratic fiction of the
1930's and 1940's, whether as originally published in *Weird Tales, Wonder
Stories,* and other magazines of the 1930's, or as subsequently gathered in
those of his major prose collections that Arkham House put out during
the 1940's, to wit, *Out of Space and Time* (1942), *Lost Worlds* (1944) and
Genius Loci and Other Tales (1948).

Although books bearing his name continued to appear, Ashton
Smith wrote little in the final decade of his life. He died on 14 August
1961 at the age of 68 at Pacific Grove on the Monterey Peninsula, and
thus before the neo-romantic resurgence of the latter 1960's and afterwards. Although he did not live to see this resurgence or to know that
wider recognition which his earliest admirers first predicted for him some
seventy-odd years ago and which eventually came about thanks to paperback and foreign publications, he at least had the satisfaction of knowing
that he had put up a good fight on behalf of what he valued in creative
literature. In mid-August, 1985, a memorial plaque honoring Ashton
Smith and his artistic achievement is to be erected with appropriate
speeches and ceremonies at the new Auburn Placer County Library in
Auburn, California, through the agency of a group of admirers and
friends. But perhaps the most touching memorial had been that accorded
him by his widow (also now deceased), Carol Jones Dorman Smith (as
recorded among some notes that she compiled toward writing a biography of her late husband under the title *The Man Who Treads the Stars*): "His
body, cremated, was mixed with the earth of his homeland, and buried
below a huge rock, lichen-covered, as he had wished." However, the true
memorial to Ashton Smith is to be found, of course, in his writings.

Whether in poetry or fiction, sculptured or pictorial art, Ashton
Smith's complete extant *oeuvre* represents a major and unique statement on
behalf of the unfettered and free-wheeling imagination. His varied body of
writing at least provides clear evidence that Smith continued, and ensured
the survival of, his own Biercean and Sterlingesque tradition, his elder inheritance of wonder and beauty and fear, but a legacy now immeasurably
deepened, expanded, and enriched. Ambrose Bierce's imaginative imperative had somehow survived into some kind of more general acceptability
by the late 1960's and the years following. The Biercean ethic/aesthetic

had indeed endured beyond "the last of sunset" for each of its three main promulgators, the theorist/creator and his two main poet-followers. Their ultimate faith in the immortality conferred within the world of literature had surely found a rich and neo-romantic justification.

(For permission to quote excerpts from the letters Clark Ashton Smith and George Sterling, cordial acknowledgement is hereby made to the Henry W. and Albert A. Berg Collection / The New York Public Library / Astor, Lenox and Tilden Foundations [the physical proprietors and custodians of the Sterling-Smith correspondence, together with related MSS. and artwork]. Ashton Smith wrote from "Auburn, Cal.," and George Sterling from the Bohemian Club in San Francisco.)

Note: This essay "A Statement for Imagination" first appeared in a slightly altered form as "An Issue for Imagination" in the magazine *Nightshade* for August 1, 1977. It has been corrected for its appearance in *The Romantist*, No. 6–7–8, 1982–83–84, published 1986.

The Last Lutenist:
Christian Gottlieb Scheidler

The lute, it seems, has long figured in one way or another as a subject for fantasy, for imaginative projection and extrapolation, whether in art or literature, especially during the century or so of its eclipse from around 1800 to around 1900 or somewhat later. We are speaking here principally of the European, short-necked lute. It has also figured, and probably to a much greater extent, as a subject for comparatively accurate representation in art, whether in painting or sculpture. The lute originally came into Southern Europe as the result of two large-scale religious and social movements. The first of these was the spread and ultimate extension of Islam out of Arabia across the Middle East into northeast India in one direction, and then into Egypt and across Northern Africa into Spain in the opposite one. The principal military bridgeheads, as well as cultural and musical ones, thus established in Europe, appear to have been the Iberian Peninsula, the Sicily-Malta-Tunis land-and-water connection, and finally (and initially to a lesser extent) Asia Minor and Greece. However, the real ineluctable catalyst for military and cultural exchange between East and West, as well as for the introduction of the lute and other Oriental instruments into Europe, was the second of these large-scale religious and social movements, which was the series of some seven or nine Crusades during the eleventh, twelfth, and thirteenth centuries.

It is true that, as carvings attest, various long-necked lute-like instruments figured in the musical activity of ancient Egypt, Assyria, and Babylonia. However, insofar as the relatively meagre documentation currently available in the Western World from the early period of Middle Eastern history allows us to make a definite statement, it appears that the Persians invented and perfected the original ancestor of the modern lute during the period of the Sassanian Empire (c. 226–641). The Persian model possessed the original four single strings of gut tuned to intervals of fourths and played with a plectrum (essentially one portentous note at a time), usually a large quill, but other substances were also used, such as an eagle's claw. This lute already possessed its distinctive form as constituted by its characteristic body, or sound chamber, shaped like half a pear (cut lengthwise) with the back or rounded portion made up of narrow strips of wood, and with a flat top pierced by a "rose" or sound hole (often elaborately carved). Apparently independent of Islam, this particular model travelled east across the trade routes of Central Asia into China where it survives to this day as the *pipa* with the original four single strings played with a plectrum; however, oddly enough, the body has no sound hole. In turn, it crossed the sea from China into Japan where it became the *biwa*, also played with a plectrum, and like the *pipa* it survives to this day in something closely approximating its original form. Both the *pipa* and *biwa* figure prominently in the classical music of their respective countries. In the original home itself of the ancestor of the modern lute, that is, in Persia or modern Iran, the instrument is apparently no longer played, or but minimally.

With the fall of Persia before the advance of Islam after the death of Mohammed (570–632), much of Persian culture became assimilated by the Arabs. Thus, although the lute is originally a Persian invention, we owe its widespread adoption, adaptation, and propagation to the religious, military, and cultural ascendancy and domination of Islam during the Middle Ages. Indeed, virtually all the names for it in the standard European languages derive from the Arabic expression *al-Ud* (the noun is also transliterated as *Oud*), meaning "the wood," the definite article in Arabic becoming part of the various European words designating the instrument. Sometime during the fourteenth century the original four single strings of the European model became doubled, doubtlessly for the heightened tone that this conferred, and towards the end of the fifteenth century other doubled strings, or "courses," were added. By the late 1400's or early 1500's the regular short-necked lute had six courses, usually doubled, but with the *chanterelle*, the highest-pitched string, remaining as a single.

Sometime around the beginning of the 1500's, or somewhat before, European lutenists abandoned the use of the plectrum, thus freeing the fingers to play relatively complicated polyphonic music, especially all the notes in any given chord more or less simultaneously. This technical innovation increased the range of lute music enormously, and during the 1500's and the first half of the 1600's the lute developed into, and remained, the standard musical instrument of its time, equivalent to the role later played by the harpsichord and then by the modern piano. Starting in the first decade of the 1500's in Italy, an enormous amount of musical literature in the form of tablatures was published and made available to virtuoso and amateur performer alike. When we consider the difficulties of stringing and tuning the lute with gut strings, and when we consider as well the relatively limited ambitus of the instrument, its widespread popularity during the 1500's on into the first half of the 1600's remains an astonishing phenomenon. The Renaissance lute in general had six courses tuned (from highest pitch to lowest), as follows: G, D, A, F, C, G. By the end of the 1500's many lutenists had added other basses, usually fretted like all the other courses, and often tuned to F, D, E, or C.

We should note that in Spain during the 1500's and early 1600's (but apparently not after that) the plucked instrument of predilection was the *vihuela de mano,* shaped like a guitar, but tuned like a six-course Renaissance lute. For some reason or other, because of the lute's association with the Moors who dominated southern Spain for many centuries, the Spaniards may have had an aversion to the lute itself, which they called the *vihuela de Flandes,* and which they may have regarded as a symbol of their former overlords of a different religion. Be that as it may, virtually all the music created for the lute during the 1500's may be played on the *vihuela de mano,* and vice versa.

New tunings and added bass courses came into use on the European lute as time went on. The added courses were usually carried on an added neck or an extension of the principal neck, and this type of lute, or *arciliuto,* was usually known as a theorbo, or theorbo-lute. By the middle or later 1600's, and definitely during the 1700's, the lute's last active century in Europe before its eclipse around 1800, the Baroque model had thirteen or fourteen courses with the tuning based on the D-minor arpeggio (from the highest pitch to lowest), as follows: F, D, A, F, D, A, and with the bass courses diatonically, as follows: G, F, E, D, C, B, A, etc. Apart from the two highest pitched strings, all the other courses were doubled on this particular model.

The characteristic manner of playing at the various European courts during the Baroque period, as well as the consequent style of music, became increasingly elegant and stately, as well as even languorous, that is, in terms of the sound but not of the playing! Whether slow or fast, the performer had plenty to keep him busy, and by this time the lute with all its wooden tuning-pegs had developed into an immensely difficult instrument to tune and play, seeming to be actually more a species of harp than anything else. The principal centre for the continuing creativity of the lute in the late 1600's and during most of the 1700's had shifted from France and Italy to Germany. However, relatively isolated pockets of high-quality lute-playing and lute-composing yet remained in both France and Italy, where published tablatures still made occasional appearances. In Italy various long-necked archlutes of many courses, strung with brass or bronze wire, retained the original tuning of the Renaissance lute, but with the inevitable (and characteristic) added bass courses tuned diatonically. These oversized archlutes, usually of the type called *chitarrone*, or large *chitarra* (a word derived from *kithara*, a type of Greek lyre), had first come into existence in the late 1500's. A group of eminent Italian lutenists, lute-composers, and lute-theoreticians had deliberately invented this new type of lute, partially to overcome some of the difficulties and handicaps inherent in the use of gut strings, but primarily to create (through the use of wire strings) a relatively loud instrument of the lute family which could hold its own in terms of sonorousness in the then-evolving orchestra used for accompanying the earliest forms of Italian opera. In such an ensemble the wire-strung archlute principally furnished the basso continuo, but it also provided both solos and solo accompaniment to the singing. There existed certain types of *chitarrone* with as many as nineteen or twenty-one courses in all. The sound of the *chitarrone* is distinct and pungent, rather resembling the sound produced by some of the earliest kinds of harpsichord.

Whether during the period of the Renaissance lute or that of the Baroque one, the instrument had many outstanding practitioners who functioned as players, composers, teachers, as well as makers. The comparatively recent rebirth of interest in the lute began in the late 1800's with such figures as the musicologist Oscar Chilesotti, and continued on in the early 1900's with such makers as Arnold Dolmetsch. The names of many of the formerly eminent lutenist-composers, whether of the Renaissance or of the Baroque period, have once more become fairly widely known via this rebirth of interest. We need mention only a few of these names: in Spain such vihuelist-composers as Luís Milán, Enriquez de Valderábano, Luís de Narváez, and Alonso de Mudarra; in England, Francis Cutting, John Dowland, Thomas Campion, Francis Pilkington, Anthony Holborne, John and Robert Johnson, Philip Rosseter, and Thomas Mace (Mace's tome *Musick's Monument* [London, 1676] is devoted principally to a rare account of the English lute in Mace's time, that is, at the period of its decline in Britain, shortly before its demise there); in France, Adrien Le Roy, Robert Ballard, Ennemond and Dennis Gaulthier, Charles Mouton, and Robert de Visée; in Italy, Francesco da Milano, Vincenzo Capirola, Vincenzo Galilei (the father of the famous astronomer), Cesare Negri, Michelangelo Galilei, and

Alessandro Piccinini; in Germany and Austria, Hans Neusidler, Elias Mertel, Esaias Reussner, Jacques Bittner, Adam Falckenhagen, David Kellner, Sylvius Leopold Weiss, Ernst Baron, Carl Kohaut, and Johann Friedrich Rust. Another figure, equivalent in stature whether as virtuoso or composer to the greatest of names already cited, was the brilliant Hungarian musician Bálint Greff-Bakfark (1507–1576).

The new tunings, of course, had come into existence concomitantly with new styles of music. Starting in the early to middle 1600's, lute music became less contrapuntally polyphonic, and more harmonic, a process whereby the simpler rhythmic vitality of the Renaissance (reflecting the lute's long-term use for dance purposes) yielded to a more complicated rhythmic approach (now often reflecting a non-dance purpose), one in which the chords were broken up (as it were), creating a new type of music, the so-called *style brisé*. However, one feature of lute music remained constant almost all through its entire span of existence in Europe, from late Mediaeval lute practice (what little we actually know of it) on through the Renaissance and then through the Baroque period. Right up through the extant works of the last virtuosos (around the mid-1700's), lute music never completely lost its contrapuntal character. The two main melodic lines of treble and bass were always emphasized in such a way whereby the music could always be identified as belonging to the lute. Also, as befitting the sounds produced by such a harp-like instrument, it never lost its distinguishing arpeggiated character either.

Among the great German composers Bach (Johann Sebastian, of course), Handel, and Haydn wrote some outstanding lute music. Even if he may not have played the instrument himself (as far as is known or can be ascertained), Bach in particular created a sizable body of work for it, an unusual feat for someone who was not a lutenist-composer. In addition to composing some excellent lute music, Bach had lutenists as both friends and pupils, including (as a friend) the greatest lutenist of the late Baroque period, Sylvius Leopold Weiss. During the last half of the 1700's, while still retaining some vestiges of the Baroque manner, the final type of music for the lute was developed, the so-called *style galant*, a style equivalent to that of such early Classical masters as Haydn and Mozart. However, after the compositions of such figures as Falckenhagen, Kellner, Weiss, Baron, and Rust, the remaining music that survives from the last years of the European lute before its demise around 1800 consists of just a few, simple, rather guitar-like lute solos or lute parts in duos and trios with woodwinds and bowed instruments.

With the retirement or death of the very last practitioners of the lute, the instrument then lapsed into dormancy with a number of notable exceptions. It appeared on display in various European museums. It was featured as a colorful and picturesque prop on the stage. Or it figured as the guitar-tuned, guitar-strummed, six-single-stringed German *Volkslaute*, also known as the modern lute. This folk-lute was played either solo, to accompany some singer, or as part of folk-music ensembles. The *Volkslaute* had come into being in a rather curious way. However, whenever it was first created sometime in the latter 1700's (possibly no later than the 1770's), it possessed a single *chanterelle* and five doubled strings, just like the typical Renaissance lute or the then emerging classical guitar. This represented a simplification of the late Baroque model, which was losing its few remaining practitioners, and which apparently had become too complicated to learn and play without proper instruction by an appropriate master. Later the five doubled courses of the folk-lute became simplified to five single strings like those of the classical guitar. This happened around 1800 when technically superior strings were first being manufactured, the three trebles being of silk and the three basses being of silk wound with fine silver wire. As a matter of course, the then early *Volkslaute* adopted these same strings just as the folk-lute made in this century utilizes the regular ones employed on the classical guitar.

II.

The preceding summary of the long historical evolution of the lute in Europe is all by way of preamble to an account and consideration of Christian Gottlieb Scheidler, who has been truly called "The Last Lutenist," performing as he did as an official court lutenist, and on a thirteen-course, late Baroque lute. Our excuse for prefacing our words on behalf of Scheidler with this résumé, is that the history of the European lute is still not that well known, and without our summary this composer and his position in the long cavalcade of music would otherwise make little sense. Scheidler thus becomes a figure for fantasy, for imaginative projection and extrapolation, simply because we know so little about him, and because so little of his music apparently survives. He also becomes a figure worthy of the attention of the discriminating Romantist (or Romanticist), because there is always a certain romance and a very definite poignance to any last surviving representative of almost any art, certainly one with the emotional, imaginative, and poetic potential of music.

Although the precise years of Scheidler's birth and death, as well as the places in which they occurred, are not officially recorded in such few reference works as mention him even marginally, a recent Schwann Catalog of recorded classical music (spring 1987) gives these years as 1752 and 1815. Such possibly reflects some recent research resulting in some definite information which has not yet reached, or been prepared to appear in, such reference works as do contain an entry on him. If these dates are indeed firm data that we can trust, they do not belie the older authorities which list his birth as happening around the middle of the 1700's and his death as sometime after 1814.

We know nothing about Scheidler's early life and education. He may have come of a musical family, and he may have been born at or near Mainz where he later held an official appointment. However, we can assume that his musical education and training began early on, as was characteristic of most musicians at this time in history, and as it certainly was as well before the 1700's. We do not know with what master or masters of the lute he studied, but we can hazard a guess that they were at least thoroughly competent and professionally adequate.

Let us place his birth, his early life, and his main career within the known historical background of the lute during the middle and latter eighteenth century. Johann Sebastian Bach (born in 1685) died in 1750. The amazing and ingenious Sylvius Leopold Weiss (born in 1686), the last of the unconditionally great lutenist-composers and a genuine music star of extraordinary prestige and undeniable glamour, also died in 1750. Ernst Baron (born in 1696) died in 1760. In addition to being quite a creditable lutenist and theorbist, Baron authored the only known history of the European lute before the twentieth century, to wit, the *Untersuchung des Instruments der Lauten* (1727). Adam Falckenhagen (born in 1697), one of the last lutenists whose music is significant (albeit mostly of simple structure in two main melodic lines), died in 1761. His first volume of works appeared in 1740, and his second one in 1742; exceptionally, both of them were published in regular musical notation rather than in the usual form of tablatures. David Kellner, a lutenist-composer of the same general period as the preceding figures, and one of the lute's last virtuosos, authored one of the last tablatures to appear for solo lute (published in 1747). After the death or retirement of these virtuosos, Carl Kohaut (alive and active evidently in the middle to latter 1700's) was accounted the single finest lutenist of his own time, the latter 1700's. He came of a family of Bohemian musicians, and passed much of his career in Vienna. Kohaut wrote symphonies as well as lute solos and several concertos for lute and a few bowed instruments. (The lute concertos at least are preserved in the Staatsbiblothek, Preussischer Kulturbesitz, Musikabteilung, Berlin.) His lute concerto in F-major, speculatively dated around 1760, has been recorded by the superlative lutenist and arranger Julian Bream along with other musicians. Apart from Scheidler, the only other known lutenist-composer of the 1780's and 1790's is Johann Friedrich Rust whose extant compositions appear primarily to be simple but attractive sonatas for the lute in conjunction with one or two other instruments.

The preceding résumé represents some of the presently known historical background of the lute during the middle and latter 1700's, and against which we should perceive Scheidler's life, education, and career. Apart from the lute, Scheidler's general musical education was apparently not neglected since it also included training which led to a professional mastery of both cello and bassoon, and much later, evidently quite on his own, a similarly professional mastery of the guitar. His lifespan thus encompasses quite a few dynamic changes both in music style as well as social and military history! In the musical sphere, this would have included what we now term the late Baroque, the *style galant*, the early Classical, and early Romantic. In the social and military sphere, this would have included the French Revolution, the rise to power of Napoleon I, the concomitant establishment of his Empire, the dissolution of the old Holy Roman Empire, the Battle of Waterloo, and the end of Napoleon's Empire and of Napoleon as the Emperor of it!

But, we are anticipating. Let us return to the early life and musical career of one Johann Christian Gottlieb Scheidler. By 1768, when he would have been sixteen years old (had he indeed been born in 1752), he already had a reputation as a cellist. By 1778, ten years later, when he would have been twenty-six years old, he had secured the official position of Court Lutenist to the Elector of Mainz (invariably the same as the Archbishop of Mainz for as long as Mainz had functioned as an Electorate of the Holy Roman Empire, that is, since the 1200's). An old and celebrated locale since the time of the Romans (who had established on the site of an old Keltic settlement a fortress and township which became the capital of Germania Superior), Mainz was that same city-state where Johann Gutenberg had been born, and where he had later used movable metal type to print his instantly famous Bible around 1456. Scheidler as Court Lutenist would have played both solo and as part of the chamber-music ensemble maintained at the Court of the Elector. In addition to the lute, he also played both cello and bassoon with the same chamber-music ensemble as part of the same official appointment. These three positions are all authenticated, and are officially recorded as part of the history proper to the Electorate of Mainz. Scheidler thus enjoyed this official appointment from at least 1778 until 1797, when he was forty-five years old. This represents a period of relatively secure employment for almost twenty years, a generally comfortable situation for an active musician. As a lutenist (according to the present available information) Scheidler was the last creative practitioner of that rather specialized kind of music. Apparently continuing on even after the other known lutenist-composer of the late 1700's had ceased his activity or had died, this being Johann Friedrich Rust, Scheidler thus figured as the very last, solitary representative of an already almost forgotten art.

Our last lutenist's only surviving work for lute (a work, moreover, for lute solo) stems from around the middle of his appointment at Mainz, which undoubtedly constituted the best, the happiest, the most stable, and the most creative part of his life and career. This composition consists of a theme by Mozart followed by twelve variations by Scheidler, as conceived on and for a thirteen-course, late Baroque lute. The original surviving manuscript in the Staatsbiblothek, Preussischer Kulturbesitz, Musikabteilung at Berlin is in the form of a French-style tablature, and bears at the beginning of it this identification written by the composer in French: *Thème de Mozart varié par Scheidler*. The work originated in a perfectly logical way. The world premiere of Mozart's magnificent opera *Don Giovanni* had taken place in Prague in 1787, and the local première in Mainz occurred some two years later on 13 May 1789. At the world première in Prague the cast had sung in the usual Italian; at the local première in Mainz the cast had sung in German, the first such performance of *Don Giovanni* anywhere in Germany. Since Mozart was definitely one of what we would call today the "hot" musicians of his time, it was only natural that Scheidler would have based some composition or series of improvisations on one or more of the melodies in that opera, particularly after Mozart's work had made its local début. Indeed, Scheidler composed his variations around 1790. The theme chosen by our Court Lutenist is the lively main melody, marked *Allegro*, of the *Champagnerlied*, a delightful drinking song; the melody has two sections, each one being repeated. We present the theme in guitar notation (written one octave higher than it sounds).

Both the theme as quoted by Scheidler, as well as his variations, are cast in the key of F-major, a relatively easy one to negotiate on the late Baroque lute since the tuning for the six highest-pitched courses for this instrument is based upon the D-minor arpeggio. The form of Mozart's theme (at least as quoted by Scheidler)—that is, in two sections, with each one being repeated—dictates the form for each variation. It is all relatively simple music, pleasant, soothing, sweetly pastoral, and generally *munter*, or *lively* (as Wilhelm Tappert has accurately characterized it), with some of it (quite naturally) markedly Mozartean; more than a few of the variations are almost "jazzy" and might lend themselves quite well to jazz improvisation. In fact, the little pieces are of such uncomplicated structure, especially in the bass, and are so patently guitar-like, that they might just as well have originated on the then-emerging classical guitar as on the late Baroque lute!

In such unpretentious music as this, with its simple bass generally reduced to the role of supporting the lovely and often enchanting melodiousness in the treble, we are closer in some respects to folk music, perhaps, than to any other kind. We are also closer in structure and feeling to the simple but well-crafted compositions of Adam Falckenhagen and Johann Friedrich Rust. We are as far from the rather grandiose late Baroque style of Bach, Kellner, and Weiss on the one hand as we are from the full-blown *galant* expressiveness of Carl Kohaut on the other. Also, we should not assume just because he had written his variations down in a certain form, that Scheidler would have restricted himself to performing them as is. A skillful lutenist could, and probably would, have used any or all of them as a *point de départ* from which to spin some longer and more complicated improvisation on the spot, perhaps a tripping *Allegretto*, a languishing *Adagio*, or a sustained *Larghetto*.

Thus, of all the compositions that he created during this over-all time whether for cello, bassoon, or lute—and we have it on good authority that they were numerous, covering as they did a period of almost twenty years while he held his official appointment in the city-state of Mainz—we have only these twelve little variations for lute solo. While not *the* very last work for lute especially in conjunction with other instruments, they could very well represent *the* last work for lute solo that is extant. In the observation of the musicologist Lionel de la Laurencie, the lute expired while breathing forth a melody by the divine Mozart.

Due mostly to the rise to power of Napoleon I, the late 1700's and early 1800's witnessed the rearrangement of much of the political map of Europe, including the final dissolution of the Holy Roman Empire, that peculiar mediaeval patchwork of principalities and city-states. Despite its name the Holy Roman Empire was actually the empire of the German-speaking peoples of Central Europe. It had more or less officially begun with the crowning of Charlemagne as Emperor of the West at Rome on Christmas Day in 800, and it was now coming to an end during the reign of Francis II (1768–1835), who ruled much of Central Europe as the last

Holy Roman Emperor from 1804 to 1835. With the dissolution of the Holy Roman Empire came also, of course, the dissolution of the system of Electors by which the Holy Roman Emperors had been chosen, as well as the dissolution of the concomitant system of Electorates by which that same Empire had been maintained. Mainz thus lost its ancient status as an Electorate of the old Empire in 1797, and thus both the principality and the court proper to the Elector of Mainz also came to an end. This meant among other things that the position of Court Lutenist at Mainz ceased to exist, and after steady employment lasting almost two full decades, poor Scheidler was "out of a job." He followed the former Lord High Chancellor of Mainz, Carl Theodor von Dahlberg, to Aschaffenburg, not far from Frankfurt am Main, and then evidently around 1800 to Frankfurt itself, where Scheidler proceeded to create a new life for himself built around the increasing preference for the classical guitar occurring at that time in Germany. From this point forward until his death in 1815, that is, during the latter part of his life, he devoted himself almost completely to the guitar, whether playing it, composing for it, or teaching it. As far as we can infer from the evidence, he must have taught himself the guitar, and mastered the instrument, around the start of his residence in Frankfurt, that is, around 1800. For a classical lutenist the guitar as then extant would have presented no technical problems whatsoever. [The Holy Roman Empire ended in 1806.]

Although it had been in existence in one form or another for quite a long time, at least as long as the lute itself, and although it had already enjoyed previous periods of considerable popularity—albeit with different tuning and stringing—what we now call the classical guitar with the characteristic tuning in E-minor had been slowly coming once again to the fore as a plucked instrument during the last half of the 1700's. Indeed, it was already producing a series of characteristic maestros, e.g., Carcassi, Carulli, Giuliani, etc. Around 1800, or sometime shortly before, the doubled courses of the guitar became simplified to single ones thanks to the manufacturing of technically superior strings of silk and of silk wound with fine silver wire. This major double innovation made possible the creation of an instrument that was comparatively easy to string, to tune, and to play, but perhaps most importantly, easy for the non-professional player to learn. As one result of this major double innovation, the classical guitar, also starting around 1800, became quite popular in Germany, among other countries, and rapidly gained propagation there. The reader may wish to compare the tunings for Renaissance lute, Baroque lute, and classical guitar by means of the diagram that we present below.

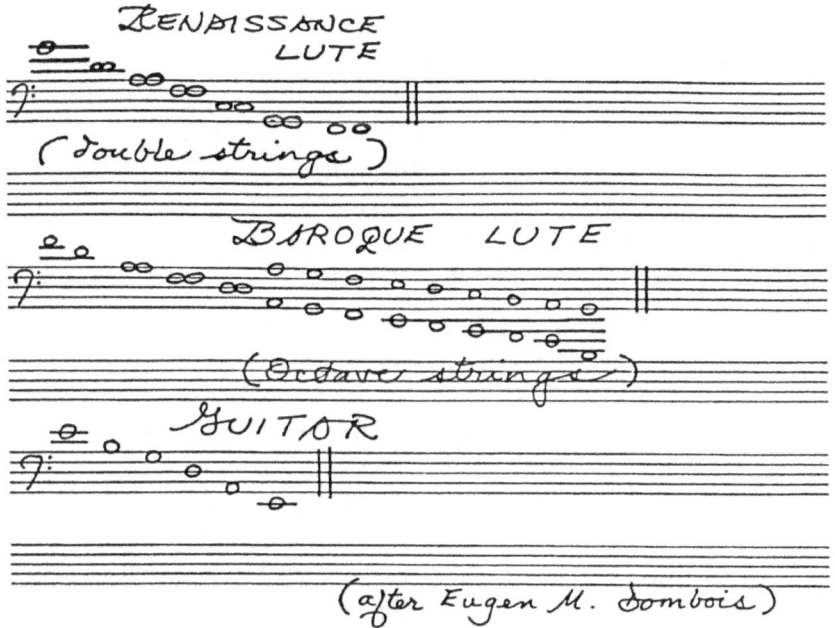

Contemporary accounts c. 1800–1815 praise Scheidler as a guitarist of superior worth. The reader should consult particularly the *Leipzieger Zeitung*, etc. However, he seldom let himself be heard in public, and otherwise in no way concerned himself with the publication of his numerous compositions for the guitar. Between 1812 and 1817 many of them were announced in the contemporary press. Only one opus apparently survives from this quite active period of his life, the Sonata in D-major for guitar and violin. Everything else, including his unpublished works for cello, has been authoritatively reported as being lost. However, the then widespread preference for guitar in Germany exhibits this maestro very much as a musician of his time, as does also the style of his unassuming, instrumentally appropriate compositions. Even allowing for the fact that Scheidler was not a composer of the highest rank, the loss of most of his creative output from this period constitutes an important gap in our knowledge and understanding of the history of the early nineteenth-century guitar, inasmuch as this composer evidently figured as the German equivalent of such Italian maestros as Carcassi, Carulli, and Giuliani.

The only known portrait of Scheidler, painted by Johann Xeller, dates from sometime between 1811 and 1813, and surprisingly exhibits the composer with his thirteen-course, late Baroque lute, rather than with a guitar or any one of his other instruments. This posing with his lute could only have happened at the instigation of the musician in question himself, and patently indicates that he still considered himself at this time a lutenist above all else. Among his rare public appearances at this general period of time, we may cite the one at the concert of the Frankfurt cellist Herr Arnold on 22 January 1806. On this occasion Scheidler with his pupil Fräulein Jung performed his Variations for Two Guitars. Reporting on this concert, the critic writing for the *Allgemeine Musikalische Zeitung* (published in Leipzig), stated of the composer, in the issue for 26 February 1806, that: "Er is nicht nur der erste Lautenist and Virtuos auf der Gitarre in Deutschland, sondern auch ein wackerer Komponist." ("He is not only the first lutenist and virtuoso on the guitar in Germany, but also a worthy composer.") The portrait of Scheidler posing with his lute, coupled with the statement from the periodical cited above, leads us to speculate whether he still played his late Baroque lute for himself in private or (more importantly) for others in public, during that period of his life when his guitar-playing had taken the ascendancy over his other instrumental abilities—that is, c. 1800–1815. We mention this possibility simply because how else would the critic of the periodical in question have known that the composer was still the first, or leading, lutenist in Germany? Such lute-playing, especially after 1800, if it indeed happened (as it possibly may have), would have formed the last authoritative activity on behalf of the European lute as it was going (if indeed it had not already gone) into eclipse during most of the 1800's.

Modest and simple enough, Scheidler's only surviving compositions, the twelve Variations on a Theme by Mozart for lute solo, and the Sonata in D-major for guitar and violin, are constructed according to the general models extant at that time in musical history, whether considered as classical or early Romantic. In the opinion of Ernst Ludwig Gerber (1746–1819)—the German music scholar, organist, and composer who, however, is justly and genuinely celebrated as a great collector and lexicographer—Scheidler's compositions are "brilliant enough, but plainly betray no great master of counterpoint." This statement would lead us to believe that Gerber had probably heard Scheidler play on at least one occasion, probably during one of his rare public appearances when he would have performed some of his own music.

Although he may have been distantly related to them, a direct association between our Scheidler and the famous and quite successful Scheidler family of musicians in Gotha does not seem to have happened. They were nevertheless aware of each other. Johann David Scheidler, the renowned cellist as well as the father of Ludwig Spohr's wife, heard Christian Gottlieb perform (on guitar or lute) on at least one occasion, and may have been duly impressed. The very last that we hear of "The Last Lutenist" is when he became conspicuous in 1814 in the orchestra of the principal theatre in Frankfurt, whether as cellist, bassoonist, lutenist, or guitarist (our sources do not indicate). His death is recorded as occurring in Frankfurt, and as either sometime after 1814 or during 1815. Scheidler presumably died in the *Pension* where he had resided, and where he had taught guitar. The rest is silence for almost a hundred years. The classical European lute to all intents and purposes had died, and had slipped into almost complete oblivion insofar as the general public was concerned.

Then in the late 1800's musicologists became interested in the now-defunct classical lute, and began to investigate the immense amount of music still extant for it in museums and music libraries mostly in the form of tablatures. Foremost among these musicologists was Oscar Chilesotti who published a number of large and excellent anthologies of such music as arranged in guitar notation during the 1890's. Subsequently distinguished luthiers and musicians appeared who began to make, and perform on, copies of the historical lutes surviving in museums and music libraries. The names of such figures as Arnold Dolmetsch as luthier in Britain and Walter Gerwig as lutenist in Germany earned a high place of honor in the history of the early revival of the classical lute. The huge vogue for the classical guitar which happened after World War II, and for which Andrés Segovia was largely responsible, also helped to stir interest in the lute, vihuela, etc., as well as their respective literatures. In the history of the more recent revival of the classical lute such names as the lutenists Julian Bream, Eugen Müller-Dombois, and Paul Odette have earned an equally high place of honor.

Although to some extent an odd-man-out in terms of the enchanted circle of historical lutenist-composers, even Scheidler has modestly figured in this historical revival, beginning in 1906 when the publisher Leo Liepmannsohn in Berlin made available Wilhelm Tappert's important pioneering monograph *Sang und Klang aus Alter Zeit*. The author not only devotes considerable space (whether in his foreword, contents, or main text) to the then-known facts of Scheidler's life and career as "Der letzte Lautenist" ("The Last Lutenist") but moreover reproduces (on page 127), both in French tablature and in regular staff notation, the *Thème de Mozart varié par Scheidler* (marked *Allegro*), and then (as a very nice and charming touch) he closes his book by quoting in full (in regular staff notation) Variations Nos. 1, 3, 7, and 8 from Scheidler's only surviving work for lute. Then, in 1926, two of these variations also appeared in H. D. Bruger's anthology of lute music, *Schule des Lauten-Spiels*, published in Wolfenbuttel. Finally, in 1970, the variations found a complete reproduction (a fact authoritatively noted by the editor in his preface dated "Vienna, June 1970"), albeit in guitar notation, when published by the Hermann Schneider Musikverlag in Vienna, and as edited by the renowned guitar-professor and editor of guitar music Robert Brojer.

However, in general, Scheidler's variations for lute solo are but rarely mentioned among our serious present-day lutenists, and when they are, it is usually with condescension. Simple music of the second or third class is apparently seldom appreciated by advanced musicians! The variations are not available from Donna Curry's Music, Lute and Vihuela Specialists, at Topanga, California; this business constitutes the single most important and complete service of its type in the United States west of the Mississippi River. We mention this only to show to what an extent poor Gottlieb Scheidler is indeed an odd-man-out in musical terms, and surely not to cast any blame on Donna Curry's Music, or Donna Curry herself, a formidable musician, an exceptional contemporary lutenist, and rare lutenist-singer who has mastered the exceptionally difficult art of singing lute songs while accompanying herself on the lute. (A fine long-playing disc features the lute-playing of Donna Curry and entitled *Since I First Saw Your Face*, was formerly available from Klavier Records of North Hollywood, California.) However, Scheidler's variations as arranged for the standard guitar tuned in E-minor may still be obtained from Vienna.

Scheidler's other extant composition, the Sonata in D-major (Opus 21) originally for guitar and violin, is also a simple and unassuming work of considerable charm, and consists of three movements: *Allegro*, *Romance*, and *Rondo*. A modern edition made by J. Zuth was published by Kohler in Karlsbad in 1931. However, the arrangement for two guitars made by Karl Scheit, first published in Vienna in 1949, has enjoyed a great popularity for decades. Rather surprisingly, it has also been arranged as a duo for flute and guitar, and as such it has been recorded twice by the current and immensely popular flautist Jean-Pierre Rampal, the first time with guitarist Ragossnig Linde, and the second time with guitarist Alexandre Lagoya. As performed by such a distinguished and highly visible musician as Rampal, the sonata has evidently become a standard repertory piece! The edition for two guitars made by Karl Scheit is still available from the Österreichische Bundesverlag in Vienna.

Although an individual and relatively distinguished figure in the long cavalcade of music, even if he is patently not a composer of the highest rank, Christian Gottlieb Scheidler—whether as the very last European lutenist before the lute's eclipse around 1800, or whether apparently as the first composer-virtuoso of the guitar in Germany—has no entry in the *New Grove Dictionary of Music and Musicians* (published in December, 1980). He does, however, have an entry in the standard German equivalent of Grove's musical encyclopedia, to wit, *Die Musik in Geschichte und Gegenwart*. The apparent loss of most his compositions and the relative lack of attention given to him in even specialized histories of music are perhaps typical of the posthumous fate often accorded musicians of less than the greatest rank. Inasmuch as the vast majority of his music has disappeared, it is not only unfair but is impossible to make an adequate judgment of Scheidler as a composer on the basis of his two extant works. *Requiescat in pace, unser liebe Scheidler*, and thank you for creating some lovely, albeit unpretentious, musical moments with your pen! You were much too modest for your own posthumous good!

Note.

Principal sources for information on C. G. Scheidler: Wilhelm Tappert, *Sang und Klang aus Alter Zeit* (Liepmannsohn, Berlin, 1906), *passim*. *Die Music in Geschichte und Gegenwart*, Vol. 11 (Bärenreiter, Kassel-Basel-London-New York, 1963), pp. 1625–1626. C. G. Scheidler (Robert Brojer, editor), *Zwölf Variationen uber ein Thema von W. A. Mozart* (Hermann Schneider, Vienna, 1970), see the editor's *Vorwort*. We are especially indebted to our German-born friend Gerda Hoefert Kennedy (originally of Kulsheim, Germany, but now of Sacramento, California) for her help in regard to certain fine points of translation from the German of our principal sources in preparation for this article. We are happy to record our grateful indebtedness to Frau Hoefert-Kennedy. [D. S.-F.]

Addendum.

Of course, despite the eclipse of the classical European lute in its various forms during the 1800's, the lute in general never died out elsewhere. Its non-European progenitors and relatives continued to thrive as they had for centuries, and as they do so today. In Europe the German or modern Volkslaute as well as other types of folk-lute filled the gap while the classical instrument languished or lay dormant. In the Balkan counties one can still find the short-necked lute with four doubled courses played vigorously with a quill; this particular instrument is virtually the same as the mediaeval lute of the 1300's and 1400's. Although the lute is apparently no longer played in Persia where it originated, the *pipa* and *biwa*, directly descended from this ancestor of the Arabian lute, continue to flourish in China and Japan, respectively, as we have already noted at the beginning of our article.

Throughout the modern Islamic world—from Morocco across Northern Africa on into Egypt and both the Near and Middle East, including Turkey, Syria, Lebanon, and Iraq—the Arabian lute, the progenitor of the classical European one, is indeed alive and well whether in classical or popular music. Incidentally, the line between the two forms of music is much less easy to draw in the world of Islam than in the West. Islam still boasts outstanding lutenist-composers, equivalent in stature to any of the great figures in their own past or in the history of the European classical instrument. We should mention a few of these representative modern masters. First, and best known because of his recordings for Lyrichord, there is H. Aram Gulezyan, who has performed extensively in Egypt, and who is the master of a number of plucked instruments, not only the regular *oud* but the similar, wire-strung, *sultania*, as well as the *sarod* and the *sitar*, both native to India. Gulezyan has established an unique reputation whether as an original composer or as a tasteful and profound adaptor of folk-melodies particularly as found throughout both the Near and Middle East. The *oud* played by Gulezyan, usually with a quill, possesses five courses with four of them doubled and with the *chanterelle*, the highest-pitched course, as a single string. Somewhat unusually for the music of the Near and Middle East, Gulezyan's adaptations and compositions are often chordal and ingratiatingly melodious; while metrically clear and often subtle, they are much less pounding in rhythm than so much of Near and Middle Eastern music.

In Iraq there is the formidable figure of Jamil Bachir, who has been recorded on the French label Arabesques, and who is master of the traditional *oud*, as well as a distinguished and highly creative composer in his own right, not only of the shorter pieces traditional to the lute almost everywhere it is played but especially of an unique Concerto for Oud and Orchestra (apparently first performed in the Soviet Union in 1970). The *oud* played with a quill by Bachir possesses six courses with five of them doubled and with the *chanterelle* as a single string, thus comprising an instrument which, while different in tuning, is otherwise virtually the same in size, in shape, and in stringing (of gut) as the Renaissance lute.

There is Hamza el-Din, originally of Nubia, and like Gulezyan and Bachir an unique and formidable performer on the traditional *oud* in addition to being highly creative. Both a lutenist-composer and lutenist-singer, Hamza has had a number of outstanding albums recorded on the Nonesuch label. Born and raised in Nubia, he received his musical education in Egypt, specializing in the *oud* so that he could subsequently adapt his own native melodies to it; this represents the first time that Nubian melodies have thus been adapted to the ambitus and resources of the traditional *oud*, and constitutes an act of genuine creativity. The original sounds thus brought into life comprise a new music, as haunting as it is unique.

Now that the classical European lute, whether Renaissance or Baroque, has returned to life, thanks to the ministrations of divers musicologists, luthiers, and lutenists, perhaps one or more quite original modern musicians who are also lutenist-composers will yet appear, and will bring the lute back to life in higher terms, that is, in terms of its own vital and completely necessary creativity, a creativity analogous to that displayed in the living art of Gulezyan, Bachir, and Hamza el-Din. Without this vital and necessary creativity the classical European lute, in whatever form that it may take, can never completely return to life. If it does not regain its own creativity, it will remain on the level of ultimately mere antiquarianism, and it may become defunct once more. Let us close with a fervent hope that the creative potential of the classical European lute will yet emerge once more, and restore it to the rank that it anciently enjoyed as the Regina Instrumentorum, or the Queen of Instruments.

N.B. Within the last year or so (1989/1990) various virtuosos in the European (revived) tradition of the short-necked lute have had their own brand-new compositions for lute announced for publication and/or actually published. Our fervent wish has been granted.

Francis Marion Crawford:
A Neglected but not a Forgotten Master

F. Marion Crawford? The name rings curiously down the halls and scattered byways of one's memory. Back to one's earliest remembered browsings in used-book stores. Always in the fiction section one could find either a few, or quite a few, titles by a certain F. Marion Crawford. Usually an *In The Palace Of The King* ("illustrated with scenes from the photoplay"), two or three editions of *Zoroaster*, and at least one *The Witch of Prague*, among other books whose titles have since slipped from easy recollection. Thus we first became acquainted with Crawford's name even if we did not read any of his books at that time.

Later, we actually took up a dozen different books by "F. Marion" and eagerly read a now much-neglected master of narrative fiction. The titles? Some of the best-known as well as some of the more obscure. (We list the titles below.) But in no individual case were we disappointed. As pointed out by Dr. Edward Wagenknecht, Crawford "never wrote a book that wasn't worth reading," a truth that validated itself for us at least in terms of the twelve books purposefully encountered.

We mean Crawford no disrespect or disservice when we call him a now much-neglected master. Although not as neglected as he was after World War I, he is still generally overlooked, at least by most readers—and to their loss, it may be added. However, it must be noted that his comparative prolificness and his once considerable popularity (from the early 1880's up to World War I) have assured his name of some reasonable survival just in purely physical terms, so that he is definitely not forgotten. His once-wide popularity guaranteed many printings and reprintings of his numerous novels. There are therefore still many libraries and used-book stores across the U. S. A. (as well as in Great Britain) which stock his titles.

His supernatural stories (gathered into the posthumous collection *Wandering Ghosts*, the British and Continental editions being entitled *Uncanny Tales*) have also helped to keep his name alive. "The Upper Berth" and "The Screaming Skull" have consistently appeared in anthologies of short uncanny fictions, and have assumed the status of genre classics. No less an authority on the supernatural tale than H. P. Lovecraft (discussing them as well as others by Crawford in his now-standard study *Supernatural*

Horror In Literature) has ranked these tales in particular as at once unusually powerful and expertly crafted. The novelistic equivalent of these shorter fantasies is (evidently) to be found in *Khaled, The Witch of Prague,* and *With the Immortals,* among other titles.

It might be mentioned in passing, just as one example of how sensitively and selectively Crawford reflected the new developments and current events of his time, that *The Witch of Prague* (subtitled "A Fantastic Tale") really rates consideration as a kind of science-fiction or science-fantasy: it is based upon, and extrapolated from, the far-reaching possibilities of the then-new science of hypnotism. All descriptions of this tale seem to indicate that Crawford's use of it is not merely decorative, but pivotal, and it motivates and moves the story irresistibly forward in the best tradition of the genuine "scientific romance" as first conceptualized and magisterially exemplified by Jules Verne.

Before we pass to our discussion of the twelve novels by Crawford we have purposefully encountered to date; we should give some cursory consideration to the Romanticism and the so-called (concomitant) genteel tradition of the late 1800's. Whether defined in the most general or in the most radical sense, it would be difficult to find a more thoroughgoing Romanticist in his time than Francis Marion Crawford, our eminent "Romantist" under discussion, and the term "Romantist" is (after all) his own expression. And this assertion may be made in terms of both his life and his written works. In addition to his mastery of the Romance languages (plus that of quite a few more), Crawford was intimately conversant. with the Latin civilizations of the Mediterranean, past and present, and above all else, with the very source and center of all Romanism—or Romanticism for that matter—to wit, the great and enduring metropolis of Mother Rome herself. Moreover, some of his greatest achievements in fiction, qua fiction (rather than Romanticised history, such as he produced in the latter part of his career), concerned themselves with Italian, and specifically Roman (metropolitan), life. Indeed, in the last decade or so of his life, he either had become side-tracked from his main vocation of fictioneering or he was actually evolving into an unique "Romantic-style" historian working toward a complete history of Rome (and the Papal States) from her legendary beginnings with the wolf-nurtured twins Romulus and Remus up to Crawford's own day. This was the great project on which he was actively working at the time of his death and of which he had unfortunately accomplished only a few volumes before he died.

Within the so-called genteel tradition, Crawford has often been vaguely defined as a major, if not the major, fiction purveyor of his time (the latter 1800's and the very early 1900's), at least in English, almost as if his fictional output (and his own best values) constituted a major kind of rearguard defense and apology for this tradition. Nothing could be further from the truth, since Crawford for all his Romanticism was also very much a practical realist. If he indeed did work within the genteel tradition (as did most of the writers of his time, including some titanic figures of patent literary genius), his sense of realism (and reality) compelled him to be honestly and ruthlessly critical of that same tradition, whenever the occasion seemed just.

We venture that this genteel tradition might be defined as the set of understood assumptions, attitudes, preferences, values, rules, regulations, and prejudices proper to the people of taste, property, and class (middle-to-upper) during Crawford's own era. While this tradition had its excesses, flaws. and shortcomings (as do all traditions or power-blocs), yet it did serve many useful purposes in its heyday. It operated more or less from the middle 1800's up to World War I.

So we come now to the twelve novels by Crawford purposefully encountered by us to date. We have arranged the titles chronologically by publication, as this was the order in which we more or less actually read them. The twelve books are as follows: *Mr. Isaacs* (1882), *Zoroaster* (1885), *A Tale of A Lonely Parish* (1886), *Saracinesca* (1887), *Paul Patoff* (1887), *Greifenstein* (1889), *Sant' Ilario* (1889), *Don Orsino* (1892), *Casa Braccio* (1895), *Whosoever Shall Offend* (1904), *Arethusa* (1907) and *Stradella* (1909).

Mr. Isaacs, or "A Tale of Modern India" (as the subtitle runs), is Crawford's first novel and his first great success. This book garnered for him a considerable popular following which was to increase with the years and then only to wane after the author's death (1909) and just after the Great War of 1914–1918. It is written from the perspective of the American writer and journalist Paul Griggs, who symbolizes the author himself. The time is apparently the late 1870's or early 1880's and the story concerns one Mr. Isaacs (or to give him his Persian name, Abdul Hafiz ben Isak) an immensely wealthy merchant dealing in gems, gold, silver, art objects, etc. The narrative is fairly direct and straightforward compared to many other novels of the same period. Our narrator Mr.

Griggs meets Isaacs in Simla (or Shumla) high in the mountains whither the Indo-British government retires every summer from the hot plains of northern India. Griggs and Isaacs socialize with Currie Ghyrkins, a high government official, and his niece Katherine Westonaugh; and the author depicts typical scenes of the life at Simla. Isaacs and another suitor, Lord Steepleton Kildare, are soon competing for the hand of Katherine but of course in a totally gentlemanly way. Although not a Westerner, Isaacs clearly outclasses Kildare, and Katherine makes her preference for Isaacs unmistakable. Kildare and Isaacs have suggested a tiger hunt on the plains south of the mountains. Soon a party is formed that includes Griggs, Isaacs, Kildare, Ghyrkins, Katherine and her brother John. They travel south and set up their camp in an area called the Terai. After a successful week or so of shooting tigers, Isaacs is called away on "business" and after his departure Griggs receives a request from him to join him in the mountains. The tiger-hunt camp is broken up and the rest of the party return to Simla, awaiting the return of Isaacs and Griggs. Aided by Griggs and Isaacs' "adept" friend Ram Lal, Isaacs—through his immense wealth and through his own discrete activity—rescues Shere Ali, the former Amir of Afghanistan deposed by the British and officially an outlaw. The Maharajah of Baithopoor has been secretly holding Shere Ali in prison but Isaacs, who has the Maharajah in his debt for a huge amount of money, forces him to give up his prisoner. The whole action is a delicate one because Isaacs must effect Shere Ali's rescue in secrecy since what he is doing is technically against the British rule. He sends Griggs north with a supply of gold and silver for Shere Ali with Ram Lal as his guide out of the orbit of the British Raj. Isaacs with Griggs then returns to Simla where they find Katherine dying from fever contracted while on the tiger hunt. She dies, and Isaacs who has deeply loved her is roused from his grief by Ram Lal, who also returned from the North. After a long transcendental peroration by Ram Lal and a moving farewell by Isaacs, both disappear from Griggs' life forever. The scenes of Indo-British life draw upon Crawford's extended experience of living in India and give the novel considerable authenticity. Mr. Isaacs was a real person and the main events in the novel reflect actual happenings. Much of the novel's artistic and popular success clearly derive from the civilized tone and genteel sensitivity of the narrator as well as from the accurately observed scenes of Indian life, then quite exotic to many Americans and British.

Zoroaster is what would have been called at the time of its original publication an "archeological" novel due to its being set principally during the early reign of Darius 1. It details not "the eternal triangle" but the compelling quadrangle formed by Darius the Great King of the Persian Empire, his queen and chief wife Atossa, his faithful military-officer-for-all-purposes Zoroaster, and the Hebrew princess Nehushta, Atossa's rival for the hearts of both Darius and Zoroaster. In a manner at once opulent and grand-operatic, but always clear, concentrated, and fast-moving, the novel describes the highly-colored and melodramatic events leading to Zoroaster's renouncing of secular life and his assumption of that religious existence by which, according to history, he exercised a considerable influence on his fellow Persians. The book's opening is distinguished by a magnificent exposition of Belshazzar's feast in Babylon as well as by the delineation of the strong and forceful character of the prophet Daniel. Crawford evidently conceived much of Zoroaster as a drama; and aptly enough the then widely popular French composer Jules Massenet adapted it as a highly effective grand opera *Le Mage* (*The Magus* or *The Magian*).

A Tale of a Lonely Parish in style and incident is at the opposite extreme from *Zoroaster*. The time is "contemporary"—that is, sometime well into Queen Victoria's reign. The setting is a remote and presumably uneventful village, Billingsfield, in Essex—the fictional name for Hatfield Broad Oak, Essex, where Crawford studied during the early 1870's. The characters: a vicar, Augustin Ambrose, who supplements his small annual income from his parish by tutoring a few dull but wealthy students; his superficially severe but actually benevolent wife; one genuinely promising but impoverished student, John Short, who leaves the vicarage to perform brilliantly as a classical scholar in Cambridge. Into this quiet and remote ambiance there enters, with her daughter Nellie, the presumed "widow" Mary Goddard, a lady of some means but under a cloud of unhappiness and oblique scandal, seeking purposefully the quietude and seclusion of Billingsfield. Enters next one Charles James Juxon, the new squire of Billingsfield Hall, an estate that has just finished languishing in court (or "Chancery") for forty years, "ever since the death of the old squire…" Enters somewhat later one Walter Goddard, Mary's presumably dead husband, a disgraced gentleman turned criminal, but now an escaped convict impelled possibly by revenge, murder, and personally achieved justice… Crawford's adroitness as a fictioneer is as marked in *A*

Tale of a Lonely Parish as it is in the instance of *Zoroaster*, but it is here employed in a totally different set of circumstances. This constitutes no mean feat of imagination as well as experience (the novel draws upon Crawford's own experience of scholasticism and village-living in England as a young man).

Saracinesca, Sant' Ilario, and *Don Orsino* all form part of the truly remarkable Saracinesca Trilogy; *Corleone* (1897) can be validly considered a fourth novel in this series. The first two novels give a graphic picture of Roman society during the last days of the Pope's temporal power (the mid-1860's) with the principal focus aimed upon the noble Saracinesca family. The third novel describes the "new Italy" which follows after the dissolution of the Papal States (some twenty years later) but mainly through the figure of the young Don Orsino who represents the third generation of the Saracinescas to be chronicled by Crawford. All in all, these three novels present an important study of Italian (and specifically Roman) life, customs, and conditions during a period of time virtually contemporary with the author's first fictional successes but one which present-day readers will now regard as "historical." Each one of these novels fully justifies very careful reading and offers exceptional enjoyment in many ways: in the fascinating absorption which only good or great fiction can provide; in the wide spectrum of skillful and shrewd characterization which only a large and variegated dramatis personae can reveal; in the interest of faithful historical accuracy; and in the decided charm of a crisp, clear, and uncomplicated style. Certainly the Saracinesca Trilogy must rank as the masterpiece of Crawford's fictional expertise wherein, as in all of his greater works, he deftly and ingeniously joins the art of Romance with the art of realism, surely a considerable achievement.

Paul Patoff, like a number of his novels, is based in part upon some real incidents in Crawford's own life. Our journalist-friend Paul Griggs is both narrator and minor actor in the story. Paul Patoff is in the diplomatic service in Istanbul, or Constantinople. His younger brother Alexander, a strikingly handsome but rather empty and maternally overindulged young man, joins him for a visit. Paul arranges various diversions for him, and these include their watching the Mohammedan services ending the feast of Ramazan from the gallery high up in the mosque of Hagia Sophia. Alexander suddenly and completely disappears, rather to the dismay of his brother who not only feels responsible for his irresponsible sibling but, because of some ill feeling between them, fears that he will be suspected of murdering him. The search for Alexander furnishes most of the momentum for the story. But no one can find him, search they high or low, publicly or privately. Paul Patoff does all he can but to no avail. He leaves Constantinople for awhile and has a series of adventures in Germany and England. Eventually he returns to Istanbul, and by chance he uncovers at last a clue to the whereabouts of Alexander. His brother is located and clandestinely rescued. It appears that he has been kidnapped as a kind of joke and then kept prisoner in a Turkish harem due to the widespread alarm over his disappearance. The animosity between the brothers is based, at first, on their English mother's extreme partiality for Alexander and then, later, on their competition for a young English woman's love. In the end their mother, who cannot any longer conceal the fact that she hates Paul, becomes insane largely because of the tumultuous jealousy and frustration she feels about Paul's triumphant suit for the hand of the young English woman.

All in all, Paul Patoff makes a typical example of novelistic entertainment. It scores on a number of grounds. First, it is reasonably plausible and certainly designed to appeal to a distinctly adult preference for amusement. Then it is a yarn of adventure, intrigue, and suspense. Additionally it is a study of exotic local color, and with its cast of characters of various nationalities it is definitely one of Crawford's "cosmopolitan" narratives, which represent the closest he approached the "international" novel of Henry James. Fortunately his characters are not given overmuch to introspection and self-analysis (in the manner of the overly civilized persons in Henry James' novels), or if they are, then the author deals summarily with this aspect of their makeup. The over-all yarn is brimming with incident and with interesting, vigorously delineated persons and personages. The scenes of purely Turkish life, the descriptions of the Constantinople extant in the late 1800's, the interaction between the Europeans and the natives of the Near East, all these draw upon Crawford's own personal experience and succinct observation. Allowing for the differences in fashionable taste and fictional technique between his time and ours, one would be hard pressed to find a better introduction to Crawford as an entertaining novelist than *Paul Patoff*.

Greifenstein must rank with the Saracinesca Trilogy as one of our author's most singular and expertly realized fictions, and moreover one "the greater part of which," or so Crawford himself tells us, "is a matter of history," truly "a strange case" which actually happened sometime during the author's own century. This strong and somber story describes the isolated existence of two related noble families, the still wealthy Greifensteins and the impoverished but still proud Sigmundskronen, and with both families still living in their ancestral castles within the beautiful but gloomy depths of Germany's Black Forest. With relentless and unforgettable force, Crawford details just how both families work together to save their mutual family honor—stopping at nothing, not even murder—when a long-dead scandal comes back to life (involving the Herr von Greifenstein's dishonored brother Kuno von Rieseneck). As a contemporary critic expressed it, and very well, writing in the then *New York Tribune*, "There is nothing weak or small or frivolous in the story. The author deals with tremendous passions working at the height of their energy. His characters are stern, rugged, determined men and women, governed by powerful prejudices and iron conventions, types of a military people, in whom the sense of duty has been cultivated until it dominates all other motives, and in whom the principle of noblesse oblige is, so far as the aristocratic class is concerned, the fundamental rule of conduct. What such people may be capable of is startlingly shown." When all the emotional storm and stress finally subside which have been created by these families in saving their precious family honor, it seems a miracle to have at least the traditional, time-honored "happy ending" of Romance. Never could it have occurred at greater cost to the suffering people involved!

Casa Braccio forms (among other things) the story of Paul Griggs, Crawford's fictionalized "alter ego," who usually represents his own personality, opinions, and general attitudes. Like many of his better "contemporary" narratives dealing with Italian and American life, *Casa Braccio* is a family novel of then-modern Italian society, and is one of his longest productions. Considering that the background of the story is nineteenth-century Italy, it is all the more striking and unexpected that the first part of the novel details the account of a Catholic nun who deserts her convent to elope with her British lover and to accompany him back to Great Britain. In the second part the former nun's daughter, Gloria Dalrymple, comes to Italy and marries the young artist Angelo Reanda. However, she leaves her husband for Paul Griggs who loves her but has had no idea that she would actually do such a thing for him. For a variety of reasons Gloria feels that she cannot return to Angelo, even though later she desires to do so. After the birth of her and Paul's natural son, she becomes more and more depressed, hiding these feelings nonetheless, and then finally poisons herself. However much grief stricken, Paul finds happiness in the memory of what he has considered to be their perfect love until he discovers (via some letters that she had written before her death to her husband but that she had not sent) that she had really loathed him. This is, of course, a great blow to his psyche; nevertheless, he continues writing and living but with no more vivid sensations of pain or pleasure. He has become in a sense, "dead" to the world. The story abounds with excellently observed scenes of Italian (and specifically Roman) life, which the author knew from protracted first-hand experience. It ends with a grippingly underwritten description of a brutal but quietly efficient murder in a Roman church, a development as unexpected and striking in its way as the earlier one of the Catholic nun deserting her convent and eloping with her lover. *Casa Braccio* must take rank with some of Crawford's best fiction, another adroit amalgam of realism and Romance.

Whosever Shall Offend is another of Crawford's novels of at-once family and Italian life. It is not a major work nor is it particularly a minor one, but somewhere in between. The narrative turns on the mysterious disappearance of the youth Marcello Consalvi from his family's seaside hunting lodge outside Rome. The same day he disappears, his mother dies, presumably because of emotional stress brought on by her son's disappearance, but actually through the agency of a poison which leaves no trace and which she takes thinking it to be headache medicine (both compounds having the same physical appearance in the form of pills). Despite an exhaustive search instigated by Marcello's stepfather Folco Corbario, neither the authorities nor some privately-hired detectives can find the young man. After a period of weeks Marcello re-emerges in the charity ward of a Roman hospital as an almost complete amnesiac because of an apparent injury to his head. He had been found and cared for by the remarkably beautiful peasant girl Regina Spalletta who loves him and who has managed to bring him to Rome. He regains his former memory after a successful operation but does not remember what happened to him during his period of amnesia, that is, during his disappearance. He takes over his inheritance from his mother's estate and resumes his life with stepfather Corbario who urges him to travel, secretly hoping he will destroy himself through dissipation. Eventually, after much difficulty and complication, after much auctorial plotting and counterplotting Corbario is revealed as the murderer of Marcello's mother and as the engineer of his disappearance. He is sentenced to life imprisonment rather than death. Regina Spalletta conveniently dies of a malarious fever, and in true Romantic fashion Marcello is reunited at the end of the story with Aurora dell' Armi, his childhood sweetheart. Of particular fascination, as always, apart from the narrative but giving it cogency and verisimilitude, are the closely observed customs and vignettes of Italian life—from the aristocratic to the rustic. Crawford's main concern in this Romance, as in all his novels, is first, last, and always that of entertainment; and in this he succeeds admirably.

The remaining two novels, *Stradella* and *Arethusa*, need not detain us overlong, for the most part, beyond a few general remarks and a few pointed details. Both are among Crawford's lesser-known titles; both are comparatively minor works; both are essentially their author and his family's main new meal-tickets for the years in which they were published; and yet both are eminently worth reading simply as entertainment. They bear out again Dr. Wagenknecht's contention that the author never wrote a book that wasn't worth being read.

Arethusa is the lesser as well as the less adroit of the two; Crawford sets this historical novel during the latter history of the Eastern Roman or Byzantine Empire (the 1370's); and in the character of Arethusa herself he scores a palpable triumph. She is a young woman who finds herself, at the start of the story, in both adverse and reduced circumstances because her father and hence her family had incurred the disfavor of the then-reigning emperor, Andronicus. Arethusa's portrait probably constitutes the novel's most notable feature but as in all of Crawford's fiction there is ample evidence of the author's shrewd psychology in both narrative and characterization, often heightened by a delightful sense of humor as well as by light satirical touches, even if the narrative is malproportioned rather noticeably in places.

Stradella forms a more notable achievement than *Arethusa*, and Crawford has presumably based the story on a real incident in the life of the seventeenth century composer Alessandro Stradella (ca. 1645–1681), originally of Naples. The tangled skein of the narrative ends happily of course for both Alessandro and his highborn, runaway lover Ortensia, with none other than the then Pope himself acting as the *deus ex machina*. Crawford's skills in characterization remain as expert as ever, and the plotting, especially the actual shape of the narrative itself, is markedly superior to that of *Arethusa*.

Crawford himself (as remarked by his friend the celebrated operatic soprano star Nellie Melba) possessed an excellent singing voice (he was a tenor), and in addition was an all-around accomplished, even if nonprofessional, musician. (According to La Melba, Francis Marion could have made a career as a professional singer, should he have had that ambition.) This comes forward most particularly in his description of the lutes handled by both Oretensia and Alessandro, and indicates as well the unusual care with which he conducted his historical research, since by the time he wrote *Stradella*, the lute had been extinct for over a hundred years, apart from a few dilettantes who had played it during the nineteenth century but not necessarily in the correct historical style, and apart from a sizable number of guitarists who favored the German Volkslaute, or six-stringed lute-guitar (also known as the "modern" or, also and paradoxically, "Gothic" lute). When we first meet Ortensia, Crawford describes her as holding "a lute with eleven strings, but of the shorter kind with the head of the keyboard [*id est*, fret-board] turned back at a right angle."

(This would be the basic Renaissance lute of eleven strings, or six "courses," with the chanterelle, or highest pitched course, as a single, and with the others doubled.) Shortly thereafter Ortensia's uncle, the Venetian Senator Michele Pignaver, ushers in Maestro Stradella himself (carrying "a musical instrument in a purple bag"), whom the Senator has engaged in order to give his niece a few lessons in both voice and lute. Crawford's description is noteworthy for its accuracy: "He carefully withdrew his lute from the purple bag and began to tune the strings. It was a fine instrument, made in Cremona. . . . It was differently designed, too, being much longer, with a double fret-board [*id est*, a double neck] and no less than nineteen strings." From the detail of the double neck we can gather that Stradella plays some kind of archlute, probably a theorbo (or "theorboed" lute), with the main neck carrying the strings on the fretboard, and with the subsidiary neck carrying the longer "open," or drone, bass strings.

The nineteen strings would indicate a ten-course instrument, with the top single, and with the others doubled. as well as with the top six courses upon the main neck fretted, and with the four bottom-most, or open, courses carried on the secondary neck. By the time of which Crawford writes—circa 1670—the lute, although no longer as popular as during the 1500's, and although passed over due to its difficulty by most amateurs for the much easier guitar, still enjoyed the attention of virtuosi such as Stradella; and while its seventeenth-century vogue (such as it was) was now occurring mostly in Paris, some instrumentalists did still play it in Italy, especially in its form as the metal-strung chitarrone in the then Italian opera orchestra, where it found employment furnishing the basso continuo or thorough bass. Now Crawford could only have known what he did about the historical lute from his own digging into musical archives located in Italy and elsewhere, since the lute had not yet begun its present comeback and renaissance, and since even most musicians and musicologists in the first decade or so of the twentieth century knew almost nothing about it themselves.

One further especially noteworthy feature of *Stradella*: those unforgettable rogues, the professional bravoes Trombin and Gambardella, who (while certainly far more hard-hearted) do anticipate in a general way the two professional fighting-men Fafhrd and the Gray Mouser in the notable saga created around them by the well-known contemporary writer of fantasy and science-fiction Fritz Leiber.

Before we close, our examination of the twelve novels by Marion Crawford just discussed can permit us to make some general observations on him as a fiction writer, especially in regard to his contemporaries, as well as in regard to his successors, particularly in the field of popular Romance. The criticism which charges that he may have written too much or too rapidly also needs a brief consideration.

A contemporary critic discussing *Greifenstein* had occasion to remark in praising it that "it… shows that he has not been tempted into careless writing by the vogue of his earlier works…" What then could have caused Crawford to become comparatively careless in some of his later novels? First, the sheer necessity to provide for his wife and family who lived very well indeed in an elaborate domestic establishment (in Italy where he lived most of his life), which Crawford had set up (understandably) during his earlier period of success. (Crawford himself lived very simply; his writing studio in an isolated tower was monastic in its austerity; and he never desired luxury for himself, only security and considerable comfort for his family.) Second, his passion for history (both original research and writing), which caused him to become sidetracked from his main vocation of fictioneering, which (to judge from his letters as well as from his comments in various novels) he evidently felt was lacking the dignity and seriousness of the official "historiographical" profession. Crawford was not the first, nor will he have been the last, to disregard the means by which he had gained his principal fame and income in favor of "something else" of presumed greater dignity and seriousness. It is a phenomenon that the diligent student can observe in many separate fields of endeavor and genuine accomplishment. Possibly he may have been mistaken but he died with his fictional powers still very much intact as clearly instanced by the posthumously published romance *The White Sister*. Possibly he may have written too much but the necessity to earn a living and to provide for his family in what was generally considered then a befitting manner, was as compelling a reason at least as any and probably more so than most others. Possibly he may have written too rapidly; but this is a charge which does not really require serious denial, since he wrote some of his best books and some of his less distinguished ones with equal speed and fluency. Possibly, too, had he lived, he could have adapted to the altered conditions in the fiction market and in people's changing tastes, those altered conditions which were attendant on the catastrophic events taking place in Europe just before, during, and after the Great War of 1914–1918. It must remain a moot question since his rather early death (in part caused by overwork) brought that possibility, of course, to a decided end. Actually Crawford was only middle-aged when he died.

How does our notable Romantist compare to some of his equally prominent contemporaries?—that is, those working in the same or similar fields? While not always on the same level as Joseph Conrad or Mark Twain, he does hold his own with A. Conan Doyle and possibly has an edge over H. Rider Haggard. He is markedly superior to both Robert W. Chambers and Winston Churchill (the novelist, not the later English politician). We personally find him far more interesting than William Dean Howells, the defender of a very limited kind of realism, and admittedly a totally different sub-species of writer.

Although only marginally recorded in his correspondence, Henry James considered Crawford's type of Romantic fiction "bad art"—and yet James was infinitely less versatile and adventurous than Crawford whether in life or literature. Crawford went to great lengths in his historical research and in such deliberate learning experience as proved necessary in order to treat adequately certain professions and styles of life in his fiction (for one salient example, he purposefully mastered the basics of silversmithing over a period of months so as to do justice to his descriptions of the same in *Marzio's Crucifix*). Even allowing for the differences in their respective overviews of life, James could certainly have learned a number of beneficial things from the author of the Saracinesca Trilogy, especially in the latter's faculty of narrating a story in a clear, compact, and straightforward manner. At his worst, James in his "inevitable prolixity and pomposity" (to use H. P. Lovecraft's phrase) makes a rather poor showing compared to Crawford's more simplified presentation. Crawford, it must be said to his credit, did not by any means despise James as a person or a writer, and fully admitted the brilliance of James' more noteworthy artistic successes. However, because of his more limited experience of life, James did not possess the wide sympathy for all humanity (particularly the poorer classes) that Crawford did. Further, our Romantist's own biography reads literally like a fantastic Romance.

Crawford's prose is almost never marred by the worst rhetorical excesses of the so-called Mauve Decade but is generally lucid, vivid, and refreshingly simple. There is very little of period "foolishness" in his overall output except, possibly, a too-great reliance on some of the traditional stock-in-trade of Romancers in general (e.g., the contrived happy ending, the deus ex machina, the useful but basically unrealistic coincidence, etc.)—although Crawford does usually go to some pains to impart at least a superficial verisimilitude even in his less-adroitly created novels.

He is far more diversified, plausible, and genuinely interesting in an adult way than such later popular Romancers as Edgar Rice Burroughs, Zane Grey, James Oliver Curwood, Peter B. Kyne, Rafael Sabatini, et al. It is Crawford's very real depth, his very real powers of characterization, dialogue, psychology, and so forth, which make him superior. In short, he may still be comparatively neglected, but he is not forgotten; and he definitely ranks as some kind of master, at least within his own chosen genre of Romance-realism.

F. Marion Crawford: Romantist Nonpareil

F. Marion Crawford. On how many books and on how many copies of those books in how many editions has that name appeared! Although his once-vast audience has decidedly diminished in size, yet a select and steady readership keeps his name alive, still as a *living* author (that is, *living* in the minds of those readers), even though his mortal corpus has long since disappeared with all due pomp, reverence, and regret. From about the mid-1880's until his death in 1909, he functioned as the most adroit and successful Romantic novelist in the English language, garnering a wide popularity in both the U. S. A. and the British Empire. A cosmopolite of American parentage who was born and who lived most of his life in Italy, and a truly astonishing linguist (among many other accomplishments), he counted some of his staunchest admirers from the ranks of the so-called genteel society of his time in English-speaking countries. He came to write his first novel at the highly sensible suggestion of an uncle, and the book developed into a major critical and popular success.. He had paid his dues, as the current phrase expresses it; he was luckily gifted, and he maintained his pre-eminence into the year of his death, the same week that witnessed the passing of the great lyric poet Swinburne. No mean achievement for a writer whose work the novelist Henry James deemed "bad art." But then, James did not especially care for the great French poet and arch-translator of Edgar Allan Poe, Charles Pierre Baudelaire, whose own particular creative accomplishments seem to have completely escaped the worthy Mr. James's perception.

However, despite this negative reaction to his novels (one of the few such at the time), and despite the considerable decline in their popularity, the sheer size of the printings for his novels guaranteed the survival of at least Crawford's name in all manner of bookshops, second-hand stores, libraries, and special collections. And it is curious that, where his works have survived in active reprinting, this owes nothing to any of them having attained the status of children's classics, like some of the best-known books by H. Rider Haggard, Robert Louis Stevenson, Edgar Rice Burroughs, Jack London, or Zane Grey, among others. Crawford's appeal today remains primarily for adults as it did in the time of his greatest vogue. Incidentally, in the ranks of Crawford's fellow Romancers, Stevenson significantly numbered himself as definitely one of his admirers.

266

The one area in which Crawford has been reprinted and anthologized time and time again is the genre of fantasy and the weird. This might have surprised him, as these stories were at best only peripheral to his main work, with the exception perhaps of the novel *The Witch of Prague* (subtitled *A Fantastic Tale)*. Yet their author evidently felt compelled to write them. The posthumous collection *Wandering Ghosts* contains such tales as "The Upper Berth" and "The Screaming Skull." The late great *doyen* of the cosmic and the supernatural, H. P. Lovecraft, rates these particular tales very highly in his monograph *Supernatural Horror in Literature,* and indeed they have assumed the definite status of genre classics. Like the best of the more recent productions in this class of highly specialized but imaginative fiction, Crawford's examples are notable for the simple, straightforward style in which he couches them. However, his novels are fortunately conceived in the same direct manner. No baroque or Late Romantic ambiguities or curlicues for his works overall.

But what then of the great mass of his novels, which after all makes up most of his work? Ah, then, what indeed! Let us choose precisely one dozen, out of the forty or so novels bearing the name of F. Marion Crawford. Arranged in chronological order, this selection includes *Mr. Isaacs (1882), Zoroaster* (1885), *A Tale of a Lonely Parish* (1886), *Saracinesca* (1887), *Paul Patoff (1887), Greifenstein* (1889), *Sant' Ilario* (1889), *Don Orsino* (1892), *Casa Braccio* (1895), *Whosoever Shall Offend* (1904), *Arethusa* (1907), and *Stradella* (1909). This makes a good cross section of his work, since it contains both major and minor novels, as well as fiction of intermediate quality. From a reading and re-reading of these books, we can immediately perceive one main concern on the part of their author, that of the novel as entertainment, first, last, and always. While Crawford was by no means unaware of the novel as high art (the achievements of Gustave Flaubert, for one example), the principle of entertainment dominates in his works. In the final analysis, despite all the talk by fiction elitists of "artistic construct," of fiction as psychological or metaphorical projection, of narrative as a deliberate and tightly controlled symbolic scheme, or even as a psychiatric case history, fiction must first of all succeed as a story, as entertainment. From this first condition or principle Crawford rarely strayed, and all in all we can pronounce this as a very good thing, indeed. Nonetheless, if he did put his own books together with considerable artifice (perfectly allowable), he employed considerable art (a nice bonus) in their construction as well.

Let us look then at our selection of a dozen representative novels. It includes his earliest book, *Mr. Isaacs*, three historical Romances, *Zoroaster*, *Stradella*, and *Arethusa*, the latter two being among the last books Crawford lived to complete; one novel of contemporary English life, *A Tale of a Lonely Parish*; one novel of contemporary German life, *Greifenstein*; and one novel of contemporary Euro-Turkish life, *Paul Patoff*. The remaining five novels, including the magnificent *Saracinesca* trilogy, detail contemporary Italian life. This choice of novels gives us considerable indication of our author's range and abilities.

Mr. Isaacs provides a graphic picture of Indian life under the British Raj, distinguished here and there with both subtle and overt satirical touches. This first novel still stands up quite well to critical scrutiny after all the years since its first publication. The description of Indo-British life is based upon Crawford's own experience living there, and Mr. Isaacs was a real person. *Saracinesca*, *Sant' Ilario*, and *Don Orsino*, which make up the *Saracinesca* trilogy, form the full-fledged but compact chronicle of the aristocratic Saracinesca family during the dissolution of the Papal States and afterwards. Featuring a large and variegated cast of characters, it probably represents the crown of Crawford's fiction expertise, highlighting as it does his own unique amalgam of realism and Romance. Another major novel with an Italian milieu, *Casa Braccio*, one of his longest and strongest productions, ranks in importance virtually next to the *Saracinesca* trilogy. The novel begins rather startlingly with a nun (Sister Maria Addoloratta) eloping from her convent to accompany her Scottish lover out of Italy and back to the British Isles. Years later, their daughter Gloria Dalrymple comes to Rome, marries and then deserts an artist, takes up with a journalist, and finally during a long siege of depression commits suicide. Crawford explores the moral and emotional implications of the heroine's plight *vis-à-vis* the compelling taboos and attitudes of Roman society of that day. The plot of *Whosoever Shall Offend* revolves around an aristocratic youth's mysterious disappearance as well as his mother's equally mysterious death. Although a work of only intermediate quality, it does nonetheless provide a good "read" and is well worth the fiction-devotee's time and effort. Like the other novels of Italian life discussed here, it is based upon Crawford's long experience living in Italy and evidently is quite accurate and realistic in its depiction and observation of everyday life there during the late nineteenth century. All these five books with an Italian background are novels of family life, a genre wherein their author excelled.

A Tale of a Lonely Parish, another family novel, demonstrates how the undercurrents and private passions of life in an obscure and lonely English village in late Victorian times did not always match its quiet and idyllic surface. A family novel again, *Greifenstein* details the isolated existence of two related noble families living in their ancestral castles in the depths of the Black Forest and examines how ferociously feudal codes of honor operate almost to destroy their everyday human happiness. *Paul Patoff* describes the perils that a young diplomat in Constantinople undergoes when his younger brother joins him for a visit and is mysteriously kidnapped. A sophisticated adventure novel, the narrative brims with exotic local color and with the often unexpected complexities of life inherent in the cosmopolitan setting of late nineteenth-century Constantinople.

The remaining stories under consideration are all historical novels but are as full-fleshed and full-bodied in their way as their author's novels of contemporary life. *Zoroaster,* an operatically opulent narrative, details the compelling quadrangle formed by Darius I, the Great King of Persia, his queen and chief wife Atossa, his general Zoroaster, and the Hebrew princess Nehushta, Atossa's chief rival for the hearts of both Darius and Zoroaster. Highly dramatic and full of contrasts, the story was adapted as the basis for the grand opera *Le Mage* by the then widely popular French composer Jules Massenet. *Stradella* and *Arethusa* are both minor works but bear out Wagenknecht's point that Crawford never wrote a book that was not worth reading. Set in Constantinople during the latter history of the Byzantine, or Eastern Roman, Empire, the most notable feature of *Arethusa* is the character and characterization of the nobly-born Arethusa herself whose father and family fall from the imperial favor. Crawford presumably based *Stradella* upon a real incident in the life of the composer Alessandro Stradella (c. 1645–1681), originally of Naples. The tangled skein of the narrative ends happily, of course, for Alessandro and his highborn, runaway lover Ortensia, with none other than the Papal Majesty himself acting as the *deus ex machina.* One particularly noteworthy feature of *Stradella* remains those unforgettable rogues, the professional bravoes and swordsmen, Trombin and Gambardella.

These novels do indeed then give us a considerable indication of our author's range of abilities. He excels in the creation of individual characters. Here we have a consistently interesting cast of actors and characterizations, from Mr. Isaacs all the way to Maestro Stradella, from shrewd peasants, gossiping servants, and other so-called simple folk, all the way to either decent and humane aristocrats or decadent and corrupt nobles. Crawford's extensive travels and upper-class mobility gave him a broad perspective on, as well as a broad sympathy for, all classes of society and all manner of activities and occupations, some of which he assumed himself for a while in order to describe them all the better in his novels. Many of the events and people detailed in his books reflect real events and real people, and this undoubtedly aids in imparting considerable verisimilitude to his narratives.

Where does one begin just to list the characters who spring to mind? First there is Abdul Haifiz ben Izak, or as he styled himself, Mr. Isaacs, that supremely capable businessman and fascinating mixture of Eastern and Western culture, extraordinarily handsome, sophisticated, multi-languaged, and thoroughly experienced in all manner of derring-do and adventure. Then there is the journalist Paul Griggs, appearing in *Paul Patoff, Casa Braccio,* and elsewhere, and representing the author himself, modest, self-deprecating but perfectly capable. There is the strong, beautiful, naive, but immensely likable peasant girl Regina Spalletta in *Whosoever Shall Offend,* as well as the seemingly harmless but devious and unctuous villain Folco Corbario. *Zoroaster* gives us a whole gallery of remarkable actors: we need only mention the stern patriarch and prophet Daniel, the manly and straightforward Zoroaster himself, the no less manly Great King, Darius, the master of all men in his empire except perhaps his own general, and the outwardly cool and composed but inwardly complex and passionate Atossa. *A Tale of a Lonely Parish* boasts quite a cast of characters but we should single out the gracious and wistful Mary Goddard and the solid, stolid, and steady Charles James Juxon, squire of Billingsfield Hall. *Greifenstein* is compact of absorbing characters and narrative: Chief among them are the seemingly frail but stern, strong, and amazingly self-sacrificing Frau von Sigmundskron; her daughter Hilda (a child of the isolated depths of the Black Forest), who is one of Crawford's most memorable heroines, so noble, constant, and brave; the equally stern, silent, grizzled, tough and stiffly courteous Herr von Greifenstein; his wife, the twitchy, nervous, affected, and superficially silly Clara von Greifenstein; their son, the handsome and truly manly "Greif," as he is nicknamed; and Greif's half-brother Rex, the novel's tragic hero.

In addition to such remarkable individuals as Trombin and Gambardella, *Stradella* offers us, among others worthy of special mention, the composer's own Sancho Panza-like servant, the clever and accommodating hunchback Cucurullo, whose antics are as comedic and sympathetic as his rather droll name. The villains in these tales are unmistakably that, but their creator usually shades them enough so that we can perceive them still as full-fledged human beings in their own right (or wrong). These, and many other characters are much more than types or personages. They are genuine persons, most of them belonging unmistakably to their class of society, but exhibiting nonetheless as much individuality as, if not more than, anyone living today. Characterization is more succinct in Crawford's novels, generally, than in the earlier, and often more sprawling, Victorian narratives by other authors. His novels do indeed contain a wide spectrum of *dramatis personae,* and in fact Crawford conceived of the novel in dramatic terms, that is, as a miniature theater with similar principles of dialogue, action, characterization, and so forth. His dialogue is generally apt and compelling, as well as characteristic of the individual speaking. The author's background work is usually skillful, to the point, and gracefully worked into the narrative at large, with relatively few set pieces *per se.*

How does our notable Romantist compare to some of his equally prominent contemporaries, that is, those working in the same or similar fields? While not always on the same level as Joseph Conrad or Mark Twain, he does hold his own with such immensely popular scriveners as A. Conan Doyle and H. Rider Haggard. He is markedly superior to both Robert W. Chambers and Winston Churchill (the novelist, not the later English politician). We personally find him far more interesting than William Dean Howells, the champion of a very limited kind of realism, and admittedly a totally different species of writer.

Although only marginally recorded in his correspondence, Henry James considered Crawford's type of Romantic fiction "bad art"—and yet James was infinitely less versatile and adventurous than Crawford whether in life or literature. Crawford characteristically went to great lengths in his historical research and in such deliberate learning experience as proved necessary to treat certain professions and styles of life adequately in his fiction (for one salient example, he purposefully mastered the basics of silversmithing over a period of months so as to do justice to his description of same in *Marzio's Crucifix).* Even allowing for the differences in their respective overviews of life, James could certainly have learned a number of beneficial things in the art of fiction from the author of the Saracinesca Trilogy, especially in the latter's faculty of narrating a story in a clear, compact, and straightforward manner. At his worst, James in his "inevitable prolixity and pomposity" (to use H. P. Lovecraft's phrase) makes a rather poor showing compared to Crawford and his more simplified presentation. Crawford, it must be said to his credit, did not by any means despise James as a person or a writer, and fully admitted the brilliance of James's more noteworthy artistic successes. However, because of his more limited experience of life, James did not possess the wide sympathy for all humanity (particularly the poorer classes) that Crawford did. If F. Marion Crawford did not write a *Golden Bowl* or a *Wings of the Dove*, then neither did Henry James write a *Marzio's Crucifix*.

Crawford's prose is almost never marred by the worst rhetorical excesses of the so-called Mauve Decade but is generally lucid, vivid, and refreshingly simple. There is very little of period "foolishness" in his overall legacy except, possibly, a too great reliance on some of the traditional stock-in-trade of Romancers in general (for example, the contrived happy ending, the *deus ex machina,* the useful but basically unrealistic coincidence, and so on), although Crawford does usually go to some pains to impart at least a superficial verisimilitude even in his less adroitly created novels.

He is far more diversified, plausible, and genuinely interesting in an adult way than such later popular Romancers as Edgar Rice Burroughs, Zane Grey, James Oliver Curwood, Peter B. Kyne, and Rafael Sabatini. It is Crawford's very real depth, his very real powers of characterization, dialogue, and psychology that make him superior. In short, he may still be comparatively neglected, but he is not forgotten; he definitely ranks as some kind of master, at least within his own chosen genre of Romance-realism.

In all truth Crawford never wrote the greatest book that he had lurking potentially within him. He lived it instead. All biographies of him are perforce but pale reflections of his own life, which literally reads like the most fantastically realistic Romance that one could imagine. And what sober and industrious biographer could do justice to that? Relatively few, we must admit.

It is very easy to say that Crawford deserves rediscovery and revival for his output overall. However, individual scriveners and scholars do not determine that possibility; only the general reading public does. But, if it ever does rediscover F. Marion Crawford, then that same public has many enjoyable, and oftentimes even astounding, hours of entertainment in store for it and from a veritable treasure-house.

Robert E. Howard:
Frontiersman of Letters

Among those writers who contributed to *Weird Tales* from 1923 to 1954 and helped make it memorable, there were at least five who more than any others truly made it *The Unique Magazine* (as its quondam subtitle ran) and who gained thereby an unique reputation for themselves: Henry St. Clair Whitehead (1882–1932), Howard Philips Lovecraft (1890–1937), Clark Ashton Smith (1893–1961), Robert Ervin Howard (1906–1936), and Ray Bradbury (born 1920). The two outstanding poets of this group, whether in verse or in prose, were the Californian, Clark Ashton Smith, and the Texan, Robert E. Howard. Smith had gained an outstanding reputation for himself as a lyric poet before he began to contribute regularly to *Weird Tales*. Howard may have made his first reputation through *Weird Tales* but he went on to write successfully for virtually every major type of pulp magazine of his time—a considerable accomplishment. Moreover he used his writings not merely to make a living as a pulp-writer but also to express his life-attitude and life-philosophy. His death at the age of thirty is often held to have cut short a career of great promise, but many commentators underestimate the fact that he had had a career of considerable achievement by the time he died. In Howard's best prose and verse, there inheres a wonderful and liberating sense of imagination and adventure, an uniquely healthy gesture reaching outward, as well as a pulse, a rhythm, that is as vigorous as it is invigorating.

Howard was descended of pioneer forebears and one senses a certain Homerical quality of the frontier and the frontiersman in his best writings. Just as much as his Texas forebears, Howard was a pioneer, but in his own way. Where they had hewed and fought with axe and gun to build a life for themselves from an often hostile environment, Howard in his turn used his typewriter to wrest a living for himself in the face of what was assuredly not a sympathetic environment. He showed his fellow citizens of Cross Plains, Texas, that a man could make a living for himself through his writing. What sweat and tears and blood the dedicated writer of vision and responsibility must sometimes shed, so that through his pain he can create pleasure and enlightenment for others, only the initiated can discover and know for themselves. But where the old pioneers had at least enjoyed a hearty and warm companionship in their adventure, Howard had in his adventure virtually no kindred spirits living near him, and in an interior sense he lived virtually alone, sustaining himself spiritually through literature, his own or that created by others, and through correspondence with a few of his fellow writers for *Weird Tales* and other magazines. The amazing thing is that, with or without the immediate physical presence of kindred spirits, he managed to create as much as he did in the short period of time at his disposal as a professional writer.

Today, more than ever before, there is a large and growing audience for Howard's fine adventure stories. Just as his finest verses—with their pulsing rhythm, their incantatory rime, their vivid and colorful imagery—make one think instinctively of the poet in his primal role as a witch-doctor or magician invoking spirits good and evil for the benefit of his people or to the harm of their enemies human or otherwise; so do Howard's finest stories evoke for us the presence of the campfire narrator, or the antique bard in flowing bardic robes, who keeps his fellow tribesmen or adventurers enthralled and thrilled with epic narratives of men battling against seemingly insuperable odds, perhaps eventually to triumph or, even if defeated, to triumph still in their own dark will. More than any other writer except perhaps Jack London (one of his favorite authors), Howard stands alone in twentieth-century literature in his ability to envision and portray elemental red-blooded struggle in "perilous untried barbaric lands." He is often unsurpassed in his power to invoke primordial gods or forces greater and older than man. His best short stories—with their vigorous and rhythmical prose, their sense of a larger context than man's own immediate environment, their strong and sweeping narratives, their often striking and poignant imagery—are akin to the plays and poems of the Elizabethans—with their similar sense of adventure spiritual and physical, with their sense of breathless discovery and exploration, and with their consciousness of the vastness and of the macrocosmos. Some of his best stories such as "The Mirrors of Tuzun Thune" are virtual prose-poems in the manner of Poe's masterpiece, "The Masque of the Red Death."

Akin to Howard's best prose fiction is his unique sequence of prose-poems, *Etchings in Ivory*, the very titles of which open up magic portals of mystery and imaginative speculation: "Flaming Marble," "Skulls and Orchids," "Medallions in the Moon," "The Gods that Men Forget," "Bloodstones and Ebony." Verily, these are titles to conjure with! Consider the opening lines of "Medallions in the Moon": "There is a gate whose portals are of opal and ivory, and to this gate I went one silent twilight when the amber sky was deepening to pale blue on the world rim and the great unlighted houses were basaltic monsters carved in the sky." Or these lines from "The Gods that Men Forget":

> One day I climbed the leafy green fastness of the dreaming and mysterious hills where no man ever went. Higher and higher I climbed where the silence brooded like a sleeping god and I went on wary toes lest I should wake the drowsing leaves which carved out the tourmaline shadows. And at last I stood against the topaz sky and saw the coiling green serpent that men call the sea spread beneath me from horizon to horizon, and the distant white sails that hung against the skyline like a splash of white flame on a turquoise girdle.

According to Glenn Lord, literary executor for the Howard estate, the author created his poems in prose comparatively early in his career as a professional writer, sometime around 1928 or 1929, to judge from the manuscripts. From where did Howard derive his models for these prose-poems? One is tempted at first glance—noting similarities in vision, in rhythm, in subject matter, in the love of color and of picturesque detail, even in titles—to see something of an influence from the prose-poems of Clark Ashton Smith, twenty-nine of which were first published in 1922 in Smith's *Ebony and Crystal*, in the final section entitled "Poems in Prose." By virtue of these last, Smith had shown himself as the sovereign master of the prose-poem in English. However, it was not until the early summer of 1933 that Howard bought himself a copy of *Ebony and Crystal* directly from Smith; although he may have seen a copy earlier. But, to judge from Howard's considerable—and highly favorable—reaction to this book of poetry as evidenced by his letter to Smith postmarked July 22, 1933, there would have been some reflection or mention of it in his correspondence if he had seen such a copy earlier. Howard wrote:

> I can hardly find words to express the pleasure—I might even say ecstasy–with which I have read, and re-read, your magnificent *Ebony and Crystal*. Every line in it is a gem ... so many of your images stir feeling of such unusual depth and intensity, and bring back half forgotten instincts and emotions with such crystal clearness.

In the charming inscription he penned on the flyleaf of the copy he sold to the younger writer, Smith addresses Howard as a brother:

For Robert E. Howard
These litanies to Astarte
and Hecate and Dagon and
Demogorgon.
With fraternal good wishes,
July 4th, 1933   Clark Ashton Smith

Howard's probable models, if he needed any, were such prose-poems by Edgar Allan Poe (one of Howard's favorite writers whether in verse or prose) as "Shadow—A Parable," "Silence—A Fable," and "The Masque of the Red Death." Since Aloysius Bertrand (1807–1841) had first introduced the prose-poem in French literature with *Gaspard de la Nuit* (published posthumously in 1842), the form had become a standard and favorite one with French writers. But in English, even though the form had been created in the language comparatively early in the nineteenth century by Poe (1809–1849), it had never caught on in the way it had in France. The work in this genre done by the English Decadents and Symbolists is largely weak and superficial, apart from a few outstanding pieces by Arthur Machen, the author of *The Hill of Dreams* and "The Great God Pan." Only Clark Ashton Smith, modeling himself principally after Poe and Baudelaire and Sir Thomas Browne, has produced a body of work in English that, for both quantity and quality, equals, and often surpasses the work of the French Symbolists as well as the Russian Symbolists, the most successful rivals as a group of their French progenitors.

Just as much as his fellow *Weird Tales* writers H. P. Lovecraft and Clark Ashton Smith, Howard had a remarkable sense of the cosmic-astronomic, which Lovecraft defined as the "capacity to feel profoundly regarding the cosmos and the disturbing and fascinating quality of the extraterrestrial and perpetually unknown." His prose-poems display this insight, and "Bloodstones and Ebony" is especially noteworthy for its evocation of cosmic splendors in a comparatively small compass.

Like its title, this particular piece remains a beautifully strange dream-piece, haunted and haunting; yet all of Howard's prose-poems are noteworthy in one way or another. For their color, their imaginativeness, their vivid delineation, their strangeness, and their dream-like rhythms, these Howard pieces are equal to some of the finest prose-poems of Clark Ashton Smith. As a succession of fantastic imageries, they would not prove unworthy of a place in the great imaginative poem "A Wine of

Wizardry" by the California Romantic George Sterling. As a prose-poet in English, Howard is second only to Smith himself. One can only regret that he did not write other similar sequences of poems in prose, and yet we can be grateful for his unique *Etchings in Ivory* and for the same poetic pulse that enlivens his fiction.

Robert E. Howard: Epic Poet In Prose

My long acquaintance with Howard's creativity goes back to the mid-1950's. The first story of his that I read was "The Black Stone" in some anthology edited by August Derleth, and I continued coming across the occasional story by the Texas fictioneer in other anthologies edited by the same owner-editor of Arkham House. I was fulfilling my obligatory military service during October 1953 through August 1956, and at that time was stationed at the U.S. Marine Corps Air Station, Opa-Locka, Florida, located in then northwest Miami. I came across these and other stories in these and other books as I found them in the air-conditioned base library, strangely well-stocked with books either edited by Derleth or published by Arkham House, which eventually prompted me to send to Sauk City, Wisconsin, for some publisher's catalogs. All the stories by R.E.H. made an indelible impression on me, and as powerful (albeit different) as that left on me by the stories of H.P.L. and C.A.S.

Most of all, Howard struck me as *epic*, in a thrillingly vigorous mode expressed far too rarely these days. In a human world and civilization that has become increasingly "womanized"—where there exists much less range and scope for the male characteristics of decisive and straightforward physical action—Howard's tales of personal combat and epic struggle serve to remind us not only of the violence released in war, but above all of what real fighting is like, as it was pursued in earlier times, possessing an existential edge that most of us have forgotten. In former times, perhaps because of the fear involved, the fear that heightened their perception, many men delighted in fighting, in killing, even in the mere threat of being killed, provided it turned out to be quick—a level of primal intensity native to the male of our species, but not to the female, who wants everything to be safe, routine, predictable, and pleasant. However, despite the efforts of many men and women toward that end, they have not succeeded in making everything safe and "nice," nor will they ever succeed in doing so. Life, the unpredictable, will defeat them at some point. Although our present civilization is the end result of myriad epic battles, it is not, *alas!* despite its great scope and size, an epic world, but one in which the "nice" and the trivial alone appear to have triumphed so far.

It became inevitable, therefore, when I sent in for my first major order from Arkham House (which order came to me in two big boxes), that I ordered the R.E.H. omnibus *Skull-Face and Others*. Oddly enough, I came to know the contents of *Skull-Face* only rather gradually, or sporadically, while I was later going to college—I attended UCLA on the GI Bill from September 1956 on through the winter of 1960–61. At that period in my life I would read one story, absorb it, *ponder* it, before going on much later to the next one. I wanted to *savor* Howard's unique blend of savage power and dreamlike poetry.

However, when I started to buy and branch out into other hardcover volumes with his name on it, such as the Conan stories not published by Arkham House, as were then easily available, I soon lost interest because of the then impossibility of reading Howard's fiction as he himself had written it. Too much of it—apart from that purveyed by Arkham House—appeared to be finished, edited, or otherwise diluted by writers who temperamentally could not have seemed more different from Howard! Although I have now gone on to read and reread material by R.E.H. both old and new, I have never forgotten the keen disappointment that I felt at being unable in the late 1950's and early 1960's to continue reading Howard, and only Howard, the pure and unique Howard, undiluted by others, a situation rather spectacularly rectified since then.

In no small part because of the two feature films made from them, Howard has gained his greatest fame as the author of the stories that he wrote about Conan the Cimmerian. August Derleth is clearly mistaken when he writes in his Foreword to *Skull-Face and Others* that "the earlier Howard wrote more skillfully than the Howard who created and exploited the popular Conan." Rereading the not quite half-dozen Conan tales in *Skull-Face*, in conjunction with the invented pre-history "The Hyborian Age"—some forty years after first reading them—leaves this critic with the very strong conviction that, when scrivening his Conan stories, Howard was very much at the top of his form. One sign of this is the facility and pleasure with which he wrote all of them. These tales overall contain some of his best and most vigorous prose, not to mention some of his best and most fertile concepts, exhilarating for writer and reader alike. Fritz Leiber in his critical pieces on R.E.H. rightly assays the Conan tales at their true and certainly high value.

According to H.P.L., the author conceived his first heroes in early boyhood, thus long before incorporation into any piece of fiction. They are thus epic heroes existing in a space almost beyond our world, into which they descend, or in which they make their appearance like visitors from some superior dimension. Epic heroes of towering stature, strength, and size, independent of any characteristic story or other epic setting. Perhaps this explains the freshness and novelty and power of such heroes, undiluted by irony or cynicism or any jadedness. Howard never felt it necessary to vitiate such primordial conceptions with any puerile revisionism or insipid second thoughts that might have tamed them down, or might have anticipated today's vapid and pseudo-pious political correctness.

Skull-Face and Others appeared in the summer of 1946. Neither Derleth nor the less-appreciative critics who greeted this omnibus seem to have grasped in what lay Howard's originality, or could have foreseen just what a gold mine Howard's writings represented in terms of later bestsellerdom of an unprecedented kind: as the work of the creator of so-called Sword-and-Sorcery stories, thus of an unique modern type of heroic fantasy— although heroic fantasy, properly defined and understood, has existed since the epic poems of Homer, Virgil, Ariosto, Tasso, and especially Spenser, among other works. Like those masters, Robert E. Howard was an epic poet of unique originality, but one who strongly realized his most heroic visions and characters through the medium of *prose* fiction.

An *epic* is a very long narrative poem, carefully conceived and structured, on a grand heroic scale, dealing with and united through a chief character—usually male—of heroic proportions, although a few female figures, whether human or divine, may play a strategic or sustaining role, but often just out of the spotlight or foreground. The earliest epics in Greek constitute the very beginning of our extant Western literary traditions, and as such have been revered since antiquity. These expert narratives in verse the audience apprehended strictly through their ears, which *modus operandi* dictated that the narrative remain as clear and cogent as possible.

Given the reverence in which the Greeks themselves have always held them from antiquity on into modern times, as probably the highest expression of their literary genius, it is not hard to trace the influence that these epics have exercised on much subsequent literature, whether in Greek and Latin, or in medieval and modern languages. The traditional Homeric pattern or model, with all its divine apparatus as exemplified in *The Iliad* and *The Odyssey*, is later perfectly exemplified in *The Argonautica*, by Apollonius of Rhodes of the third to second centuries B.C., narrating the story of Jason's quest for the Golden Fleece, and ending with the dire love affair between Jason and Medea. The single greatest Latin epic is *The Aeneid*, divided into twelve books, by the Roman poet Virgil, who successfully assimilates and extrapolates the Homeric model to create a new literary paradigm, the *deliberately composed or constructed epic*, one glorifying the adventures of the Trojan hero Aeneas as he travels from Troy to Africa and then Italy, inspired by his divine mission to found what will evolve into the future city-state empire of Rome.

Many centuries later, Dante created yet another new genre with *The Divine Comedy*, a *religious epic* whose structure and style are unique, given the verse form—the *terza rima*—that he employed. This marvelous epic led to the later religious epics of the Renaissance and beyond, such as *La Muse Chrétienne* and *La Création du Monde* by Guillaume du Bartas, *Les Tragiques* by Agrippa d'Aubigné, and *Paradise Lost* in twelve books (1667) and *Paradise Regained* in four books (1671) by John Milton—whose characterization of Lucifer makes him into a kind of cosmic adventure hero!

Parallel to the medieval epics and romances, or actually preceding them in several instances—especially the cycles of stories around Charlemagne first and then King Arthur later—there flourished the genre of the so-called *folk epic*, which more often than not had a single composer or compiler at some point, who either began it or pulled it together in the final stages of its evolution. In this category fall such works as the Anglo-Saxon *Beowulf*, the Finnish *Kalevala*, and the Teutonic *Nibelungenlied*—all remarkable and individual creations. Meanwhile, evolving out of the medieval romances, covering a period of time from the middle 1400's to the late 1500's, there emerged a small but select series of strikingly original Renaissance epics, the *Orlando innamorato* by Matteo Boiardo, the *Orlando furioso* by Lodovico Ariosto, the *Gerusalemme liberata* by Torquato Tasso, and—last but not least—*The Faerie Queene* by Edmund Spenser (1552? - 1599), which among much else assimilates medieval romance and Renaissance epic, utilizing all of the poetic and scholarly lore behind these last, wide-ranging works of the Italian Renaissance. We should also probably mention that equally curious and variegated opus that preceded *The Faerie Queene* by half a century, the *Gargantua and Pantagruel* in five books (published 1532–1564), a kind of enormous and satirical epic in prose written by Rabelais, but also a wide-ranging fantasy that wielded enormous literary influence throughout Europe of the Renaissance.

Did Robert E. Howard imbibe any of these works? Yes, he did, at least some of them. Although Howard attended public schools wherever his parents happened to be living in Texas, and then finally Howard Payne College, he remained essentially a self-educated individual, an autodidact. The Texan apparently read both of Homer's epics, and given his love of full-bodied, not to mention fantastic, adventure stories, I suppose he may have also read *The Argonautica* and *The Aeneid*. In a letter to Harold Preece postmarked January 4, 1930, he links his own heroic ideal to Homer's masterworks:

> The first Greeks, the Achaeans or however it's spelled, were Celts. You will note a striking resemblance between Greece's heroic age, sung by Homer, and the Red Branch Cycle of the Irish legends. Achilles, Patroclus, Ulysses, and Ajax were indubitably Celts in word, action and thought.

To Howard, Homer's epic heroes echoed throughout history. Of the western outlaw Henry Brown—whose exploits inspired Howard's "The Vultures of Wahpeton"—R.E.H. wrote that "Utterly without fear, he shot his way out of traps and confronted perils with heroism worthy to be sung by Homer—and again he killed causelessly and in cold blood, simply to see his victims fall and quiver." Even modern times appeared rife with the thematic progeny of Achilles—in January 1932 Howard quipped to H.P.L.: "But football; that's straight, clean and Homeric. I've seen no less than heroism on the football field."

We know that R.E.H. started reading in early life, both prose and poetry. Without direct evidence, but cognizant of his constant and variegated reading, we can intelligently speculate as to what he may have perused in the genre of the epic poem. Already by the late 1800's and early 1900's many fine translations existed of the Greek and Latin epics, not to mention those originating in other cultures and languages. Exactly how many of these long narratives in verse, or great epic poems, Howard actually read and assimilated is a moot question, but he certainly would have read some of the greatest of them, at least in part, not excluding the epics of Homer, Virgil, Dante, Spenser, and Milton. These are not only some of the greatest poets in any language, but some of the greatest minds in poetry fomented by some of humanity's greatest cultures.

Since R.E.H. mastered many of the features and shorter forms of the traditional prosody in English, it is of direct interest to speculate what he might have achieved in a serious vein, had he attempted, not necessarily an epic poem (the most difficult genre), but simply a long narrative in verse like, say, *Snowbound* by J. R. Lowell, or *The Courtship of Miles Standish*, *Evangeline*, and *Hiawatha* by H. W. Longfellow. He surely had the skill and ability to have succeeded in trying his hand at such demanding, as well as more protracted, genres of poetry. We find evidence of this in such serious, and often-cited, longer lyrical poems of his as "Which Will Scarcely Be Understood," "Lines Written in the Realization that I Must Die," the poignant masterpiece "Solomon Kane's Homecoming," not to mention such a depiction (in poetic terms) of elemental struggle as "The King and the Oak."

That he had obviously read at least *some* of the great epic poems as those that we have mentioned, is manifest. To my mind, the chief proof of this inheres in such typical, amazing, and larger-than-life characters as Conan the Cimmerian, King Kull, Solomon Kane, and Steve Costigan, who besides being wanderers like Odysseus or Aeneas are about as heroic or epic as any hero of fable, myth, or history. This group of characters also includes such a figure as Breckinridge Elkins, who functions as the parodistic—and, we might add, insanely humorous—exemplar of the same epic or heroic archetype.

To see some of these epic elements actively in use, we need only review the pieces included by August Derleth in *Skull-Face and Others* (Arkham House, 1946), the first and probably still the best anthology of Howard's mostly fantastic fiction. Add some of the earliest stories published in *Weird Tales*, starting in the summer of 1925 and leading up to the astonishing efflorescence that began in 1929, and one gains a renewed perspective of the epic-mythic-heroic archetypal characters that animate his best and/or most fantastic fiction. To reread those stories—as I recently did—in the order more or less in which they first appeared in published form in magazines, is to see more clearly the emergence of Howard's unique talent—or if you will, pure genius—at relating stories in a vivid and action-filled manner.

An *epic* manner, and an *epic* hero-type:

Howard's earliest stories published in *Weird Tales* seem like professional work. But while the aficionado who genuinely enjoys all of Howard's output is happy to read them and have them, they are often not exceptional and—apart from "In the Forest of Villefere," "Wolfshead," and "Red Shadows"—give us no real inkling as to the rare narrative power, atmosphere and mood of the remarkable tales that would flood forth from 1929 onward. However, taken in conjunction with Howard's earliest published but not professional stories as presented in his high-school newspaper *The Tattler*—of which "'Golden Hope' Christmas" and "West Is West" furnish us with good examples—as well as with what is

technically his juvenilia (according to the critical consensus of those readers who have inspected Howard's very beginning fiction), it would appear
that, at the minimum, R.E.H. was a natural-born storyteller who merely
needed several years of actual practice or experience to develop into the
top-notch and profoundly serious entertainer that he became. The catalyst for this characteristic evolution came in the form of Solomon Kane,
one of the several epic heroes that the author first conceived in early
boyhood. First Solomon Kane, then Steve Costigan and King Kull, next
Conan, then the Texas-frontier tough guy Breckinridge Elkins, along
with others, all opened the floodgates of Howard's imagination.

With each successive epic hero whose exploits R.E.H. chronicled,
the Texas fictioneer's vogue among the readers of "The Unique Magazine" flourished, and increased incrementally, if not spectacularly, so that
by the late 1920's and early 1930's he had established himself as one of
the leading writers for *Weird Tales* and other pulps. Moreover, with their
fast-paced action and vigorous but poetic prose his highly individual stories not only stood out by themselves but ranked equally well next to
those by Lovecraft, Ashton Smith, Whitehead, and others of equivalent
merit and popularity. This represented quite a feat for someone who
never had the advantage of belonging to a sympathetic circle or coterie of
like-minded fellow scriveners.

While Howard's narrative impetus has affinities with the flux of imagery in a typical action movie of the 1930's, it has even greater affinities
with the flux of imagery in an epic poem, or in some other type of long
narrative in verse. Whether consciously or unconsciously, R.E.H. uses
many of the narrative and other devices typical of such poems, whether
of the folk type or of the "art" category, i.e., especially created or composed, as *The Aeneid*. Such epic devices appear, of course, in other types
of fiction—for example, as in adventure stories—but they particularly do
this in a classical or folk epic, where they tend to make their appearance
in a somewhat predictable, ritualistic manner.

Among these epic devices are:

Solemn invocation of or to the Muse, in this case usually Calliope, the
muse of eloquence and heroic poetry. This is to stress the noble or solemn purpose of the story to be told.

The need for an elevated style (employed with taste and restraint, however, to avoid unintentional humor or parody).

A necessity to begin "in medias res," that is, right in the thick of whatever narrative is taking place. The actual beginning will have its exposition later, in due or prescribed form.

A hero of mythic or legendary proportions. The author often makes use of epic, heroic, or Homeric simile—an extended comparison that may last several (or more) lines—that tends to appear in a certain set formula.

The featuring of heroic battles with divine intervention into the hero's actions, or into those of some other leading character.

Epic lists or catalogues, as before or during a battle, or other major event: for example, the different nations or tribes lined up on either side of a pitched battle or other struggle. The epic catalogue can also take the form of a medieval or Elizabethan pageant, particularly as in Spenser's epic, where it becomes something extra special indeed.

The pathetic or meteorological fallacy, whereby the weather or other heavenly phenomenon is often correlated closely with the hero's actions, his moods, etc., and their consequences.

Although he never *solemnly* invokes the Muse in and of herself in the prescribed epic fashion—such, of course, would have been completely out of place in writing for a pulp magazine, except perhaps for *Weird Tales!*—Howard at least invokes her *indirectly* by making serious use of poetry to head either stories overall, or the individual chapters making up the stories. Incidentally, he reveals in this manner a deep and sophisticated knowledge of poetry, at least in English.

Almost all the chapters in "Skull-Face" (the novelette) begin with appropriate epigraphs culled from such figures as Omar Khayyám, Poe, Swinburne, Kipling, Chesterton, and others. The unique Conan novel *The Hour of the Dragon* begins with a substantial verse paragraph of Howard's own devising. Indeed, quite often, the epigraphs featured are of his own skillful invention, attributed to poets like Justin Geoffrey, or to the generic military folklore of his own self-invented Hyborian Age, as in quite a few of the Conan series. This represents quite a fancy procedure for a writer too often dismissed as "a mere pulp-magazine hack" during the 1940's, 1950's, and 1960's. It also stresses the fact that—contrary to what some critics have contended—R.E.H. was very much a serious artist, and rightly regarded himself in this way. It is the author or the artist who first must take himself or herself seriously before others will, including the traditional "carping critics."

In the epic, the solemn invocation of the Muse tends to stress the noble or elevated purpose of the story to be told: hence, the need for an elevated or heroic style, and on occasion a certain solemnity of statement. Of course, this allows a much greater freedom, if not a greater sense of play. After all, as just one of many subjective definitions, one of the finest has it that poetry represents at its best the sense of "serious play" for which our own species, no less than other primates, has gained an enviable notoriety. The adroit author can easily suborn or subvert this serious or solemn style for the purpose of satire, parody, humor, or irony. Like H.P.L. and C.A.S., R.E.H. was a master of rhetoric, of diversified styles, and many of his tales are marked here and there by a deliberate rhetorical overkill.

One of the best examples of rhetorical excess, as employed for the purpose of achieving a pristine vividness, occurs during the breathtakingly action-filled narrative of "Skull-Face," which remains one of Howard's best longer fictions, and a model of what shape a fast, but relatively short, novel may assume. After Costigan has escaped from the malign clutches of Kathulos, unperceived by the inimical forces everywhere around him, he plans with his immense physical strength to rescue Gordon before moon-dawn if he can. However, he is more than uncertain how to proceed, given the alternatives at his option. He is in fact quite ambivalent. To quote Howard's incomparably distinctive language: "He reeled back from the parapet, *rent in twain by indecision*." (Italics added.) The language is so strong that it invites an almost humorous response, the same humor used with repeated effectiveness in the Sailor Steve Costigan and Breckinridge Elkins tales. But it certainly captures the protagonist's mental and emotional state (at that moment in the narrative) to perfection.

Whether or not Howard's tales always begin *in medias res*, they almost always commence at a strong or striking place in the narrative, which at some point soon after its announcement the author (like the superb adventure writer that he is) will explain to let the reader know just what has already transpired that has led up to this dramatic moment. Such a technique betrays the skilled hand of the author as an instinctive romanceer, fictioneer, storyteller, entertainer *par excellence*. Tightly interwoven with this technique is another: the author invariably depicts his narrative through a fast-moving body of images, *pure imagery*, that remains astonishingly poetic, and specifically like that of epic narration in its circumstantial detail.

Some of the passages in "The Hyborian Age" are extraordinarily evocative, as are certain related passages in some of the stories. For example, as when the king Cormac of Connacht (sometime after the start of "Kings of the Night") is thinking as he and his companions walk through the camp of the Picti, "Can the old legends be true—that they [now savages, but still giant dwarfs] reigned in a day when strange cities rose where now the sea rolls? And they survived the flood that washed those gleaming empires under, sinking again into that savagery from which they once had risen?" Passages like this as they occur throughout Howard's *oeuvre* possess (in passing) unusual depth and power, and serve to trigger the imagination on into strange but enjoyable musings. If we perceive Time and History as the Sea (both the sea of waters that girds our planet and the sea of stars through which the planet has been swimming almost since the beginning of time), then we may similarly perceive the previous ages (often as unrecorded as they are unrecordable) as the ever-changing Tides of that same Sea. Although we do not generally find in R.E.H.'s fiction extended or elaborate comparisons that could qualify as classically Homeric simile, we do find—and in abundance—Howard's unerring use of epic metaphor. Such usage came as instinctively to him as to the Celtic bard that spiritually he remained all his life.

Epics usually feature the direct or carefully concealed intervention of the given society's gods and goddesses into human affairs—not just in the hero's actions, but especially in the heroic or major battles in which the hero takes part. Sometimes this happens baldly in the form of the *deux ex machina*, or more subtly through the divine agent often appearing disguised in humble, human form. Certainly we have divine intervention, whether via good or bad agents, in much of Howard's weird fiction. This does not mean that the hero ever has an easy time of it in his personal combat (hardly!), but he must reckon on, and concomitantly struggle with, powerful forces rarely benign and more often malign. Moreover, the tales prominently feature such characters as wizards, demons, sorcerers, and sorceresses, all of whom play quite an important role in the unfolding of a typical Howardian weird story.

One of the most characteristic of the epic devices is the epic listing or catalogue, often featuring the names—typically highfalutin or exotic or both—of the different armies or tribes making up the fighting assemblage on either side of a pitched battle. As in the divertissement—the long and elaborate suite of dances in a full-length classical ballet (with a linear narrative)—the epic catalogues can take the shape of an involved and multi-sectioned pageant, as in Spenser's epic, ostensibly directed at some leading character in the story, but just as much at the reading audience. Behold Howard's catalogue from the story "Spears of Clontarf":

> They were an array of war-eagles: Murrogh, Brian's eldest son, the pride of all Erin—tall, broad-shouldered, mightily muscled, with wide blue eyes that were never placid, but danced with mirth, dulled with sadness or blazed with fury; Murrogh's young son Turlogh, a slender, supple lad of fifteen with golden locks and a frank eager face—tense with anticipation of trying his hand for the first time in the great game of war. And there was that other Turlogh, his cousin—Turlogh Dubh—Black Turlogh, who was only a few years older, but who had already his full stature and was famed throughout all Erin for his berserk rages and the cunning of his deadly axe-play. And there was Meathla O'Faelan, prince of Desmond or South Munster, and his kin— the Great Stewards of Scotland, Lennox, and Donald of Mar, who had crossed the Irish channel with their wild Highlanders—tall men, somber and gaunt and silent. And there was Dunlang O'Hartigan, and O'Hyne, chief of Connacht. But O'Kelly, brother chief of the O'Hyne, and prince of Hy Many, was in the tent of his uncle, King Malachi, which was pitched in the camp of the Meathmen, apart from the Dalcassians, and King Brian was brooding on the matter. For since the set of the sun, O'Kelly had been closeted with the king of Meath and no man knew what passed between them.

I marvel that Farnsworth Wright rejected the rewrite of this story, "The Grey God Passes," in part because, "the reader loses interest in a confusion of proper names." Of course, it is just such passages that grant the tale its profound verisimilitude. As Howard wrote vainly to Harry Bates, another editor who may have had little use for mythic archetypes, "Those days of war and rapine represent an age crammed with vital drama, enough to supply a hundred thrilling volumes. In writing ['Spears of Clontarf'], I have dipped deeply into both history and legendry, striving to interweave historical facts and folk-lore myths in a realistic and logical manner."

We now come to a supreme epic device: the *pathetic fallacy*, which I prefer to call the *meteorological effect*. This is an effect—spelled out strongly on the stage—whereby the weather or other heavenly phenomenon is often correlated closely with the hero's actions, his moods, and their consequences. It comes in especially well when correlated with the break of day, or above all with a sunset, and can serve to mark the finale of some interior act with due solemnity. We have become so many times over-accustomed to this device, and moreover have seen how too easily it lends itself to parody, that we tend to forget how very effective it proves when utilized with taste, skill, and sincerity.

The single most striking example of Howard's use of the pathetic fallacy is found in one of his single most imaginative and powerful stories, the aptly titled "Kings of the Night." King Kull of Atlantis emerges from an incredibly distant past to fight all day alongside fellow barbarians, only then returning to his own faraway existence. But it is Howard's unique manner of transporting Kull to and from Bran Mak Morn's contemporary world that captures and holds our attention, and fires our imagination. At daybreak of the big battle, as the sun's disk rises—*just when it sits right on the horizon*—the massive and mighty figure of Kull suddenly materializes out of, or "against" the disk, as against an enormous round battle shield; and in all his dread majesty he strides into the midst of the confederates fighting on the side of Bran Mak Morn! This then is the king that Bran has promised the Norsemen, summoned forth from an aeon beyond ancient, and even beyond archaic, time.

After the valiant Norsemen, standing and fighting with Kull, have all perished, Kull still hangs on, although bleeding from numerous wounds. The sun is meanwhile sinking in the west, and *as its disk sits right on the horizon once more*, Kull returns to his own incredibly remote epoch. Once more his figure stands against that disk and vanishes back into the sun. At the same time that he describes the scene with perfect and understated skill, the author adumbrates in a dazzling kaleidoscope of imagery the enormous passage of time separating Kull's period from that of Bran Mak Morn, and also manages to suggest the tremendous unknown powers invoked to make Kull's participation in the battle possible. The evocation of Kull first out of the sun, and then back into that same disk, constitutes to my taste one of the supreme moments in all of literature. Kull's vanishing represents a masterstroke of pure genius: it is then that the reader realizes with a thrill the supreme irony of the story's title—the futility inherent in all toil, battle, hard work, and struggle—"Kings of the Night," indeed! Like faerie gold magically presented and experienced at night, nothing remains of that magic and that experience, for who will recall in future ages the tremendous battle fought here? As usual, Howard the Epic Poet Working in Prose Fiction excels.

Clearly the single most important feature of an epic poem is the spotlight that invariably falls upon a hero of mythic or legendary proportions. The epic hero by definition invites upon himself the central focus. But is it not here above all—in this central feature or element, the epic hero—that R.E.H. excels with a freshness and a vigor unsurpassed, at least in the modern literature of his own century, the 1900's?

Most, if not all, of Howard's protagonists are obviously larger than life, clearly epic heroes, clearly and inherently *heroic*. Moreover—like Odysseus in *The Odyssey*, like Aeneas in *The Aeneid*, like Prince Arthur and his brother knight-heroes in *The Faerie Queene*, like Orlando in *Orlando furioso* and other typical heroes of epic—those of Howard are *wanderers*, either involved in some difficult or impossible quest, or seeking some goal or eminence of power, some worthy personal fight or epic battle, some old or new home, some place of heart's desire, or some splendid warrior's doom. Which of Howard's major heroes does not fit this description, all of whom are wanderers of one type or another?

What Howard managed to achieve, in his poignantly short life, continues in place, and eternally to his credit. It is the instinctive poet deep inside the hard-bitten Texas romanceer who is responsible for the mastery observable in his best prose fictions. It is precisely the Celtic bard— or epic poet that spiritually he remained all his life—who created those unforgettable narratives of his.

How Two-Gun Bob's imagery lingers in the mind, aided by the music of his rhythmic and evocative prose, and long after the reader has read and experienced the given story! "Skulls in the Stars," with Solomon Kane, tall and rangy, garbed in his somber Puritan costume, striding across the moonlit moors on the way to Torkertown, tracking an unknown horror that is also tracking him. The valiant hunter Niord in "The Valley of the Worm," standing atop his lone column as he faces down the macrocosmic wormlike entity coming up out of the great hole in the ground that lies at the heart of the massive ruined temple. Bran Mak Morn struck with astonishment in "Worms of the Earth" as he beholds the Roman fortress, the Tower of Trajan, now reduced to a mere colossal pile of shattered stone and crumbled granite thanks to the subterranean cooperation of the titular creatures. "The Fire of Asshurbanipal" and its savage Bedouin riders pursuing the soldiers of fortune Steve Clancy and Yar Ali, who themselves stagger forward afoot, bereft of their camels, going south over the burning sunlit sands while indistinct hills slowly take shape as an enormous Assyrian metropolis built of black stone in the middle of the trackless desert!

Or recall the grandiose apotheosis-like revelation at the end of "The Cairn on the Headland," when the disdainful and ignorant Italian, Ortali by name, having dug into the cairn down to where Odin lies quiescent in only seeming death, brings the god inadvertently back to life—Ortali had thought to find some rare treasure, indeed!—as the gigantic winged form rises up with its grisly head bathed in the *outré* splendors of the *aurora borealis*. Marvel at the mighty and massive figure of Kull as a disillusioned king in "The Mirrors of Tuzun Thune," sitting on the throne-like chair in the House of a Thousand Mirrors by the Lake of Visions, as he looks day after day deep into those very same mirrors that seem to reflect either the ultimate illusion or the ultimate reality, thus adumbrating an eternal and fascinating philosophical ambivalence. Weep at the ineffably strange and alien scene between Conan and Yag-Kosha in "The Tower of the Elephant," lair of the elephant-headed creature from another world, as they hold converse within the golden-domed chamber, a scene so full of aching pathos that it becomes near unbearable.

We could multiply such examples many times over, each indicating the richness and abundance of the epic poetry that Howard has distilled and instilled into his unique Otherworldly stories. One is palpably struck by the author's unique individuality, by the vividness, the thoughtfulness, and the gorgeous action-filled narratives peculiar to his fiction. They not only still read as well as they did seven decades ago but, like all great epics, become stronger and more individual with the passage of time. Howard need not fear for his laurels, even when placed side by side with the redoubtable Tolkien, who by the way seems to have admired the Conan stories. Reflect for a moment on just how much living and writing Howard managed to pack into his relatively short life-span, the thirty years or so between his birth on 22 January 1906 and his death on 11 June 1936—prodigious! and prodigious, indeed!

R.E.H. yields in no way to H.P.L. or C.A.S. as a romanceer of the Otherworldly, but absolutely takes equal rank as a fictioneer of the weird and fantastic. Although he shares a certain fatalistic and futilitarian philosophy with them, no less than other affinities, Howard's own personal stance as projected through his chief protagonists is *ab incunabulis*. In his verve, imagination, and power of language, Robert E. Howard successfully evokes the epic ancients, creating as they did timeless parables of Otherwhere.

The Alleged Influence of
Lord Dunsany on Clark Ashton Smith

Fritz Leiber has recently brought to my attention the article "Conan's Great-Grandfather" by L. Sprague de Camp in *Amra*, vol. 2, no. 17. In this article Mr. de Camp states in passing that Lord Dunsany influenced the writings of Clark Ashton Smith. Since Mr. de Camp has mentioned this in print on at least three other occasions (*Science Fiction Handbook*, Hermitage House, New York, 1953, page 79; *Lost Continents*, Gnome Press, New York, 1954, page 260; *Amra*, vol. 2, no. 17, in the review of Smith's collection *The Abominations of Yondo* under the heading "Scrolls & Such"), I assume it is a carefully considered opinion, and as such worthy of serious attention. I would, however, like to present a divergent point of view.

In the *Lost Continents* citation Mr. de Camp states that Smith's style is "based ultimately on Poe and Dunsany." While I admit to something of a superficial similarity between the respective subject-matters of Dunsany and Smith, I cannot admit to the style of Smith being based on that of Dunsany. However, Mr. de Camp is correct in singling out Poe as one of the authentic stylistic influences on Smith, as Smith himself acknowledged the influence of Poe, as well as that of Baudelaire.

Smith once told me that he first read some of Dunsany's output about 1920, but a mere reading is not sufficient to act as a profound influence on a writer—especially such a writer as Clark Ashton Smith, who chose his literary models very carefully—and Dunsany simply was not among them. Long before 1920, Smith had been creating poems wherein exist many themes and backgrounds similar to those of his later tales— circa 1925–1937.

There is a logical and unmistakable evolution in Smith's writing from his first juvenile efforts in prose (at the age of 11 Smith wrote imitations of fairy tales and *The Arabian Nights*, and later "long adventure novels dealing with Oriental life"), through his first professional short stories ("The Malay Krise," "The Ghost of Mohammed Din," "The Mahout," "The Rajah and the Tiger" in *The Overland Monthly* and *The Black Cat*, 1910–12), through his published poetry, through his poems in prose, and finally on through his later tales, many of which are extended poems in prose. By the time Smith read Lord Dunsany, he was already gravitating toward the creation of tales set in imaginary worlds. He may have noted how Dunsany handled his materials and how Dunsany's style helped him to present his imaginary worlds, but Smith had already formed his prose style well before 1920—at least as early as 1914—and by 1920 he had already perceived, even if somewhat vaguely, the subject matter for his later tales (to judge from the poems in prose of his *Ebony and Crystal*).

The superficial similarity of Dunsany and Smith forms an example of independent and (almost) parallel evolution. Such examples are not rare in the field of literature. For example, Alexander Montgomery and Edmund Spenser evolved a similar sonnet form of interlinking rhymes quite independently of each other. Many of the themes and backgrounds which appear in Smith's three major poetry collections—*The Star-Treader and Other Poems* (1912), *Ebony and Crystal* (1922), *Sandalwood* (1925)—reappear in his later tales, and this logical development in Smith's creative evolution had nothing to do with any influence from Dunsany.

Space would not permit the citation of all possible examples from the three aforementioned collections and the comparison of same with examples in Smith's later tales, and so a few generalizations will have to suffice, and two or three examples.

Through all three collections runs the theme of what may be called the cosmic-astronomic—this theme was undoubtedly suggested to Smith by the example of the poems of a similar nature by George Sterling—or the interplanetary and the interstellar; but the theme is treated most expansively by Smith in *The Star-Treader*. Also present are many poems dealing powerfully with the themes of death, destruction, and night, especially in *The Star-Treader* and *Ebony and Crystal*. *Ebony and Crystal* and especially *Sandalwood* contain many poems dealing with love in a manner of rare poignance. And in all three are poems dealing with figures of classical (i.e., Graeco-Roman) mythology, as well as a few poems dealing with the "lost continents" of Atlantis and Lemuria (*The Star-Treader*: the sonnet "Atlantis"; *Ebony and Crystal*: the sonnet "In Lemuria"; *Sandalwood*: the quatrain "Lemurienne," this last was added later to the printed volume; and in bits and snatches of other poems in all volumes).

Thus, Smith's preoccupation with death and imageries of death began very early in his literary career, and continued not illogically in the majority of his tales. When Smith came to write in the 1930's what may nominally be termed science-fiction, a science-fiction of interplanetary and interstellar themes and backgrounds, he was merely utilizing material he had handled fifteen to twenty years earlier. From handling figures and gods of classical mythology in his poems, it was but a short and simple step for Smith to utilize in his tales, whenever the need or inspiration or both presented itself, gods of his own creation. And almost needless to mention, Smith uses lost continents as backgrounds for about one-fourth or one-third of his later tales.

Let me cite an example of continuity of theme, that of the Gorgon Medusa. In *The Star-Treader* there are the poem "Medusa" and the sonnet "The Medusa of the Skies," and in *Ebony and Crystal* there is the sonnet "The Medusa of Despair." And among Smith's later tales we find "The Gorgon."

Let me cite an example of continuity of background, that background of Smith's creation which features multiple suns. In the title poem of *The Star-Treader* Smith mentions a world "Where colored skies of systems triplicate / Bestow on planets weird, ineffable,/ Green light that orbs them like an outer sea,/ And large auroral noons that alternate / With skies like sunset held without abate."—and in *Ebony and Crystal* we have *Triple Aspect* (dealing obviously enough with three suns—each of a different hue) and in the sonnet "Desire of Vastness" Smith mentions a "trinal noon" (indicating a noontime of triple suns). For a continuation of backgrounds with multiple suns among his later tales, see "The City of the Singing Flame" and the Inner Sphere wherein the sky is "filled with many-coloured suns, like those that might shine on a world of some multiple solar system"; see "The Curse of Aforgomon" and the planet Hestan with its "four small suns; see "The Maze of the Enchanter" and "The Flower-Women" and the three suns of amber, emerald, and carmine; see "The Demon of the Flower" and the planet Lophai with its double suns of "jade green and balas-ruby orange."

Finally as an example of continuity of character-type, let me cite from *Ebony and Crystal* the poem "The Nereid," who "dwells forever, ocean-thralled,/ Soul of the sea's vast emerald." Consult the tale "Sadastor" and compare the above nereid with the nereid-like siren Lyspial, who—born of the waters of the planet Sadastor—must die with those same waters.

Generally overlooked is the fact that a great many of Smith's so-called "tales of horror" are just as much tales of love. The theme of love so powerfully sounded in *Ebony and Crystal* and *Sandalwood* continues with equal force in his later tales, especially in such extended poems in prose as "A Night in Malnéant," "The Planet of the Dead," and others.

As for the crowning poem in *Ebony and Crystal*—a poem only describable as a telescoped epic—"The Hashish-Eater; or, The Apocalypse of Evil:" it is a veritable catalogue of things to come in Smith's later tales. The tremendous efflorescence of imagination in Smith's later tales, especially those of 1930–1934, is strikingly and unmistakably prefigured in the seemingly exhaustless flood of invented wonders presented in this, the longest of his poems. To list subject-matter and episodes (many of which are compressed tales in themselves) would be like reading an author's commonplace book, so pregnant is it with themes and backgrounds used in his later tales. The cosmic-astronomic element seen here is combined with extrapolations of monsters of classical mythology and with an entire repertory of objects of evil used by Poe, Baudelaire, and the French Symbolists; the whole poem being unified by the central figure of the Hashish-Eater, i.e., "the emperor of dreams" (which figure has its analogies with "the Man-God" of Baudelaire, actually a very ancient concept). This extraordinary poem Smith composed in 1920, and its preview of things to come in later tales owes nothing to Dunsany. Something of its imagery and structure was suggested to Smith by George Sterling's "A Wine of Wizardry," which poem Smith first read in 1907 when he was almost 15, two years after Smith discovered the poetry of Poe.

Perhaps even more significant to the student of Smith's later tales is the inclusion in *Ebony and Crystal* of the twenty-nine poems in prose, a number of which Smith had composed prior to 1920, such as "Ennui," first published in 1918 in *The Smart Set*. Already much of the characteristic subject-matter of Smith's later tales is foreshadowed as a few titles will show: "The Traveller," "The Flower-Devil," "The Princess Almeena," "In Cocaigne" (this French-medieval imaginary land of idleness and luxury has its obvious analogies with Atlantis), and "From the Crypts of Memory." In fact, two of these—"The Flower-Devil" and "From the Crypts of Memory"—later served as the nuclei for the tales or extended poems in prose, "The Demon of the Flower" and "The Planet of the Dead," respectively.

From these poems in prose it was but a short step to the creation of the extended poems in prose, "The Abominations of Yondo" and "Sadastor," both composed in 1925, and from them to Smith's later tales. The first of these does have a slight Dunsanian flavor in its first paragraph, especially in the phrase "Yondo lies nearest of all to the world's rim," and in the first paragraph's concluding sentence: "Things have crept in from nether space, whose incursion is forbid by the gods of all proper and well-ordered lands [which seems especially Dunsanian]; but there are no such gods in Yondo, where live the hoary genii of stars abolished, and decrepit demons left homeless by the destruction of antiquated hells [but this phrase has more a flavor of the wit of Voltaire or William Beckford than that of Lord Dunsany]."

This brings us to a discussion of certain essential differences between Dunsany's tales and those of Smith, differences in style and subject-matter. First, note the dissimilarity between the imaginary worlds created by Dunsany as background for his tales and those created by Smith for his. Dunsany's worlds or lands are "beyond the East" and "at the edge of the world"; they are deliberately vague, with no pretension of geographical existence, on our globe or any other. Despite their fabulous creatures and events, Smith's worlds could exist or could have existed as real places on our planet (given as true that Atlantis-type lost continents existed). As for Smith's tales not laid on lost continents, they are placed either in *real* locales or in interplanetary, interstellar, or interdimensional lands that, while imaginary, pretend to exist as *definite* places.

To point up a further difference between Dunsany and Smith, consider a passage from Mr. de Camp's article "Conan's Great Grandfather:" "Dunsany was a master of the trick or surprise ending. Many of his stories are mere anecdotes built around such an ending." The trick or surprise ending per se is rare in Smith's tales. While an ending might come as a surprise to the reader, the effect of surprise is subordinated to the overall mood of the tale. Smith usually sought to tell a story with the utmost control; and the effect of inevitability, the result of such control, is what gives many of Smith's tales their characteristic power and impact, which could scarcely have been achieved with purely trick or surprise endings.

Mr. de Camp's definition of Dunsany's tales as "children's fairy tales but on a sophisticated adult level" is a very apt one. What saves Smith's tales from becoming such, despite their outward trappings, is the extraordinarily intense conviction of belief and the depth of feeling they carry. Such conviction of belief and such depth of feeling are usually lacking in Dunsany, who seems to have the air of a worldly-wise and ingenious *raconteur* relating agreeable entertainments to a sophisticated audience. This is true not only of Dunsany's later Jorkens tall tales but even of much of his earlier and more sincerely intended prose, wherein Dunsany's creation of an elaborate mythology often appears to be an ingenious game, a game which does not evoke deep emotions in the reader. On the other hand, while one cannot systematically consider Smith's tales in their entirety as allegories (although they might be such in part), yet are many of his tales somber and stately parables of death, destruction, and darkness; of love, beauty, and wonder; of grief and nostalgia; of horror, terror, and fear; of hate and revenge; and of destiny and deity; and with many of these themes, especially those of love and death, combined in poignant and baroque synthesis, spiced occasionally with a strange humor and a merciless irony.

Dunsany's style, particularly of his earlier and perhaps best work, was modelled directly upon the King James Version of the Bible. Smith's style, while it may offer some slight affinities with a "Biblical" style, was manifestly not modelled after Dunsany, but after Poe (see especially Poe's "Shadow—a Parable, Silence—a Fable," and above all "The Masque of the Red Death," which is the closest thing in the canon of Poe's works to a tale by Smith) and after Baudelaire (see particularly the *Petits Poèmes en Prose*). Dunsany's prose style at its best achieves a gossamer quality. Smith's general prose style is one of serious and very stately pomp. Many of his tales, viewed theoretically as short stories, might indeed seem written in an "euphuistic" style. However, viewed as extended poems in prose, the tales no longer seem written in such a style but in one perfectly suited to the subject matter. True euphuism à la John Lyly's work *Euphues* often deliberately twists the subject matter to suit the rhetorical extravagances; Smith manipulates his seeming "rhetorical extravagances" to suit the subject matter. In Smith, the form exists for the subject, not the reverse. (Apropos Smith's style, it is interesting to observe that the last chapter of Sir Thomas Browne's *Hydriotaphia* has often been cited as the ultimate in stately splendor of style. Yet Smith in many, many instances easily surpasses Browne in this regard.) Smith's style, for all its depth of feeling or "Romantic" affinities, may best be described, I believe, in view of its strict control and elaborate rhetoric, as "baroque".

I do not mean to disparage the literary achievement of Lord Dunsany, but he was certainly not "the first fully to exploit the possibilities of heroic fantasy." I think that distinction lies with Edmund Spenser, who in his extraordinary epic *The Faerie Queene* created an entire world of Faëry—of fancy, of fantasy, of the imagination—a world rife with imaginary courts, queens, knights, ladies fair, monsters, and with deities and figures of classical and Hebraic mythologies. Although to be perfectly fair, one must not forget Ariosto and his *Orlando Furioso*, no less than Tasso and his *Gerusalemme Liberata*, both of whom served as inspiration to Spenser. Yet, in spite of Ariosto and Tasso, Spenser, possibly influenced by such dream-allegories as *Le Roman de la Rose*, was the first to create an entire imaginary setting or background, i.e., "*Faerie* lond" (Spenser's italics).

Dunsany's important innovation, in my estimation, was the creation of a body of romance with his own deities taking the place of the gods of classical or other mythology, all with a system of proper names more elaborate and more scientific than the nomenclature systems of his predecessors. However, Dunsany, contrary to many of his predecessors, was not content merely to use an occasional god in his stories; his earliest volumes have as their manifest purpose the creation of an *entire* mythology. Smith's tales, although they may occasionally feature some invented deities, do not have as their purpose the creation of a mythology per se. Surely the superficial similarity of kings, queens, kingdoms, palaces, temples, etc., in the works of both men is not enough to warrant calling Smith's tales "Dunsanian," merely because Dunsany preceded Smith by one or two decades in prose fiction.

As a final example of the essential differences between Smith and Dunsany, consider the difference in their attitude toward death. Smith relentlessly emphasizes the carnal qualities of death and dying; Dunsany does so never. In Dunsany, the change from life to death seems no more than the casting off of a garment. While Dunsany may make use of witches, he does not feature necromancers and necromancy in his tales as Smith does in many of his. Actually the importance of necromancy in Smith's works cannot be over-emphasized; it is another manifestation of "the Man-God," one of the principal themes unifying the entire output of Smith from *The Star-Treader and Other Poems* to his last published volume of poetry, *Spells and Philtres*. Since necromancers have the power to raise the dead and bring them back to a pseudo-life, a life that is not life (a baroque ambiguity), and since the bringing back of the dead to life or pseudo-life is presumably one of the prerogatives of deity; necromancers may be considered, at least in part, further versions of the Man-God.

Mr. de Camp has not been the only commentator who has alleged an influence of Dunsany on Smith. Edward Wagenknecht, well-known man of letters, once called Smith Dunsany's "American disciple (after a fashion)." To Anthony Boucher "the echoes of Lovecraft and Dunsany drown out [Smith's] own voice." In view of Smith's own creative evolution, whereby he came to the writing of his later and most characteristic tales as a logical development which had nothing to do with Lord Dunsany, I find myself unable to agree with Messrs. de Camp, Wagenknecht, and Boucher. And I must conclude that they came to their opinion because they lacked sufficient knowledge of Smith's earlier creative evolution. Smith's tales are no more "Dunsanian" than they are, say, "Arthurian" or "Spenserian"; and to describe them as such is misleading to the uninformed reader.

Klarkash-Ton and E'ch-Pi-El:
On the Alleged Influence of H. P. Lovecraft on
Clark Ashton Smith

It has been considerably bruited about in certain quarters, and indeed, even taken very much for granted, that H. P. Lovecraft, one of the modern masters of the macabre, exercised an extensive influence on the late Clark Ashton Smith and his writings. August Derleth and Donald Wandrei in their introduction to Smith's first major prose collection, *Out of Space and Time*, tell us that "in prose Smith was constantly encouraged and influenced in large part by...H. P. Lovecraft." Anthony Boucher, in his review of the above Smith volume (see *Unknown Worlds*, 4/43), calls Smith "the outstanding disciple of H. P. Lovecraft." And Zelia Bishop, in her *H. P. Lovecraft: A Pupil's View* (see *The Curse of Yig*, Arkham House, 1953), calls Lovecraft "the spiritual father of a group of devoted followers" and then proceeds to list Smith as one of these "devoted followers."

The assertion of a Lovecraftian influence on Smith has been made principally on the grounds of Smith's contributions to and borrowings from the Cthulhu mythology invented by Lovecraft. Now it is a matter of fact that Smith and Lovecraft maintained for about seventeen years a friendship through correspondence, from about 1922 until Lovecraft's death in 1937. It is possible that they began their correspondence through the suggestion of their mutual friend, Samuel Loveman (to whom Smith dedicated his third volume of poetry, *Ebony and Crystal*, in 1922). By the time that they first made each other's acquaintance through the medium of letters, Lovecraft had already gained a considerable reputation in the United Amateur Press Association (which he had joined in 1914), although it wasn't until 1923, with the founding of *Weird Tales*, that Lovecraft began to acquire his wider fame as a writer of macabre tales. Smith had made his début in the Bohemian literary and artistic circles of San Francisco, Carmel, etc., in 1912 with his first volume of poetry *The Star-Treader and Other Poems*. Since that year he had become a recognized poet of considerable stature, at least in his native state of California. In 1918 the Book Club of California had published fifteen of Smith's poems in a deluxe edition entitled *Odes and Sonnets*, and later presented to him, in recognition of his services to literature, a bronze plaque designed by the noted sculptor Edgar Walter, an honor bestowed only on such distinguished literary men as George Sterling and Edwin Markham. The correspondence-friendship of E'ch-Pi-El (as Lovecraft would characteristically sign himself) and of Klarkash-Ton (as Lovecraft was in the habit of addressing Smith) must have been an unusually rewarding and mutually stimulating relationship as the two men evidently shared many similar views, tastes and opinions. Lovecraft's *Selected Letters*, the first volume of which will be published in 1964 will reveal at least Lovecraft's side of this long-time correspondence; what has become of Smith's letters to Lovecraft this writer has been unable to discover.

The fifteen-year-long correspondence of Lovecraft and Smith is thus a matter of fact. But the nature of Lovecraft's "influence" on Smith, if such it may be called, is more difficult to determine. Smith himself once indicated the extent and nature of his contributions to and borrowing from the Lovecraft mythos, in a letter dated July 21,1953, (in *Howard Phillips Lovecraft: Memoirs, Critiques, Bibliographies*, SSR Publications, 1955) in which he listed those stories of his which could be considered as more or less related to the Mythos.

These tales, ten in number, are listed as follows: "The Coming of the White Worm," "The Door to Saturn," "The Holiness of Azédarac," "The Nameless Offspring," "The Return of the Sorcerer," "The Seven Geases," "The Tale of Satampra Zeiros," "The Testament of Athammaus," "Ubbo-Sathla," and "The Weird of Avoosl Wuthoqquan." Smith then states his contributions to the mythos as being the god Tsathoggua and *The Book of Eibon*, both of which Smith himself invented and which Lovecraft promptly adopted into his myth-pattern. To determine the precise extent of any Lovecraftian influence on Smith, let us systematically catalogue, story by story, both Smith's uses of his own contributions to the Cthulhu Mythos as well as Smith's uses of his borrowings from it.

"The Coming of the White Worm," Smith informs us, is an entire chapter from his invention, *The Book of Eibon*, but there are no mentions of Lovecraftian deities, or any implicit connection with same. In "The Door to Saturn" Smith's own invention, the god Tsathoggua, plays some part.

In "The Holiness of Azédarac," *The Book of Eibon* has a pivotal role, and Tsathoggua as Sodagui and the Lovecraftian deity Yog-Sothoth as Iog-Sotôt, are both *mentioned*, thrice, as follows : "[Brother Ambrose] has...beheld the veritable manifestation of Lilit, and even of Iog-Sotôt and Sodagui, those demons who are more ancient than the world...." Or,

"... the *Book of Eibon*, which contains...the secret, man-forgotten lore of Iog-Sotôt and Sodagui, is now missing." Or, "again he shuddered at the trans-galactic horror of the demon Sodagui, and the ultra-dimensional hideousness of that being known as Iog-Sotôt to the sorcerers of Averoigne."

Smith uses a quotation from the *Necronomicon* of Lovecraft as a heading to *The Nameless Offspring*, a quotation invented by Smith himself. There is no mention of Tsathoggua or of Lovecraftian deities either in the quotation or the story itself.

In "The Return of the Sorcerer," the *Necronomicon*, alone, has a featured role, and within the story occurs a Smith-invented quotation from the book, without mention of any Lovecraftian or his own gods.

Smith's own invented deity Tsathoggua plays some part in "The Seven Geases," and plays a fairly prominent role in "The Tale of Satampra Zeiros." And in "The Testament of Athammaus," Knygathin Zhaum, descended from Tsathoggua and the "swart, Protean spawn...from the elder worlds," has a pivotal role.

In "Ubbo-Sathla," Smith's own *Book of Eibon* has a fairly prominent role, and the *Necronomicon* is *mentioned*—once. There are two quotations— from the first-named book, the first used as a heading to the story, the second within the story's context. In the second quotation there is no mention of deities, although in the first Smith's Tsathoggua as Zhothaqquah, and Lovecraft's Yog-Sothoth as Yok-Zothoth and Cthulhu as Kthulhut, are all three mentioned once, as follows: "Before the coming of Zhothaqquah or Yok-Zothoth or Kthulhut, Ubbo-Sathla dwelt in the streaming fens of the new-made Earth...." As for the *Necronomicon*: "Tregardis [the protagonist] had collated the French volume [*The Book of Eibon* in a medieval French translation] with the frightful *Necronomicon* of the mad Arab Abdul Alhazred."

In "The Weird of Avoosl Wuthoqquan," the entity in the cavern who circumstances the death of the protagonist, is described as being "outrageously unhuman" and definitely non-terrestrial in appearance. Tsathoggua is *mentioned* once, in an oath by the entity, as follows: "'By the black altar of Tsathoggua, 'tis a fat money-lender....'" There is no evidence, however, that this entity is related to Tsathoggua, the relationship only being inferred.

Finally, in Chapter III of Smith's unfinished (and so far unpublished) novel *The Infernal Star*, Lovecraft's *Necronomicon* is mentioned once, as follows: "…he [the protagonist, Oliver Woadley] had already begun the study of certain excessively rare tomes, such as *The Necronomicon* and the writings of Hali." (This last is a reference to the writings and writer invented by Bierce for a quotation preceding Bierce's tale "An Inhabitant of Carcosa.")

Let us summarize then the uses Smith in his own tales has made of two of Lovecraft's own invented gods and of one of Lovecraft's own invented books. (We may safely ignore the uses to which Smith, in his stories, puts the god Tsathoggua and *The Book of Eibon*, as Smith has Tsathoggua and his other invented gods enter into the action of his tales in a manner quite different from that in which Lovecraft manipulates his gods in his own fictions. And Smith certainly possessed a perfect right to feature, in his very own stories, the god Tsathoggua or *The Book of Eibon*, as had not Smith himself invented them, contributions though they might be to Lovecraft's mythology?) Yog-Sothoth is mentioned three times in one story. *The Necronomicon* is mentioned once in one story and once in another—twice, altogether. Cthulhu is found only once. Another quotation from the *Necronomicon* is featured prominently—in one story.

Featuring Lovecraft's *Necronomicon* in one story, quoting two Smith-written passages from it, mentioning the book twice in other stories, mentioning two of Lovecraft's gods altogether less than a dozen times in all his stories, and adding one god to Lovecraft's ultra-mundane pantheon, and one book to Lovecraft's library of forbidden texts—is this any evidence of a *genuine* literary influence by Lovecraft on Smith? If all the enumerated data above are evidence of such an influence, then it is, at best, a very superficial one. But let the following figures speak for themselves. Smith wrote about 140 stories; ten of these, by Smith's own reckoning, are more or less related to the Cthulhu mythology of H. P. Lovecraft—that is, *less than one-seventh* of Smith's total short story output.

As a footnote to the preceding it might be added that the only place in which Smith attempts to tie in systematically any of his deities with those of Lovecraft's creation is not in one of Smith's tales but in a letter written by Smith to R. H. Barlow sometime before Lovecraft's death. This letter was later published in *The Acolyte*, Summer, 1944, and republished in *The Shuttered Room and Other Pieces* by Lovecraft. In this letter Smith postulates for a few of his deities (used in his Averoigne and Hyperborean tales) a genesis in the Lovecraftian universe, in "Azathoth, the primal nuclear chaos."

In Smith's story "The Dark Eidolon," laid in Zothique, the last continent of Earth, the "older gods" and the "elder demons" are mentioned in paragraph one as having returned to man, the gods and demons of Hyperborea, Mu, and Poseidonis but, however, with different names. But which of these "older gods" and "elder demons?" Smith does not say; and there is little or absolutely no justification to tie them in with any Lovecraftian deities.

It may be mentioned that Smith, unlike Dunsany or Lovecraft, seemed to have been little concerned with or interested in creating any over-all mythology or any cosmogony. While some of Smith's gods are inter-related, the bulk of them appear to have no relation to one another. There was no intent to create a myth pattern. Rather, within a given tale, Smith would invent and use, whenever need and inspiration arose, one or two gods, usually with strong symbolic overtones.

In only one tale, "The Monster of the Prophecy," does Smith theorize any cosmogony, and then only within the terms of the ultra-mundane culture featured therein. The tongue-in-cheek cosmogony is apropos "Cunthamosi, the Cosmic Mother," to wit: "Cunthamosi was worshipped as the source of all things: her maternal organs were believed to have given birth to the sun, the moon, the world, the stars, the planets, and even the meteors that often fell in Satabbor." (Satabbor is a planet of the sun Sanarda, known to terrestrials as Antares.)

The real influence of Lovecraft on Smith, if "influence" it may be called, was that of a friend who encouraged Smith to write short stories. Lovecraft had been inspired to do this upon examining certain poems in prose by Smith, some of which are essentially condensed short stories. But there is *no* evidence that Smith might *not* have written short stories without Lovecraft's suggestion. Indeed, there is fairly good evidence that Smith was gravitating toward the creation of short stories purely under the urging of his own personal daemon.

There can be relatively little serious discussion, then, of any genuine Lovecraftian influence upon Smith—any more than of *his* influence upon Lovecraft—unless we recognize it as a mutual "influence," which, again, does not seem to be the right word. This writer is of the considered opinion that the correspondence-friendship of Lovecraft and Smith may be best characterized as one of mutual stimulation, encouragement, advisement, admiration, and appreciation.

Unlike so many of Lovecraft's correspondence with others, often characterized by a teacher-pupil relationship, the Lovecraft-Smith correspondence was distinguished by the fact that the two men, when they met through letters, met on equal ground, as equals, and with many similar views, tastes, and opinions. Lovecraft considered himself inferior to Smith.

In his excellent study *Supernatural Horror in Literature*, Lovecraft before his death rendered an eloquent homage to Smith's genius, and after Lovecraft's death Smith paid homage to his friend in two beautiful poetic tributes, "To Howard Phillips Lovecraft" and the sonnet "H.P.L.;" and in a letter to "The Eyrie" in *Weird Tales*, July 1937, and in a letter to Claire Beck published in "A Note from the Editor" in *The Science Fiction Critic*, April 1937. But long before Lovecraft died, Smith had already paid public homage to him by contributing (at E'ch-Pi-El's urging and invitation) to Lovecraft's ingenious Cthulhu mythology one god and one book, and by adopting into some of Smith's own tales a few of Lovecraft's inventions from this same mythology. And thus it is as a fitting and poetic tribute to the genius of his great friend E'ch-Pi-El that we may best regard Klarkash-Ton's Cthulhu Mythos borrowings and additions.

P.S.

Apropos the following excerpt from the letter of Harry Warner, Jr., in *Hindsight*: "The Fryer article disappointed me somewhat. He evaded completely the big job, that of attempting to prove or disprove stylistic inheritance, and confined himself to safer ground cataloging provable matters on which his opinion could not be challenged...."

(See *Mirage*, No. 7, 1965.)

Mr. Warner's criticism has caused me to reconsider carefully, yet one more time, the Smith-Lovecraft question, as to who influenced whom, and as to the area of influence. Let me repeat: "This writer is of the considered opinion that the correspondence-friendship of Lovecraft and Smith may be best characterized as one of mutual stimulation, encouragement, advisement, admiration, and appreciation." It honestly never occurred to me that there could be any serious question of a "stylistic inheritance." Contrary to what Mr. Warner writes, I did not evade "completely the big job..."—precisely because, for me at least, the "big job" did not, and still does not, exist to be "evaded!"

If we acknowledge the possibility of such a stylistic inheritance, when would such have operated, and to what extent? The date of the start of the H.P.L.–C.A.S. friendship/correspondence is established in Lovecraft's *Selected Letters I* (Arkham, 1965). I refer Mr. Warner to the letters numbered 109, 112, 114, 115, 116, 123, all addressed to Smith; I also refer him to letters 95, 106, 110, and 134, which, while not addressed to Smith refer to him...Smith evidently first read a tale by H.P.L. sometime during or shortly before August, 1922, and would continue to read H.P.L.'s mss. before publication up until shortly before Lovecraft's death. If any stylistic influence did operate, it would have to have done so c. August, 1922–March, 1937....The letters to Smith clearly reveal that H.P.L. recognized Smith's superiority in handling certain fantastic and cosmic-astronomic themes in verse that Lovecraft was attempting to treat in prose (see in particular letters 95, 109, 110, 112, 116, 123, and especially the last paragraph of number 115)....

Since Smith did not commence writing extended prose fictions in any quantity until 1929, the period of greatest influence should have been c. August, 1922-December, 1929, when Smith could have studied H.P.L.'s style and fiction techniques at his leisure; this would clearly have been reflected in the writing of 1929–1938. But Smith wrote few tales obviously patterned after Lovecraft's, apart from a small handful in almost a hundred or more stories (such as "The Return of the Sorcerer" and "The Hunters from Beyond"). As his chronology makes clear, Smith's extended prose fictions grew quite obviously out of his earlier poems in verse and in prose c. 1911–1922, sans any cognizance of H.P.L. and his work. A few examples:

"The Planet of the Dead" (pre-1932), derived both as to plot-germ and to phraseology from the prose-poem *From the Crypts of Memory*, first published in *Bohemia*, 4/17.

"The Demon of the Flower," composed October 1931, derives from the prose-poem *The Flower Devil*, composed before 9/29/20.

"The White Sybil," written July 1932, owes something to the prose pastel *The Muse of Hyperborea*, composed 12/22/29.

Smith had formed his prose style in his first serious prose, the prose-poems of 1915–1921, included in *Ebony and Crystal*; i.e. before 1922 when he first read a tale by H.P.L. And since the style and the imagination of Smith's prose-poems lead very logically and demonstrably to his later fiction, I can honestly see no place in his creative evolution whereat a Lovecraftian stylistic influence could have operated.

A better case might be made for, say, Smith's evident "stylistic inheritance" from Baudelaire (whom Smith first read and studied in June-July 1912, even if only in translation, while staying at George Sterling's place in Carmel) for the years 1922–1929, specifically apropos Smith's later short stories.

It may be noted that Smith's tales differ for the most part quite sharply from those of Lovecraft, especially in regard to narrative structure (a perceptive observation made by Bill Blackbeard, of the Los Angeles Science Fantasy Society, in February, 1964) .

There is a strong emphasis in the work of both men on mood and atmosphere. Both derived a good deal from Poe and certain writers of the 1600's and/or 1700's. For example, one may cite Poe, William Beckford, Sir Thomas Browne, and Baudelaire as some of the principal influences on Smith's prose style. One may certainly cite Poe as possibly the greatest single influence on Lovecraft's prose style, also Lord Dunsany, Arthur Machen, and some of the leading stylists of England's Augustan Age. It is not surprising that there should be some resemblance between the two men, stylistically and otherwise, but I believe them to be more of coincidence than of anything else, stemming from the fact that they were kindred spirits. Undoubtedly H.P.L. himself would have been the first to have dismissed the idea of any serious "stylistic inheritance" from him to Smith.

I do not care to discuss this issue any further except to refer Mr. Warner to the previously cited letters in *Selected Letters I*, to my essay on Smith, "The Sorcerer Departs," in *In Memoriam: Clark Ashton Smith*, and especially to my introductory essay, "Clark Ashton Smith: Poet in Prose," in *Poems in Prose* (Arkham, 1965). In the last cited I treat, in somewhat greater detail, the question of Smith's serious prose style. I hope Mr. Warner will find these divers materials illuminating.

Nora May French:
Somewhere Between
Eulalie and Edna St. Vincent Millay

Reading again the entirety of the extant poems by Nora May French (1881–1907), especially following a long period of relative neglect, say, two or three decades, has proven in the present instance not just a richly rewarding experience in sheer poetic terms but a profoundly moving one in personal terms as well. Albeit in my own case I memorized some half-dozen of her lyrics over thirty years agone, and indeed have often performed them in recital whether in Great Britain or in the U. S. A. since then—spreading the gospel, as it were, of her especial muse—re-reading all the others in her one and only collection (The Strange Company, San Francisco, 1910), simply titled *Poems,* and feeling again the full impact of her unique poetic presence, revives for me once more the over-all poignant story that is her life and career, however brief they may have turned out. Although I first learned of this poet through a volume by Clark Ashton Smith in the spring of 1958, it was not until sometime in 1960 or 1961—when I was conducting the earliest researches in depth on behalf of my Clark Ashton Smith bibliography (and compendium of other but related information as well), but not to be published until many years later, in 1978, by Donald M. Grant—that I managed to find and look at a copy of her collection (published posthumously), and to read all or most of the selections included therein.

Both Ashton Smith and his great poetic mentor George Sterling, together with many other and highly diversified admirers, thought quite highly of the poetic gifts evidenced by "Phyllis," as Nora May styled herself among her friends first in Los Angeles and then in San Francisco as well as in Carmel. Whether as a tragic figure or as a poet of extraordinary talent, she has inspired a kind of legend, the legend of a poet of great promise who did not live long enough to fulfill that promise either as a poet or as a person, given her comparatively short life and career. As a California Romantic whose highly imaginative poetry reveals here and there an overtly cosmic perspective—however simple (but not simpleminded) that poetry may seem at times—Nora May French stands out among that group of writers who gravitated around George Sterling and Jack London, and who yet stands apart from them as a poet, moreover one singularly uninfluenced either by Sterling as the then poet laureate of the Far West of North America, or by Ambrose Bierce as poetic mentor to Sterling and indirectly via Sterling to those poets influenced by Sterling as the most prominent poet on the West Coast but before the advent and later prominence of Robinson Jeffers.

As another member of that group who lived in Carmel and sometimes in San Francisco during 1906–1907, and who moreover came to know Nora May both as person and artist at Carmel, the mystical and fiercely independent Mary Hunter Austin (1868-1934), a fine and pioneering writer on both early-feminist and Amerindian subjects, thought quite highly of Phyllis as human being and creative person. In her autobiography *Earth Horizons* (Boston: Houghton Mifflin, 1932), Mary Austin states unequivocally that Nora May French was "the only woman of the group with an equivalent talent to London and Sterling."

During the early part of his correspondence and friendship with Sterling (1911–1926), Clark Ashton Smith spent his first considerable period of time away from his parents' home (southeast of what is now Old Auburn) as of when he was the elder poet's especial guest in Carmel during late June through late July of 1912. This visit lasted a month or so, and marked a major step forward for Smith both as person and artist-poet. First and foremost came the impact of the Monterey region, a place of great natural beauty then largely undeveloped, and with a natural forest cover dominated by pine trees and Monterey cypresses, but with the character of everything involving the terrain itself, especially the rocky coast, completely formed or transformed long since by the ocean, which undoubtedly furnished the greatest source of revelation to Smith, who had lived almost all his life up to that point in a foothill or mountainous area far inland.

Sterling's library also provided new revelations: Smith now first experienced the poetry of Baudelaire, even if only in translation, probably that of Arthur Symons (1865–1945). However, whenever it was that Smith first encountered Nora May French's poetry, the impact on him from it could not have proven any less great than that from Baudelaire's own output, inasmuch as Phyllis had used the same native language as Smith did, and American literary usage tended at that time, at least in California, to be strongly influenced by British forms and norms.

As it turned out, Smith had first encountered Nora May's *oeuvre* during the spring of 1912, apparently before his discovery of Baudelaire. Writing to Sterling on March 24, Ashton asks after Nora May's only volume. Responding to his question on April 12, George assures him that he will send him one of the extra copies that he still has. This he does, and Ashton gratefully responds on June 9, expressing his great pleasure over the volume. Finally, on June 11, George responds positively to Ashton's reaction, and explains that, if the book is beautiful, it is because "we her friends published it."

Oddly enough, the one eminent person and critic who did not seem particularly to like Nora May's poetry for whatever cause was Ambrose Bierce, who along with Sterling and Ashton Smith despised the sentimentality that larded so much of the popular literature before World War I. We stress that "oddly enough" because Nora's poetry is comparatively "lean" considering her general time-frame, and remarkably free of the sentimental fat so typical of the popular poetry created in the late 1800's and early 1900's. Although Smith writes of Bierce in passing that he was an almost infallible critic, the considered opinion held by Mary Austin is probably much more the infallible one in regard to Nora May's distinctive, thoughtful, and profoundly felt lyrics. But, digging further, we now know that Bierce did not dislike her poetic work at all, but fully felt the tragic poignance of it as well as of her suicide.

On the other hand, standing out in opposition to the cult of admiration that exists in Northern California, particularly the Bay Area, relative to her poetry, is the position of Jack Foley, the poet and the contemporary doyen of California poetry critics. While not in any way denigrating the quality of her work, Foley does not find her poems as remarkable as her persistent and often feminist admirers obviously do. Certainly the exalted opinion concerning Nora May held by Sterling and Smith counts for some real weight in any appraisal of her extant work.

Following Sterling's death on 17 November 1926 in his chambers at the Bohemian Club, Ashton Smith wrote two memoirs of his great friend and mentor. The first, written in late 1926 or early 1927, appeared in *The Overland Monthly* for March of 1927 as "George Sterling—An Appreciation." The second, written around 1941 under the title "George Sterling: Poet and Friend," did not see publication until its first appearance in magazine form in *Mirage* for Winter of 1963–1964, and then its first subsequent appearance in book form in *Planets and Dimensions: Collected Essays of Clark Ashton Smith*, edited by Charles K. Wolfe and brought out by Mirage Press in 1973. The second of these two memoirs is the more personal, and contains an extended and unusual report on Nora May but as emanating from the elder poet who had known her very well (as a close friend but not as a lover) during her brief but fatal residence in Northern California, starting in San Francisco during August of 1906 and ending in Carmel during November of 1907, hardly more than a year later.

> He often spoke of Nora May French, that strange and tragically gifted girl who had ended her life with poison in the same bed in which I slept nightly. She had, it seems, previously attempted to shoot herself with his revolver and had brought him a tress of her ashen-blonde hair clipped away by the bullet. He showed me the very spot beside the path up the ravine where this attempt had occurred, according to her statement. But, oddly, there had been no powder marks on her hair. I do not recall that he attributed her suicide to unrequited love for James Hopper; but there had been other reasons... perhaps sufficient ones.
>
> She was, he said, the most changeable person he had ever known: incredibly radiant and beautiful at times; at others, absolutely dull and colorless in her appearance. One day he brought out a manuscript of hers dictated during the delirium of illness. It was full of an otherworldly weirdness; but I can remember nothing of it, but that it was "such stuff as dreams are made on," and therefore immemorable as dreams. On one occasion, I recall that George told me to keep the cabin door shut at night. "If you don't," he warned, "the cat will come in and jump on the bed. You'll think it's Miss X— trying to climb into bed with you, and you'll be scared." "Oh, no," I rejoined, "I'll probably think it's Nora May's ghost, and I won't be scared at all. I'm sure that her ghost would be a lovely one." "You certainly have an imagination," he commented, half admiringly, half deprecatingly.

One cannot help but wonder what ever became of that manuscript! From Smith's description it would seem to be a companion piece to Nora May's little poem in prose, "Think Not, O Lilias," which she recalled out of a dream. This marvelous and revelatory visit with Sterling that lasted for a month or a little more, the closeness that he felt instinctively for Nora May via Sterling, and Smith's first extended sojourn by the ocean at Carmel, highlighted by the then pristine beauty of the undeveloped Monterey peninsula, all this coalesced in the alembic of the poet's imagination, and then culminated in his outstanding tribute "To Nora May French," appearing for the first time in book form ten years later when Smith published his second major collection *Ebony and Crystal* in December of 1922. This is a supreme elegy in blank verse, making it at almost an exact century of lines (98, to be precise) the single most extended of all Smith's poetic tributes to anyone at all. At almost 100 lines it is not only the longest but also the most elaborate of all the tributes ever paid to Phyllis, or Nora May, and of all the tributes created by Smith to various poets whether personal friends or historical figures. Only Henry Anderson Lafler's tribute "The Pearl" is longer. Smith wrote a number of outstanding memorial poems, some of them shorter by one fourth or one half than the one to Nora May French—we cite here especially "To Omar Khayyam," "To George Sterling: A Valediction," and "To Howard Phillips Lovecraft"—but even among these deeply felt pieces of poetic homage the one to Phyllis claims a certain pre-eminence in a personal and professional way difficult to define.

Although Smith could not have met her by the time that she died (he was only fifteen, and would not meet Sterling himself until 1911–1912), the younger poet came to know her thus directly through Sterling acting as a kind of medium. The latter had indeed lived very close to her, even if more in the manner of an older brother. He was never the lover of either Nora May or of her sister Helen, who had accompanied her older sibling when she moved to Northern California, but who had returned to Los Angeles by the time of her sister's demise. Although rather long for a short poem in blank verse—it has never seen much circulation—Smith's tribute clearly deserves to be quoted in full here in this essay-memoir. It not only pays to read and con it, but it especially repays to reread and reread it. It is a profound, majestic, and magnificent monument in that most intangible medium, "mere" words.

I first read this poem among others after I had acquired copies of all Smith's volumes of early poetry during the spring of 1958, including a copy of *Ebony and Crystal*, of course. Even during that first acquaintance with the volume in question Smith's tribute stood out among so many superb pieces of inspired craftsmanship. But the note by Smith immediately following it focused my attention on Nora May in an uniquely distinctive manner. The poem is quoted here as it appears in *Ebony and Crystal*, but not as it does in the *Selected Poems*, Arkham House, 1971. The differences between the two versions are few and insignificant. However, Smith did slightly modify the note following the poem. The phrase "the most gifted poet of her sex that America has produced" reads in its later incarnation as "one of the most gifted women-poets of America." It is important to note that Smith does not call her the greatest or one of the greatest female poets, but only the most gifted, or one of the most gifted, obviously keeping in mind the fact that she did not live long enough to fulfill herself either as person or as poet.

To Nora May French

I.

Importunate, the lion-throated sea,
Blind with the mounting foam of winter, mourns
To cliffs where cling the wrenched and labored roots
Of cypresses, and blossoms granite-grown
Lose in the gale their tattered petals, cast
On bleak, tumultuous cauldrons of the tide
Where fell thine ashes. **** Past the bay
The morning dunes a dust of marble seem —
Wrought from primeval fanes to Beauty reared,
And shattered by some vandal Titan's mace
To more than time's own ruin. Woods of pine
Above the dunes in Gothic gloom recede,
And climb the ridge that arches to the north,
Long as a lolling dragon's chine. The gulls,
Like ashen leaves far-off upon the wind,
Flutter above the broad and smouldering sea,
That lightens with the fire-white foam: But thou,
For whom the sea is urn and sepulchre,
Who hast thereof a blown, tumultuous sleep,
And stormy peace in gulfs implacable,
What carest thou if Beauty linger there,
Clad with the crystal noon? What carest thou
If sharp and sudden balsams of the pine
Mingle for her in the air's bright thurible
With keener fragrance proffered by the deep
From riven gulfs resounding? *** Knowest thou
What solemn shores of crocus-colored light,
Reared by the sunset in its realm of change,
Will mock the dream-lost isles that sirens ward,
And charm the icy emerald of the seas
To unabiding iris? Knowest thou
The waxing of the wan December foam –

A thunder-cloven veil that climbs and falls
Upon the cliffs forever?
                                        Thou art still
As they that sleep in the eldest pyramid —
Or mounded with Mesopotamia
And immemorial deserts! Thou art one
With the wordless dumb conspiracy of death —
Silence wherein the warrior kings accord,
And all the wrangling sages! If thy voice
In any wise return, and word of thee,
It is a lost, incognizable sigh,
Upon the wind's oblivious woe, or blown,
Antiphonal, from wave to plangent wave
In the vast, unhuman sorrow of the main —
On tides that lave the city-laden shores
Of lands wherein the eternal vanities
Are served at many altars; tides that wash
Lemuria's unfathomable walls,
And idly sway the weed-involvèd oars
At wharves of old Atlantis; tides that rise
From coral-coffered bones of all the drowned,
And sunless tombs of pearl that krakens guard.

                    II.
As none shall roam the sad Leucadian rock
Above the sea's immitigable moan,
But in his heart a song that Sappho sang,
And flame-like murmur of the muted lyres
That time hath not extinguished, and the cry
Of nightingales two thousand years ago,
Shall mix with those remorseful chords that break
To endless foam and thunder; and he learn
The unsleeping woe that lives in Mytelene,
Till wave and deep are dumb with ice, and rime
Hath paled the rose forever—even thus,
Daughter of Sappho, passion-souled and fair,
Whose face the lutes of Lesbos would have sung,
And white Erinna followed—even thus

The western wave is eloquent of thee,
And half the wine-like fragrance of the foam
Is attar of thy spirit, and the pines
From breasts of secret, melancholy green,
Release remembered echoes of thy song
To airs importunate. No wraith of fog,
Twice-ghostly with the Hecatean moon,
Nor rack of blown, fantasmal spume shall rise,
But I will dream thy spirit walks the sea,
Unpacified with Lethe. Thou art grown
A part of all sad beauty, and my soul
Hath found thy buried sorrow in its own,
Inseparable forever. Moons that pass,
Immaculate, to solemn pyres of snow,
And meres whereon the broken lotus dies,
Are kin to thee, as wine-lipped autumn is,
With suns of swift, irreparable change,
And lucid evenings eager-starred. Of thee,
The pearlèd fountains tell, and winds that take
In one white swirl the petals of the plum,
And leave the branches lonely. Royal blooms
Of the magnolia, pale as Beauty's brow,
And foam-white myrtles, and the fiery, bright
Pome-granate flowers, will softly speak of thee,
While spring hath speech and meaning. Music hath
Her fugitive and uncommanded chords,
That thrill with tremors of thy mystery,
Or turn the void thy fleeing soul hath left
To murmurs inenarrable, that hold
Epiphanies of blind, conceiveless vision,
And things we dare not know, and dare not dream.

Note: Nora May French, the most gifted poet of her sex that America has produced, died by her own hand at Carmel in 1907. Her ashes were strewn into the sea from Point Lobos.

Smith's note certainly piqued my interest and (inferentially) my potential awe but from the late 1950's on into the earliest 1960's the discovery, exploration, and assimilation of Smith's own poetic *oeuvre* (and beginning in 1961, those of Spenser and Swinburne as well) so preoccupied my mental horizons that I let the discovery of Nora May French's extant output of poems remain an unfulfilled project until a more convenient occasion. Meanwhile, primarily through my two visits with Ashton Smith at Pacific Grove north of Carmel in 1958 and 1959, respectively, I had also come into a deeper acquaintance with and knowledge of Smith's great mentor George Sterling, that is, with the latter's own poetry above all. Among other selections in Sterling's own second and third major collections, *A Wine of Wizardry* (1909) and *The House of Orchids* (1911), I had noted the elder poet's own beautiful tributes, respectively: the exquisite and powerful sonnet "Nora May French" and "The Ashes in the Sea / N. M. F.," a somewhat longer and possibly even more poignant piece of posthumous homage.

The first tribute Sterling redacted in late 1907 while still at Carmel. In fact, with his wife Carrie, he remained that winter of 1907–1908 in Carmel for the most part. Nora May's suicide certainly had affected the mood of the artists' colony there.

Nora May French

I saw the shaken stars of midnight stir,
    And winds that sought the morning bore to me
    The thunder where the legions of the sea
Are shattered on her stormy sepulcher,
And pondering on bitter things that were,
    On cruelties the mindless Fates decree,
    I felt some shadow of her mystery,
The loneliness and mystery of her.

The waves that break on undiscovered strands,
    The winds that die on seas that bear no sail,
      Stars that the deaf, eternal skies annul,
Were not so lonely as was she. Our hands
    We reach to thee for Time—without avail,
      O spirit mighty and inscrutable!

It is a little strange that in his second and final tribute to Nora May he addresses her, not as Phyllis, but as Evadne, a Greek name meaning fortunate. Did he mean fortunate in beauty and poetic talent? Surely he did not mean fortunate in terms of her life and career. Why would he have made what seems like an ironic use of such a name? "The Ashes in the Sea" remains a potent and poignant mixture of the real world at Carmel adroitly referenced with the cosmic-astronomic and the other-worldly. This tribute first appeared in book form when Sterling included it in *The House of Orchids* (1911), but inexplicably he deleted the final powerful stanza when he included it in his excellent volume of *Selected Poems* (1923). Did he think that it might seem sentimental? Sentimental it is not. Strong and emotional it is, and bereft of any conventional mawkishness.

The Ashes in the Sea

N. M. F.

Whither, with blue and pleading eyes,—
   Whither, with cheeks that held the light
Of winter's dawn on cloudless skies,
     Evadne, was thy flight?

Such as a sister's was thy brow;
   Thy hair seemed fallen from the moon—
Part of its radiance, as now
     Of shifting tide and dune.

Did Autumn's grieving lure thee hence,
   Or silence ultimate beguile?
Ever our things of consequence
     Awakened but thy smile.

Is it with thee that ocean takes
   A stranger sorrow to its tone?
With thee the star of evening wakes
     More beautiful, more lone?

For wave and hill and sky betray
   A subtle tinge and touch of thee;
Thy shadow lingers in the day,
     Thy voice in winds to be.

Beauty—hast thou discovered her
   By deeper seas no moons control?

What stars have magic now to stir
    Thy swift and wilful soul?

Or may thy heart no more forget
    The grievous world that once was home,
That here, where love awaits thee yet,
    Thou seemest yet to roam?

For most, far-wandering, I guess
    Thy witchery on the haunted mind,
In valleys of thy loneliness,
    Made clean with ocean's wind.

And most thy presence here seems told,
    A waif of elemental deeps,
When, at its vigils unconsoled,
    Some night of winter weeps.

However, it was not until 1960–1961, when preoccupied with those earliest researches on behalf of my Clark Ashton Smith bibliography, that I finally, but finally, became acquainted with Nora May's poems, it would now seem almost incidentally. During the late summer of 1960, as I was finishing up my summer job as night-watchman at the old Mendelson-Zeller fruit-packing shed out on Nevada street west of Old Auburn, and immediately south of the long-established Auburn Cemetery (this was all before I would return to my studies at UCLA during the regular school year of 1960–1961), I began looking through the old bound volumes of the *Auburn Journal* in the possession of the Carnegie Library. Dear Dorothy Sanborn, now retired (and since deceased) but then the head librarian, facilitated my painstaking research, page by page more often than not, looking for materials whether about or by Clark Ashton Smith, by permitting me to borrow the volumes overnight on an unofficial basis, in addition to letting me conduct a search through them in the special downstairs or ground-floor chamber devoted to them and other bound newspapers in those pre-microfilm days. Dear Ethel Heiple had spoken on my behalf to Dorothy, who proved perfectly willing to help me this way, many blessings upon both Ethel and Dorothy. I soon ran out of available volumes, and realized that I would now need to continue my search among the complete set of bound volumes in the possession of the California State Library.

Thus, before I returned home to Los Angeles to continue my studies at U. C. L. A., I went down from Auburn to Sacramento in order to reconnoitre the holdings in that institution. The task that lay before me was evidently not one that could be done in a day or so, and I realized that I would need to come back up north from the Southland to spend a whole week sometime that winter of 1960–1961 in order to finish up the job. There was also the more selective research to conduct in the *Placer Herald.* It was during this final part of the search that winter that I happened to come across Nora May's one and only volume of *Poems.* Towards the end of that final week of research, I realized that I would now have time to do a few incidental things while working in the then California Section. I looked up the volume in question, and then spent the major part of an afternoon reading and assimilating Nora May's poetry. I read through the entire volume with the exception of the remarkable long narrative in verse, the tragic love story called "The Spanish Girl," at which I only glanced at that time; the volumes of the *Auburn Journal* still beckoned.

Nevertheless, I had read enough to be both deeply moved and impressed by the poems themselves, and the book itself remains an enchantment, a little masterpiece of Art Nouveau typesetting, printing, and binding. The title page has the letters printed in silver, including not only the title and the author's name, but at the bottom the publisher's name: The Strange Company, San Francisco, 1910. But what caught my attention first and foremost was the frontispiece, a striking photo-portrait of Nora May herself, the most famous photograph of her, uncredited but by Arnold Genthe. She is wearing a dark blouse, and staring intently at the viewer. Her beautiful eyes possess an eerie, near preternatural, intensity. She has a lovely oval face, not over-full, and well-marked and well-proportioned features. Her hair is relatively short, not quite shoulder-length, but gathered to cover her ears. A beam of light extends down across her forehead from her hair parted in the middle to her eyes, in such a way that the light appears to emanate from the eyes themselves. She seems a brunette in the photograph, but we know from Smith's description that she had dark blonde hair. Her image as projected by the portrait would be considered beautiful by any standard, and we know that she had a robust and quite attractive physique. Her sister Helen reported that they both loved to take vigorous hikes together, striding over grasslands and other open terrain. No wonder that she had so many fans and would-be lovers!

The poems are copyright 1910 by The Strange Company, and a note below the copyright informs us that the volume was "Printed by / The Stanley-Taylor Company / San Francisco." However, according to authoritative accounts it was the critic and printer Porter Garnett who did the actual typesetting; he was obviously a fine printer. Whoever typeset the book did an excellent job. As mentioned earlier, this volume of poetry remains a little masterpiece of Art Nouveau book production. Right after the title and copyright pages, on a page all its own, the following rather stark announcement appears:

NORA MAY FRENCH

WAS BORN AT AURORA, NEW YORK, APRIL THE TWENTY-SIXTH, 1881, AND DIED AT CARMEL, CALI-FORNIA, NOVEMBER THE FOURTEENTH, 1907, AGED TWENTY-SIX YEARS.

The volume officially has 91 pages with 53 mostly short lyrical selections: first, a group of 22 poems; then the long narrative in verse "The Spanish Girl" (it occupies just over 30 pages); last, a group of 30 poems. The notes (but for only a few of the poems) appear on page 91. The final information on that page lets us know that Henry Anderson Lafler edited the poems, and assembled the notes, and that he did so with the assistance of George Sterling and Porter Garnett. "The Spanish Girl," Nora's longest and most ambitious poem, has three parts: Part I has seven subsections; Part II also has seven subsections; and Part III has eight subsections. The verse paragraphs making up the subsections vary in length, and the form used throughout the narrative is the quatrain riming A B A B, which achieves more often than not a rather laconic and understated effect, and which definitely contributes to the emotional impact.

A special mention should be made here on behalf of "The Spanish Girl," the extended narrative in verse which—an observation deserving repetition and special emphasis—remains Nora's longest and most ambitious poem, which I read, re-read, and studied, but only much later. Dolores is the Spanish maiden of the title, but obviously more a vital young woman than a girl. The locale appears to be some Hispanic ranch or farm in California, probably way before the Gold Rush of the late 1840's (however, it is not thus identified specifically). The other characters in the narrative are José, Marta, and some unnamed young man, but obviously not Hispanic. The story is told indirectly, and the reader must piece together much of the story and the characters wherever such is not explicitly detailed.

In Part I we make our first acquaintance with Dolores, and with her much older companions: José, the caretaker on the property and man of all jobs, but who behaves in a fatherly or grandfatherly way towards Dolores; and Marta, the domestic and cook, but who behaves in a motherly or grandmotherly way towards the same young woman. A girl of passion and spirit, Dolores feels quite stifled whether by her Catholic religion or by her out-of-the-way environment or by the weight of tradition and custom. She yearns to love and to be loved, to feel really alive. She prays to the Virgin Mary, in whom she trusts and believes completely. For emotional release Dolores can go riding at liberty (apparently she is a skilled horsewoman), but she also relieves much of her frustration by tending her garden, into which she brings plants from outside the ranch's compound.

In Part II what is obviously a handsome young man arrives at the ranch, a stranger from beyond the sea. Often he sings and plays guitar. Could he be an Anglo from New England, such as sometimes arrived in California before the Gold Rush? The young man and the young woman fall in love. Apparently José and Marta do not realize that the two young people are (in fact) in love. For the first time the young woman finds genuine fulfillment by being in love. (Of course, the narrative does not reveal the degree of physical intimacy.) In Part III the situation has changed, even though Dolores only knows this by intuition. Although the handsome and apparently sincere stranger does reassure her that he loves her, yet she senses that he is remembering some woman in his own far-away land, and that both woman and land are calling him back.

Inevitably the stranger makes his departure, presumably still professing his love for Dolores. Of course, she is grief stricken, and in her depression and latent frenzy she goes on a horseback but wild and hazardous ride, which releases her tension, and which she survives. José and Marta do not suspect the burden of grief that the young woman bears, but eventually Dolores becomes quite ill from her profound grief. Marta keep vigil by her bedside, but at last the hapless and unhappy Dolores dies of love for the departed stranger, and the story reaches its conclusion. Immediately following "The Spanish Girl" in the collection, "The Garden of Dolores" as a kind of sequel brings a poignant closure to this tragic tale about some Hispanic maiden in old California, presumably sometime before the secularization of the missions in 1834 and the much later flood of adventurers ushered in by the Gold Rush of 1848–1849.

The indirect manner in which the tale is adumbrated, the limited cast of characters as in a Greek tragedy, the lack of specificness as to geographical place or historical period -- not to mention, as to firm "reportorial" detail—the intentionally fateful tone of the narrative itself, all these help impart a kind of timelessness to the story, no less than a poignant sense of tragic predestination. Quite apart from the high quality of her lyrical poems, it is the high level of technical accomplishment, of subtle and sustained storytelling by inference, in "The Spanish Girl," always using the simplest means, that hint at what Nora May French might have achieved had circumstances allowed her to live longer, and to continue developing as a poet, no less than as a person. And it is this, even more than her tragic death, that has helped to inspire and form her particular legend, the legend of a poet of great promise who did not live long enough to fulfill that promise whether as a poet or as a person.

Just as the result of that first reading and perusal of her posthumously published book of poems, I learned by heart a handful of lyrics, instant and poignant favorites, of such a nature that I was able to memorize them with no real effort: "The Outer Gate" (the opening selection), "The Mission Graves," "A Place of Dreams," "The Mourner," and "Ave Atque Vale" (the closing selection). Many of Nora May's poems reflect her love of gardening, and the nurturing of helpless little things, references which she turns to touching effect. We quote here a dozen selections, all of them highly characteristic of her poetic art, some intended obviously for publication in contemporary magazines, and others, quite autobiographical, and hence intended only for her own contemplation, or that of lovers or very close friends. Poetry a hundred years agone at the turn of the century from the 1800's on into the 1900's, we are clearly reminded, had not yet become, as primarily so much of it is today, autobiographical revelation and/or cryptic or obscure puzzles.

Some special information on these present selections must precede their citation in full, almost all of it taken from Lafler's notes, with the exception of that relating to the Californian Missions. "The Outer Gate:" this renowned sonnet on death was written a year and two months before the poet's own demise. "The Mission Graves:" many of the missions in Alta California, if not in fact most of them, found themselves in a state of advanced ruin or neglect by the start of the 1900's. "Think Not, O

Lilias:" relative to this little (spontaneous) poem in prose, Lafler's note reads: "These prose lines were recalled out of a dream. They are included here because of their singular beauty." "Yesterday" and "The Mourner:" these are the two very last poems that Nora wrote before her death. "Ave Atque Vale:" this final selection was written some two years before the poet died.

Apart from what seems like the obsession with death, Nora May French is keenly sensitive to all the manifestations of the beautiful in everyday life, it is quite evident. Like Sterling, or like Swinburne for that matter, she identifies instinctively with the sea, its vastness, and its miracle-working power to create life, and to sustain it, in unending variety. Like Sterling, but in her own way, she likewise identifies with that incommensurable sea beyond, the sea of stars, and of infinite space, expanding since the beginning of time, and still expanding at a ferocious rate. The directness, power, and simplicity of certain lines by this poet are nothing short of breathtaking, and her poetic gestures are truly grand and magnanimous, and always lead outward, from her own introspection out into the cosmos at large. Although not fantasy per se, her poetry is nevertheless highly imaginative. and achieves a fantasy-like effect, universal and liberating.

The Outer Gate

Life said: "My house is thine with all its store;
    Behold, I open shining ways to thee—
    Of every inner portal make thee free:
O child, I may not bar the outer door.
    Go from me if thou wilt, to come no more;
    But all thy pain is mine, thy flesh of me;
And must I hear thee, faint and woefully,
Call on me from the darkness and implore?"

Nay, mother, for I follow at thy will.
    But oftentimes thy voice is sharp to hear,
    Thy trailing fragrance heavy on the breath;
Always the outer hall is very still,
    And on my face a pleasant wind and clear
    Blows straitly from the narrow gate of Death.
        Best-Loved

It was a joy whose stem I did not break—
     A little thing I passed with crowded hands,
And gave a backward look for beauty's sake.

Of all I pulled and wove and flung aside,
     Was any hue preferred above the rest?
I only know they pleased me well, and died.

But this—it lives distinct in Memory's sight,
     A little thing, incurving like a pearl.
I think its heart had never seen the light.

Vivisection

We saw unpitying skill
     In curious hands put living flesh apart,
     Till, bare and terrible, the tiny heart
Pulsed, and was still.

We saw Grief's sudden knife
     Strip through the pleasant flesh of soul-disguise—
     Lay for a second's space before our eyes
A naked life.

The Garden of Dolores

The garden of Dolores! Here she walked.
     When fretted in the twilight's pallid space
The trees were black and delicate as lace,
     And palms were etchings, sharp and slender-stalked.

Now riots summer in these magic closes,
     And life is rounded in the frailest spray....
Dolores, cold and buried yesterday,
     Is it thy spirit here among the roses?

For restless murmurs through the garden seek;
     To shadowy caress the flowers unclose;
A blossom in the dark magnolia glows —
     Or leaning pallor of an oval cheek?

Upon the dusk is borne a strange long cry,
  And one quick sob of wind the air has moved.
Ah, perfect garden that Dolores loved,
  Her soul has called to thee... a far goodbye.

When Plaintively and Near the Cricket Sings

Now evening comes. Now stirs my discontent...
  Oh, ache of smallest, unforgotten things!
How sharp you are when day and dark are blent,
  When beetles hurry by with vibrant wings,
  And plaintively and near the cricket sings.

The sighing garden calls me from the door;
  Above the hills a little crescent swings —
Above the path where you will come no more
  When beetles hurry by on vibrant wings,
  And plaintively and near the cricket sings.

The Little Memories

My thoughts of you... although I strain and sigh
  At stubborn roots, at boughs that tear my face,
No plants in all my garden grow so high,
  Nor fill with sturdier life a wider place.
It pleases me, and wakes an old delight,
  To go with wordy shears in idle times
And trim them as a patient gardener might,
  Clipping the thorny boughs to curves and rhymes.
If these were all, opposing strength with strength
  To make my hurt an easier thing to bear;
If these alone usurped my garden's length,
  It would not be so hard—I should not care.
But close against the ground, oh, small and weak!
  The trodden flowers, the little memories, grow.
Uprooting fingers press them to my cheek....
  Dear heart, I love you, and I miss you so.

The Mission Graves

By man forgotten,
Nature remembers, with her fitful tears.
The wooden slabs lose name and date with years,
And crumble, rotten.
The Padre there,
On Saint's day, from an evening rite returning,
Set for each unknown soul a candle burning,
With muttered prayer.
Glow-worms, they shone —
Strange, spectral-gleaming through the lonely dark.
Whose nameless dust did each faint glimmer mark —
Skull, crumbling bone?
Ah, the Dead knew!
The grateful Dead, far-called from voids of space,
Each by the tiny spark that gave him grace,
Watched, the night through.

A Place Of Dreams

Here will we drink content, comrade of mine—
   Here, where the little stream, to meet the sun,
Flows down a yellow rock like yellow wine.
Here will we launch a leaf to distant shores,
   And in it shut a word for Wonderland—
The blue Unknown beyond the sycamores.

Think Not, O Lilias

   Think not, O Lilias, that the love of this night will endure in the sun. Hast thou beheld fungi, white, evil, rosy-lined, poisonous, shrivel in the eyes of day?

   In this wilderness of strange hearts it is not thine alone that concerns me. Many brave hearts of men are more to me than thine. The hearts of men breathe deeply. As for thy heart, it runs from me, it is quicksilver, it does not concern me greatly.

Yesterday

Now all my thoughts were crisped and thinned
    To elfin threads, to gleaming browns.
Like tawny grasses lean with wind
    They drew your heart across the downs.

Your will of all the winds that blew
    They drew across the world to me,
To thread my whimsey thoughts of you
    Along the downs, above the sea.

Beneath a pool beyond the dune —
    So green it was and amber-walled
A face would glimmer like a moon
    Seen whitely through an emerald —

And there my mermaid fancy lay
    And dreamed the light and you were one,
And flickered in her sea-weed's sway
    A broken largesse of the sun.

Above the world as evening fell
    I made my heart into a sky,
And through a twilight like a shell
    I saw the shining sea-gulls fly.

I found between the sea and land
    And lost again, unwrit, unheard,
A song that fluttered in my hand
    And vanished like a silver bird.

The Mourner

Because my love has wave and foam for speech,
    And never words, and yearns as water grieves,
With white arms curving on a listless beach,
    And murmurs inarticulate as leaves—

I am become beloved of the night—
    Her huge sea-lands ineffable and far

Hold crouched and splendid Sorrow, eyed with light,
    And Pain who beads his forehead with a star.

Ave Atque Vale

It gathers where the moody sky is bending;
    It stirs the air along familiar ways —
A sigh for strange things dear forever ending,
    For beauty shrinking in these alien days.

Now nothing is the same, old visions move me:
    I wander silent through the waning land,
And find for youth and little leaves to love me
    The old, old lichen crumbling in my hand.

What shifting films of distance fold you, blind you,
    This windy eve of dreams, I cannot tell.
I know they grope through some strange mist to find you,
    My hands that give you Greeting and Farewell.

Although her poetry seems imbued with an inspired and even classical simplicity, Nora May's life itself turned out much more complicated,
however poignantly brief. Who was the young woman behind these laconic verses? Contrary to the general reaction to her volume of poems
after publication, she was in truth no more obsessed with death than is
the average but sensitive young woman or young man at any period in
history. Her life as well as her career, such as they were, while not unduly
harsh for the most part, had nevertheless endured their due share of
hardships and struggles. Aurora, the town in which Nora May was born,
lies on Cayuga Lake among the eastern reaches of upscale New York's
big western "panhandle" that lies between Lake Ontario to the north and
Pennsylvania to the south. Not an unusual name, neither is French exactly a common one. Several distinguished individuals born in the mid-
1800's already bore this last name but whether or not they were indeed
related to Nora May's family is not known. The immediate French family
to which she belonged appears to have been solidly middle class with social and economic aspirations upward, as is often the case.

The Frenches—father, mother, two brothers, two sisters—moved
from New York to Southern California during the big land boom of the
mid-1880's, in which the father himself had invested heavily, and thus,

when that boom went bust, he suffered financial reverses. The family, having settled in Pasadena, somehow managed to survive. The two sisters, Helen and Nora, had a warm and close relationship, and received their education in the Los Angeles public school system. Nora May went east, to study art in New York City, using some of the skills that she learned in art school to hold down a continuing job in a leathercraft factory. While in New York, she lived with close relatives including a handsome first cousin. They fell in love, and to avoid any major problems that their continued nearness might engender, their mutual families decided to separate them. Nora was compelled to return to California, and meanwhile she continued to find solace by creating her simple but idiosyncratic poems. As is often the case, she wrote them on a sporadic basis, and had them published in such periodicals as Charles Lummis's *Out West*, no less than *Sunset Magazine*, among others.

Through correspondence regarding her magazine submissions, Nora May became involved with Henry Anderson Lafler, the editor of the *Blue Mule*, a magazine specializing in short stories, and he helped her place her poems in other West Coast periodicals including *The Argonaut*, at that time a distinguished publication also sold in London and New York City, by no means a common occurrence for California-based journals, reviews, and so forth. Disaffected from his wife, Lafler came down from Northern California to Los Angeles. He visited the beautiful young woman, and they fell in love. It was only a matter of time then before she decided to move up north, where she had already established a reputation as a poet through her magazine appearances. In fact, thanks to Lafler, one of her private sayings had already found itself printed in a public place up north, even before she moved there.

Located in the celebrated Montgomery Building, or Monkey Block, in San Francisco (between Montgomery and Sansome on one hand, and Washington and Clay on the other), Coppa's Italian restaurant by the turn of the century had become famous not only as the most important Bohemian hangout but also for its colorful and unorthodox murals, including exotic, whimsical, irreverent, or sagacious inscriptions of all kinds as quoted from, or high-lighted by, the local artists and scriveners. Before her arrival in "The City," Lafler took a sentence from one of Nora May's letters, and added it to those curious murals and inscriptions which occupied the upper half of the walls at Papa Coppa's. It is worth quoting: "I fancy that all sensible people will ultimately be damned." This finds a kind of echo much later among the "Epigrams and Apothegms" included by Clark Ashton Smith to close his second Arkham House collection of poems and translations *Spells and Philtres* (1958). "It is a ghastly but tenable proposition that the world is now ruled by the insane, whose increasing plurality will, in a few generations, make probable the incarceration of all sane people born among them."

Meanwhile the great earthquake and fire struck San Francisco during April of 1906, but once the Bay Area had recovered from the shock and the terrible mess, the then chief metropolis at once began rebuilding. In August of 1906 Nora May moved to San Francisco, her sister Helen following somewhat later, in March of 1907. Preceded by her reputation as a very talented poet, Nora May, or Phyllis, immediately became a conspicuous figure because of her beauty, her poetic gifts, her keen intelligence, as well as her considerable charm and charisma. Many handsome and gifted men (alas! too many of them already married) courted her with varying degrees of success during the period that she lived in "The City:" George Sterling, Alan Hiley, Jimmy Hopper, and Bruce Porter, among others; but she seems to have maintained a kind of loyalty to Lafler. It is important to note, however, that although San Francisco's Bohemians warmly welcomed the two lovely sisters into their midst, and quite accepted them as part of their anarchic world—a world marked more by high jinks than by truly decadent or depraved behavior—Helen and Nora had received their education and personal formation in Los Angeles, and therefore in one sense remained the product, even if highly individual, of the then Southern California of the latter 1800's and earliest 1900's.

Late that summer of 1907 the two sisters went down to Carmel, to stay for awhile at the home of George and Carrie Sterling. It was in 1905 that the Sterlings had settled in this beautiful but then largely undeveloped community that occupies the southern part of the Monterey peninsula. There they bought a sizeable lot, and built on it a comfortable bungalow. Later Sterling built a cabin behind it, where he could lodge guests, and sometimes he would erect a tent to catch any overflow. Nora May and Helen (the latter only briefly) stayed in the cabin, and soon became a welcome addition to the artists' colony that had grown up in the wake of the Sterlings having moved there. It was George and George alone whose presence had caused the little town to become a haven for artists and other free spirits who had abandoned San Francisco. Sometime soon that summer or autumn Helen returned to Los Angeles, but her sister stayed on in Carmel. Apparently she had one or more serious medical problems that she had not discussed with anyone but Helen, problems more serious that anyone realized, information which her sister apparently suppressed. Although she had, of course, discussed the problem with her sister, but evidently with no one else, Nora did not know quite what to do. Suicide, an irrevocable decision or solution, must have seemed to her the only way out of her predicament.

Nora tried several times to commit suicide. First she borrowed Sterling's revolver without his knowledge, but succeeded only in shooting off a tress of her beautiful hair, a tress that she gave to the elder poet. Next she obtained some cyanide of potassium from a local druggist ostensibly to clean some silver. Instead, she put enough of it in a glass of water, and then drank the mixture down. Nora died almost at once on 14 November 1907. The Sterlings at once informed the authorities, as well as Nora's family in Pasadena, and Helen hurried back to Northern California. Nora's body was cremated at some facility in San Francisco, and Helen with a group of their friends at Carmel dispersed the ashes into the Pacific Ocean from Point Lobos. This quasi-pagan ritual apparently scandalized certain edgy relatives in the French family at large, although to a purely aesthetic perspective nothing might appear more appropriate and more beautiful. Nora herself would probably have approved: she was not a stickler for conventional proprieties, as it should be evident by now.

The loss was a profound one. Nora had not by any means attained her full development whether as poet, person, or pictorial artist. The loss was felt not just by her family, particularly her sister, but by all of their friends at Carmel and San Francisco. Following the ceremony, Helen returned to live in Pasadena, but she kept in touch with many of her former friends in the Bay Area and elsewhere in Northern California, especially with George Sterling. Once he had realized that he could not have either sister as a lover, the now poet laureate of the West Coast had regarded and always treated both Helen and Nora May with notable tenderness, as if they were his own siblings. He offered his especial sympathy to Helen in several letters. Although now departed irrevocably, Nora May French had left a legend behind her, a legend that could only increase with the passage of time.

Nora had already assumed near-mythical status by the time that the young Ashton Smith visited George in Carmel during June and July of 1912. George was letting a family in temporary financial difficulties, actually some close friends, live in his house while he lived in the little cabin that he had built himself expressly for Nora May, or so the report goes. He now gave the cabin to Smith for his use, while George slept in the little tent that he sometimes would have one or more of his guests use themselves. These gestures on Sterling's part are yet further instances of his noblest characteristics, his generosity and ready help towards others. Thus it came about that the young Smith found himself sleeping in the same bed where Phyllis, or Nora May, had breathed her last, per his own report.

Meanwhile in 1910 her sister Helen had married a handsome expatriate Englishman by the name of Hunt, and living in a colony of other British expatriates in Pasadena, Helen enjoyed a long and happy married life with her husband. At some point in the latter 1960's following Mr. Hunt's death, that indefatigable scholar and researcher Randal Alain Kirsch Everts located Helen living at that time in an apartment in South Pasadena. This is the same Everts Kirsch, or Kirsch Everts, who has rescued so many valuable research materials from their owners concerning the famous writers to whom these owners were related, or sometimes from the famous writers themselves (in the genre of the modern fantastic tale or novel), and who has thus preserved them for posterity. His discovery and locating of Nora May's own sister was undoubtedly a major and startling development for all the persons to whom he introduced Helen, myself included.

The present writer remains very grateful to Randal for going out of his way to introduce me to Helen French Hunt, first through letters and shortly after that through a personal visit. Helen would come up from Pasadena and South Pasadena a few times almost every year to pass one or more weeks in the Bay Area, visiting old friends and acquaintances. I was living at that time in an apartment in a house in the first block of Divisadero Street, an apartment that I shared with a few friends. (The first two blocks of Divisadero run parallel to the last two blocks of Castro Street, one block to the east of Divisadero.) Randal was in the Bay Area at the same time as Helen, having come north at the same time from Los Angeles like Helen; and possessing a car, he picked up Helen from her hotel in downtown San Francisco, a small but choice hostelry. The three of us had a very cordial visit together, not over-long, and we went out to eat lunch at some restaurant near her hotel. The chief subject of conversation, of course, was her sister the poet. At least we had broken the ice, and I subsequently visited Helen at her hotel downtown one or more times during that sojourn of hers in "The City." This all took place in the winter of 1967–1968. Helen emerged as a remarkably intelligent, quite cultivated, and singularly beautiful woman, all the more noteworthy for being in her mid-eighties. She remained an extraordinary person in her own right, quite apart from her gifted poet-sister.

This new friendship would endure (with several ups and downs, but not too severe, I hasten to add) from that winter of 1967–1968 until her death in April of 1973. Every time that Helen carne north to the Bay Area, we would have one or more extremely pleasant visits, and in turn I introduced her to such close friends in San Francisco as could appreciate knowing such a fine and wonderful person as Helen had become. She had a great sense of fun, and could match enthusiasm for enthusiasm. Thanks to a series of exercises given her by a doctor years before—she performed these faithfully every day as health permitted—Helen remained in extraordinary shape, all the more notable for her age.

At that time, among many other activities, I was finishing up the slow and laborious process involved in creating my own first collection of poetry, the first series of *Songs and Sonnets Atlantean* (published by Arkham House in June of 1971). I had begun the collection in March of 1961. In addition to the quaint and curious conceit that many of the poems were translations from the language and literature of ancient Atlantis, the book drew for its own immediate tradition and inspiration (at least in English) on the poetic output of the California Romantics, 1890–1930, a group that had included Nora May herself and her classically simple and understated lyrical poems.

For me, directly and personally, Helen brought an entire earlier world of California's "Bohemia" to life, whether centered in San Francisco or on the Monterey peninsula. Thus through her occasional sojourns to the Bay Area (once or twice a year), staying sometimes in "The City" or at other times at some fine old-time hotel in Sausalito over in Marin Country due north of San Francisco—but just as much through her warm and incisive letters—she put me at once in contact with California's fin-de-siècle and with its immediate aftermath that had produced such outstanding writers as Sterling and Ashton Smith, along with others, following more or less in the wake of Ambrose Bierce. Helen thus "humanized" my grasp of my own immediate poetic tradition, and brought me that much closer to her dear and beautiful sister. Nora May French has had many posthumous lovers, and I am happy to count myself among them!

However, far more than that, Helen herself became a valued and uniquely cherished friend, one who gave inspiration, encouragement, personal criticism, and (on occasion) monetary assistance to me, who was just managing to live during most of my residence in San Francisco by a combination of odd or part-time jobs or by my wits, an adventurous mode of existence, but not one to recommend to others, especially to younger people, except with the gravest reservations. (I lived almost entirely in the Bay Area, mostly San Francisco, from January of 1966 on into June of 1975.) After her death in April of 1973 I discovered through some relatives of hers in Los Angeles that Helen had helped other young persons over a considerable period of time—nor were all of them struggling poets and beginning writers! Also after her death (on 9 April 1973), some of her closest relatives special-mailed me a small box of memorabilia (left to me by Helen as a special bequest) largely relative to her sister, and recalling the tragic circumstances of Nora May's death. Due to the unsettled circumstances of my life at that time (an extreme understatement), I did not retain this cherished box but gave it over into the care of certain close friends in San Francisco (to whom I had introduced Helen). Later they gave the box to the Bancroft Library.

The circumstances of Helen's death emphasize to what extent she was indeed an extraordinary person in her own right, quite apart from her gifted poet-sister. In the many conversations that I shared with Helen and other friends, she had mentioned more than once her distaste for convalescent homes, in addition to her hope that fate would spare her ever needing to go into such places. However, as fate would have it, she fell, and broke her hip during February or March of 1973, while still residing in her then apartment in South Pasadena. Helen had moved into this apartment about the time that she sold the house where she had enjoyed such a long and happy married life with her expatriate husband. To her horror she was now forced to move into a room in some convalescent home nearby. However, she remained firm in her resolve not to stay there by whatever means lay in her power. She refused all food, and at her age and in her weakened condition she hardly lingered a month after her fall. On one occasion the nurses or other helpers moved her from her bed to a chair nearby, and while they were attending to some chore (making up her bed or whatever), turning their heads away but briefly,

Helen Augusta French Hunt gave up the ghost, and thus left the convalescent home, as she had resolved, as soon as possible.

Had Helen lived on into the summer of 1973, she would have turned ninety on 4 August. Born in 1883, she was thus Nora May's younger sister, and apparently was born just a few years before the French family moved from upstate New York. Helen's willing me the small box of memorabilia relating to her sister had, of course, profoundly touched me as its recipient; that she would have chosen me for such an honor had even amazed me. It contained letters to, from, and about Nora. Here were pictures (photos) of her as an adolescent and adult in California, as well as of her family. Here also were pictures of her family and of Nora (as a child) in Aurora, New York. Here was a poem entitled "Poppies," written in her own hand. Here was one or more letters from Sterling with a draft of his first and best memorial poem to Nora, the sonnet beginning "I saw the shaken stars of midnight stir," a poem especially cherished by Helen. And here was also—perhaps most moving of all, and genuinely magical—the sterling silver napkin ring with an elegant Art Nouveau design of mermaids on either side of a scallop shell. In the middle of this is engraved the single name of Nora, who had used this napkin ring as a child in New York, as well as later in Los Angeles.

I had long cherished the desire to create my own suitable memorial poem to Nora May, and meeting Helen in the winter of 1967-1968 quickened this long-suspended wish into reality, and between then and the end of that year I composed and then "tested" over and over (sounding it aloud) an apt "monument" in words not too unworthy of Phyllis. Although I "published" it by word of mouth late in that year to a few friends, I could not regard it as truly completed until I had gone down to the Monterey peninsula to consecrate it by declaiming it aloud out over the Pacific Ocean from some appropriate vantage point at Point Lobos, just five miles or so south of Carmel on the peninsula. I made arrangements to bus down to the area sometime soon after Christmas, staying overnight with some friends whom I had known earlier in the hippie years then happening in San Francisco, and who were living in an apartment in some unpretentious neighborhood in Monterey. I telephoned these friends from my pad in "The City," and explained my objective. They warmed at once to the idea, and since they had a car, they could take me to Point Lobos around or somewhat before mid-morning, and then pick me up a few hours later.

I believe that I had already mailed to Helen some preliminary version of this tribute to Nora May, explaining my plan to consecrate the poem at Point Lobos late that year. She read it, and in general gave it her warm approval. The plans were thus all in place, and on 30 December I took the Greyhound bus down to Monterey, arriving there in the late afternoon. My friends picked me up, and we spent a fine evening together. They had prepared a lovely meal, which we all ate eagerly, accompanying it with wine and other beverages, but not in excess. Nor did we stay up late. They had to go to work in the morning, and I wanted to be fresh for the supreme event, my solo consecration of the memorial poem to dear Nora May. It functioned just as well as a tribute to Helen in her capacity as her long-lived sister.

The morning of 31 December dawned bright and clear, and after we had all arisen and breakfasted, my friends took me on their way to work, and then dropped me off at the entrance to Point Lobos, the original Punto de los Lobos from the times of the Spanish and then Mexican domination of California. A picturesque and grandiose promontory (or series of promontories), Point Lobos juts out into the Pacific Ocean, and the entire area is, of course, a nature preserve under the care of the California state park system—truly a dramatic and spectacular region. Also, something not realized until one goes there, Point Lobos covers a considerable, and variegated, geographical terrain, and is not restricted to the single most spectacular view generally chosen for photographic or artistic depiction. I walked on deep into the region, eventually found an appropriate spot by the ocean, and after due meditation and contemplation I proceeded to declaim the memorial poem to dear Nora May, together with other appropriate pieces. I had worked myself up into a heightened emotional state, and by way of cooling down, I began walking around the nature preserve—exploring, discovering, exulting in such sublime natural beauty. I returned to the entrance and my friends came by in their car around noon (I did not have long to wait), we returned to their apartment, and ate a token lunch. I thanked my hosts warmly for their help and hospitality, readied my overnight bag, we all got into the car, and then they dropped me off at the Greyhound bus station in Monterey, from which I returned to "The City" that afternoon. I was very happy that, although somewhat cold and windy, the weather had proven a real ally by not raining. Over-all the outing had emerged as a fine and satisfying adventure.

While out at that chosen spot on Point Lobos, I had also read or recited other tributes to Nora May, including not only George Sterling's two poignant and powerful pieces, but also major parts of Ashton Smith's own "To Nora May French." I ended my reading or "concert" of poetic homage by declaiming in full the second stanza from Swinburne's perfect elegy to Baudelaire, the "Ave Atque Vale," one of the greatest memorial poems to anyone at all in any language whatsoever. I had chosen to declaim Swinburne's own stanza last because of the references to Sappho as "the supreme head of song," and because of the obvious correlation with Nora May as a "Daughter of Sappho, passion-souled and fair," to quote from Clark Ashton Smith's own magnificent elegy:

> For always thee the fervid languid glories
> > Allured of heavier suns in mightier skies;
> > Thine ears knew all the wandering watery sighs
> Where the sea sobs round Lesbian promontories,
> > The barren kiss of piteous wave to wave
> > That knows not where is that Leucadian grave
> Which hides too deep the supreme head of song.
> > Ah, salt and sterile as her kisses were,
> > The wild sea winds her and the green gulfs bear
> Hither and thither, and vex and work her wrong,
> > Blind gods that cannot spare.

Even though some connoisseurs would not agree with me, I personally consider the elegant, laconic, powerful, and limpid poems of Nora May French—mostly lyrical, mostly short—to be on a par with the pitifully few poetic fragments by Sappho that survive from the ancient Graeco-Roman world. This exalted opinion of Nora May's work explains, of course, the sentiment animating the third line of my own tribute to Nora May, "We muse on Phyllis and her Sapphic glory." In terms of Californian and (U. S.) American poetics, Nora May French obviously stands somewhere between Eulalie and Edna St. Vincent Millay. Millay needs no introduction to lovers of modern poetry (cast in traditional forms, etc.), but Eulalie is not so well known. Born in New Richmond, Ohio (not far from Cincinnati), Mary Eulalie Fee (married name Shannon), 1824–1854, ranks as California's first woman poet in English, and became celebrated in the over-all region of Auburn, Sacramento, and the general gold-mining area thereabouts.

Eulalie came to California following her marriage to John Shannon in late January of 1854, when her husband returned to Auburn in late winter or early spring of that same year. Her husband featured her poems on a regular basis in his newspaper *The Placer Democrat* during her first and only year of residence in Auburn. In November of 1854 the publishers Moore, Wilstach and Keyes brought out her one and only collection of poems *Buds, Blossoms and Leaves* at Cincinnati, and they probably dispatched some copies to California whether by stagecoach overland or by ship and other modes of transport via Panama.

Although she lived in Auburn but a poignantly brief period of time, from March or April of 1854 until her death in the throes of childbirth in late December of the same year, Eulalie had become fairly well known in the gold-mining area centered in Auburn by the time of her death, indeed becoming known as the Auburn Poetess. While not retiring like Eulalie, and belonging to a later and more audacious generation, Nora May French was no less idealistic than Eulalie in her expectations of love, even though her experiences in such adventures unfortunately led to her death. At least we can retain her poetry as the precious heritage that it is in fact. I close with my own poetic tribute to her memory.

"Thy Spirit Walks The Sea"

Dedicated to Nora May French, in memoriam.

Standing upon this lyric promontory
Which rises up beside the western sea,
We muse on Phyllis and her Sapphic glory:
Since that same time when you but seemed to flee
And in these waves they cast your ashes free,
Now more than half a hundred years have passed:
Beyond this world, its impure grief and glee,
You hold a greater world... the ocean's vast...
With whose untrammeled realms your spirit shall outlast:

Within what sunken colonnades and gardens do you roam,
Amid what palaces of some deep Atlantean past?...
Whose regal ways you have returned to claim once more as home:

And have you found—beyond this planet's barriers and bars –
Those greater spheres and realms... deep in the Ocean Sea of stars?

Point Lobos: 31 December 1968.

Appendix of Lesser Reviews and Miscellanea

Addendum: Another "Smith"

Schmidt, Franz. *Fourth Symphony* (in C major). Zubin Mehta conducting the Vienna Philharmonic Orchestra. London Records (English Decca), released in February 1973.

Toward the end of the review-essay "The Last of the Great Romantic Poets," mention was made in passing of the Austrian (post-Mahlerian) symphonist Franz Schmidt (1874–1939), as one of several "late great romantic figures." In terms of the older classical-romantic music Schmidt is indeed some kind of "last great romantic composer"—all proportions guarded—and since Schmidt's position in the world of music is roughly analogous to that of Clark Ashton Smith in the world of poetry, it is apropos to alert the readers of *Nyctalops* to both this composer and this new record. During the mid-1950's Philips released a symphonic disc of the Fourth Symphony conducted by Rudolf Moralt; however, this release received little publicity, but those collectors who happened upon it have treasured it ever since. The only other music by Schmidt that has been generally available is the incredibly beautiful *Intermezzo* from his first opera *Notre-Dame*. Herbert Von Karajan has recorded this twice—first, with the London Philharmonic for Angel—and then with the Berlin Philharmonic for Deutsche Grammophon—both times as part of an over-all collection entitled *Opera Intermezzi*. Angel is deleting its release from the Schwann catalogue; however, the recording with the Berlin Philharmonic is the superior of the two, as the London orchestra is absolutely no match for the Berlin, especially in the string section, an all-important part of the Schmidt symphonic ensemble.

To date (April 1973) no review of this new release has appeared in either *Stereo Review* or *High Fidelity and Musical America*—are they deliberately ignoring both this record and this composer?—but two leading English record magazines *Gramophone* and *Records and Recording* published highly favorable reactions in their issues for February (by John Warrack and Antony Hodgson, respectively). The present reviewer has no idea how this recording has sold in England but it appears to be doing well in America; recently (6 April 1973), whilst looking for it in Boston, he was unable to find a single copy in any of the record stores in the whole downtown area; the initial shipment had completely sold out. The American release is a handsomer production than the British one, and features a reproduction of Gustav Klimt's painting *Death and Life* on the front cover of the record jacket together with some attractive and appropriate Art Nouveau lettering. The British release features a reproduction of what appears to be a painted portrait of the composer; this gives no indication of the kindness and gentleness apparent in photographs of Schmidt.

As possibly the last major figure in the line of the great Viennese symphonists, the position in musical history of this Austrian cellist, organist, pianist, and composer seems clear-cut to us today in retrospect. He is regarded in his native Austria as the most important Austrian composer of his time, and in a popularity poll conducted in Vienna, Schmidt once came second only to Bruckner himself.

Born in 1874 in Pressburg (the Hungarian frontier town between Vienna and Budapest), today called Bratislava, the composer had a hard struggle in his youth but managed to attend the Vienna Conservatory (today the Vienna Academy of Music) from 1889 through 1896, studying composition and counterpoint with Anton Bruckner, ere the elder composer died in 1896. As a student Schmidt came to know not only Bruckner but Johannes Brahms as well, who died in 1897. He idolised both Wagner and Bruckner, both highly controversial at that time. At 22, upon successfully completing his course of study at the Conservatory, Schmidt was appointed cellist in both the Vienna Opera and the Vienna Philharmonic, positions he was to hold for 14 years (1896–1911), principally under the direction of the outstanding composer-conductor Gustav Mahler (who died in 1911). The budding composer attained to the first chair in the cello section, and hence he played all the cello solos in the standard operatic and symphonic repertoires then maintained. Thus he witnessed, and directly participated in, the end of the great Late Romantic movement in music. During the years 1896–1900 he conducted his own intensive studies in music theory; the first fruits of these studies crystallized into his First Symphony in E major (created 1896–1899), first performed in Vienna in 1902. This First Symphony firmly established Schmidt in the musical and artistic world of Vienna, and the Gesellschaft der Musikfreunde (the Vienna Philharmonic Society) awarded it their Composition or Beethoven Prize of 2,000 kronen (id est, crowns) in the same year as its first performance. There is much more to this First Symphony than what may be gleaned from the rather flip (but amusing) capsule-description of this work as "four Brahmsogenic movements with herophiliac excrescences" found in Nicholas Slonimsky's monograph *Music Since 1900* (see page 26 of the Fourth Edition, Charles Scribner's Sons, New York, 1971). In this First Symphony Schmidt has given a magnificent and eloquent expression to nothing less than the late 19th-century romantic movement in all its variegated splendor. And it forms a superb summary of that movement.

By the time he died in early 1939, Schmidt had achieved an output by no means enormous but certainly sizable, in which every work had received the maximum of compositional care. In all, 4 symphonies, 2 operas, 1 oratorio, 2 piano concertos, 5 pieces of chamber music, 1 cantata, divers variations for orchestra, and numerous pieces for organ, amongst other compositions. Like Max Reger, he was a master of the fugue and contrapuntal writing in general; and we must emphasize here the general contrapuntal weaving of the texture in Schmidt's music. A special word must be said about Schmidt's greatest achievement, the climax of his creative life, and the last major work he lived to complete: this is the magnificent apocalyptic oratorio *Das Buch mit sieben Siegeln* (*The Book with Seven Sigils*, premiered in 1938, shortly after the Anschluss)—based upon the Revelation of Saint John the Divine—wherein oratorio, opera, symphony and medieval mystery play merge to create a new dimension in music.

The creation of as large an output as Schmidt did manage to achieve, is all the more remarkable, considering the amount of time that he had to devote to both teaching and playing. He taught cello at the Vienna Conservatory. He appeared in the concert hall as both solo pianist and accompanist. He played organ in divers churches. He performed chamber music for his own pleasure. He retired from his orchestral appointment to join the Vienna Academy of Music in 1910 where as professor he taught piano and composition. He was President of the same Academy from 1925 into 1927. And he was director of the Hochschule für Musik from 1927 into 1933. In addition he also taught music to private students. He retired from teaching in 1937 to devote his remaining years to composition.

Music Since 1900 supplies the basic facts about most of Schmidt's major works. Harold Truscott in the latest edition of *The Symphony* (published in England) provides excellent analyses of Schmidt's symphonies (Truscott must be some kind of pioneer in the appreciation of, as well as in the dissemination of information about, Schmidt's music in non-

German-speaking countries). At least two books have been written on Schmidt (in German), as follows:

Andreas Liess. *Franz Schmidt. Leben und Schaffen*. Hans Böhlau, Graz, 1951.

Carl Nemeth. *Franz Schmidt. Ein Meister nach Brahms und Bruckner*. Amalthea, Vienna, 1957.

One other of Schmidt's symphonies won an unusual prize. In 1928 the Columbia Gramophone Company of New York and London sponsored a contest for the composition of a symphony dedicated to the memory of Franz Schubert—to mark the celebration of the 100th anniversary of Schubert's birth. Schmidt's Third Symphony (composed in 1928) was awarded the "First Prize for the Austrian Section" and was performed for the first time in December of the same year in Vienna and on the same program as the Sixth Symphony by the Swedish composer Kurt Atterberg (born 1887)—this last work was awarded the absolute first prize, world-wide.

But now let us turn our attention to the principal matter at hand, Schmidt's Fourth Symphony, a remarkable and profoundly moving work, inspired by the death of his only daughter, and hence also known as the Requiem Symphony. With great good taste the notes by Erich Graf (translated from the German by Kathleen Dale), who personally knew the composer, make no mention of this latter title, thus avoiding even the suspicion of any sensationalism. In the present reviewer's considered opinion, Schmidt's Requiem Symphony is not only a requiem for his daughter but—just as much—a requiem for the noble Viennese classical-romantic musical tradition, the so-called First Vienna School, of which it thus forms some kind of ultimate flowering.

The form of the symphony is ingenious: an expanded sonata wherein the first movement *Allegro molto moderato* represents the exposition, the two middle movements *Adagio* and *Molto vivace* represent the development, and the last movement *Poco sostenuto* represents the recapitulation. The symphony opens and closes with a trumpet solo of a strange and melancholic type, which leaves one with a feeling of haunted and haunting inevitability. Thus, the work forms an integrated whole without any breaks and with a kind of cyclic unity; an *ur*-symphony if there ever was one. It is constructed around two principal subjects: the second principal subject possesses an Hungarian folk quality, and magnificently lends itself to some gorgeously opulent and lyrical adagio development; the first principal subject first appears in the opening trumpet solo; and all the other themes are ingeniously created from the first principal subject. At the center of the work stands the magnificent *Adagio*, one of the most impassioned and yet restrained passages in modern musical literature—fully worthy of the Brucknerian and Mahlerian heritage. At the center of the *Adagio* is the compact but overwhelmingly passionate threnody expressive of the composer's grief over his daughter's death—this is a passage of unforgettable intensity. The *Molto vivace*—wherein everything seems to melt into everything else!—is another miracle of pure tone. The recapitulation at the symphony's end becomes a triumphant reaffirmation of faith over tragedy and grief. As the final trumpet solo fades away after sounding its very last note, we realize we have experienced the art of a great and unique musician.

To those who listen to music only as texture and who want music only as an agreeable background, a word of warning: please do *not* buy this record. Unless the listener is prepared to have some intellectual grasp of sonata form in general, and to have some appreciation of how Schmidt manipulates the same deliberately for his own ends, then quite frankly that listener is wasting his time and his money. Also: this music benefits by being played on a superior high-fidelity phonographic set.

The record itself is technically of a high quality, and the performance by the Vienna Philharmonic under the leadership of Zubin Mehta is inspired. Mehta has known Schmidt's music since Mehta's earliest days as a student at the Vienna Academy of Music. This is the orchestra in which Schmidt himself played and for which he specifically composed. The Viennese are of course excellent at playing almost any kind of music, but this is music they both understand and love in a special way, and it shows.

Schmidt composed this Fourth Symphony during 1933 (it was premiered in early 1934 by the Vienna Symphony under the direction of Oswald Kabasta, to whom the score is dedicated), the same year that the Schola Cantorum Basiliensis was founded in Basel, Switzerland (4000 Basel...Leonhardtstrasse 4...Switzerland), as an unique "Institute for the teaching and research of old music." "Old" means here music from the Middle Ages into the 18th century. More specifically, for example, one course of study "Historical Composition" outlines the practice of composition from the 1200's through the mid-1700's, thus paralleling much of the same spectrum of time as the romance tradition itself. Thus, just as

Schmidt's creativity sums up a very important over-all cycle of music (including the contrapuntal innovations of both Bach and the lutenist-composers who preceded Bach), the Schola Cantorum Basiliensis was founded to discover and disseminate much of the same tradition that preceded Schmidt's own final contribution. Vienna, a capital of music for over 1,000 years, also played host to the lyric poetry of the Middle Ages. It will be recalled that Walther Von der Vogelweide (c. 1170-c.1230), the minnesinger-poet, and the greatest German lyric poet of the Middle Ages, began his career as a court poet in Vienna at the brilliant ducal court of the Babenbergs. Walther compassed in his poem-songs both the elegancies of court society and the natural affections of village folk.

It is more than pertinent to note here that Schmidt was born in 1874, the same year as Arnold Schoenberg, the founder of atonal music and the twelve-tone system, who thus deliberately broke away from the Viennese classical tradition. It remained for Schmidt, as his unique historical destiny, to carry the tradition forward after Bruckner and Mahler, and then to bring it to its end, in a completely fitting and noble way. Schmidt thus worthily upholds the great symphonic tradition of Schubert, Brahms, Bruckner, and Mahler.

Through his teaching and playing, Schmidt directly passed on his own musical heritage to many musicians and composers. One of these is Theodor Berger (born 1905), who studied composition with Schmidt in Vienna from 1926–1932. Berger is regarded in Austria as one of the most significant among Austrian composers born in the 20th century. His music, like that of Schmidt, is remarkable for its passionate exuberance and its almost Mediterranean pleasure in pure sound.

Schmidt's final years, although clouded by both physical and emotional pain, were filled with honor. In 1936, the University of Vienna conferred an honorary doctorate on the composer then at age 60. After his death in Perchtoldsdorf (near Vienna) in early 1939, all of musical Vienna united in heartfelt respect to pay him the final honors. Schmidt was thus just spared the horrors of the Second World War. In 1949 the Franz Schmidt-Gemeinde (id est, Society) was founded in Vienna for the dissemination of his music as well as of information regarding the composer and the performances of his music. Readers interested in Schmidt (as well as anyone interested in joining the Gemeinde) should write to the following: Dr. Friedrich Jölly...Generalsekretär der Franz Schmidt-Gemeinde...Hegergasse 17/1/3...1030 Wien...Österreich (Austria).

Those readers who would like to obtain further long-playing records of Schmidt's music, should write to the following: "Gramola"...1010 Wien 1, Graben 16...Österreich. Among other items available from *Gramola* are: his 5 pieces of chamber music, his complete organ music (a considerable portion of his over-all output) on 6 discs, his *Saint Hubertus Mass*, and his magnificent oratorio *Das Buch mit sieben Siegeln* (this last on the *Amadeo* label), featuring a superb performance superbly recorded. These records, it should be mentioned, are expensive even by American standards; however, both the performances and the quality of recording are equally excellent.

1974 will mark the 100th anniversary of Schmidt's birth. This event will be celebrated in Vienna, Munich, and elsewhere, with many performances of his music. It would be very much worth the while of those music-lovers who treasure great symphonic music, to make the pilgrimage to Vienna in 1974, to participate in the celebrations that will honor this composer. Of all the Late Romantic composers—Alexander Glazunov, Gustave Fauré, Alexander Scriabin, Kurt Atterberg, Hans Pfitzner, Max Reger, etc.—Franz Schmidt is absolutely one of the most remarkable. And he is at the same time undeniably "modern"... make no mistake about that. At long last the world is catching up to Franz Schmidt and his music. There *is* cosmic justice, after all.

Don Herron: Echoes and Yet Again Echoes

Don Herron. *Echoes From the Vaults of Yoh-Vombis. A Compendium of the Life of George F. Haas.* Dawn Heron Press, St. Paul, Minnesota, October 1976. Total printed pages: 53. (Edition: 500 copies.) $3.75 per copy. (Interested readers may buy directly from the author-publisher himself: Don Herron /537 Jones St., Box 9207 / San Francisco, CA. 94102)

George F. Haas is best known in the world of fantasy and science-fiction for his two excellent memoirs of the poet and fictioneer Clark Ashton Smith, *As I Remember Klarkash-Ton* and *Memories Of Klarkash-Ton.* ("Klarkash-Ton" is pronounced simply as "Klar Kash Ton".) Apart from Smith's wife, George was Smith's closest friend in the last seven years or so of Smith's life. This wonderfully good-humored and alluringly written compendium of George's life indicates an abundance of reasons why this should have been so.

The present writer was uniquely fortunate in being able to introduce George Haas and Don Herron to each other on the evening of February 28th, 1974. Almost two years later, and after innumerable visits by Don to George's chambers in Oakland, Cal., this book appeared, the final result of that first meeting and then of the subsequent and continuing friendship. With the bemused approval of the original poet-author himself, George appropriated the title of Smith's interplanetary horror story "The Vaults of Yoh-Vombis" for George's library-den around the middle 1950's, and after the death (in Mexico) of Robert Barlow who had previously used the title to designate his closet (filled with old copies of *Weird Tales* and other treasures) in his then apartment in Berkeley.

The present reviewer is both delighted and honored to write this appreciation of Don Herron's book, even though he is going modestly *à rebours* or "against the grain" in writing it—that is, in this case, against the unwritten taboo which dictates a writer should not write a review, especially a favorable one, about a book in which he himself appears, and especially in a favorable aspect. This is a taboo which we would ordinarily respect but *Echoes* is above all about George Haas, and only peripherally about one D. Sidney-Fryer. We had the unique pleasure of watching this book being born and grow and come to completion, a book moreover that—we had long felt—needed to exist, for the benefit and memory of George's many friends. The monograph turned out much better than we

350

had any right to expect, and Don Herron merits every credit for writing and then publishing the book himself. Taboo or no, the taboo deserves to be broken in this particular case, and the book itself deserves to be praised and celebrated.

The chapter headings alone are most inviting, and forthrightly indicate the fabled nature of the contents: "To the Vaults," "The Inhabitant Therein," "Sandalwood and the High Seas," "Magick and Mysteries," "Lord of the Trees, King of the Mountain," "Before Kerouac," "Friends," "Klarkash-Ton's Epithalamial Hauntings," "Bigfoot Investigator," "Crater Ridge" (plus a most proper bibliography of George's considerable writings, and a most proper and useful index). These headings promise much but they live up totally to that promise. This is the real McCoy—a kind of written documentary - and not an imitation of anything else previously existing.

The material is fascinating and can bear endless rereading. At best, however, this selection of anecdotes from, and mostly about, George is but the tip of the iceberg. "Compendium" is the right word to describe the contents. As anyone knows who is lucky enough to have him as a friend, George is a veritable encyclopaedia of uncommon lore and wisdom.

Visiting George is very much like reading one of the magisterial stories of wonder and mystery penned by the Anglo-Welsh writer Arthur Machen. There is the same initial cozy ambiance (a visit to someone's "chambers"), then the gradual adumbration of wonders and marvels, then (probably) a more explicit "manifestation", then (possibly) a shattering denouement (usually described tangentially), and then (finally) a quiet and reflective ending, after which none of the participants or narrators of the story can ever again perceive "reality" as they had before the story occurred.

Apart from the absence of an occasional shattering denouement (such as would actually threaten the physical life of his hearers)—for which let there be many thanks!—George is a superb host and an excellent raconteur, and his chambers are at least as inviting as any found in Machen's stories. Machen whether in Wales or in London was an inveterate walker, and this is abundantly reflected in both his autobiographical and purely creative writings. George is also a seasoned walker, and any promenade with him is properly Machenesque. We believe Machen himself would have enjoyed walking and "communing" with George; Clark

Ashton Smith certainly did. Any walk or visit with George usually leaves the visitor with his sense of wonder refreshed and recharged, and with his sense of reality considerably expanded, if not outright turned upside down!

This book is essentially a collaboration, with George supplying the material, the atmosphere, and much of the tone, and then with Don writing it down, shaping it up, and then putting it all together. To echo Don's own words, "this booklet acts in some ways as a memoir of the author's reactions to the fascinating anecdotes of the Inhabitant of the Vaults and in other ways as a biographical account of Haas' life." What results (with much refreshing tongue-in-cheek and twinkle-in-eye) is a kind of *cinéma-vérité* journalism: the facts are real but the facts presented are so unusual, and the treatment itself is so evocative of fabulous things, that the end product reads like fiction. Although George naturally dominates the book (since it is, after all, devoted to him and his life), yet we also sense Don's own personality. Don achieves this primarily through an interesting mixture of styles, partly scholarly, partly colloquial, partly pastiche. One example, from the very beginning of the book, will suffice:

> To locate the aura of [Clark Ashton] Smith, I found it necessary to enter the Vaults of Yoh-Vombis and to encounter the Inhabitant Therein.
>
> Early in the afternoon of the twenty-eighth, Don Fryer knocked on my door and asked, "Would you like to visit George Haas later this evening?"
>
> Unsuspecting of the otherworldly experience awaiting me and never thinking of saying "no"—how Lovecraft would have loved me as a protagonist in one of his tales!—I answered, "Sure."
>
> Night was soon to fall and the air was chill when we took an East Bay transit bus across the San Francisco-Oakland Bay Bridge.

One of the leading Bigfoot investigators in the world, George has led, and continues to lead, a life wonderfully rich in experience of all types, from the ultra-mundane to the antipodean, as this monograph amply demonstrates. There is an eye-opening middle section of ten pages with photographs showing George at various stages of his life as well as exhibiting divers sculptures by Clark Ashton Smith (and all part of the Inhabitant's grand collection, one of the best ones of its class anywhere in the world).

The format of this soft-bound book is tasteful, commendably simple, and withall handsome and well thought-out. The attractive cover features some apt and nicely done artwork surrounding a photograph of George sporting a serious and no-nonsense expression. The total production with its singular contents will certainly stir the reader's sense of wonder and marvel in the best manner of imaginative fiction or extraordinary fact.

Great credit is due Don Herron for the dedication, love, and outright skill with which he has presented his compilation-collaboration; and even greater credit is due George Haas for choosing to live so refreshingly liberated and fascinating a lifestyle. In this book we are luckily light-years away from American middle-class materialism and banality. All in all, this is an unique and moving tribute, and a very human (and humane) document.

For the serious aficionados of fantasy in life and literature, the innumerable associations with Clark Ashton Smith would alone justify their collecting this book. But for the cosmic humanist, it provides a no less necessary and vital experience. In one word: Delightful!

L. Sprague de Camp:
The Art of Modern Enchantment

L. Sprague de Camp. *Literary Swordsmen And Sorcerers: The Makers of Heroic Fantasy.* Arkham House, Sauk City, Wisconsin, 1976. Pages, xxix, 313. Price, $10.

This book, containing eleven chapters in all, has as its main concern those writers who, virtually single-handedly, created modern fantasy. A number of them have also made significant contributions to modern science-fiction and science fantasy. In Chapter I, "The Swords of Faerie," De Camp traces the evolution of the modern genre (for "modern" read "late nineteenth and early to middle twentieth century") from its antecedents in classical, medieval, and early modern literature (for "early modern" read "Renaissance and afterwards up to the early eighteenth century"). In Chapters II through X, he deals with important individual writers. And in Chapter XI, "Conan's Compeers," he presents an account of some half-dozen authors, the most outstanding being C. L. Moore, Henry Kuttner, and the very much alive and creatively active Fritz Leiber.

In Chapter II, "Jack of All Trades," De Camp makes a seemingly plausible case for William Morris as the inventor of stories laid in purely imaginary lands and worlds, or (what is in essence) pure mental space (literally a totally unbounded realm of reference and speculation). In long (and rather long-winded) prose narratives Morris presumably laid the foundation for modern heroic fantasy. (Incidentally, his verse narratives are much better formed and paced.) Well, yes and no. The prose narratives seem to have had almost no influence on any of the subsequent scriveners in the genre, but they did come first, and Morris did write them as novels. And it is good to have De Camp focus our attention on this fine Pre-Raphaelite poet just as a prose fictioneer, one aspect of Morris which had virtually sunk into total forgetfulness and neglect until De Camp and Carter's revival of him.

In Chapter III, "Two Men in One," De Camp sketches in full the life and multifaceted accomplishments of Lord Dunsany. One could make a much better case for Dunsany, rather than Morris, as the father of modern fantasy (id est, largely created in the twentieth century), especially in the short story form, following the lead here of Edgar Allan Poe.

Dunsany's plays as well as his tales became rather widely known during the first quarter of our present century. He was very much self-conscious of doing something different and new in at least the short story; he acknowledged no tradition or influence from William Morris; and his short fantasies had some undoubted influence, just by the simple fact of their existing as an example of what could be done in pure style and concentrated form, on H. P. Lovecraft and (to a lesser extent) perhaps on Clark Ashton Smith. His later novels proved to be as fine and innovative in the genre of heroic fantasy as his earlier short works, and they are surely more easily understandable and accessible for the average aficionado than such idiosyncratic examples as *The Worm Ouroboros* by E. R. Eddison or *A Voyage To Arcturus* by David Lindsay, no less credit to these last-cited titles because of such a fact.

Of course, the towering figure as a novelist of heroic fantasy is E. R. Eddison whose magnum opus *The Worm Ouroboros* is almost as fine an achievement as a prose narrative produced in the twentieth century as Spenser's epic *The Faerie Queene* is as a verse narrative appearing in the (late) Renaissance. In Chapter V, "Superman in a Bowler," De Camp gives this work a very high rating indeed, and fills us in on Eddison's other fantasy novels, which (while admittedly inferior to his masterpiece) are nonetheless interesting and well worth experiencing. In his high assessment of Eddison's *meisterwerk*, we most heartily concur with De Camp.

In Chapters IV and VI, "Eldritch Yankee Gentleman" and "The Miscast Barbarian," the two longest sections of the book, De Camp details the lives and literary careers of H. P. Lovecraft and Robert E. Howard, respectively. For these chapters De Camp draws upon his previous writing on these same figures. The true HPLophile and REHophile who have not liked De Camp's former treatment of these figures, will probably not thank him for his present accounts; although in the case of Lovecraft he has heeded some disparate criticism and has accordingly made some changes and additions. However, to be perfectly fair, De Camp always reaches his conclusions about these controversial and influential writers on his own, and he bases his opinions objectively on his own rigorous and careful researches. While the present reviewer holds his own ideas and opinions about H.P.L. and R.E.H., he finds De Camp's account of them refreshing, lucid, and stimulating; and that is after all a large order of things for which to be grateful.

In Chapter VII, "Parallel Worlds," De Camp details something of his collaboration with Fletcher Pratt, who led a fascinating career indeed as a fantasy and science-fiction writer on the one hand and as an official military historian on the other. A thorough-going individualist, Pratt created two novels of heroic fantasy, *The Well of the Unicorn* and *The Blue Star*, to which De Camp and other experts accord a high rank, somewhat below Eddison's *meisterwerk*, but more than holding their novelistic own with the non-Ouroborian competition.

In Chapter VIII, "Sierran Shaman," De Camp presents a crisp, straightforward account of Clark Ashton Smith's life and his career as a man of letters but falls somewhat short in dealing with the actual literary output per se (especially in regard to his poetry). We feel De Camp could have devoted much more time and space to Smith than what he actually does; his treatment is basically adequate in regard to the main events in Smith's life but is otherwise disappointing. We discuss the apparent reasons for this below.

In Chapters IX and X, "Merlin in Tweeds" and "The Architect of Camelot," De Camp gives over-all a very decent accounting of the lives and prose fictions of J. R. R. Tolkien and T. H. White, respectively, by far the two most popular fantasy novelists of the twentieth century in English. In Chapter IX, among other things, De Camp takes on the problem of Edmund Wilson's negative criticism of Tolkien's massive narrative of Middle Earth, and without being in any way vituperative, petulant, or ungentlemanly, he comes up with some very good reasons why Wilson may not have liked *The Hobbit* and *The Lord of the Rings*. ("Oh, those awful Orcs," indeed!) As August Derleth has written apropos of Wilson's negative reaction to Lovecraft, Wilson virtually did in fact have a blind spot when it came to most fantasy. Wilson simply was not the best authority to come to critical grips with Tolkien's inspiring literary achievement which, more than any other, helped prepare the way for the current renaissance of interest in fantasy.

In Chapter X, De Camp does quite a nice job on T. H. White and his fantasy novels, which output is to date almost unique in having inspired a Walt Disney animated cartoon (*The Sword in the Stone*) and a Broadway musical (*Camelot*) and the subsequent film adaptation of the Lerner and Loewe musical play. Although not quite in the same way as Tolkien, Messire White's prose fictions have also helped spark the current fantasy renaissance.

In Chapter XI, "Conan's Compeers," De Camp deals with some half-dozen writers, three of whom were new to us (to wit, Leslie Barringer, Clifford Ball, and Norvell W. Page) and the other three of whom are easily the most outstanding: Catherine Moore, Henry Kuttner, and Fritz Leiber. These last three writers have also made highly significant contributions to science-fiction and science fantasy, as have Lovecraft, Ashton Smith, Dunsany, Pratt, and Sprague de Camp himself.

Fritz Leiber, who is not only very much alive but still creatively active as well, has attained to a new prime and a new literary excellence. His Saga of Fafhrd and the Gray Mouser is possibly the best heroic fantasy now happening or continuing, and his science-fiction and science fantasy are distinctive for the very real and alive characters he creates for them. The dramatis personae inhabiting his heroic fantasy narratives are notable in particular for their pungent, hairy-sweaty, nitty-gritty qualities, thus producing some of the most realistic fantasy ever, if such a statement is not a contradiction in terms. His science-fiction and science fantasy have made many important contributions to the American literary scene, and have been just as much honored by his co-writers and co-fans in a series of Hugoes, Nebulas, et alia. His distinguished stories of supernatural wonder and horror have similarly met with equally distinguished recognition in the horror-fantasy field. His recent novel *Our Lady of Darkness* (1977) is set in the San Francisco of both haunted past and haunted present. A further volume in his Fafhrd and Gray Mouser series will be shortly appearing. Besides all this, Leiber ranks as one of the best informed, most insightful, and most versatile critics and commentators in the various genres in which he also writes creatively.

The author of *Literary Swordsmen and Sorcerers* has himself led a very active and variegated career to date in the genres of which he speaks—both as a critic-scholar and as a creative writing force—as we are kindly reminded by Lin Carter who supplies the "Introduction: Neomythology," most of which he quite properly devotes to "Quixote with a Pen," who is none other than one L. Sprague de Camp. Most of the author's best qualities as a scholar-popularizer are apparent in the present volume but in regard to Clark Ashton Smith, for example, they fall short. There is a distinct continuity between Smith's early poetry and his later fiction; this is hardly more than mentioned in De Camp's treatment. In pointing out the practical exigencies of ordinary or artistic life, De Camp is always a steady and dependable authority, but the present observer has generally found Messire De Camp short on literary theory, and so he finds him in this present case. We think that just a little more of such overt aesthetic would have improved the Ashton Smith section in particular and his present book-length study over-all.

And what of the term "heroic fantasy" to designate the modern concept of fantasy, i.e., stories laid in purely imaginary lands and/or worlds, or (what is in essence) pure mental space? The great grandfather of modern fantasy in this last pivotal sense is of course Edmund Spenser who purveys it abundantly in his epic-romance-allegory *The Faerie Queene* (1590, 1596, 1609). His influence on the English Romantic and then on the English Victorian poets was enormous, and contributed tremendously to the state of mind which could conceive of "faery lands forlorn" (to use that much too convenient phrase by Keats) wherever they just might happen to be. So, like the term "Swords and Sorcery," heroic fantasy has found wide acceptance in the field because it is a sensible and useful expression. It is, incidentally, quite apt to note that De Camp did some important literary pioneering back in the 1950's, helping to keep fantasy literature alive during an otherwise unremarkable decade with both his own stories and with such scholarly book-length studies as *Lost Continents*, a now classic discussion and compilation on the Atlantis theme in life and literature.

De Camp is very good indeed within the self-imposed limitations of his present study. However, like Lin Carter, we would have preferred a section on James Branch Cabell, a singular omission. But there are very few studies like *Literary Swordsmen and Sorcerers* presently available, and so De Camp's useful monograph fills a real need, and it does this with clarity, simplicity, and considerable balance, no mean feat, it must be admitted. In addition to bringing a great deal of otherwise scattered information together in a convenient form, De Camp especially excels, as he goes along, in providing many clear-cut, useful, and ingenious definitions, thus in the best tradition of the modern popularizer.

With its welcome discussion of Catherine Moore's work—the only woman so represented—his present study, however, does forcibly remind the aficionado just how few women have come to the fore in the genre until recently. Although there are alive and active in the field many able and even outstanding male writers, it may be maintained that the best writers of fantasy (and science fantasy) today—considered as a group—are women. We need only think of Evangeline Walton, Joy

Chant, Ursula LaGuin, Marion Zimmer Bradley, André Norton (that grand and genuine spinner of tales), and (among other newcomers) Tanith Lee. It bodes quite well for the genres of imaginative fiction that the feminists in them have now come to the forefront. It is, in addition, significant and encouraging that Fritz Leiber has nonetheless remained— despite "all the changes coming down"—one of the most intelligent and articulate male feminists in fantasy and science-fiction all along.

Literary Swordsmen and Sorcerers concludes with a proper section of notes as well as with a very useful index. This is a plus. Also, like most Arkham House productions that have appeared since James Turner became managing editor, this book seems to be virtually free from typographical errors. This is another plus. An even further one is the reproduced frontispiece, a piece of art by Sidney Sime, the famous illustrator of a number of Dunsany's early books. The front-cover design on the dust-jacket is a charming group of fantasy figures done by Tim Kirk in his characteristic and attractive style. The photograph of De Camp on the back inner flap of the dust-jacket is by E. B. Boatner, and we must say that the author looks unusually fit and certainly much younger than his stated sixty-eight years. Over-all then, *Literary Swordsmen and Sorcerers* is highly recommended as a sane, good-humored, entertaining, and well-balanced survey of some of the outstanding figures in the modern fantasy-literature field, and written by one moreover who is a skilled and urbane practitioner therein himself. This book is a decided bonus.

Frank Belknap Long, *In Mayan Splendor*

Frank Belknap Long. *In Mayan Splendor*. Dustjacket and illustrations by Stephen Fabian. Arkham House, Sauk City, Wisconsin, December 1977. Pages, x, 66. Price, $6.00.

This book is pure unalloyed gold together with some silver of similar quality. For once, amid the busy production of fantastic verse, we have here at last the real McCoy, verily the genuine article. What a relief! what a pleasure! what a joy! Along with the work of George Sterling, Clark Ashton Smith, Samuel Loveman and others, this must rank with the more notable imaginative poetry of the twentieth century. Belknap Long's fine craftsmanship permits us to enjoy, unsullied and unflawed, his poetic visions, narratives, and outpourings. The volume is physically slender but the contents themselves are ponderous in quality. Endlessly notable and endlessly quotable, these poems cover a wide spectrum of mood and emotion: from the opening sonnet *In Mayan Splendor* ("In misty dreams and shadowed memories / Of fabled cities I have dwelt apace.") to the final selection, the touching memorial sonnet H. P. Lovecraft ("Sublimer beauty never dwelt with Poe, / Or walked with Shelley in the white dawn's glow.") our poet ranges far afield indeed. We have here such wonderfully imaginative and narrative lyrics as *A Knight of La Mancha*, *A Man of Genoa*, *The Magi*, *Ballad of St. Anthony*, *An Old Tale Retold*, *The Goblin Tower*, *The Marriage of Sir John de Mandeville*, *The Horror of Dagoth World*, *Ballad of Mary Magdaline*, *Great Ashtoreth*, and *An Old Wife Speaketh It*. To quote from *When We Have Seen*:

> Let us mount gorgeous horses…
> For sea-girt cities beckon
> And we go Troyward soon.
> Yes, but let them be *Stallions of the Moon*!
> Mystic beasts of Sibyl,
> Fed on golden oats,
> More than Spartan finish
> On their moonspun coats.

Belknap Long's own poem titled *The Hashish Eater* is quite different from Ashton Smith's towering magnum opus of the same name but it is nonetheless appealing and certainly surprising in its own way:

> The boat was waiting; seas like foaming wine
> Curled round its prow; the moon was full and red.
> "I go," he laughed, "to lie upon her bed
> And kiss her mouth until desire is dead,
> For I am Caesar, and the world is mine'"
> He shrieked, and woke upon a cross; his bands
> Were dripping blood upon the yellow sands,
> And far below a harlot wrung her hands.

Our own first introduction to Belknap Long's fanciful and sensitive muse came via H. P. Lovecraft's monumental essay *Supernatural Horror in Literature* in the latter's discussion of the Anglo-Welsh fantaisiste Arthur Machen and his works. Within his discussion H. P. L. quotes in full the superb sonnet *On Reading Arthur Machen*; by virtue of which we became an instantaneous but permanent fan of Belknap Long's. We in our turn cannot resist quoting this poem in full yet once again:

> There is a glory in the autumn wood,
> The ancient lanes of England wind and climb
> Past wizard oaks and gorse and tangled thyme
> To where a fort of mighty empire stood:
> There is a glamour in the autumn sky;
> The reddened clouds are writhing in the glow
> Of some great fire, and there are glints below
> Of tawny yellow where the embers die.
>
> I wait, for he will show me, clear and cold,
> High-raised in splendor, sharp against the North
> The Roman eagles, and through mists of gold
> The marching legions as they issue forth:
> I wait, for I would share with him again
> The ancient wisdom, and the ancient pain.

Shades of the (British) Masterpiece Theatre production of *I, Claudius*, that emperor under whose rule Britain was added to the *Imperium Romanum*! Could there be any better allusion to, and summary of, the unique feeling and attraction characteristic of Machen's *oeuvre* than this? We doubt it. Or in another and more contemporary mood Belknap Long can charm us with such a simple, tranquil, delightful lyric as *A Time Will Come*:

> A time will come when we shall share
>   The wonder, dear, together,
> Of flaming candles on a shrine
>   In gray and golden weather.
> And we shall kneel with avid eyes
>   To watch a shining chalice
> By children borne across the nave
>   Of some cathedral-palace.
> And we shall rise, and go away
>   With eager lips that cling,
> Unmindful of the strumming choirs
>   And every living thing.

It seems incredible to us that Belknap Long could have created *Exotic Quest* at the age of thirteen! But as fine as are these more fanciful effusions, in such pieces as *In Hospital, Manhattan Skyline, W. W.,* and *Subway,* our poet effects his own unique and literally neat amalgam of classic form with contemporary allusion and subject-matter, the past and present nicely immingling for present as well as future delectation. Withal, his characteristic touch and treatment are light, but not slight; we might even say lightsome in the best sense of something nimble, buoyant, lively, graceful, cheerful, and lighthearted but also in the sense of something literally luminous and bright.

Since much imaginative poetry of the past and present has had a distinct and distinctive tendency toward the massively, but not necessarily unattractively, ponderous in effect, Belknap Long's achievement in his own verse must be seen as all the more remarkable.

We understand that the contents of this volume, collecting as it does his early poetry, has been subjected to some judicious and recent revision, thus making *In Mayan Splendor* in some sense as much a product of the mature Belknap Long as of the earlier poet before the age of thirty. While there is frankly far less cosmic-mindedness, or cosmic-astronomic-mindedness, such as we associate with H. P. L. or Ashton Smith, there is instead a far-ranging fancy which, in the final analysis, has its own incidental touches and elements of cosmicism. Together with the chiseled and incisive prose of Samuel Loveman's Preface, and with the simply gorgeous illustrations by Stephen Fabian—my, wouldn't the designs for *Stallions of the Moon* and *The Goblin Tower* make equally gorgeous posters?!—*In Mayan Splendor*, truly a cyclic recapitulation of Belknap Long's lyrical youth, forms a perfect little book, truly a delightful gift for yourself or for some fortunate friend. It ranks as one of the handsomest books Arkham House has yet produced under the aegis of the current managing editor James Turner. *By all means!*

Celeste Turner Wright, *Seasoned Timber*

Celeste Turner Wright. *Seasoned Timber* (Selected Poems). Dust-jacket by Jeanne Thompson. The Golden Quill Press, Francestown, New Hampshire, December 1977. Pages, 80. Price, $5.00

To turn from Frank Belknap Long's volume to that by Celeste Turner Wright, is to turn from the poetic rapture and exaltation of a young man (such rapture and exaltation do not after all last forever) to the carefully guarded and painstakingly nurtured ecstasy of a mature woman who has sustained her poetic passion into a rich and rewarding seniority. A young person would see primarily the enchantment, excitement, and exuberance of life. The older person would acknowledge all that vital delirium but would also perceive causes and effects beyond the young person's vision simply because the older person had lived and experienced life over a longer period of time.

Frank Belknap Long is an overt "fantasy author"—surely, one of the more admired and profoundly respected "elder" figures in our field of fantasy and science-fiction, and all the more honor to him for that. Celeste Turner Wright superficially would be considered a "mainstream" writer and poet, and in her own particular "genre" she has received many honors for her literary and academic accomplishments. Arriving there in the latter 1920's (to quote from the dust-jacket of her book), "Dr. Wright was the first woman professor at the University of California, Davis, and also the first Ph.D. of either sex to teach in the humanities there. For twenty-seven years she was chairman of the English department. In 1973 the university dedicated to her a grove of cedar trees near the library. Since retirement, she has been annually reappointed to teach Shakespeare and creative writing."

Obviously Dr. Wright is not a "fantasy poet" per se but her work is distinguished by that strong sense of imaginativeness that used to characterize much "mainstream" writing. Thus, basically, her poetry is at least as imaginative, qua imaginative, as Belknap Long's but it is of course different and in its own way singularly rewarding and attractive. It compels re-reading and re-studying not only for its fine surface features and unusually careful craftsmanship but above all for its acute and often subtle insights.

Like Belknap Long, Dr. Wright by preference utilizes as her vehicle or form both metre and rime. She handles these with a skill that can only be termed consummate. She ranks in a technical sense as near perfect a master as one could ever hope to find; since the use of both metre and rime has become far less common today than what formerly obtained, such mastery is rare, indeed, and one cannot emphasize this enough. Luckily her craft serves not to obscure but primarily to communicate and illumine her image, metaphor, statement, message, or highly non-platitudinous moral. Incidentally, it might be mentioned that her previous (or second) volume of verse, *A Sense of Place* (Golden Quill, 1973) was accorded a silver medal by the Commonwealth Club of California (San Francisco).

Dr. Wright was born and grew up in Maine but went to college in California. Apart from her trips to Europe and to divers parts of the U. S. A., she has spent most of her adult life in California. Her poetry reflects her travels as well as her mixed Yankee and California heritage. The twenty-six selections from her first volume of verse *Etruscan Princess and Other Poems* (Alan Swallow, Denver, 1964) are here made available again (and could there be anything quite so perfect and moving in its way as *Etruscan Princess?*); while the remaining twenty-two selections appear here in book-form for the first time, including the final piece, the remarkable narrative cast in Spenserian stanzas, *Bread and Roses.*

All of Dr. Wright's best qualities and major characteristics as a poet stand forth in this her third volume of verse. Her mastery of the sonnet-form is displayed in the following selection, as well as her insightfulness.

THUMBPRINT
California

Almost reluctant, we approach the block
Cleft from a stout sequoia; calculate
By arches, loops, concentric rings the date
Of Hastings, Plymouth, Gettysburg; the shock
Darkens our eyes. As dying men a clock,
We read the scornful summary of fate—
Elizabeth an inch—and estimate
How it will scant our chronicle and mock.

Redwood has fingerprinted Time, the seams
Of his gigantic thumb: a circle grew
With padres' grapevines; when this curve was new,
The miners waded California streams.

Can all our aspirations and our dreams
Leave but a filamentous line or two?

Or she can capture a rare mood and a rare moment, as in the following:

INCIDENT ON A PETAL

Today I split my sides and crept
Out of my chrysalis and stepped
Forth into April, where my wing
Unfolded. How bewildering!

Or she can combine the human and the cosmic into a rare and even
inspiring mixture:

SATELLITE
Sputnick: October 4, 1957

Sleepless upon the hill,
Dispirited by chill,
We searched the frosty heavens for a light,
Till swifter than a star,
Foreknown as comets are,
Magnificent it glided through the night...
And then diminished; on our town
Once more the dark descended and the cold crept down.
A comet seems a fraud:
It flaunts itself abroad
   To awe the generations visited –
But only while its run
Swings hopeful toward the Sun;
   He scorns it, and its radiance is hid.
The aureole tonight enzones
No comet's petty mystery of frozen stones.

Starlight deludes our gaze
With dead nostalgic rays
From galaxies extinguished long ago;
Now bivouac has brought
Us no such backward thought,

But the Infinity that men shall know:
A micro-planet lost in space
No more restrains the wings of our nurturing race.

Though frail his flesh and soft,
Man shall be borne aloft
By conjugation of his steel and brain
Until the planets rock
Responsive to his clock,
The rhythm of the ardent human vein —
Where constellations drift like sand
And he can sift the stars like jewels through his hand.

The final poem *Bread and Roses* in a series of twenty-seven Spenserian stanzas bespeaks a mediaeval tale of the landgrave Louis and his beneficent wife Elizabeth who brings food and "stout" clothing to cold and starving peasants in the winter. The narrative is climaxed by the miracle of blooming "Roses in winter!" Dr. Wright's technical expertise and command show forth from the very first stanza.

BREAD AND ROSES

Germany: The Wartburg

High in Thuringian forest, from the seas
Of restless evergreen ascends a hill
Topped by a castle. Through the surge of trees
The battlements are turned unsmiling still
Upon the valley—lidless gaze and chill
Even in Junetide. Foemen never scour
The fields today; only the hunter's trill
Echoes; but the untenanted watchtower
Is legacy of feuds and monument to power.

Celeste Turner Wright has been called one of modern America's major poets. We heartily concur, and we urge this profound but unassuming volume upon all aficionados of genuinely imaginative literature.

William Hope Hodgson, *The Dream of X:* A Creative Alternative to *The Night Land*

William Hope Hodgson. *The Dream of X*. Dustjacket, endpapers, decorations, and illustrations by Stephen Fabian. Donald M. Grant, West Kingston, Rhode Island, 1977. Pages, 140. Price, $15.00.

This reasonably effective condensation of Hodgson's vast and minutely narrated saga *The Night Land* comes to us, once again, by means of Donald M. Grant, of West Kingston, Rhode Island. If nothing else, it demonstrates that an author himself can do a much better and more sensitive condensation that those professionals who do condensations for, say, the *Reader's Digest* et alia. The present reader personally found this novella, or novelette, version of *The Night Land* to be quite moving, but: would we have done so without our memories of the complete version to fill the condensation in here and there, and to draw upon for a greater emotional resonance? We honestly don't know. We only wish some enlightened publisher would issue the entire prose epic in a format as gorgeous as this that Donald Grant has made available to us.

Hodgson manages to give us much of the atmosphere of the original. We have here the description of the Great Redoubt, the super-pyramid in which most of humanity is concentrated in the extremely far future. Then we have the going-forth of the Hero to find the Lesser Redoubt and his Beloved, whom he has been seeking through aeons of evolution and incarnations; the wonderfully emotion-filled meeting of the lovers (this moved us to tears, as in the original); the peril-beset return to the Great Redoubt; the seeming death of the Beloved; her unexpected return to life; and then, at last, the final happiness of the lovers. The main narrative has of course been drastically reduced but it manages to convey something of the original's mood of breathless expectancy. Stephen Fabian's art is undoubtedly some of the best we have ever seen in a modern production of fantastic literature—he evidently has a strong sense of identification with Hodgson—and the whole book is a marvellously sensitive *édition de luxe*, a veritable work of art as have been so many of Donald Grant's productions, and certainly able to rank with some of the better products of both the Heritage Club and the Limited Editions Club of New York City. Considering that Grant has far more limited means than those publishers, his accomplishment seems to us all the more worthy and the more creditable.

As a romance, *The Night Land* is one of the most romantic romances imaginable, if not the ultimate romance in the most archetypal terms ever. Contrary to H. P. Lovecraft who considered it to be a clumsy archaic imitation, we have always found the style, *qua* style, in which Hodgson narrates it, to be both effective and highly original. Also contrary to Lovecraft, we find the story of the lovers to be singularly moving, within the terms of "a love that is more than love"—of an extraordinary sentimentality beyond all other sentimentality—in the most Poesque sense conceivable. Without a doubt, Hodgson is one of the rare titans in the field of fantasy and science-fiction, and in the limited genre of the sustained fantasy novel of supernatural horror he has no true equal. We are indebted to Donald Grant for granting us this production, well worth every penny of the asking price.

Jesse F. Knight, *The Romantic Revival*

Jesse F. Knight. *The Romantic Revival. Setting the Record Straight. A Conversation with Frank Cooper.* Walkerton, Indiana: Lion Enterprises, 1979. $5.00.

This excellent little book, handsomely produced in soft covers, goes a long way toward explaining for us precisely what has been happening with Romanticism and its revival in the art of music, and particularly in the art of the performing of music. Let us be frank: the Romantic revival in music has probably furnished the main impetus in the current Romantic revival over-all. Jesse Knight in his Introduction defines the important role (pivotal in all respects) played by Frank Cooper in this Romantic revival: "More than any other individual Frank Cooper is responsible for the Romantic Revival that has revolutionized the musical scene in recent years. Writing, recording, promoting, through the Romantic Festival, which he founded in Indianapolis, and the new Festival of the Centuries, which he is in the process of creating in Miami, Cooper has provided vital impetus for a number of valuable excursions into the field of romanticism."

The author lets Mr. Cooper take over in this published conversation (as is right and proper), and interpolates himself only to ask tasteful, apt, and intelligent questions and to put the over-all discussion into a unified structure. Even those lovers of music who consider themselves conversant with nineteenth-century music and performing practises will have much to learn here from Mr. Cooper's informed definitions and examples as well as from his refreshing enthusiasm.

The nineteenth century was rich in major, minor, and in-between composers, performers, etc. Going back to study the lesser figures in particular has helped us to put the major ones in perspective, since any art to be healthy and alive needs an abundance of variety at any one time, and this diversity the nineteenth century furnished in a truly amazing abundance. This booklet also serves to illustrate that musical Romanticism, far from being the exclusive property of just the nineteenth century, is very much active in the twentieth, performing-wise as well as creatively in terms of composition: the at-once arch-Romantic and arch-classical symphonist Franz Schmidt (1874–1939), although not mentioned here—whose techniques are nonetheless thoroughly modern—could only have happened in the twentieth century, at least in regard to the most mature phase of his musical development; yet paradoxically the modern techniques only throw the nineteenth-century elements into greater, and more poignant, relief.

A useful section of notes on composers, writers. compositions. performers. etc. (compiled by Mr. Knight), rounds the booklet out in proper fashion, and altogether then the well-intentioned Romanticist, or Romantist, is clearly doing himself an injustice if he does not become acquainted with this exemplary publication. If Frank Cooper deserves a great deal of credit for his role in the Romantic Revival (and he clearly does), then Jesse Knight has rendered us a real service in putting it all down in book form. Heartily recommended!

Clark Ashton Smith, *The City of the Singing Flame*
(Introduction.)

Poet of the Singing Flame. (Clark Ashton Smith. *The City of the Singing Flame*. Timescape Pocket Books, New York, 1981.)

Upon the death of his poetic mentor George Sterling in November of 1926 (as well as his great and good friend for sixteen years), Clark Ashton Smith deepened his friendship with Genevieve K. Sully of his own native Auburn, California. They had first met in Autumn 1919 but it was principally the gap left by Sterling's death that impelled Clark to know her better as a worthy friend and a rare kindred spirit. Sterling's death not only closed a major period in California's literary and artistic history—that older Bohemia centered in San Francisco and later, thanks to Sterling, in Carmel-by-the-Sea on the Monterey peninsula—it virtually marked the end of Smith's own first phase of poetic productivity, that for the years 1911–1926. Born on January 13, 1898, he had begun to write both prose and verse early in his teens; and he wrote his first mature poetry at the age of eighteen. Three major collections of poetry—*The Star-Treader* in 1912, *Ebony and Crystal* in 1922, and *Sandalwood* in 1925—had won him on one hand the admiration of critics, fellow poets, and patrons of the arts, that is, in the West of the United states; but had garnered him on the other hand only a minimal income at best, in addition to a meager reputation with the critics of the East Coast establishment who knew Smith, if they knew him at all, only as an imitator rather than the innovator that he truly was in the Ambrose Bierce and George Sterling tradition of pure poetry. His personal life and his literary career had both reached an impasse but through his friendship with Genevieve he was to find a way out of this dead end into fruitful new directions.

In July of 1927, while on a camping trip with her and some other friends in the Sierras, Clark visited for the first time the Donner-Pass-and-Summit area, as well as Crater Ridge nearby. Crater Ridge (now known officially by a different name, Boreal Ridge) is a fascinating and beautiful ambiance with several unusual geological features (as duly observed by him later in his fiction), and it comes as no great surprise to learn that Clark, while on his first visit onto the Ridge, had a profound imaginative experience. From this experience, during late 1930 and early

372

1931, would evolve two of his greatest science-fantasies, *The City of the Singing Flame* and *Beyond the Singing Flame*, later combined and gathered by the author under the title of the first story for the first hardcover collection of his fantasies, *Out of Space and Time* (Arkham House, 1942).

As recorded years later (in 1967) by Genevieve:

> One hot summer—that of 1927—when we were all wilted and tired of the heat, we invited Clark to go with us on a camping trip to the mountains in the Donner-Peak-Summit region.
>
> After a few days of short walks, we proposed a longer, walk—to Crater Ridge—where we had gone many times in the past, but now we were going with a companion who came under a spell of strange thought, transforming the scene into a foreboding and grotesque landscape which Clark later used in his now-famous story, *The City of the Singing Flame.* Clark wandered about among the boulders, studying the rocks and general terrain. We could all see that he was deeply affected by the place.
>
> Later in the afternoon while Clark was still feeling a strange influence, after we had sat down to look at the views which combine to make this place especially beautiful, I suddenly suggested that he use his powers of writing for fiction, which would be more remunerative than poetry. His financial situation at that time was critical, and some practical advice seemed in order. This prodding led to Clark's writing of weird fiction and, thus, the walk to Crater Ridge started the flow of work which has made Clark the well-known writer that he is.[1]

(Later, in August of 1937, to be precise, Ashton Smith plotted a sequel to *Beyond the Singing Flame* under the title *The Rebirth of the Flame*; but he evidently never finished it since no manuscript or typescript of it was found among the stories left unpublished at the time of his death on August 14th, 1961.)

Although his poet-friend Eric Barker acknowledged that Smith was "a poet of genius," he tempered this recognition by writing further: "albeit one out of touch with his times." According to Eric: "In his personal life as well as in his writings he was as far removed from contemporary life as a poet could possibly be." The same friend summed up Smith's historical rôle as a poet in this way: "His unique and particular genius was to play upon the old harps more musically than almost any poet since François Villon, a poet whom he resembled in some respects."[2]

Despite this poet-friend's opinion, it can be cogently argued that Ashton Smith and his lyric predecessor George Sterling—with their pioneering developments in poetry (and prose) of "cosmic-astronomic-mindedness," and with their near-constant emphasis on the environing wonder and mystery of the cosmos—were infinitely more in touch with their times and their world, in a profound and universal way, than many other contemporary writers whose work and perspective remain rigidly, and unimaginatively, anthropocentric. When we look back from the early 1980's out over the immense and multifaceted panorama of literature in the earlier twentieth century, we see many scriveners once considered vital, important and very much "with it"—who seem today at once empty, irrelevant and singularly dated. Sterling and Smith's intense preoccupation with the cosmic-astronomic once inspired poet-critic Witter Bynner to dub them the Star-Dust Twins. While we can chuckle at the wit behind this nickname, it should not deter us from noting how curiously prophetic their pre-occupation has proven to be of humanity's increasing fascination with—as well as intrepid exploration into—the cosmos at large in our current Age of Space.

The multiple suns and skies, the dimensions within dimensions, the revelations behind revelations in *The City of the Singing Flame* typify particularly well Ashton Smith's own especial class of cosmic-astronomic-mindedness. Also, as pointed out by Fritz Leiber, the story showcases an uncommon concern on Smith's part for life battling doom, a concern absent from most of his other fiction. Archetypally, in cosmic fable after cosmic fable, Ashton Smith's main leitmotif is one of alienation, death and exotic metamorphosis. His viewpoint is that of the cosmic outsider, the grisly specter at the feast, the grim and sardonic Master of Ceremonies who has arranged for our amusement some elegantly lethal diversions. Nonetheless, the other keynotes in the Smithian leitmotif remain those of beauty and adventure and irony—and, yes, love.

Unlike his friend H. P. Lovecraft, much of whose fiction skillfully weaves an elaborate and self-sustaining tapestry of myth, Smith postulates no overall Cthulhu Mythos, or Yog-Sothoth Cycle of Myth. His gods and goddesses are there for possibly related but still different causes. Unlike another of his correspondent-friends, Robert E. Howard, who typically and cannily created whole series of stories around certain central characters (one of the principal reasons for his particular popularity), Ashton Smith only rarely has a series of connected tales built around a central character or characters. A double example is collected in this book. "The Tale of Satampra Zeiros" and "The Theft of the Thirty-nine

Girdles" feature that beguiling rogue and master-thief Satampra Zeiros. The other mini-series spotlights the omniscient and omnipotent enchanter Maal Dweb in "The Maze of Maal Dweb" and "The Flower-Women." Here, as well, are some other fabulous narratives of Smith's own lost worlds, Hyperborea, Averoigne and Zothique, with hints of that Orient which exists now only in *The Arabian Nights*, William Beckford's *History of the Caliph Vathek*, and similar literary milieux.

Here then, in these thirteen stories, is something of the metaphysical range and imaginative spectrum of one Clark Ashton Smith, poet, visionary and cosmic master artist.

NOTES
1. Letter-memoir, p. 190, *Emperor of Dreams, A Clark Ashton Smith Bibliography*, compiled by D. Sidney-Fryer, published by Donald M. Grant, West Kingston, Rhode Island, 1978.
2. Memoir, "Clark Ashton Smith—In Memory of a Great Friendship," pp. 29–31, *Emperor of Dreams*, u.s.

Clark Ashton Smith, *The Last Incantation*
(Introduction.)

The Last Enchanter. (Clark Ashton Smith. *The Last Incantation*. Timescape Pocket Books, New York, 1982.)

At the beginning of the Depression in 1929, the poet and visionary, Clark Ashton Smith, commenced writing fiction in some sizable quantity. During the years 1929–1938, he created over one hundred short stories, half of them belonging to various series located in his fabulous lost worlds of the Singing Flame, Hyperborea, Atlantis, Averoigne, Zothique, Xiccarph and the Orient. Many of his novelettes and short stories are virtually condensed novels; and his fiction overall grew, stylistically and imaginatively, out of his poems in verse, as well as his poems in prose, for the years 1911–1926.

When one considers that Smith characteristically wrote about five drafts of each story (and this is true for most of his fiction), and that he typically packed his tales with as much fantastic adventure and as much meaning as he could manage (while still keeping the requisite clarity and sense of balance which normally distinguishes decent prose), his more than one hundred examples in the short-story form represent much more hard labor than what the casual reader might surmise.

A word or two is in order here as to Ashton Smith's method in writing a story. First he would sketch the plot in longhand on some piece of notepaper, or in his notebook, or commonplace book, *The Black Book*, which he used circa 1929–1961. (Deciphered and transcribed by Rah Hoffman and Donald Sidney-Fryer, and edited and annotated by. the latter. *The Black Book* first appeared in published form from Arkham House, 1979.) He would then write the first draft, usually in longhand but occasionally directly on the typewriter. He would then rewrite the story some three or four times (this was his own estimate); this he usually did directly on the typewriter. Also, and just as important, he would subject each draft to considerable alteration and correction in longhand, taking the manuscript with him on a stroll and reading it aloud in some secluded spot on or near Boulder Ridge (also called Indian Ridge) not far from his cabin just outside Old Town, Auburn, California. Thus, this careful rewriting in a manner not dissimilar to that of Gustave Flaubert, or the Roman poet

Virgil, for that matter, accounts (at least in part) for the extraordinarily polished style characteristic of Ashton Smith's finest prose fantasies.

There is one phase of this compositional process which deserves especial discussion here. Like any self-respecting veteran poet, Clark was long accustomed to the habit and necessity of reading his own poetry aloud and of literally testing its interior and exterior sonics. Particularly for a poet like Smith who created in an intensely bardic spirit of wonder, nobility, and awe, this testing of the poetry's music and magic, by declaiming it over and over again (whether aloud, or within "the inner ear" of the poet), formed, perhaps, the single most crucial part of the poetic process. So, too, the procedure of proving and testing his prose by reading it expressly aloud became equally important in the composition of his narratives. These tales clearly owe their success to the sonority of the style which Smith devised for them, a style where meaning and music go hand in hand, as in such other archetypal fantasy as *The Faerie Queene* by Edmund Spenser. Rather like Malygris the magician in "The Last Incantation," Smith must have been one of the last major literary figures of his type who literally chanted ("chaunted" or "enchaunted") his poetry and especially his prose in the manner that he did, reading it aloud to the birds, bees and blossoms within whatever woodland glade he found himself. Ashton Smith, in this distinctly literal sense, must have been "The Last Enchaunter."

In explanation of the deliberately self-aware and elaborate style typical of most of his fiction, as well as of his poems in prose. Smith once commented as follows, in his letter to S. J. Sackett dated July 11th, 1950:

> As to my employment of an ornate style, using many words of classic origin and exotic color, I can only say that it is designed to produce effects of language and rhythm which could not possibly be achieved by a vocabulary restricted to what is known as "basic English." As [Lytton] Strachey points out [in his essay on Sir Thomas Browne], a style composed largely of words of Anglo-Saxon origin tends to a spondaic rhythm, "which by some mysterious law reproduces the atmosphere of ordinary life." [In Strachey's essay, the original wording reads: "which seems to produce (by some mysterious rhythmic law) an atmosphere of ordinary life."] An atmosphere of remoteness, vastness, mystery and exoticism is more naturally evoked by a style with an admixture of Latinity, lending itself to more varied and sonorous rhythms, as well as to subtler shades, tints and nuances of meaning—all of which, of course, are wasted or worse than wasted on the average reader, even if presumably literate.

As to coinages, I have really made few such, apart from proper names of personages, cities, countries, deities, etc., in realms lying "east of the sun and west, of the moon." I have used a few words, names of fabulous monsters, etc., drawn from Herodotus, Mandeville and Flaubert which I have not been able to find in dictionaries or other works of reference. Some of these occur in "The Hashish-Eater," a much misunderstood poem, which was intended as a study in cosmic consciousness, drawing heavily on myth and fable for its imagery. It is my own theory that if the infinite worlds of the cosmos were opened to human vision, the visionary would be overwhelmed by horror in the end, like the hero of this poem. I hope I have made it plain that my use of rare and exotic words has been solely in accord with an esthetic theory, or, one might say, a technical theory.

Be that as it may, the average reader who is honestly prepared to meet Ashton Smith solidly on his own terrain should not, by any means, feel cheated. The eighteen stories in this collection will richly repay the reader's -careful attention. "The Last Enchaunter" comes by his music and magic quite honestly, that is, through his own hard work.

In "The Last Incantation" and "The Death of Malygris" we have another rare example of a Smithian mini-series built around the same central character: in this case, Malygris, another of Ashton Smith's archimages, a figure at once omniscient and omnipotent in the manner of Maal Dweb.

One more story should be individually mentioned here. "The Vaults of Yoh-Vombis," one of the most purely horrific stories that Smith ever created, introduces the reader to another of the author's lost worlds: his own conception of the planet Mars. This horror-science-fiction thriller has its obvious parallels with such Lovecraftian masterpieces as "The Color Out of Space" and "The Shadow Out of Time," as well as with such a recent "Lovecraftian" film as *Alien*. In such stories mood and atmosphere are just as important as the plot, and characterization is succinct and secondary to the central artistic effect of the overall narrative. A tightly plotted and well-constructed suspense-thriller like *Alien* in particular seems very much like a Smithian or Lovecraftian story of cosmic horror and ever-mounting dread from the pulp magazines of the 1930's and 1940's, but with their narrative rhetoric brought up to date for the 1970's.

Here then are some further stories of Hyperborea, Atlantis, Averoigne, and other lost worlds as uniquely chronicled by one Clark Ashton Smith, "The Last Enchaunter."

Clark Ashton Smith, *The Monster of the Prophecy* (Introduction.)

Lyricist of Lost Worlds. (Clark Ashton Smith. *The Monster of the Prophecy.* Timescape Pocket Books, New York, 1983.)

In spite of his long friendship with him through correspondence, and in spite of his considerable admiration of his novels and stories, Clark Ashton Smith never felt any need to unify his own fictional output by creating an overall mythology in the manner of the Cthulhu Mythos, or Yog-Sothoth Cycle of Myth, embodied in the fiction of H. P. Lovecraft; although gods and goddesses certainly inhabit Smith's verse and prose, whether as active agents or as possible background. Nor did Ashton Smith feel impelled to create whole series of stories around certain central characters in the manner of Robert E. Howard, another of his correspondent-friends. Instead, half of Smith's published fiction falls into appropriate series or subdivision according to the culture, country, continent or planet to which a given story belongs.

In addition of the dimension (or dimensions) of the Singing Flame, these worlds or imagination principally include Hyperborea, that first continent (or civilized continent) of Earth; Atlantis and Poseidonis, that last isle remaining from the main submergence of Atlantis; the mediaeval province of Averoigne in France; Zothique, the last continent of Earth; the planet Xiccarph; and that half-mythical Orient that seems to exist primarily in the fiction of the Western World; and numerous other milieux, terrestrial as well as non-terrestrial.

August Derleth, his friend, correspondent and publisher for many years, once summed it up very well when he wrote that, more than most other writers, Ashton Smith had captured in his prose and poetry the beauty and terror of fantastic worlds of dream and the imagination, and that he had created not one but many worlds of his fanciful device in his resplendent and terror-full stories, written only as Smith could write them, in a weirdly beautiful prose whose rhythms and patterns are not easily forgotten Indeed, the combination of a highly concentrated and fantastic narrative with a studied, rich and allusive style produces a type of story with few parallels or precedents elsewhere.

Just as most of his poetry comes from his first phase of poetic productivity, that of the years 1911–1926, then so does most of his prose fiction come from the years 1929–1938. For both his poetry and his prose Aston Smith had a carefully developed philosophy and *raison d'etre*. We can peruse his critical remarks, preferences and statements that relate specifically to his fiction for 1929–1938 in the posthumous volume *Planets and Dimensions, Collected Essays of Clark Ashton Smith*, edited by Professor Charles K. Wolfe (The Mirage Press, Baltimore Maryland, 1973). But we can read his own case for his poetry (and for imaginative art in general) here and there in his correspondence to George Sterling in the years 1911–1926 (preserved together with related papers in the Berg Collection of the New York Public Library).

The charge of irrelevance and escapism so often heaped on the fantaisiste by proponents of literal-minded realism in the arts is refuted, or, rather, corrected in Smith's letter to George Sterling dated October 27, 1926. In this letter Ashton Smith makes a very important statement on behalf of imaginative poetry (but it applies just as well to all imaginative art and literature), that imaginative poetry, properly regarded, does not constitute an escape from life so much as an extension of it. "Anything that the imagination can conceive of becomes thereby a part of life," embodies a profound observation, indeed, and explains much of his attitude toward his own work.

It is a logical hypothesis (in lieu of any other evidence) that Ashton Smith in a very general sense was working out in his mind his own individual worlds of imagination (shortly to be developed in his fiction for 1929–1938) sometime after Sterling's death (in late 1926) but before 1929/1930. Indeed, we have some kind of a clue in the last letter, dated November 4, that he wrote to Sterling before his great friend and dear poetic mentor was to die on November 17: "... My fondest hope is to find a Hyperborea beyond Hyperborea, in the realm of imaginative poetry. I have the feeling that my best and most original work is still to be done."

Smith did in fact realize his fondest hope; he did in fact find his Hyperborea beyond Hyperborea, together with many other worlds besides. Only the realm of imaginative poetry had become transmuted into the realm of imaginative or fantastic prose. He had in truth deployed his poetical genius, but adapted to the medium of prose fiction, in the form of those fantastic narratives which must rank with some of the best and most original work that he accomplished.

In the creation of his own individual realms of imagination Smith had discovered specific hints for a few of them from his deep and multifarious reading. Not only from Greek and Roman legend but just as much from Theosophic lore had he gleaned some important suggestions for his conception of Hyperborea as well as that Hyperborea beyond Hyperborea—Mhu-Thulan, the northernmost peninsula of the Hyperborean continent. Similarly he had taken hints for his Atlantis from Plato but for his Poseidonis he had garnered again, specifically, from Theosophic lore. From his own native Auburn, California and from Auvergne, that old province in central France, he seems to have devised his Averoigne. With playful but profound insight Smith's friend and fan Rah Hoffman, who visited his hermitlike abode on Boulder Ridge just outside of Old Auburn during the 1940's, rightfully insisted that the vernal woods and hills around the Smith cabin were nothing less than the fabulous forest of Averoigne. Whereas Hyperborea is the first civilized continent, Zothique the last continent shall arise only in the latter cycles of Earth; for this conception Smith seems to have taken hints from no one or nothing except his own poetic divination, and from the hot, dry, dun-colored summer landscape of California. Last, the half-mythical Orient he employs in some dozen published stories draws from *The Arabian Nights* and William Beckford's *Vathek*, as well as from the travel memories and reminiscences of his father Timeus, who squandered a large patrimony through gambling while traveling around the world as a young man before he finally settled in the Auburn-Long Valley area.

These notes all explain to some degree the spirit in which Ashton Smith created his prose fantasies, but the beginning of one of his Atlantean fables, "A Voyage to Sfanomoë," illustrates even better his own attitude and approach as a story-teller:

> There are many marvelous tales, untold, unwritten, never to be recorded or remembered, lost beyond all divining and all imagining, that sleep in the double silence of far-recessive time and space. The chronicles of Saturn, the archives of the moon in its prime, the legends of Antillia and Moaria—these are full of an unsurmised or forgotten wonder. And strange are the multitudinous tales withheld by the light-years of Polaris and the Galaxy. But none is stranger, none more marvelous, than the tale of Hotar and Evidon and their voyage to the planet Sfanomoë, from the last isle of foundering Atlantis. Harken, for I alone shall tell the story, who came in a dream to the changeless center where the past and future are always contemporary with the present; and saw the veritable happening thereof; and, waking, gave it words.

Here then, in these fourteen stories, is more of the metaphysical range and imaginative spectrum of one Clark Ashton Smith. Here then is *The Monster of the Prophecy*, as well as other fabulous narratives, from the pen of our lyricist of lost worlds.

G. Sutton Breiding, *Autumn Roses*
(Introduction.)

G. Sutton Breiding. *Autumn Roses.* Silver Scarab Press, 1984.

Although he was born in West Virginia, and although he has lived elsewhere, G. Sutton Breiding is very much a San Francisco poet and man of letters. He ranks as a modern example of the same California Romantics who much earlier on in our century included such remarkable figures as Ambrose Bierce, George Sterling, Nora May French, and Clark Ashton Smith. The work of this group, which has included others only a little less remarkable, has re-emerged in the past few years to renewed interest, fresh appraisal, and merited approval. The dedication—with appropriate speeches and ceremonies, and aptly enough at noon on Saturday, 10 July 1982—of a new plaque on Russian Hill in San Francisco to the memory of the elder poet George Sterling signalizes perhaps best of all the re-emergence of this group's collective *oeuvre.* Just as important, the specific tradition of their work has endured and has been continued.

Despite the peripheral or underground status of their work for many years, the California Romantics represent something very special, indeed, in the vast over-all tapestry of Californian and/or American literature. Although unlikely to be the subject of mass adulation and popularity, or even of academic acclaim, the particular essence or quality of this group has proven extremely tenacious. Despite other schools, cliques, and movements of writers it has retained all its individual characteristics. Despite succeeding fads and fashions in the world of literature, it has remained true to its own self or quintessence, and has quite definitely survived. In particular, these autumn roses from the atelier of Sutton Breiding indicate emphatically the unusual tenacity and vitality of the California Romantics and their tradition, which is definitely one of imaginative and often otherworldly panache.

Beginning with "Prelude: The Lost Poets" and ending with "Postlude: The Immortal Lover" (who in this instance is Loneliness), the reader will remark an immediate and immense affinity not only with such poets as Swinburne, Sterling, and Ashton Smith but also and generally, with the concomitant fin-de-siècle bridging the nineteenth and twentieth centuries. It is anomalous, if not indeed fabulous, that we should have right now—in the long Atlantean afternoon which is the latter half of the twentieth century—such marvellous and refreshingly unfashionable effusions as "Lines to a Wandering Courtesan," "Dreams in a Wineshop," "A Necklace of Pearls," "Babylonian Suite," "Prayer" (and to Dionysus!), "Requiem of Ecstasy," "The Old Wine Genius," "The Hermit's Folly," "Fables," "Ode to Omar," "The Minstrel's Dream," and "I Long for Her, and "Babylon."

However, for something related to, but different from, these poems mentioned above (noteworthy for their rich and often recondite imagery), we should turn to such productions as "Black Leather Vampyre," "Lovepoem," "Breathing Death," and "Entreaty." Here, in such thoroughly modern poems, treading the fine thin line between pornography and genuine erotic art, Sutton Breiding does indeed accomplish something new. In a manner at once audacious, heartily lustful, and imaginatively graphic, he depicts some notable amorous adventures. We discover in "San Francisco" another notable love poem, one of the best and most attractive evocations of that lovely city poised between its own great bay and the Pacific Ocean.

Thus, for a variety of reasons, there is so much to enjoy and appreciate in this handsome collection. As the editor and publisher Harry O. Morris, Jr. has aptly written, we can like Sutton Breiding's poems for their cultivated taste of melancholy, for their pains and pangs of loneliness, for their depths of despair and horror, for their heights of euphoria as expressed in the wonderful imagery of cities by the sea as well as of love eternal, and always for the elusive thread of dreams that the narrator pursues. Behind their colorful and even sometimes lurid imagery— behind their outrageous invocation of impossible amours—there inheres, obviously enough, an equally outrageous sense of humor and irony which subtly mocks all the outrageousness but which does not vitiate in any way the desperate sincerity of the poet's fervid lyricism.

We might never guess from these poems that Sutton Breiding has paid and continues to pay his dues (to use that current phrase), both in the humdrum workaday world, as well as in that of poetry-publishing. He has worked at a variety of jobs, including those of foot messenger and file clerk in the stone and glass wilderness of San Francisco's financial district. For some ten years or more now, he has published extensively, whether in other people's magazines or (more appropriately) in those of his own manufacture. Nonetheless, despite or because of this broad experience, whether or not it has directly influenced his own work in verse and prose, his poetry achieves at times an extraordinary rhapsodical strength. However modern his style may be at times, the essence of Sutton Breiding's art is clearly one with that of his literary progenitors; his own poetry makes an exciting congener to that of Ambrose Bierce, George Sterling, Nora May French, and Clark Ashton Smith, among others.

Here, in these more than two dozen poems, our bardic host invites us into his own inner dimensions as well as such evanescent (and yet artfully palpable) ones as Atlantis, Cockaigne, and Cimmeria.

Sacramento, California.

H. P. Lovecraft, *Fungi From Yuggoth*

Fungi From Yuggoth read by John Arthur. Cassette recording from Fedogan & Bremer, 1988.

Fungi From Yuggoth, a sonnet cycle by H. P. Lovecraft, read by John Arthur with Music by Mike Olson, Directed by Lawrence A. Russo, Produced by Philip J. Rahman. This Dolby cassette is available for $10, plus $1 for postage and handling from Fedogan & Bremer / 5116 39th Ave. So. / Minneapolis, Minnesota 55417. (The tape is available in two mixes, one by the director favoring the performance by John Arthur, and one by the composer emphasizing voice and music more equally; the customer should specify if he has a preference.)

Dating from December 1929 and January 1930, when their author composed these sonnets in a major burst of inspiration and creativity, the cycle *Fungi from Yuggoth* remains Lovecraft's greatest poetic achievement. In regard to the present recording (the first such one devoted exclusively to Lovecraft's poetry, so far as we know)—while completely professional in every respect and refreshingly serious in approach (no mere "high camp" here, thanks be to Cthulhu, Nyarlathotep and Azathoth!)—it must be emphasized at once that this production is the result of much more than ordinary care, and has evidently been put together with considerable personal commitment on the part of all the contributors. The *Fungi from Yuggoth* has become in this instance a major poetic revelation, reflecting enormous credit on everyone concerned, and focusing our attention in an aptly portentous manner on Lovecraft the poet, *qua* poet, and not as a mere versifier. How rare in modern poetry that the words alone can be heard and understood at the first exposure!

This collaboration of music and verse is not only a superb format for the presentation of Lovecraft's masterful sonnet cycle, but harks back to the most ancient roots of poetic expression and performance. Although imperfectly chronicled and understood, the tradition of poetry read aloud, declaimed, proclaimed, or otherwise performed and accompanied by music is a venerable one. This tradition goes all the way back at least to the times of the ancient Egyptians, Greeks, and Romans when poets would chant or intone verses to the accompaniment of lyre, harp, or the earliest form of lute.

During the Middle Ages the various types of troubadour-poets in the different European countries would sing their poems or poetic songs to their own music made on lute or *vielle*, i.e., the viol, the precursor of the modern viola. Similarly the jongleurs would recite romance or epic or lay, usually to their own music made on the *vielle* quite often with one long-held bass note per line. These figures were in turn succeeded by the so-called poetic rhapsodists of the Renaissance, who recited lyrics or some favorite section of an epic while improvising on the lute to some well-known tune or "ground" often used for that purpose.

Concomitantly certain highly talented lutenist-composers created and performed their new-style lute songs or "ayres," which were poems created as songs and set to especially composed accompaniments which were often contrapuntal in nature. The performance on lute and with voice constituted in itself alone a particularly difficult and studied art. However, this efflorescence of poet, singer, composer, and accompanist all in one did not survive the 1600's. After this brilliant period the poets who followed seemed to concentrate their efforts on the musicality inherent in the spoken verse divorced from the accompaniment provided by a musical instrument. Sung poetry as such was taken over by the professional singer within the new art form called opera which enlisted the full talents of specialist composers and librettists. But for certain rural bards rumored to still exist in obscure parts of Russia, who chant long narrative poems to the accompaniment of some plucked instrument, the tradition is dead or dormant among most modern poets.

A live performance to a musical accompaniment, and/or as recorded in some form at the same time, is perhaps the ideal manner in which to experience poetry; and a revival of this form is certainly the ideal manner in which to experience this particular poetry by Lovecraft. In this instance the expressly composed music by Mike Olson—new in style, but lyric in effect, and refreshingly accessible—adds enormously to the poetic and emotional impact, not only enhancing the specific dramatic or narrative content of the individual poems but, much more than that, extending or expanding the over-all mood or moods as the sonnet cycle grows, builds, becomes diverse, and yet remains constant in accordance to its inner essence. The multinuanced sonnets find a consummate expression in the multi-accented performance of the actor John Arthur, who also does justice to the musicality of the verse forms themselves, rather a rare thing among actors and dramatic readers who tend to sacrifice poetic music to dramatic effect.

In a formal sense it might be argued that this sonnet cycle is not a connected narrative sequence, but paradoxically it holds together as some kind of a narrative unit amazingly well, proceeding along its own original itinerary, whether in mood or imagery, ringing its variety of changes on its principal emotions of love and fear. This is achieved in a startlingly simple way by means of the one constant in the over-all sequence of poems; the poet himself who is the dreamer-adventurer-narrator. The over-all feeling is less one of horror than of mature contemplation, the purely horrific sonnets nicely balancing with ones of bucolic charm, poignant yearning, breathless expectancy, profound nostalgia and especially wonder and mystery on a cosmic scale. In places, for the sensitive listener, the poetry in conjunction with the music achieves an almost unbearable and heartbreaking sincerity.

There can be no doubt that Lovecraft *meant* this poetry in a deeply personal way, and this quality certainly communicates itself to the listener. We are fortunate that by the time he came to the creation of this corpus of poetry he had become a singularly deft and accomplished versifier in terms of the traditional prosody. The result is much more than a lighthearted, tongue-in-cheek imitation of eighteenth century poetic practice, but rather a modernism that is uniquely Lovecraft's own.

This recording forces us to react to Lovecraft's sonnet cycle as an over-all entity, rather than in bits and pieces, and thus in this particular form the *Fungi from Yuggoth* is unequivocally revealed to be some kind of great poetry. For this revelation alone all the contributors involved in this production deserve every praise. Can we possibly hope for some future recording of Clark Ashton Smith's monumental compressed epic of cosmic-astronomic-mindedness *The Hashish-Eater,* similarly enhanced by some original music, from the same production team?!

"Klarkash-Ton" versus "Clark Ashton": A Minor Issue for Controversy

By Rah Hoffman and Donald Sidney-Fryer

In the first of the two memoirs that he penned of Clark Ashton Smith, "As I Remember Klarkash-Ton" and "Memories of Klarkash-Ton" (collected in *The Black Book of Clark Ashton Smith*, Arkham House, 1979), George Haas indicated that "Klarkash-Ton" is pronounced simply as "Clark Ashton: that is, "klark-ASH-t'n." He probably intended well, but perhaps he understated the case. Smith's correspondent H. P. Lovecraft was wont to use fanciful or humorous nicknames in his letters, such as Comte d'Erlette for August Derleth, the Satrap Pharnabazus for *Weird Tales* editor Farnsworth Wright, Two-Gun Bob for Robert E. Howard, and even Eich-Pi-El for himself. The spellings of these whimsies were sometimes varied, and so the pronunciations themselves were subject to some variance. His name for Clark Ashton Smith, Klarkash-Ton, suggesting an exotic, possibly even alien language—and entity—would seem to be pointless were it to be given vocal utterance in mundane everyday tones. How else to instill the essence of mystery into sound other than altering the spoken syllables? Thus KLAR-kash-TON', *ton* rhyming with *anon* or *salon*. Rah Hoffman and Donald Sidney-Fryer both recall that Clark, and his wife Carol as well, used this pronunciation, heavily accenting the last syllable, which seems to be the way that most Klarkash-Tonphiles and other aficionados utter the term. The *o* in TON would thus have the sound of *o* in such words as *not, odd, tonic*, or a string of proper names, such as *John, Don, Tron*, or even the sometime Presidential *Ron!*

Being an unusually gentle and nondogmatic individual, Clark Ashton Smith, when pressed, did not insist on just one pronunciation for any of the names that he invented for persons and places in his prose fictions. The French-sounding names that he used or created for his Averoigne (AV-er-won or AV-er-ron) stories do not generally give many problems in pronunciation, especially to those familiar with the French language, even if only minimally. However, the names in his series of tales on Hyperborea, Poseidonis, Zothique. Xiccarph, etc., do provide readers with the opportunity for a variety of pronunciations. Similarly, he did not suggest that a person using H. P. L.'s term for Smith pronounce it as

KLAR-kash-TON', even though it was the way Smith himself pronounced it.

Elsewhere, Rah Hoffman has written (in *Emperor of Dreams*, Donald M. Grant, Publisher, 1978) of some of Smith's speech patterns, such as pronouncing imagery accented on the second syllable. In general, Clark Ashton Smith stated, his fictional names were accented on the penultimate (last but one) or antepenultimate (second before last) syllable, as frequently evidenced in the scanning rhythm of his story titles. Atlantean he accented on the penult (*not* the antepenult), AT-lan-TE'-an, as later demonstrated in Sidney-Fryer's *Songs and Sonnets Atlantean* (Arkham House, 1971), a title which scans beautifully in the best Smithian manner. Zothique is pronounced Zo-THEEK', as revealed by Smith in verse. Other names include Tsa-THOG-u-a, Po-SEID-o-nis, A-VOOS-l Wu-THOQQ-uan. The word eidolon—not a Smith creation—is of course properly accented on the long *o* of its middle syllable. A few of Smith's story titles as he pronounced them: "A VOY-age to Sfa-NOM-o-e"; "A Night in Malnéant"—Mal-nay-ahnt, with a hint of a stress on the last syllable; "The DIS-in-TER-ment of VE-nus" (certainly not "The Dis-INT-er-ment OF Ve-NUS"!). The scanning is usually the proper clue.

And now, if someone will please come forth to pronounce for us the name of the reviewer for *Crypt of Cthulhu* and for this magazine [*The Dark Eidolon*]—Stefan Dziemianowicz—perhaps we can all rest more easily!

G. Sutton Breiding, *Journal of an Astronaut* (Introduction.)

Wisdom From An Astronaut's Journal (G. Sutton Breiding. *Journal of an Astronaut*. Ocean View Books, 1992.)

The terrific silence of sidereal space. The ultimate loneliness at the edge of our galaxy or of the cosmos at large. The latent sense of terror and horror lying in wait in the black nothingness of the infinite area beyond the furthest reaches of the cosmos. The sheer enigma of the pure pulsating life or energy which is a star, an atom, or a human being, that medieval measure of all things that exists somewhere between the star and the atom. All these, together with much more, haunt G. Sutton Breiding's *Journal of an Astronaut,* a paradoxically spare and yet richly evocative account of one astronaut's experience amid the ultimate frontier beyond our incredibly diverse and possibly unique water planet.

But Sutton Breiding's vision spans not only the external gulfs of the macrocosmos but the internal abysses of the microcosmos as well, which is in this case the human being, especially the individual perceived as a lonely mote struggling against the indifference of the universe or even of humanity itself, rather than observed as part of the teeming billions of our species in existence on the planet Earth. We are indeed that same human species which, as of this moment in history, continues to develop and to destroy that same planet, as the species continues to increase its population almost geometrically, in response to its own hormones that it probably will never understand in their totality, until it is too late for itself and for the planet as well.

In these pages we find not only such utter alienation as might exist in the awesome outer reaches of space but also, as a strategic foil to that outer void, the homely, appealing remnants of rural Appalachian life and such of its wilderness as actually survives, remnants such as the cicada, the titmouse, the chickadee, the wren, together with the steadfast presence of old barns and old homesteads, as well as rare old stands of trees. At a cost infinitesimally smaller than what would obtain through the auspices of NASA, the reader can experience in these poems by means of imagination's both inner and outer eye a particularly modern, twentieth-century sense of dislocation, as expressed in a particularly modern style.

Here we find again that terrifying reality possibly first formulated by the French mathematician and philosopher Blaise Pascal—"those terrible spaces of the universe"—and here we also find that same infinity, but possibly no less terrifying, as enclosed within the microcosmos of the human self.

Still, beyond all despair, desolation, and dislocation, the reader will also experience, phoenix-like, an unique sense of wonder and marvel and transcendent mystery, as well as a healing sense of the wholesomeness of our planet-biosphere and of the very earth itself, the tenderness and even delicacy displayed in the infinitude of green growing things and of the fauna sustained on that flora. This journal is thus an epiphany, truly divine, which encompasses all its opposites under and through the symbolic guise of words.

O *Amor Atque Realitas!*
Clark Ashton Smith's First Adult Fiction

When *Strange Shadows: The Uncollected Fiction and Essays of Clark Ashton Smith,* as compiled and edited by Steve Behrends (together with two associate editors), was published by Greenwood Press in April of 1989, the volume brought to the attention of Smith cognoscenti for the first time what appears to be almost all of his first adult fiction, the major part of it from the first half of the 1920's, among other hitherto ungathered materials. However, in the book itself there is only one reference to this fiction, but not (we hasten to add) in the terms that we have just set forth immediately above. This one reference occurs in the first paragraph on page xxi of *A Note on the Contents,* as follows: "The reader will also find Smith's ironic fiction, composed for the most part before the 1930's." Possibly the term "ironic-romantic fiction" is more inclusive, and so this is the one that we shall use by preference throughout the present article, in addition to that of "his first adult fiction." Thus, while the fact that this ironic-romantic fiction is also his first adult fiction is not exactly obscured, neither is it exactly highlighted. It should also be pointed out that apart from this one editorial reference on the part of Steve Behrends, there is no other information on these stories in the book, whether preceding them in the section *Non-Fantastic Fiction* in which they are included, or in the excellent and extensive section *Notes to the Text* immediately following the main (i.e., Smithian) text.

The present article seeks to add to whatever other little information that we possess on these stories. The quotations that we proffer in the course of this article are taken exclusively from Smith's letters to George Sterling for the first half of the 1920's. The principal compiler and editor of *Strange Shadows* has thoughtfully included, wherever known, the extant dates of composition, or (rather) of completion of composition, for at least a few of the pieces, which with one exception (as noted below) also stem exclusively from the first half of the 1920's. The stories and their dates, as presently known, are as follows, arranged more or less chronologically:

"The Flirt"	(December 22, 1921.)*
"The Perfect Woman"	(February 28, 1923.)*
"Gossip"	(possibly Winter-Spring, 1923.)
"A Platonic Entanglement"	(ditto.)
"Something New"	(probably Spring, 1924.)

"The Expert Lover"   (possibly Winter, 1924–1925.)
"Checkmate"   (November 7, 1930.)*

    *Dates furnished by Steve Behrends

Certain additional observations should be made at once. Although not included in *Strange Shadows,* but previously collected into *Other Dimensions* (published by Arkham House, Sauk City, Wisconsin, in April of 1970), "Something New" belongs to the above group of stories. "The Perfect Woman", as extant, is much more of a plot-sketch than it is a finished short story. "Gossip" is but a fragment, and "A Platonic Entanglement" may possibly be just the beginning of a longer story, and hence, as extant, also a fragment. "The Flirt" and "Something New" are perfect examples of a "short short" story, and only "The Perfect Lover" and" Checkmate", as extant, are typical short stories of the usual length.

[Additional non-fantastic fiction includes "The Parrot" (1930) and "A Copy of Burns" (1930), both collected in *Strange Shadows.* Both are "ironic" rather than "ironic-romantic" —Editor (Steve Behrends)]

As far as our present information allows us to state, only two of these tales were apparently published in magazines during Smith's lifetime, again exclusively during the first half of the 1920's, as follows:

"The Flirt", in *Snappy Stories,* sometime probably either late 1922 or early 1923.

"Something New," in *10 Story Book,* August 1924.

It is doubtful that Smith would have mentioned these stories or prose-sketches of an ironic-romantic nature to most of his correspondents, who were never numerous even in the best of circumstances. It is possible that he might have mentioned them to fellow poet Samuel Loveman, in addition to his great friend and mentor George Sterling. During the period for 1911/1912 through 1925/1926 Smith's chief correspondents were Sterling, Loveman, and (from 1922 onward) H. P. Lovecraft. While admittedly no great masterpieces—they are frankly experimental—these tales are much more than "trite tearjerkers" as one reviewer of *Strange Shadows* has characterized them. In fact, the term is a complete misnomer. Love, death, loss, and irony are among the principal themes or elements in Smith's *oeuvre,* whether in verse or in prose. What gives his ironic-romantic fiction its characteristic and amusing tone, distinguishing it from his other and later fiction (written for the most part during the 1930's), is the complete absence of depth. Smith wrote these stories quite frankly in the hope that he might sell them to such characteristic magazines of the early 1920's as *Snappy Stories, 10 Story Book,* and other periodicals of a similar nature, and that he might thus add to his perennially meagre income. He intended them apparently as no more than deft and lightweight stories, to beguile an idle moment or two. Moreover, it becomes obvious to anyone reading Smith's letters to Sterling just for the period 1918 to 1926 that he wrote them while drawing directly upon much of his own life's experiences for the same period. Next to the epigrams, apothegms, and pensées that he contributed to *The Auburn Journal* for 1923–1926 (and in addition to his private letters, of course), his ironic-romantic stories are almost unique in his *oeuvre* for the fact that they do something that his verse and prose almost never do—these tales deliberately reflect or cultivate something of the spirit of the times, the Jazz Age and the period of Prohibition that went into effect in the U. S. A. after the Great War (i.e., World War I), with their then chic, clever, and up-to-date qualities characteristic of the then modernism and avant-gardism.

We herewith present the relevant passages from Smith's letters to Sterling. The reader should be cautioned that, in considering his own work, Ashton Smith typically often complained of its deficiencies and inadequacies to himself and to his correspondents. If the description "trite tearjerkers" might seem a complete misnomer, then it might strike us as equally anomalous that both Sterling and Smith should have considered such relatively innocent fiction to be so much "literary whore-mongering." Such magazines as *10 Story Book, Snappy Stories,* and others of a similar class were in fact the "girlie" publications of the time, but in content and by nature they were never directly erotic. They featured a typical mixture of light and lighthearted fiction combined with rather charming but certainly not directly sexually provocative photographs of attractive young women usually in a state of semidress. These periodicals were as far removed from *Playboy* magazine as they were from frankly pornographic stories and pictures. Any eroticism that such periodicals possessed was always implicit and rarely explicit.

> November 23rd, 1922:
> "Snappy Stories" has accepted a little prose-sketch of mine, entitled "The Flirt." They pay 2 cents a word for prose. Maybe I'll do some more whore-mongering, at that price.

March 7th, 1923:

As for me, I'm trying to write verse and prose-fillers, in the hope that some of them, at least, will sell. I'm doing it absolutely without inspiration, with lacerated nerves and a sodden brain.

July 21st, 1924:

Hope you received the *Ten Story Book* containing a storiette of mine. I received $6.00 for it—on publication! But the story was rotten, anyhow—except for the spanking—which was what I *ought* to have administered, some time back, to a certain badly spoiled female person.

August 25th, 1924:

I'll tackle some more fiction when the wet weather comes. Literary whore-mongering is distasteful to me; but I don't want to break my back, if I can help it—or tie myself down to a [regular] job, either. I'd rather starve than be a wage-slave for anyone in Auburn.

Collating the data in these excerpts from Smith's letters with the list of extant ironic-romantic stories, we are able to reach a number of conclusions and to make a number of statements about their composition. According to the first excerpt, "The Flirt" was thus published about a year or so after its composition. Then, according to the second excerpt, "The Perfect Woman" was one of the prose-fillers that Smith was trying to write during the winter of 1922–1923; and "Gossip" and "A Platonic Entanglement" could also very well be the others. According to the third excerpt, *10 Story Book* like other periodicals both before and since was antedated; thus the issue for August 1924, which carried "Something New," was probably produced and printed in June so as to appear on the stands in July. Even though "Checkmate" bears the date of composition, or of completion of composition, as November 7, 1930, both "The Expert Lover" and "Checkmate" could then quite likely stem from the winter of 1924–1925, according to one possible interpretation of the fourth and last excerpt presented just above.

In assessing and interpreting properly the autobiographical quotient in the make-up of these ironic-romantic stories, however, we still need to consider (at least) not only two further excerpts from Smith's letters to Sterling for the early 1920's but also certain general conditions of Smith's life during the period from 1911/1912 through 1925/1926, especially between 1918 and 1926. We should recall that, after the publication of his first volume The *Star-Treader* in late 1912, and lasting into the latter part of the 1910's, Ashton Smith suffered from generally poor health, and was consequently unable to do much mundane work in order to earn some necessary funds. Therefore his great and good friend George Sterling did all he could, either by taking from his own small store of money, or by soliciting a wide range of wealthy people in Northern California, to supplement the collective income of the Smith family.

By virtue of his unique position as the unofficial poet laureate of San Francisco and hence, by extension, of the entire West Coast as constituted at that time, Sterling had access to many persons of genuine wealth, whether as friends or as acquaintances, and he did manage to convince less than a handful of millionaires or persons close to being millionaires, who could thus well afford it, to send the young Smith a monthly or quarterly stipend, and over a period of at least a few years. Since the Smith family's needs were comparatively simple and few, the total money thus donated sufficed to take care of them. Most of these stipends would last until the latter 1910's when some of them ceased, and when circumstances thus forced Smith to return to mundane labor at least on a part-time basis. Consequently, the early to middle 1920's witnessed not only the publication of *Ebony and Crystal* in late 1922 and of *Sandalwood* in late 1925, but also the performance by Ashton Smith of such likely work as he could obtain. However, it was almost never regular jobs of a permanent nature but almost always either odd jobs or regular jobs of limited duration. Temperamentally the latter type of mundane labor suited Ashton Smith much better, because he could then continue with his own creative work during those times when he was not earning money by working for other people.

Between 1918 and 1926, Ashton Smith not only underwent a variety of physical maladies and mishaps, but also, when he was well, he performed a variety of odd jobs for some dozen or more local people principally located in and around Auburn and Long Valley. Some of this work in particular consisted in fact of quite hard labor of a physically demanding type. Recovering from "incipient tuberculosis" and a "nervous breakdown" (Smith's own terms) that he suffered c. 1918, this hard physical labor, which included woodcutting, at which he became quite expert, appears to have helped the convalescent to become physiologically stronger and psychologically more self-reliant in a variety of ways.

The two further excerpts from Smith's letters to Sterling from the early 1920's which we still need to consider are unusually revealing, not only for the light that they throw on his ironic-romantic fiction but just as much for what they tell us of his life for that period, as well as before and after. In his letter of December 27, 1920, Ashton Smith had mentioned that he might visit George Sterling in San Francisco with the clear implication that this would be soon. However, writing again on January 31st, 1921, he has now decided, after all, not to visit his friend and mentor at the latter's place in the celebrated "Monkey" or Montgomery Block situated in the downtown area of the City. (The reference below to Bologna is to the Cafe Bologna in San Francisco, a well-known haunt of creative people and their friends.) Smith continues:

> I doubt if I'll visit San Francisco, I don't feel that I can afford the trip; anyway, there wouldn't be much pleasure in it for me. I've sworn off prohibition-booze, and have no time to bother with semi-virgins of the Bologna variety. Anyway, I never make love to girls. Only married women need apply.

Later that same year Smith expatiates a little on this rule of behavior. From the context of this letter and others, as well as from the known circumstances of his life, especially during the over-all period from 1910 until 1930, this rule appears to be one which he reached after careful deliberation, and to which he more or less adhered until his last decade. When he did finally marry, it would be to a woman more or less his own age, and past the capacity to conceive and bear any further children. The next letter in which he mentions the topic again is dated September 5th, 1921:

> Marriage is an error I was never tempted to commit: I have not been in love with an unmarried woman since I was fifteen!

The reader should keep in mind that Ashton Smith had been fifteen during 1909. It is probably safe to say that, if his very first complete sexual experience with a human female did not occur precisely when he was fifteen, then it must have happened sometime between his eleventh and fifteenth years. The advantages of such a stance—i.e., making love only to married women—for a man of limited income are perfectly obvious. At best it represents a sensible and responsible compromise between his own erotic drive and the human world outside his own person. It must be recalled and emphasized that the modes of controlling human conception, even early in the first half of the twentieth century, were still relatively limited and crude, apart from actual sterilization. However, apart from the threat of conception and unwanted children, the principal problem was to avoid arousing the suspicions not only, and primarily, of the husband involved but also, and in its way just as importantly, of such of the local citizenry as were given to gossiping.

We must not forget that Ashton Smith was living if not right inside, then certainly not far from, a small town already celebrated for its gossipmongers when Ambrose Bierce was residing there, off and on, during the 1880's, just before Smith would be born in January of 1893. In such circumstances as these, a discreet young man would not go out of his way to advertise his amorous and sexual preferences and proclivities—even when they were of the accepted heterosexual variety—if he could help it! Such a stance or attitude on the part of Ashton Smith does not by any means indicate that the non-corporeal aspects of love did not have considerable importance for him. Rather, he had clearly chosen a method whereby he could enjoy those aspects of a mature loving relationship which possessed the greatest value for him, and also whereby he could minimize, biologically and socially, those potentially negative possibilities of such a regular relationship with a woman.

For anyone who can read between the lines of Smith's letters to Sterling for the first half of the 1920's, and who can correlate his behavior *vis-à-vis* his women friends with the amorous duplicity or two—as well as aligning that behavior on the one hand with the discreet cuckoldry on the other, such as he describes in this romantic fiction—it is quite obvious that Smith was directly writing out of his own life, or was directly and strictly extrapolating therefrom, when he was writing these particular stories. In other words, these richly ironical tales can make perfectly decent claims on our attention as the earliest examples of genuine realism from Smith's pen and typewriter. It is therefore appropriately ironical that, when they were finally published as a group, they should have been greeted as, inter alia, "trite tearjerkers." Making love to married women continued to claim Smith's creative attention to some degree even after he had turned his principal energies to writing prose fantasies sometime between the middle and latter 1920's. Why otherwise would he have composed, or completed, such a tale as "Checkmate" in late 1930 when such a type of comparatively realistic fiction had become much less salable for him than the type of prose fantasies that he was creating for and selling to *Weird Tales,* and by then with undoubted popular and artistic success? While it is extremely dubious that he would have gone on to become a major realist of any type—if we may judge at least by such marginal prose—yet Smith's ironic-romantic fiction will probably remain as a fascinating and not unfruitful byroad that marketing circumstances alone caused him to pursue no further than he did.

(For permission to quote excerpts from the letters of Clark Ashton Smith to George Sterling, cordial acknowledgement is hereby made to the Henry W. and Albert A. Berg Collection, The New York Public Library, Astor, Lenox and Tilden Foundations. The New York Public Library is the physical proprietor and custodian of the Sterling-Smith correspondence, together with related MSS. and art-work. For further permission to quote these same excerpts, grateful acknowledgement is likewise made to "CASiana Literary Enterprises," representing the literary Estate of Clark Ashton Smith.)

Frank Belknap Long, *The Darkling Tide*
(Introduction.)

Flotsam and Jetsam on the Darkling Tide. (Frank Belknap Long. *The Darkling Tide*. Tsathoggua Press, 1995.)

Reading and re-reading the poems of Frank Belknap Long (1901–1994) today during the mid-1990's, it is easy to perceive the qualities that must have attracted the considerable praise of such figures as diverse as George Sterling, John Masefield, Samuel Loveman, and even Arthur Machen himself. These qualities include imaginativeness, originality, craftsmanship, and especially the seemingly light but rarely trivial touch so characteristic of this poet. In short, it is good solid work worthy of extended perusal and contemplation. Belknap Long was only a young adult when his first collection appeared in 1926 as *A Man from Genoa and Other Poems*; and he was only a little older when his second collection appeared in 1935 as *The Goblin Tower*. When by reciprocal agreement, half a dozen years after the death of August Derleth in 1971 as the original editor-proprietor, Arkham House arranged with Belknap Long to republish in one volume the contents of the two earlier collections, the poet-author then in his mid-seventies apparently subjected the poems to some slight revision, and even discarded a few selections. The new volume appeared in 1977 as *In Mayan Splendor* as a singularly handsome little book with exceptionally beautiful illustrations by Stephen Fabian. Obviously such a republication of earlier work had left a considerable amount of other poems ungathered, including in this category a surprising number of later pieces in free verse as well as a small number of vignettes in prose.

Even after establishing a solid reputation as an original and all-around writer of imaginative fiction of diverse types—fantasy, science-fiction, supernatural horror, &c.—Belknap Long still continued to regard himself primarily as a poet Moreover, he took justifiable pride in his poetic output, and continued to turn out a rare piece of verse on occasion during the middle and then the latter part of his rather long life and career. His over-all output of poems would seem to be quite a bit less than one hundred titles, and—including his vignettes in prose—somewhere around seventy pieces. Whereas *In Mayan Splendor* gathered exactly forty selections (including his memorial sonnet to H. P. Lovecraft first published in 1938), there are still some thirty pieces or less remaining unharvested. These remnants Perry M. Grayson has collected into the present volume appropriately called *The Darkling Tide*, and including at least three notable poems that deal with, or touch on, the sea *Innsmouth Revisited*, *Man Is the Sea's Child*, and *The Sea's Cold Blueness*. Furthermore, in gathering then into the present volume, Mr. Grayson has rendered real service not only to the cause and reputation of the original poet-author himself but just as much to the aficionados and collectors of highly imaginative poetry. This is a type of poetry that unfortunately has become increasingly scarce, particularly as cast in the fixed forms but mutable figures of speech characteristic of the older prosody.

The survival of such poetry, generally rimed and metered and often of quite an imaginative type, has become increasingly uncertain. In fact, it is possible that, at least as practiced by major poets, this kind of poetry may very well disappear completely, or almost so, in the next quarter or half of a century, if indeed it will even last that long. Nevertheless, it is part of a continuous tradition that in one shape or another goes back at least to the High Middle Ages, and possibly even to the ninth and tenth centuries of the Christian Era, to the revival of learning that took place under Alcuin at the Court of Charlemagne during the eighth and ninth centuries at Aachen, or Aix-la-Chapelle, an over-all period that probably was distinguished most notably by the coronation of the Frankish ruler at Rome in December of 800 as Emperor of the West.

The first great efflorescence of this new poetic tradition (as distinguished from that of the ancient Greek and Roman world) manifested itself in the *chansons de geste* of the 1000's and 1100's, then in the metrical romances of the 1100's and 1200's (probably the first modern fiction), and concomitantly in the poems of troubadours and trouvères of the same centuries, poems that the poets themselves characteristically sang, or hired other people to sing for them. The new tradition produced its greatest achievements in such diverse works as *La Chanson de Roland* (c. 1100), *Le Roman de la Rose* (c. 1235 and 1280), *The Divine Comedy* (completed in 1321), *The Canterbury Tales* (created in the last two decades of the 1300's), and then the sonnets and other love poems devised by Petrarch during the 1300's as inspired by the hopeless passion that he felt for Laura. (The preceding enumeration has no pretension to being complete, of course.) In these lyrics the spiritualized passion for the ideal and also unattainable—first developed and celebrated by the troubadours and trouvères, and always concentrated on the figure of a woman—found its culminating expression and apotheosis. In turn, the love poems of Petrarch would inspire countless lovers and poets throughout Europe not only during the Renaissance but even far beyond it.

This first great period of poetry created in the new languages that evolved after the collapse of the Western Roman Empire—poetry, moreover, that often was intensely and archetypally Romantic in feeling—we might designate for convenience, in the absence of other inclusive terms, after the dominant styles of architecture that came into existence during the Middle Ages: the Romanesque of the 1000's and 1100's, and the Gothic of the 1200's through the 1400's. Although not exact, the parallel between literature and architecture during this over-all "Romanesco-Gothic" period is nevertheless close enough.

The same spirit animating this earliest Romantic efflorescence emerged again in the fantastic narratives in verse by such figures of the Renaissance (the 1400's and 1500's) as Ludovico Ariosto and Torquato Tasso, such narratives as *Orlando Furioso* (varying editions 1516–1532) and *Gerusalemme Liberata* (completed 1575, and published 1581). Such epic-romance-allegories as these had straightforwardly descended from the metrical romances of the 1100's and 1200's. The Romantic efflorescence of Ariosto, Tasso, and other poets found its ultimate expression in the last great poem of both the Middle Ages and the Renaissance, *The Faerie Queene* of Edmund Spenser (published 1590, 1596, and 1609). The same poetic fire that had burst forth in the Middle Ages, and that emerged again in the Renaissance, made its appearance possibly at its most powerful during the 1800's, the Romantic Century par excellence, but as a conscious artistic movement Romanticism really began in the late 1700's, and then continued on into the twentieth century long after the 1800's.

In English, of course, it includes all the great Romantic and Victorian poets, William Blake, Wordsworth, Coleridge, Keats, Shelley, Thomas Lovell Beddoes, Tennyson, Swinburne, &c. Needless to mention, great poets writing in almost all the European languages existed and flourished not only during the Middle Ages and the Renaissance but particularly during the 1800's. However, the modern Romanticism of such American poets as George Sterling. Nora May French, Clark Ashton Smith. Edna St. Vincent Millay, and Samuel Loveman, among many other figures, occurred largely during the first fourth, third, or half of the twentieth century, and also thus included the early collections of Belknap

Long, which reappeared in later published form during the second half of the same century. The major part of the poems in verse and vignettes in prose, collected here for the first time during the 1990's, goes back to the 1920's and 1930's, and includes quite a few beautiful, enchanting, and otherwise remarkable effusions. These lyrics directly remind us of the idealistic and imaginative type of poetry that was predominantly characteristic of the first fourth or third of the 1900's in the U. S. A.

Why has the survival of such poetry as these lyrics become uncertain, that is, in terms of an ongoing tradition that is not just alive but flourishing? The answer is unequivocal, and comes from the alternate poetic tradition (often burningly Romantic in feeling as well), that of Walt Whitman, and that has developed in the last century and a half, originating in the U. S. A. out of the general American poet's need to convey an experience of life differing from that of Europe. The poetic tradition that we have just sketched, involving as it does both rime and meter, we might call for convenience the Mediaeval Syndrome, arising as it did in the early Middle Ages and lasting through all the centuries since then on into our own modem period. When the Old World settled and colonized the New World, the emigrants naturally brought with them the literary traditions and forms of the Old World in the various European languages. However, these forms, genres and themes ultimately could only go so far in adapting to the lifestyles of the New World, and it was inevitable that new forms and modes of literature would arise, which they did, of course.

It was none other than Walt Whitman (born 1819) who began the poetic revolution in the mid-1800's with his *Leaves of Grass,* first published in 1855. This collection he revised and enlarged through nine successive editions before his death in 1892. Whitman's poetic revolution would ultimately exert an enormous influence throughout North, Central, and South America. as well as throughout Europe, whether directly or indirectly. T. S. Elliot and Ezra Pound at least in English renewed and continued this revolution in their own idiosyncratic manner, particularly in the 1920's and 1930's. In turn, highly visible in the 1950's and 1960's, such figures as Allen Ginsberg, Kenneth Rexroth, and Lawrence Ferlinghetti, among many other poets primarily centered in the San Francisco Bay Area (the so-called Beatniks of the Beat Generation), renewed and continued the same revolution in their own idiosyncratic but inclusively democratic manner, thus restoring the impetus to its original source in

Whitman. The Beatniks ultimately exerted even greater influence than Eliot and Pound.

In this new poetic development—and we are dead serious on this point—we should make considerable allowance for the equally new tradition of sung poetry presented by rock and roll music and its leading practitioners, such groups above all as the Beatles, the Rolling Stones, the Grateful Dead, the Jefferson Airplane/Starship, the Doors, &c., especially prominent and influential during the 1960's and 1970's. Indeed, Jim Morrison (or, in full, James Douglas Morrison), the leader of the Doors, as a modern Romantic poet (in feeling if not in terms of literary form), may be seen as the equivalent in the twentieth century of such English Romantic poets as Byron, Keats, and Shelley. The result of these changes and innovations is that, almost universally, poets today write in prose of extraordinary variety, but still in prose, the ultimate heritage from Whitman. Much of the new poetry since the mid-1900's became, alas! even more autobiographical than it was even during the time of the English and American Romantics of the 1800's; and although some of it inevitably remains obscure, most of it is relatively accessible, at least with some serious attention.

Since the 1950's, especially in the San Francisco Bay Area, a major poetic rebirth has taken place, inspired in part by the public readings there of the great Welsh poet Dylan Thomas on tour in the U. S. A. during 1952; and this poetic rebirth has developed its own autochthonous notion of poetry publicly performed, sometimes accompanied by music such as jazz. Another result of all these changes and innovations, and just as important, is that poetry has become accessible again to the average person, and thus concerned with the recognizable dysfunctions, problems, and joys of everyday life and existence. Although some of it remains obscure, it is today for the most part no longer arcane, or but rarely so, and rarely is it sublime. A notable exception may be cited in the extraordinary visions and effusions of the great American Surrealistic poet Philip Lamantia, who continues in a number of exceptional ways, both subtle and overt, many of the more arcane traditions represented by the epochal poetry of Clark Ashton Smith, no mean accomplishment.

The restoration of relatively accessible poetry to people at large, through the medium of public performance as much as through that of the printed page, compensates perhaps for the loss of the incisive type of speech or expression, the loss of the Romantic afflatus, no less than that of the Romantic style of imagination, all of which were so richly purveyed by metrical poetry from the Romanesque period onward. Renewed with undeniable splendor during the Renaissance and then later during the Romantic Century, the tradition of Romantic poetry is yet somehow alive after so many poetic revolutions and counter-revolutions, as witness these hitherto ungathered Romantic lyrics and other more modem effusions by Frank Belknap Long. Who knows but that we may be looking for the last time at the last of the last as we pick up and peruse this collection?! We could be wrong, and we hope that we are indeed wrong. If in fact we are looking at the last of the last, then let us cherish these remnants, and let us revel in the fun, fancy, and lyric expansiveness of a young poet who reached his coming of age just a little over seventy years ago.

Sacramento, California
The Fourth of July, 1995.

Keith Allen Daniels.
What Rough Beast, What Rough Book

What Rough Book: Dark Poems and Light, by Keith Allen Daniels. Foreword by Michael R. Collings. Anamnesis Books, Clute, Texas, 1992, 141 pp. Write to the publishers now located at P. O. Box 51115, Palo Alto, California, 94303. $12.95.

Sent me very kindly by the author himself, my copy of *What Rough Book: Dark Poems and Light* served to introduce me to a poet whose work I had not previously encountered, to wit, Keith Allen Daniels. Reading it, then reading it again, and reading it yet once again, has provided me with quite an exhilarating roller-coaster ride of one intriguing adventure after another. Daniels is outstanding on a number of immediate accounts: he writes in traditional forms with meter and rime, or his own adaptations of the same, and his work is crystal-clear and accessible. Technically assured, and more than merely competent, Daniels employs a wide range of image and vocabulary. He displays considerable originality, no less than an unusual intensity of emotion. What gives his elegantly and even humorously crafted verses their genuine distinction and authentic inspiration is Daniels' professional background in the sciences, especially chemistry and engineering, in which he holds degrees. This background thus results in a broad spectrum of subject matter, in fact unprecedented in my own experience of modern imaginative poetry, from frozen eye-balls to rat cathedrals. *What Rough Book* in particular demonstrates for me the unique strength of what for lack of a better term we may call fantasy and science-fiction poetry. To our collective good fortune Daniels' book features nothing of the debilitating introspection, the cloying autobiographica, as well as the obscure and oh-so-clever puzzlement, of much so-called mainstream poetry as produced in the late twentieth century. Over-all the touch, no less than the tone, of this especial poet remains remarkably light (that word is used here in the highest complimentary sense), and full of a refreshing and outrageous humor, the latter deployed to superb advantage in the purely macabre poems. A wonderful aura of impishness and irreverence hovers over much of these verses. *What Rough Book* provides one delicious extroverted adventure after another, from the very first selection, "All the Century Plants" (significantly invoking the centennial of H. P. Lovecraft's birth), all the way through to the very last selection, the ironically droll "Yak Attack." Furthermore, the book provides an abundance of such adventures: out of 141 pages 122 are devoted to 116 poems. Such lavish abundance bespeaks a rare, and unfashionable, auctorial generosity on the part of Daniels as the poet-inventor involved. Amid this plethora of goodies the present critic is unable to pick out a particular favorite, but he can cite a few typical examples.

We quote the last eight lines of "Black space:" "HORS D'OEUVRES. / Eyeball caviar / skewered by toothpicks, / vitreous humor dolloped / on crackers and wheat thins. / The cones and rods of poets / are the best, the tang of retinas / black with a freight of dreams." Now *that* is original, and more than nominally unsettling. Another poem, "Dead Cow of the Sierras," begins arrestingly. "Camouflaged among the boulders in a dry wash, a dead cow was sprawled with her legs in the air." It then becomes even more acutely observant, "her belly bloated taut with the gases of internal putrefaction." The reader is urged, and with glee, to read the rest of this adventure.

The haiku created by Daniels are masterful and especially well focused. Here are a few examples. "Autumn junkyard scene: / cars the color of dead leaves / rusting in windrows." Another: "Alchemy is dead / today: philosopher's stones / are found in kidneys." Yet another, entitled "Suppose:" "The moon's a portrait / of the earth, like Dorian / Gray's in the attic."

A prose-poem "Rat Cathedrals" delineates the final custodians of neglected buildings: "Rats cluster piously behind soot-painted windows— stained (or sullied) glass—and worship the shadows in cathedrals relinquished by men."

One final quotation: "Welcome to a tomb / where even rust can rot. / The camera reveals TITANIC: / a benthic nightmare / as bereft of glamor / as a hagfish. / My hands are cold and damp."

Keith Allen Daniels is evidently a young and enthusiastic person as well as poet, and I shall follow his ongoing career as an author with interest and curiosity as to what further shape it will assume. He has mastered the shorter forms and modes of poetic communication, and it will be fascinating to see just what he may accomplish as time unfolds, and especially in a longer format such as a long linear, or quasi-linear, narrative in verse. The long, tightly woven poem more or less telling a story has languished for the most part in a state of limbo, definitely out of fashion, since the earlier half of the twentieth century. Daniels could possibly accomplish something important, unique, and fresh in the genre of the long poem, that is, the extended narrative in verse. His readers are indeed fortunate in securing the expert services of such a fun-loving and innovative guide in these imaginative realms. I find only one false note in the entire book, and whoever was responsible for this was profoundly ill-advised. On the back cover, heading various and well-deserved blurbs, appears the following: "A MODERN-DAY BAUDELAIRE." Anyone who knows in depth the quite extended cavalcade of French language and literature, say, from the time of Charlemagne through the twentieth century—and concomitantly understands the unique place held by Baudelaire in that cavalcade whether in regard to poetic substance or classical French prosody (his alexandrines are not quite like those by anybody else)—would be very skeptical in regard to the considerable claim represented by the above.

Ashton Smith with some justification could be called, and has been called, "the Baudelaire of California." (Of course, Ashton Smith is much more than that.) However, whereas both Poe and Ashton Smith have each quite an unique sense of humor, Baudelaire always appears deadly serious in *Les Fleurs du Mal* (probably best translated as *The Flowers of Ill*, rather than the usual *Evil*) and *Le Spleen de Paris* (his poems in prose). In addition, Poe, Baudelaire, and Ashton Smith definitely share a certain severe and uncompromising sombreness of imagination—Miltonic in its grandeur—and I find nothing of that in *What Rough Book*. But I find many other things, and no less welcome, in the work of Mons. Daniels. I appreciate him as "a modern-day Keith Allen Daniels" with whom one could go "hiking, camping, boating, and exploring the planet," and all of that with secure pleasure. I definitely would not care to do any of that with Poe and Baudelaire (supremely urban-type of individuals), although I suspect that Ashton Smith, that expert log-splitter, might make a very good companion on a camping trip, as does undoubtedly Keith Allen Daniels—for such endeavors one picks the appropriate partners with enormous care. I recommend *What Rough Book* with the greatest of confidence to those with a taste for a genuine adventure whether macabre or otherwise as expressed in the form or condition of poetry.

In Memoriam: Keith Allen Daniels (1956–2001)

On Tuesday, 18 December 2001, in the late afternoon, a major creative presence was lost not only to the world of modern imaginative literature—in this case the world of fantasy and science-fiction—but just as much to the world of modem literature at large. After a generally successful struggle against metastatic colon cancer via chemotherapy during March through August of 2001, Keith Allen Daniels—poet, scientist, and poetry publisher—lost his final battle against the disease, a final battle that lasted from mid-September on into latter December. After being hospitalized several times in October, he died at his home in Ridgecrest, California, in the Mojave Desert, faithfully attended to the last by his loving wife Toni Luna Daniels, who had thus become his final nurse and caregiver. Previously employed as a materials engineering manager in Palo Alto while residing in San Francisco, Keith had worked as a materials engineer since May, 2000, at China Lake, the U.S. Navy missile testing center next to the town of Ridgecrest. Despite his early death at 45, the poet left behind him an impressive and unique output of his own, just as he had also brought out an equally conspicuous body of work as poetry editor and publisher, managing his own Anamnesis Press, founded in 1990, an original venture largely specializing in science-fiction poetry.

Keith Allen Daniels was born in Rantoul, Illinois, on 4 June 1956, and raised in Portsmouth, Rhode Island, where he received his early education in both private and public schools. He attended the University of Rochester, New York, where he received a B. S. in chemistry. After four years in the U. S. Navy, he attended the University of Florida in Gainesville, where he received his M. S. in materials science. Although he specialized in the physical sciences while in college, he pursued the humanities and his literary arts on his own, having never attended a college-level English class. He began writing poetry in 1967, and publishing it in 1970. While attending a science-fiction convention at San Francisco in the autumn of 1993, Keith met and fell in love with Toni Luna, where she was working as a food and beverage supervisor of the restaurant in the hotel where Keith was staying. That same autumn he relocated from Tallahassee, Florida, to San Francisco, where Toni and he lived together, and were married. They worked unusually well together as a team on behalf of Anamnesis Press, Keith as editor-publisher, and Toni as typesetter and, quite often, as cover artist for their line of handsome trade paperbacks.

Keith combined the practical knowledge of the physical scientist with the keen imagination and sensibility of the instinctive poet, inasmuch as he founded the speculative flights of his poetic output on a solid bedrock of hard science as preached by the late great science-fiction writer James Blish. Keith was that rare phenomenon, the science-fiction and fantasy poet who combined informed scientific thought with the forms and standards of traditional English prosody, including meter and rime, all of which he deployed with unusual skill, naturalness, and musicality. Audaciously clear and accessible—during a period still remarkable for much obscurantist poetry—his own poems lack neither depth nor variety, and indeed exhibit considerable virtuosity.

The many volumes of his poems demonstrate a notable and even startling range. Among other attributes they reveal a vivid and wonderful sense of humor and whimsy that not only can pop up almost anywhere quite unexpectedly, even in a serious context, but that comes to the fore most particularly in such volumes as *Haiku by Unohu*, *I Think, Therefore Iamb*, and *Loopy Is the Inner Ear*. His fine sense of wonder and marvel in face of life itself and the cosmos at large manifests at its best perhaps in his "corrections" of serious poems, distinguished in equal measure by an almost Zoroastrian dualism as displayed in the wide-ranging subject matter, now fantastic, now science-fictional, now terrific, or now horrific: *What Rough Book: Dark Poems and Light*, *Dyscrasias: Selected Poems*, *Notes from the Antipodes*, and *Satan Is a Mathematician*, possibly his single best book. The last single collection of his that he managed to publish late in 2000, and before the onset of his fight with cancer, was the elegant and slender chapbook, *Shimmarie*, a little gem of tender and sparkling imagination. Like many poets and prosateurs in the world of fantasy and science-fiction following the establishment of Arkham House, Keith derived much inspiration from the two premier modern American poets or prose-poets and science-fantaisistes H. P. Lovecraft and Clark Ashton Smith with their powerful cosmic-astronomic perspective and philosophy.

Keith's accomplishment as editor, collaborator, and publisher more or less equals his achievement as a poet and as a fine poet-reader or poet-performer. Among other recent offerings that appeared in the course of 2000–2001 he published a large and noteworthy collection of fantastic and/or science-fictional sonnets *The Weird Sonneteers*, including work by Jerry H. Jenkins, Anne K. Schwader, and himself; and most recently, and perhaps best of all, an outstanding miscellany representing 63 poets,

2001: A Science Fiction Poetry Anthology. As editor he published, among the most rewarding books long since issued by Anamnesis Press, such outstanding compilations as these: *Arthur C. Clarke and Lord Dunsany: A Correspondence*; and *With All of Love: Selected Poems* by James Blish.

Demonstrating his great love of poetry, no less than his generosity towards other poets, Keith also published a dozen distinctive poetry chapbooks by various authors. During 1996–2001 he sponsored every year a poetry contest through the auspices of Anamnesis Press. Open to all poets, this involved $1000 for the best short collection of new poems, plus its publication in the form of an attractive chapbook. Of course, this also meant a great amount of extra work, not to mention expense, for Keith as editor and publisher—he had to read as well as judge very carefully and conscientiously sometimes a total of around 400 manuscripts—but he willingly and joyfully undertook all this extra labor and expense to encourage imaginative poetry. Such altruism on the part of an established poet-publisher all on behalf of other poets and their work is quite a rare phenomenon.

As an editor with comprehensive tastes, Keith could easily compass such disparate, but not antagonistic, sensibilities as Lord Dunsany, one of the single most influential modern fantaisistes, and Arthur C. Clarke, possibly the premier modern science-fiction writer. As a fine poet-reader or poet-performer Keith made many appearances at fantasy, science-fiction, and other conventions, becoming known in the process as a distinguished poet. A member of the Science Fiction Poetry Association during 1979–1998, he is listed in *Who's Who in America* and *Who's Who in Writers, Editors and Poets*, and his poems have appeared in *Altair*, *Analog SF*, *Asimov's Science Fiction*, *Weird Tales*, *Recursive Angel*, *Air Fish*, *Talebones*, *Poets of the Fantastic*, *Once Upon a Midnight*, *Narcopolis*, and numerous other magazines, books, and anthologies. He has given readings at Barnes and Noble bookstores, several World Science Fiction Conventions, the Southwest Writers Workshop in Albuquerque, two World Fantasy Conventions, the Fort Mason Center in San Francisco, and elsewhere.

In addition to winning the National Association of Independent Publishers Fallot Literary Award for *What Rough Book* (1992) and the 1999 Zine Guild Award for Best Science Fiction Poem, his work has been nominated for the Rhysling Award (15 times), the Nebula Award, the Pushcart Prize, and the Clark Ashton Smith International Poetry Award. He was awarded the 1995 Rhysling Award (Honorable Mention,

Short Poem category) for the popular "Satan Is a Mathematician," which has since been reprinted in French, German, and Korean. His full-length collection of the same name was a finalist for the 1999 Writers Digest National Book Award for Poetry.

His wife Toni Luna Daniels, an accomplished artist in various media, has not only typeset many of the volumes put out by Anamnesis Press, but has also provided much stimulating and attractive cover art for them whether authored by Keith or by others. Toni will continue the business at least until she sells out the current stock of books. The present address is:

Anamnesis Press

P.O. Box 95

Ridgecrest, California, 93556

U. S. A.

Keith is survived not only by his wife but also by family members in New England. His body has been cremated, and his ashes have been scattered into the Pacific Ocean by his wife in a private ceremony conforming to his final wishes, on 26 January 2002.

Just as his Anamnesis Press has probably functioned as the foremost publisher of science-fiction poetry, so did Keith himself probably figure as the foremost science-fiction poet of his time—although he was obviously much more than that—a feat all the more exceptional given his cultivation of the forms and standards of traditional English prosody. As Timons Esaias has very well expressed it, in his brief but pithy foreword to *Shimmarie*, "Daniels has made a powerful poetic device of the rich vocabulary of science and technology." For the people fortunate enough to know him intimately, Keith was not only the most humane, faithful, and generous of friends but in a world where phonies and swindlers abound, he remained stalwart and steadfast, an admirably genuine person. As Keith was fond of stating in person or in print, he worked as a scientist by day, but his soul belonged to the night, where may he happily wander at his liberty, free of the body that betrayed him at the last.

Acknowledgements

Essays

"The Alleged Influence of Lord Dunsany on Clark Ashton Smith."
   Amra, January 1963.

"The Sorcerer Departs: Clark Ashton Smith (1893–1961)."
   In Memoriam: Clark Ashton Smith, Mirage Press, 1963.
   Separate booklet, Tsathoggua Press, 1997.
   Separate booklet, Silver Key Press, 2007.

"Klarkash-Ton and E'ch-Pi-El."
   Mirage, Winter 1963–1964.

"Clark Ashton Smith: Poet in Prose."
   Clark Ashton Smith. *Poems in Prose*, Arkham House, 1965.
   French edition (essay only), translated by Philippe Gindre (separate book-
   let), La Clef d'argent (Silver Key Press), 2001.

"Robert E. Howard: Frontiersman of Letters."
   Robert E. Howard. *Etchings in Ivory*, Glenn Lord, 1968.
   Don Herron, *The Dark Barbarian*, 1984; Wildside Press, 2000.

"The Last of the Great Romanic Poets."
   The Last of the Great Romanic Poets, Silver Scarab Press, 1973.

"A Statement for Imagination."
   Nightshade, August 1, 1977 (as "An Issue for Imagination.")
   The Romantist, No. 6–7–8, 1982–1984, F. Marion Crawford Memorial Soci-
   ety, Nashville, 1986.

"George Sterling (1869–1926): Hesperian Laureate."

"A Garland of Poems by George Sterling." (Selected by Donald Sidney-Fryer.)
   The Romantist, No. 1, 1977, F. Marion Crawford Memorial Society, Nashville, 1978.

"A Memoir of Timeus Gaylord."
   The Romantist, No. 2, 1978, F. Marion Crawford Memorial Society, Nashville, 1979.

"Francis Marion Crawford: A Neglected But Not A Forgotten Master."
   The Romantist, No. 3, 1979, F. Marion Crawford Memorial Society, Nashville, 1980.

"Romantist Nonpareil."
   Moran, John. (Ed.) *An F. Marion Crawford Companion*. Westport, Connecticut
   and London: Greenwood Press, 1981.

"A Visionary of Doom: Ambrose Bierce, Poet (1842–1914)."
Ambrose Bierce. *A Vision of Doom,* (edited by Donald Sidney-Fryer), Donald M. Grant, 1980.

"The Last Lutenist: Christian Gottlieb Scheidler."
The Romantist, No. 9–10, 1985–1986, F. Marion Crawford Memorial Society, Nashville, 1997.

"Robert E. Howard: Epic Poet in Prose."
The Cimmerian, Vol. 3, No. 12, December 2006.

"Nora May French: Somewhere Between Eulalie and Edna St. Vincent Millay."
(Hitherto unpublished—original to this book.)

Lesser Reviews and Miscellanea

"Addendum: Another 'Smith'."
The Last of the Great Romanic Poets.
Silver Scarab Press, 1973.

"Echoes and Yet Again Echoes."
Review of Echoes from the Vaults of Yoh-Vombis by Don Herron.
Nyctalops, No. 14, March 1978.

"The Art of Modern Enchantment."
Review of L. Sprague de Camp. *Literary Swordsmen and Sorcerers.*
Nyctalops, No. 14, March 1978.

Review of *In Mayan Splendor* by Frank Belknap Long.
Nyctalops, No. 14, March 1978.

Review of *Seasoned Timber* by Celeste Turner Wright.
Nyctalops, No. 14, March 1978.

Review of *The Dream of X* by William Hope Hodgson.
Nyctalops, No. 14, March 1978.

"Jesse F. Knight. The Romantic Revival. Setting the Record Straight. A Conversation with Frank Cooper."
The Romantist, No. 3, 1979, F. Marion Crawford Memorial Society, Nashville, 1980.

"Poet of the Singing Flame." (Introduction.)
Clark Ashton Smith. The City of the Singing Flame.
Timescape Pocket Books, New York, 1981.

"The Last Enchanter." (Introduction.)
Clark Ashton Smith. *The Last Incantation.*
Timescape Pocket Books, New York, 1982.

"Lyricist of Lost Worlds." (Introduction.)
  Clark Ashton Smith. The Monster of the Prophecy.
  Timescape Pocket Books, New York, 1983.

"Introduction."
  G. Sutton Breiding. *Autumn Roses.*
  Silver Scarab Press, 1984.

Review of "*Fungi From Yuggoth by* H. P. Lovecraft as read by John Arthur, etc."
  Nocturne, No. One (Special insert sheet), Autumn 1988.

[Article] "'Klarkash-Ton' versus 'Clark Ashton.'"
  The Dark Eidolon (The Journal of Smith Studies), No. 2, July 1989.

"Introduction."
  G. Sutton Breiding. Journal of an Astronaut.
  Ocean View Books, 1992

[Article] "O Amor Atque Realitas! Clark Ashton Smith's First Adult Fiction."
  The Dark Eidolon, No. 3, Winter 1993.

"Flotsam and Jetsam on the Darkling Tide." (Introduction.)
  Frank Belknap Long. *The Darkling Tide.*
  Tsathoggua Press, 1995.

"What Rough Beast, What Rough Book"
  Review of *What Rough Book* by Keith Allen Daniels.
  The Yawning Vortex, 1998.

[Obituary] "In Memoriam: Keith Allen Daniels (1956–2001)."
  Locus (Magazine), February 2002.
  The Western Front, Vol. 3, No. 1, Roodmas 2002.